ATONEMENT
AND THE NEW PERSPECTIVE

ATONEMENT
AND THE NEW PERSPECTIVE
The God of Israel, Covenant, and the Cross

Stephen Burnhope

◥PICKWICK *Publications* · Eugene, Oregon

ATONEMENT AND THE NEW PERSPECTIVE
The God of Israel, Covenant, and the Cross

Copyright © 2018 Stephen Burnhope. All rights reserved. Except for brief quotations in critical publications or reviews, no part of this book may be reproduced in any manner without prior written permission from the publisher. Write: Permissions, Wipf and Stock Publishers, 199 W. 8th Ave., Suite 3, Eugene, OR 97401.

Pickwick Publications
An Imprint of Wipf and Stock Publishers
199 W. 8th Ave., Suite 3
Eugene, OR 97401

www.wipfandstock.com

PAPERBACK ISBN: 978-1-5326-4646-1
HARDCOVER ISBN: 978-1-5326-4647-8
EBOOK ISBN: 978-1-5326-4648-5

Cataloguing-in-Publication data:

Names: Burnhope, Stephen, author.

Title: Atonement and the new perspective : the God of Israel, covenant, and the cross / Stephen Burnhope.

Description: Eugene, OR: Pickwick Publications, 2018 | Includes bibliographical references.

Identifiers: ISBN 978-1-5326-4646-1 (paperback) | ISBN 978-1-5326-4647-8 (hardcover) | ISBN 978-1-5326-4648-5 (ebook)

Subjects: LCSH: Atonement—Biblical teaching | Jesus Christ—Crucifixion—Biblical teaching | Jesus Christ—Crucifixion | Bible. New Testament—Theology | Atonement

Classification: BS2545 B875 2018 (paperback) | BS2545 (ebook)

Manufactured in the U.S.A. 08/09/18

Contents

Author's Preface | vii
General Introduction | xi

CHAPTER ONE
The Doctrine of Atonement | 1

CHAPTER TWO
New Perspectives on First-Century Judaism | 53

CHAPTER THREE
Atonement in New Perspective | 158

CHAPTER FOUR
The Continuing Place of the Traditional Ideas of Atonement | 229

Bibliography | 247

Author's Preface

THE DOCTRINE OF ATONEMENT has always fascinated me. From my mid-teenage years, when I first encountered and responded to the gospel, I could never quite understand how, exactly, Christ's death on a Roman cross two thousand years ago was effective in enabling a personal relationship with God. Mostly, however, as a young Christian I kept my questions to myself, given the propensity of those church leaders of whom I would occasionally make timid inquiries to respond along the lines: "We shall never fully understand these things. If we could, we would be God. You simply need to 'have faith.'" I could relate to this to a point, but I was troubled by the very shallow level at which it seemed to cut in as the default answer. The Christian world of my formative years seemed particularly concerned to warn me of the dangers of allowing my head to get in the way of my heart (which could, apparently, do grievous harm to my fledgling faith). It was only later in life, when a number of other taken-for-granted ideas in the popular realm had also stopped making sense to me, that I began to admit to myself that it was either time to give up on Christianity altogether or find more compelling answers, which I was confident were out there somewhere. I concluded that theological study was the route to finding them and am pleased to say that my expectation was rewarded.

Along the way, that early fascination with the "how?" question of salvation stayed with me. My initial discomfort with the doctrine as commonly presented concerned the commonplace Evangelical reliance on penal substitution; partly because numerous flaws seemed evident to me in its foundational assumptions and partly because it no longer seemed "saleable" in the contemporary Western world. Exploring the credentials of the penal view *versus* a "kaleidoscopic" or "multi-model" understanding was the burden of my Masters' dissertation—which happened to coincide with the heated debates taking place in the so-called "atonement wars" around the turn of the century.

That completed, however, I continued to feel that there had to be "something more." Two concerns still bothered me. One was that Christianity seemed surprisingly content to allow atonement to be defined by a multiplicity of otherwise-unrelated metaphors, each picturing "something" of the meaning of Christ's work—making it, in effect, a "bit like this" and a "bit like that." Notwithstanding that these characteristics might, individually, be valid, the absence of any identifiable common *nexus* or unifying feature drawing them together seemed strange. My other concern was that little if any Christian conceptualization concerning the atonement was being drawn from the longstanding pre-existing relationship between Israel and its God that preceded the coming of Jesus; or at least, it was not being drawn in a positive way. Any reference to Israel and Torah seemed to be solely by way of its value for a negative contrasting with Jesus and Christianity—law *versus* grace; shadow *versus* reality, and so on. Israel's role seemed simply to provide a dark background against which the light of the true gospel could shine more brightly. Torah, meanwhile, translated as "law," was roundly condemned as both ineffectual in relation to salvation and, moreover, impossible to keep. Each of these features that Christianity appeared to take for granted seemed slightly odd to me, given that God had given Torah to Israel in the first place (presumably in good faith). The failings of Israel were typically highlighted, notwithstanding that God had presciently included restorative provisions within Torah precisely in anticipation of such human failure. In short, in order to emphasize the uniqueness and significance of the Christian gospel, it seemed that what came before in relation to Israel had to be at best ignored and at worst disparaged. As R. Kendall Soulen has pointed out, the relationship of the God of Israel to the Israel of God has essentially been excised from the story—the standard canonical narrative has been foreshortened through one giant soteriological leap from Adam and the fall (as a timeless universal problem) to Christ and the cross (as the timeless universal solution).

Events of the last century, however—specifically the catastrophe of the *Shoah* and the subsequent return of a Jewish people to a land called Israel—have profoundly challenged us to re-evaluate Christianity's relationship to its forebear on a number of levels. The theological aspects of that process have been significantly impacted by recent scholarship concerning the so-called "New Perspective on Paul" and other recent research, which not only reminds us that Jesus and Paul were Jewish but also challenges longstanding assumptions about the nature of "Judaism" and "Christianity" in the early Jesus-following movement. This present work, which is the product of my PhD research, is an exploration of how our understanding of just one doctrinal matter—the atonement—might be reconsidered in the light of the new scholarship.

My context is the Evangelical and Reformed traditions, within which atonement is such a crucial doctrine and has been the subject of a great deal of passionate debate. The proposal develops in four parts: firstly, a survey of the current state-of-play in atonement theology; secondly, a review of the New Perspective and other recent research; thirdly, my substantive proposal for a "re-Judaization" of atonement theory, framed around twin poles of non-supersessionism and christocentrism, with an affirming stance towards the efficacy of the relationship between Israel and its God that preceded the coming of Jesus; and finally, a consideration of the implications of my proposal for the traditional models and metaphors by which atonement has habitually been understood.

It remains only to express my profound thanks and appreciation first and foremost to my wife Lyn, whose theological studies served as the catalyst for my own entry into the world of academia. Without her selfless support, patience, and longsuffering I would never have reached this point. Secondly, to Dr Graham McFarlane at the London School of Theology, who continually challenged my closeted thinking, devoted great time and patience to supervising my Master's dissertation and then provoked me in the nicest possible way to explore a PhD at King's College London. Thirdly, to my wonderful PhD supervisors, Dr Susannah Ticciati and Professor Ben Quash, for their patient encouragement and engaging critique. Finally, to Dr Robin Parry and everyone at Wipf and Stock Publishers. I am grateful for all of their support and contributions, and it remains only to say that any shortcomings in the end product are entirely my own work.

General Introduction

This Jesus is the stone that was rejected by you, the builders, which has become the cornerstone. And there is salvation in no one else, for there is no other name under heaven given among men by which we must be saved.[1]

JESUS SAVES . . . BUT HOW?

SALVATION THROUGH THE ATONING work of Jesus Christ lies at the very heart of Christian faith. The classic content of the gospel is that though humanity is separated from God by its sinful state, we are somehow made "at one" with God through Christ. However, the word "somehow" is indicative of a profound underlying question: yes, Jesus saves . . . but *how*, exactly? Given the significance of the answer to this simple and sensible inquiry, one would expect it to have been comprehensively addressed in the historic formulation of doctrine. Yet here we encounter one of the most puzzling features of Christian orthodoxy: we search in vain through the early Creeds of the church for definitive statements on how salvation in Christ was actually brought about.

Why might that have been? Was it simply so "obvious" to Christians in the first few centuries that no-one felt the need to record it for posterity? And if so, *what* was so obvious about it?

In discussing the atonement it has been customary to refer to a wide range of images, metaphors, and models drawn from the New Testament to express the efficacy of Christ's work. Less clear has been how, if at all, this variety of imagery should be drawn together. Can they happily be left as stand-alone ideas? Ought one theory to be understood to be central or dominant? Or does the real answer lie beyond all of the past and present theories?

---

1. Acts 4:11–12, ESV.

In recent years, debate about the atonement at both popular and scholarly levels has been particularly rife (and impassioned) within Evangelical circles—specifically, whether primacy ought to be granted to the doctrine of penal substitution.[2] Discussion of atonement has somewhat run aground on this single question, which has attracted as much heat as light. Any proposal to revisit the doctrine of atonement must necessarily touch upon this critical Evangelical debating point.

Beyond that, however, we perceive there to be something that ought to be more fundamental still to any discussion of the atonement and that might even provide some of those answers. Namely, the remarkable failure of all of the traditional explanations to situate the question in the context in which atonement doctrine—and arguably, all Christian doctrine—ought firstly to be considered: the story of Israel narrated in the Hebrew Scriptures that comprise the major part of the Christian canon. Simply put, Christian doctrinal consideration of atonement has been at best ambivalent towards, and at worst has entirely ignored, the primal context of the relationship between the God of Israel and the Israel of God. It would surely be reasonable to assume that a truly canonical view of Christ's atoning work should be understood within—and informed by—divine-human relations in the story of the people of Israel.[3] And yet, discussion of Christian doctrine has almost universally displayed what R. Kendall Soulen calls an "Israel forgetfulness."[4]

This memory lapse has been brought into sharp relief by the recent literature of the so-called "New Perspective on Paul"[5] (hereafter, the "NPP")—a

---

2. Namely, that Christ on the cross took the punishment that I am due for my sins (the penal element), standing in my place (the substitutionary element).

3. This is not, of course, to suggest that either the story of Israel or the nature and character of the God of Israel can fully and properly be understood in the absence of Christ. Nor is it to suggest that Christians should not learn to understand all these matters in the light of Christ as the center point of salvation history. These aspects are not, however, my primary focus in this work, which is to call attention to a far greater continuity than has traditionally been recognized between the ways and purposes of God in his relationship with Israel narrated in the Hebrew Scriptures and his ways and purposes revealed in Christ—a continuity that has, at best, been downplayed and at worst, denied. Thus our concern is the ways in which Christ and the New Testament can more helpfully be understood in the light of the story of Israel, the nature of the God of Israel and Israel's relationship in Torah presented in the Hebrew Bible (in particular, insofar as they concern the atonement), rather than approaching these matters almost exclusively from the opposite direction, as is commonly the case. We propose that this re-contextualization offers a fresh perspective on the nature and significance of Christ as that could reasonably have been conceived by a faithful first-century Jew.

4. Soulen, *The God of Israel and Christian Theology*, 49.

5. The "New Perspective on Paul" has justifiably been likened to "a Copernican revolution" in Pauline studies. See Hagner, "Paul and Judaism—The Jewish Matrix of Early Christianity." Hagner's article succinctly summarizes the key foundations of the

body of research that questions traditional Christian readings of Paul and the circumstances of first-century Judaism, which has become prominent in Pauline studies since the latter half of the twentieth century. Such is its importance today that the Preface to a substantial recent reference work on Paul acknowledges that its contributors "mainly stand in the shadow of this major new appraisal of Paul's attitude to the Law, the covenant and the people of Israel."[6]

The NPP challenges us in two overarching respects. Firstly, to give proper and positive recognition to the fact that both Jesus and Paul were Jewish, steeped in the existing relationship between Israel and its God. Secondly, to revisit some longstanding assumptions embedded in Christian thought; namely, that (i) Judaism was and is a religion of works-righteousness, characterized by "law" over "faith," and (ii) Jewish-Christian relations at the time of the early Jesus-following movement are to be understood in terms of two distinct and divergent competing religions called "Judaism" and "Christianity."[7]

This body of new literature on the true characteristics of first-century Jewish faith has radical implications for Christian doctrinal understanding. The burden of this book is therefore to inquire how our understanding of the doctrine of atonement might be reconfigured if one were to apply the insights of the NPP and, specifically, to allow a positive significance to Israel's relationship to the God of the Hebrew Scriptures in framing atonement thought.

SCHOLARLY CONTEXT—EVANGELICALISM

Evangelicalism has always held the work of Christ, centered on the cross, and individual human response to it, to be of fundamental significance in making a necessary, personal decision for salvation. The gospel message that Jesus saves—and hence too, the articulation of *how* he saves—performs a

---

New Perspective, including the following: Judaism was not and is not a religion where acceptance with God is earned through the merit of righteousness based on works; Paul's theology has been misunderstood because it has been read through the lens of Luther and the Reformation; Paul experienced not conversion to a new faith, not a change of religion, but a call and commission to bring the gospel to the gentiles; and, Paul had no quarrel with the law (and hence Judaism) *per se*. The New Perspective is discussed in more detail in chapter two.

6. Hawthorne, Martin, and Reid (eds.), *Dictionary of Paul and his Letters*.

7. We shall in due course address the inherent anachronism, noted by recent historians, when terms such as "Judaism" and "Christianity" are used as descriptors for the first-century context. For the time being, we will simply flag the difficulties.

crucial role in evoking that response. For this reason, the movement known as Evangelicalism and the Reformed heritage with which it is closely aligned (notably within its more conservative wing) has been adopted as a natural scholarly context for our purposes. It is also timely that atonement should recently have become such a major debating point within Evangelicalism.[8]

"Evangelicalism" itself is by no means self-defining, even amongst its adherents, but we will adopt the quasi-definition of David Bebbington in his landmark study of the history of Evangelicalism,[9] while acknowledging that the movement's precise boundaries are not material for our purposes. Bebbington concluded there to be four features that have been its "special marks": *conversionism, activism, biblicism,* and *crucicentrism*. Together, these form "a quadrilateral of priorities that is the basis of Evangelicalism."[10]

However, the question of what constitutes core Evangelical beliefs is less easily decided. Martin Lloyd-Jones's urging to Evangelicals in the mid-twentieth century that we "must be as *inclusive* as we can and yet draw certain lines which we regard as being essential" serves as a worthy rallying call but has proven challenging in practice.[11] In what has always been a loosely-defined movement, how one is to distinguish the beliefs that are to be regarded as foundational and non-negotiable, those over which there can be legitimate differences of opinion yet still qualify as Evangelical, and those that fall outside Evangelical boundaries completely and must therefore be rejected, remains a problem. The doctrine of atonement has become a particular case in point as to where Lloyd-Jones's "essential lines" ought to be drawn. And yet, however nebulous the movement may be to pin down, one of the benefits of Evangelicalism for our purposes is that it is resolutely Christ-centered and personal salvation-centered; any reconsideration of atonement that is to be viable within its boundaries, therefore,

---

8. For a short but informative review, see Tidball, Hilborn and Thacker (eds.), *The Atonement Debate*.

9. Bebbington, *Evangelicalism in Modern Britain*, 1.

10. Ibid., 2–3. Other definitions have, of course, been offered. Alister McGrath, for example, proposes an expanded six points: The supreme authority of Scripture as a source of knowledge of God and a guide to Christian living; the majesty of Jesus Christ, both as incarnate God and Lord and as the Savior of sinful humanity; the lordship of the Holy Spirit; the need for personal conversion; the priority for evangelism for both individuals and the church as a whole; and the importance of Christian community for spiritual nourishment, fellowship and growth. McGrath, *Evangelicalism and the Future of Christianity*. The term "Evangelical" derives from the Greek word *euangelion*, meaning "good news" or "gospel."

11. Lloyd-Jones, *What Is an Evangelical?* 63. On "Evangelical essentials," see e.g. Stott, *Evangelical Truth*. For a recent work that seeks to re-examine the foundational concepts of truth on which Evangelicals have based their beliefs see Hicks, *Evangelicals & Truth*.

must maintain these features. This inbuilt discipline should ensure that a christocentric salvific focus remains center-stage.

This, then, frames our scholarly context. Where we make reference to the historical perspectives of the church or Christian tradition, whether in relation to atonement or first-century Judaism (or the theological conclusions that have flowed from those perspectives), the implicit sub-text will generally be "as viewed through an Evangelical lens," notably within the Western world. At no stage therefore will we be claiming to speak for all Christian tradition. That said, self-evidently neither the doctrine of atonement nor the way in which Judaism has been viewed in Christian thought are subjects exclusive to Evangelicalism—not least because of the movement's relatively recent provenance in the overall panoply of Christian history. Accordingly, although we shall locate the discussion within the Evangelical and Reformed context, it is to be hoped that something meaningful may also be derived by other traditions.

GOD AND FATHER OF OUR LORD JESUS CHRIST: THE GOD OF ISRAEL

> Great crowds came to him, bringing the lame, the blind, the crippled, the mute and many others, and laid them at his feet; and he healed them. The people were amazed when they saw the mute speaking, the crippled made well, the lame walking and the blind seeing. And they praised the God of Israel.[12]

The theological frame for God's salvific action in Christ, as the New Testament presents it, is God's established identity as "the God of Israel." Throughout the Gospels, the ministry of Christ is situated within the sphere of God's relationship with Israel and specifically in the identification of Jesus the Son of God as Israel's Messiah. All four Gospels make mention of Jesus's fulfillment of prophetic expectations of the Messiah recorded in Israel's scriptures. According to passages such as Luke 4 and 7 and Matthew 11, Jesus himself saw his mission in terms of Isaiah 61.

When Paul writes to the Corinthians about the significance of Christ's work, he reminds them, in one of the earliest Christian creedal affirmations, of something he had previously passed on to them as "of first importance": that "Christ died for our sins according to the Scriptures" (1 Cor 15:3–4, NIV). From our contemporary vantage point, we can but speculate as to

---

12. Matt 15:30–32 (NIV).

precisely *which* scriptures Paul may have had in mind,[13] but we can be confident that they were drawn from the sacred literature of Israel that Christians today know as the Old Testament (or, Hebrew Bible)[14] and associated apocryphal writings. It seems clear that the church's first and greatest theologian found the meaning of Christ's work, as he encountered it and understood it, to be founded in the historic relationship of the God of Israel with the Israel of God that those scriptures set forth.

Against this background, it is more than surprising that the standard theories of atonement make very limited reference to the larger story of Israel by which the Christ-event is framed. Although today's ways of giving a Christian account of salvation appropriate metaphors from the first-century Jewish social and religious world—such as sacrifice and redemption—the overall relationship of the God of Israel to the Israel of God to which the first volume of the Christian canon is devoted appears to be of little, if any, substantive relevance. The commonplace theories of atonement are de-historicized and universalized. Things work equally well (or better) it seems, when the original context of divine-human relationship between Israel and its God is excised from the telling. Its omission becomes increasingly uncomfortable, however, in the light of the NPP and hence bears urgent reconsideration.

The new research should lead us to inquire how the overall story of Israel narrated in the Hebrew Scriptures may be *structurally important* for Christian theology, rather than simply providing a compendium of metaphors and stories to be drawn upon from time-to-time as illustrations of Christian faith and soteriology.

"WHAT'S PAST IS PROLOGUE"?

Shakespeare's famous phrase from *The Tempest*—"What's past is prologue"—might have been speaking of the customary Christian perspective

---

13. There is much to be said for N. T. Wright's idea that Paul is in fact referring to the grand narrative of the scriptural story as a whole: Paul "does not mean that he and his friends can find one or two proof-texts to back up their claim, but rather that these events have come as the climax to the long and winding narrative of Israel's scriptures." N. T. Wright, *Scripture and the Authority of God*, 48.

14. Already we encounter the semantic challenge of how best to describe the first part of the canon in non-pejorative terms. For the sake of narrative flow, we shall follow the practice of the *Notes on the correct way to present the Jews and Judaism in preaching and catechesis in the Roman Catholic Church* (Commission for Religious Relations with the Jews) and "continue to use the expression *Old Testament* because it is traditional (cf. already 2 Cor. 3:14) but also because 'Old' does not mean 'out of date' or 'out-worn.'"

on the relationship between Israel and its God preceding Christ. Christian thought has tended to an innate supersessionism: a "replacement" theology in which the church supplants Israel in the heart and purposes of God in consequence of Israel's rejection of Jesus as its long-awaited Messiah. A "supersessionist assumption" is embedded in the foundational thought-world within which Christian doctrine has been incubated.

R. Kendall Soulen identifies three "distinct yet mutually reinforcing forms" of supersessionism—economic, punitive, and structural—which collectively capture something broader than simply a "replacement theology":

> *Economic* supersessionism "holds that from the beginning, God's purpose for carnal Israel in the economy of salvation was destined to be fulfilled and completed by Christ's coming, after which its place was taken by the church." Thus, "everything characteristic of the economy in its [carnal] Israelite form is fulfilled and rendered obsolete by its ecclesial [spiritual] equivalent." Christ's coming means that Israel's carnal existence is "theologically obsolete."
>
> *Punitive* supersessionism "holds that God has angrily abrogated the covenant with Israel because of Israel's *de facto* rejection of the gospel. Generally, punitive supersessionism is an addition to economic supersessionism, not an alternative to it."
>
> *Structural* supersessionism, meanwhile, is the tendency to "*render the Hebrew Scriptures largely indecisive for shaping doctrinal conclusions about how God engages creation in universal and enduring ways.*"[15]

Unlike the first two types, structural supersessionism "does not ordinarily appear as an explicit body of teaching about the Jews." Rather, it "makes itself evident as a characteristic of virtually every other area of Christian thought, namely, as the quality of 'Israel-forgetfulness.'"[16] It is not simply that the church has been "absent-minded"—an active theological anti-Judaism pervades common assumptions within Evangelicalism. We shall argue that this, too, is inappropriate and requires to be countered. Supersessionism *per se* need not necessarily be anti-Judaic, but a general denigration of Israel and/or the covenant in Torah is typically a twin tendency.[17]

15. Soulen, "Karl Barth and the Future of the God of Israel," 415–17. Italics original.
16. Ibid., 417.
17. We note Roman Catholic scholars Marianne Moyaert and Didier Pollefeyt's translation of the Latin *supercedere* as "to be superior to." "Israel and the Church: Fulfillment beyond Supersessionism?" in Moyaert and Pollefeyt (eds.), *Never Revoked*, 159. Michael Vlach offers a more visual rendering—*super* (on or upon) and *sedere* (to sit):

As we progress, we shall encounter all three forms identified by Soulen and—given their mutually-reinforcing character—we are equally concerned with each. With regard to economic and punitive, we shall be denying their premises. With regard to structural supersessionism, we shall wish to turn it on its head and to argue that precisely the opposite should be the case: once supersessionist presuppositions are eliminated, God's history with Israel should provide a *decisive* theological contribution in shaping our doctrinal conclusions, in this case concerning the atonement. For simplicity's sake, we shall use the term "supersessionism" in a general sense, of the assertion that Israel has been replaced by the church in the on-going purposes of God. We shall also be equally concerned about the broader "theological anti-Judaism" that paints a deeply-negative portrait of Judaism as a religion of works-righteousness and of "the Jews" as hypocritical legalists (concerned with outward form and ceremony rather than heartfelt inward piety) and denigrates the Sinaitic covenant as an ineffectual means of knowing God. Theological anti-Judaism positions perceived negative features of Judaism over against Christianity's perceived corresponding qualities—law *versus* grace, flesh *versus* spirit, darkness *versus* light, type *versus* reality, works *versus* faith, and so on. These assumptions flow freely in Reformed Evangelicalism, at both a popular and academic level, and they are at least as problematic as supersessionism itself in eviscerating the value of Israel's relationship with its God as a resource for Christian thought.

Israel's history with the God of Israel has fared particularly badly when it comes to being credited with making any positive contribution to Christian thinking about atonement. This is because Christ's "new" soteriological work has been interpreted as enabling precisely what Israel's "old" soteriological understandings based in the law (Torah) could not.[18] In Christian thought, the words of the apostle Paul have appeared to make the point clearly enough: What Israel's faith represented by the law was

---

"one person sitting on another's chair, displacing the latter." "Replacement Theology: Has the Church Superseded Israel as the People of God?" The William R. Rice Lecture Series, March 17, 2010, 1, available at http://www.dbts.edu/pdf/rls/Vlach_ReplacementTheology.pdf (accessed February 24, 2012).

18. We shall later return to the point that "law" (as it is generally rendered in Bible translations) is an unfortunate and unhelpful translation of "Torah," which is something far more profound than the English concept of law suggests. Martin Selman's survey of the 220 occurrences of Torah in the OT reveals three main aspects of the word: (1) teaching or instruction to be learned; (2) commands to be obeyed; and (3) guidance about how to live in specific situations. See "Law," in Alexander and Baker (eds.), *Dictionary of the Old Testament: Pentateuch*, 498. Attempts to rehabilitate the word "law" present an uphill struggle due to the deeply negative overtones of "legalism" in Christian thinking.

powerless to do, God did by sending his Son (Rom 8:3). Evangelicalism has not devoted much time, however, to asking quite *why* the God of Israel would give Israel such an inadequate framework—living in accordance with Torah—within which to live as his covenant people. Why, for many centuries, he would allow them to continue in trusting and faithful dependence on its ordinances, in what would appear—in Christian hindsight—to amount to a state of self-delusion.[19]

The Evangelical tradition in particular has taken it as somehow "obvious" that Judaism and legalism are there as the dark clouds to enable the light of Christ and his grace to shine more brightly in contrast. The effect of this thinking, as Soulen observes, is that Christianity traditionally "misinterprets redemption in Christ as deliverance from God's history with Israel and the nations."[20] Influenced by the classic Reformed understanding that Luther's railing against mediaeval Catholicism was directly comparable to Paul's railing against Judaism, the logic has been that the new religion of Christianity was everything that its predecessor was not and could never be.

In consequence, the canonical Old Testament has come to occupy a strangely ambiguous place. On the one hand, it is habitually raided for stories and proof-texts to illustrate and support Christianity in ways that imply a very strong continuity. Examples include where: (a) the New Testament already offers its own endorsement of Old Testament subject-matter, such as the heroes of faith in Hebrews 11; (b) prophetic foretelling endorses Jesus being the Messiah and hence, adds the weight of the longevity of the Israelite tradition to the credibility of the Christian story; and (c) Old Testament texts seem to reflect a similar understanding of "relationship with God" to that which we see in the New Testament. On the other hand, Evangelicals also position significant swathes of Old Testament text in an essentially negative relationship to the New Testament (especially concerning the efficacy of the law) or set them aside in an almost Marcionite way.

The overarching theological framework offered by the Old Testament story of Israel and its relationship with its God is perceived mostly to be offering insights on what the relationship was not—and could never be—in a negative sense compared to that which Christianity offers. This negative

---

19. If one was incapable of living in accordance with Torah (including its provisions for relational restoration in the event of failure—"sin," in other words) then God had surely played a "cruel trick" on Israel by giving it to them in the first place and allowing them to believe in it as they did. The standard Christian explanation of Christ having "fulfilled" the law (i.e., succeeded in living in accordance with Torah, when all others had failed) does not answer this question. Still less does it tell us, except through a confessional presupposition, why Torah is thereby brought to an end. These are questions we shall endeavor to address.

20. Soulen, *God of Israel*, 110.

perception presumes the story's overarching theological framework to have nothing positive to offer as an interpretive lens for the eternal relational purposes of God with humanity over the entire span of human history; including—and most particularly—in the Christian era. Put another way, if the failure of the cosmic plan-A (i.e., Israel) explains the need for the cosmic plan-B (i.e., Christ), and if it is the inefficacy of the one that provides the basis to understand the efficacy of the other, then the primary function of Israel's story is to offer a negative salvific contrast rather than a positive salvific continuity. By driving an historical wedge between the gospel and the God of Israel, the theological significance of God's way with Israel is "fatally undercut," rather than functioning as "the permanent and enduring medium of God's work" and "the permanent and enduring context of the gospel about Jesus."[21]

A central feature here is, of course, the role and place of Torah, the law. This negative framework means that those texts that mention law in a positive sense need to have the law taken out of them! For example, Psalm 119:97—"Oh, how I love your law! I meditate on it all day long" (NIV)—is widely cited by Christians as a timeless reflection applicable to scripture in general. However, they do not mean or intend it to be taken literally, as regards the law in particular. To endorse "loving the law" would be tantamount to "loving legalism"—hence, the truth of that verse "works" only if and to the extent that we substitute "Bible" for "law." The idea that the Psalmist truly held a positive perception of the law—one that saw it as divinely-inspired, rather than naïvely-misguided—and that his words have significance for understanding the eternal ways of God with humanity is not contemplated.

The attitude of Christian religion to its predecessor could be characterized by the title of the popular song of the late 1930s that became the entertainer Bob Hope's signature tune: *Thanks for the Memory*.[22] To an extent, this is perhaps understandable—after all, the more one affirms the "old" religion of Israel, the less need or opportunity there would appear to be for a distinctively new Christianity. This is a problem to which we shall return.

This reasoning came into sharper focus from the eighteenth and nineteenth centuries, when under the influence of the Enlightenment it was perceived that

> Christians needed to prove that Christianity was superior to Judaism. Otherwise, why would it exist at all? Surely Jesus and

---

21. Soulen, *God of Israel*, 110; 112.

22. Composed by Ralph Rainger and Leo Robin and first introduced in the 1938 film *The Big Broadcast*.

Paul saw something basically and intrinsically wrong in Judaism, or there would be no new religion. [. . .] The charge of legalism perfectly fitted the Christian need to accuse Judaism of producing bad humans.[23]

And yet, as Martin Selman points out, the God of Israel expressly and unambiguously promised "blessing" and "life" to those who made the choice to obey Torah: Israel "will be blessed more than any other people" (Deut 7:14, NIV) and will enjoy an abundance of prosperity and protection that identifies Israel as his people (Deut 28). Moreover, the Old Testament associates Torah first and foremost with the person and character of YHWH rather than with statutes and regulations.[24] Indeed, if one is entitled to take God at his word, then living faithfully to Torah was by definition being in right relationship with God—"If we are careful to obey all this law before the LORD our God, as he has commanded us, that will be our righteousness." (Deut 6:25, NIV).

THE BACKDROP OF THE HOLOCAUST AND MODERN ISRAEL

Beyond purely theological considerations, events of the twentieth century have also contributed to a changed landscape. To begin with, there is the horror of the Holocaust, in which as Soulen notes, Christians have had to confess their own complicity.[25] John Gager states it more bluntly:

> The experience of the Holocaust reintroduced with unprecedented urgency the question of Christianity's responsibility for anti-Semitism: not simply whether individual Christians had added fuel to modern European anti-Semitism, but whether Christianity itself was, in its essence and from its beginnings, the primary source of anti-Semitism in Western culture.[26]

---

23. Sanders, "Jesus, Anti-Judaism, and Modern Christianity," 49.

24. Selman, "Law," in Desmond Alexander and Baker (eds.), *Dictionary of the Old Testament: Pentateuch*, 512, 509.

25. Soulen, *God of Israel*, x.

26. Gager, *The Origins of Anti-Semitism*, 13. Gager argues that the trauma of the Second World War is largely responsible for bringing the study of both pagan and Christian views of ancient Judaism into the mainstream of scholarship and for determining the direction which that study has taken (14).

As Jewish scholar, David Meyer, has observed, "The Church was not Nazi. [. . .] But nevertheless, it was in Christian soil that Nazism took root."[27] An easy and comfortable "taken-for-granted" supersessionism has therefore become increasingly awkward and uncomfortable.

Furthermore, the world has seen the recent return of a Jewish people to a real country called Israel after almost two thousand years of exile and deprivation of nation-status. No longer is the promised land of the ancient texts simply a relic of ancient history that may conveniently be consigned to a bygone era. Once again, there is a land and a nation called "Israel."[28]

And yet, many centuries of supersessionist disposition, in-built within the church's theology, is not something that can simply be jettisoned without considerable thought being given to the ramifications—not least for its reading of Pauline texts. Christian doctrine has heretofore taken for granted first-century Judaism's "calling" to be first-century Christianity's antithesis, not least concerning soteriology.

As Soulen identifies, therefore, "The rejection of supersessionism is fraught with profound implications for the whole range of Christian theological reflection, and the full extent of these implications is still far from fully clear."[29] Our special interest here is to consider these profound implications with regard to soteriology in general and atonement in particular.

With this problematic background in view, our concern is to develop a perspective on atonement that presents the God of Israel as having a unified and coherent approach to his relationship with humankind throughout the full course of canonical history. It rises to the implicit challenge of the NPP to apply a rehabilitated view of Israel's relationship with its God to Christian doctrinal thought concerning atonement—namely, how relationship with God is established, maintained, and where necessary restored both pre- and post-Christ. It invites us to consider the manner in which a positive understanding of Israel's relationship with God through Torah ought to inform our understanding of the nature of relationship with God through Christ. And it invites us to develop an articulation of how these two bases of relationship with God interact that is affirming of both.

Once relationship to God through Torah is recognized as providing a positive rather than negative point of reference for understanding relationship to God through Christ, each such relationship ought logically

---

27. "*Nostra Aetate*: Past, Present, Future," in Moyaert and Pollefeyt (eds.), *Never Revoked*, 119.

28. This is not to enter into a quasi-political debate about the modern State of Israel in either a religious or secular sense. It is simply to note that its re-emergence is an unavoidable background feature to contemporary discussion.

29. Soulen, *God of Israel*, x.

to be perceived to shine positive interpretive light on the other within one coherent whole (rather than it being "one-way traffic" solely from the Christian direction).

It is worth saying up-front that we shall not be suggesting no-one previously has proposed a connection between the story of Israel and soteriology from an Evangelical perspective. N. T. Wright, for example, is a prominent NPP scholar associated with the Evangelical tradition who has written extensively on Israel's story. However, the NPP has not as yet developed an account that grants any materiality to it in soteriological terms, at least in any positive sense. Indeed, we will argue that certainly in the NPP's early scholarship, its thinking—Wright's included—has continued to reflect a supersessionist and theologically anti-Judaic assumption. The question here is whether Israel has been granted any integral and indispensable place in the accounts of atonement that are currently on the systematic-theological map (to which the answer, we suggest, is "no"). There is a significant difference between appropriating imagery that would have been familiar to Israel—such as "sacrifice" or "ransom"—and finding the relationship of Israel and its God to be in some way indispensable to the Christian doctrine.

IN SEARCH OF A NEW PERSPECTIVE

In the course of this book, we shall be exploring answers to a number of questions:

- Can an overarching continuity be identified in God's redemptive ways that provides a "missing link" to how Christ's atoning work should properly be understood?
- Does this offer a route to a non-supersessionist theory of the atonement and, if so, what are the implications for Christian thought concerning law *versus* grace, works *versus* promise, and other dark *versus* light contrasts?
- How would this impact on an Evangelical understanding of the gospel?
- And last but not least, where would it leave the traditional models and metaphors of atonement?

The development of the argument has been structured around four substantive chapters, in the following fashion.

Chapter one, *The Doctrine of Atonement*, reviews the current state of play in existing accounts of atonement within the Evangelical and Reformed tradition.

The chapter necessarily engages at some length with the current "atonement debate": specifically, the impasse between those who insist on the hegemony of penal substitution and those who espouse a more nuanced and "kaleidoscopic" view in which all of the principal atonement ideas are allowed peacefully to co-exist, each reflecting something of the significance of Christ's atoning work. Ultimately, we find both approaches to be inadequate, drawing particular attention to some of the flaws that undermine the claims of the penal substitutionary doctrine—an important step to include, given its deeply-rooted approbation within Evangelicalism.

Having noted the strangely ambivalent approach throughout Christian history towards adopting a doctrinal position on atonement, we further note the surprising absence, in the metaphors and models by which atonement is customarily characterized, of any positive dependency upon the story of the God of Israel and his relationship with the Israel of God. The doctrine of the atonement exemplifies the "Israel-forgetfulness" inherent within Christian thought. This remains the case even in the work of some recent scholars that we review in this chapter, who may be perceived to have taken steps down this road. It is precisely a concern that the doctrine should reflect an "Israel-remembrance" at the same time as remaining christologically-centered that will shape the critical argument in our ultimate reconstruction. Both features, we suggest, should be recognized as indispensable, rather than inherently antithetical.

The chapter concludes with an outline of the "unfinished business" that we believe remains outstanding in current thinking about the atonement and the implications that may arise from our findings so far.

The title of chapter two, *New Perspectives on First-Century Judaism*, consciously echoes the New Perspective on Paul. As with chapter one, it functions as a review, during which we trace the trajectory of its thought and its principal waypoints.

We are aware that there is some quite widely variegated thinking among New Perspective scholars—it soon becomes clear that there is by no means one such perspective![30] For our purposes, however, we are looking to build upon its more-widely agreed upon findings in asking how a reconstructed view of first-century Judaism might lead to a reconstructed view of the atonement. Accordingly, we shall be taking as a basic premise that the broad conclusions of the NPP, generally shared amongst its scholars, expose an historic Christian misreading of the first-century Jewish religion that was

---

30. As Chris Tilling puts it, the New Perspective "doesn't even exist in the singular"! "Introduction," in Tilling (ed.), *Beyond Old and New Perspectives on Paul*, 1.

common amongst the people. The chapter begins by contextualizing this "new" perspective against the background of the "old."

It is important to emphasize that the subject-matter of this chapter is being approached from the perspective of its potential deployment in a systematic theological context. We are not looking to debate as historical-critical scholars, but simply to bring to bear, on the subject of atonement, some of the core findings of experts specializing in this field. However, where appropriate we shall not draw back from critiquing those scholars on the grounds of supersessionism and/or theological anti-Judaism where these may be discernible in or underlying their theology. We shall be asking to what potentially different doctrinal conclusions their findings might lead, if firstly these negative presuppositions are taken out of the equation and, secondly, we approach the reconstruction process with the expectation of a *positive* contribution from the preceding covenantal relationship of Israel and its God. Once that historic relationship—particularly as it is defined in Torah—is validated in its own terms, it could make a potentially decisive contribution to explaining relationship with God in Christ as appropriately situated in continuity rather than contrast.

Accordingly, we shall not seek to engage in the NPP's intra-disciplinary debates, either as participants or adjudicators. We shall simply act as observers, from a systematic theological perspective, raising questions only in limited measure. Our specific critique will be to question whether notable NPP commentators have failed to identify a continuing supersessionist and theologically anti-Judaistic assumption within their "new perspectives."

Finally, we include some other recent scholarly contributions drawn from outside the confines of the New Perspective *per se*, to paint a fuller picture of the circumstances of the first-century Judaism within which Christianity was incubated—particularly, insights that inspire fresh ways of thinking about the atonement.

In chapter three, *Atonement in New Perspective*, we build upon the materials assembled from chapters one and two to construct the positive case as to how one might go about repairing the fault lines in atonement doctrine.

Founded upon chapter two's findings, we take Paul's view of his own Jewish tradition to have been an essentially positive one, rather than the negative view that has traditionally been assumed. We also take as a starting point that Paul never thought he left something called Judaism for something called Christianity, citing the evidence which suggests that, during its earliest period of development, "Christianity" *was* "a Judaism" rather than self-evidently antithetical from the outset.

It is in this chapter that we are asking and answering the big question towards which we feel the NPP inexorably draws us: "If one were to start from the perspective of an affirming rather than denigrating view of the relationship between God and Israel, into which Christ came and within which his work was situated, how might this influence the way in which his atoning significance might be understood?" This will involve developing an account of atonement that is, so far as possible, free of supersessionism and that recognizes an overarching soteriological significance in God's covenantal history with Israel, alongside a continuing priority to christocentrism. Informed by the new literature, we will argue that the relationship that the covenanting God of Israel entered into with the covenant people Israel, notably in and through Torah,[31] provides the conceptual paradigm by which we can make sense of the covenant relationship that the same covenanting God entered into with the world in and through Christ. We will suggest there should be a presumed continuity, rather than a presumed discontinuity, in systematic theological thought about the atonement across both Old and New Testaments. Stated differently, it would hardly seem unreasonable to propose on the basis of the recent scholarship that a taken-for-granted positivity of the earliest Jewish Christ-followers towards their current understanding of relationship with God—specifically, in God's wonderful gift of Torah—would provide the logical first point of reference for framing their understanding of the wonderful new gift of God in Christ.

Further developing the implications of adopting a non-supersessionist view of Israel's history, we will argue that the basis of the relationship between Israel and its God as set forth in the Old Testament—and specifically, its assumptions concerning atonement—should be affirmed as fully efficacious in its own time and on its own terms, rather than only in some provisional sense contingent upon the temporally-subsequent Christ-event, as Reformed doctrine has argued.[32] A repristinated understanding of first-century Judaism to which the NPP draws our attention should underlie a repristinated understanding of atonement that begins by taking seriously Israel's covenantal relationship with its God (yet without denigrating the unique significance of Christ's work).

In theological terms, the significance of covenant is, of course, by no means a new proposition. It features notably in the so-called "Federal

31. For Jewish religious life, God's covenantal history "has meant primarily the revelation of Torah at Sinai." Eugene Korn, "Introduction," in Jenson and Korn (eds.), *Covenant and Hope*, viii.

32. Reformed thought as expressed in the Westminster Confession of Faith (1647) sees the Old Testament framework as simply offering types and ordinances "fore-signifying Christ to come," which were "for that time sufficient and efficacious" but only insofar as they "instruct and build up the elect in faith in the promised Messiah" through whom forgiveness and salvation was later accomplished in a retrospective sense. See Section V of Chapter VII, entitled *Of God's Covenant with Man*.

theology" of the seventeenth-century Reformers and remains important to their modern successors, who continue to have strong influence within Evangelicalism. Accordingly, we shall address Reformed covenantal thought and how it materially differs from the reading we are proposing. *Contra* the Reformers, we shall argue that the covenantal relationship between the God of Israel and the Israel of God was fully efficacious, including its provisions for atonement, in the period before the birth of Jesus of Nazareth. Torah therefore meant what it said, without reliance on a temporally subsequent event.[33]

Consequently, we shall suggest that the newness of the gospel *versus* Torah lies elsewhere than soteriological efficacy; rather, it is in the *nature* of the relationship now offered "in Christ" as living Word compared to that offered "in Torah" as written word. The relationship is of a different order of magnitude compared to its antecedent. The distinctives are located in the new relationship's mediator, *modus operandi*, and now-universal scope directly embracing the gentiles—as foretold by Israel's prophets.

The arguments will proceed as follows. Firstly, building upon a core conception of atonement berthed in covenantal terms, we explore Miroslav Volf's proposal that if one wishes to understand in Jewish terms what drives the Christian understanding of atonement, one should look at the Jewish notion of election.[34] We suggest a corollary between God's particular covenantal invitation to the nation (Israel) in Torah and his universal invitation to all nations (the world) in Christ. In this context, we discuss the status of the individual versus the group, and the inherent tension between covenant as "gift" and covenant as "demand."

This leads us to follow Morna Hooker by proposing a Christian understanding of God's work in Christ as a "new covenantal nomism" (based on Sanders's famous assertion of Judaism's pattern of religion as "covenantal nomism")[35]—namely, a divine covenantal invitation, to which in order to enter into the benefits of the covenant a faithful response is required to the stipulations of the covenant-maker. We argue that Sanders's rejection of the notion that the Pauline pattern of religion was a covenantal nomism results from a universalized reading of what Paul was saying and an assumption that Paul "finds something wrong" in his prior Judaism.[36] Thus, by applying a post-supersessionist criterion that assumes substantial *correspondence* in

---

33. It is of course the case that in the Christian understanding, the God of Israel and Torah was always and everywhere the Triune God, eternally active by Word and Spirit.

34. Volf, "The Lamb of God and the Sin of the World," 316–17.

35. Hooker, "Paul and Covenantal Nomism," 48.

36. See pages 179–82.

how "old" and "new" operate, rather than the traditional view of substantial *dissimilarity*, we argue that to be and to live "in Torah" functioned covenantally as the nomistic equivalent of being "in Christ."

In this, we acknowledge "Torah" as being far more than merely "law" or instruction—rather, as George Foot Moore long ago characterized it, Torah is "all that God has made known of his nature, character, and purpose, and of what he would have man be and do."[37] Exploring the insights of W. D. Davies, in particular,[38] we suggest that a "new" Torah has become incarnate in Christ (a Torah "personified") and that through the outpoured Spirit God can be known and experienced in a way that bears direct continuity with— but is also a development from—Israel's relationship in Torah. As Jenson suggests, with echoes of the Johannine prologue, "the Torah became flesh and dwelt among us."[39]

A repristinated view of Torah in first-century context leads us to suggest—though it will be for others to explore further, from an historical standpoint—that the "big debating point" for the early church on which we are eavesdroppers in our reading of the New Testament was not to do with universalized and timeless concerns over salvation by grace *versus* works, but specifically first-century concerns over the correlation of God's wonderful longstanding gift of Torah with his wonderful new gift of Christ. If we take that first-century context to be one in which Torah was held in very high rather than low regard, it would be entirely logical for Jewish Jesus-followers to be deeply concerned to determine the appropriate roles of Torah and Christ, alone or in combination, in the on-going covenantal relationship. The question would, of course, be exacerbated by their recognition of an eschatologically-significant outpouring of the Holy Spirit, by which the God of Israel has invited the gentiles to enter into relationship with himself through Christ, outside of Torah.[40]

---

37. Moore, *Judaism in the First Centuries of the Christian Era*, vol. 1, 263.

38. See pages 185–89.

39. Jenson, "Toward a Christian Theology of Judaism," 6, 12.

40. E.g., reading Gal 3:2–5, with a substantially or exclusively gentile audience in mind: "[D]id you receive the Spirit by the works of the law, or by believing what you heard? [. . .] [D]oes God give you his Spirit and work miracles among you by the works of the law, or by your believing what you heard?" Cf. the story of Peter and Cornelius in Acts 10–11: "[I]f God gave them the same gift he gave us who believed in the Lord Jesus Christ, who was I to think that I could stand in God's way? When they heard this, they had no further objections [. . .]. [M]en from Cyprus and Cyrene went to Antioch and began to speak to Greeks also, telling them the good news about the Lord Jesus. The Lord's hand was with them, and a great number of people believed and turned to the Lord. News of this reached the church in Jerusalem, and they sent Barnabas to Antioch. When he arrived and saw what the grace of God had done, he was glad and encouraged

We further develop the concept of the covenant in Christ as a new covenantal nomism within an understanding of Christ's death as covenantal sacrifice situated in Passover. This leads us to a renewed appreciation of the significance of the Eucharist in the early church and New Testament thought, as the repeated reminder and assurance of continuing atonement in Christ in the new covenant relationship. This is preceded—and further illuminated—by a short but important examination of the kinship dynamic of covenant.

Finally, having summarized these features and elements of a covenantal framework for the atonement, we come back to the question of the extent to which this repristinated reading of the story of Israel's relationship to the God of Israel can address supersessionism. Is it possible to explain atonement in a thought framework that affirms Christ's superiority—in texts such as Hebrews 8:10: "the ministry Jesus has received is as superior to theirs as the covenant of which he is mediator is superior to the old one, since the new covenant is established on better promises" (NIV)—without the hard supersessionism that treats God's prior covenantal promises as obsolete and replaced by those to the church? We articulate an understanding that seeks to "fit" with the twin objectives of rehabilitating the authenticity and efficacy of the God of Israel's antecedent relationship with the Israel of God yet at the same time gives full assent to the traditional Evangelical understanding of the unique place of the incarnate Christ in enabling for humanity an atoned personal relationship with God. Nonetheless, we acknowledge that there remains the question as to whether in seeking to meet this twin challenge we are still left with a version of supersessionism, even if it is in a distinctly softer form.

Finally, in chapter four, *The Continuing Place of the Traditional Ideas of Atonement*, we explore the implications of an "Israel-remembered" reading of how atonement is accomplished for the imagery on which the church's explanations currently rely. We suggest that all of the traditional imagery is actually addressing *ramifications* of the covenant; that the *foundational locus* of atonement is and always has been a covenantal decision in the heart of God birthed in the grace of God and accessed by faith in his word and his promises. That decision is manifested to *the nation* of Israel in its covenantal history, notably in Torah. Now it is manifested to *the nations* in the covenant in Christ. In both eras, however, we see one continuing covenantal

---

them all to remain true to the Lord with all their hearts." Acts 11:17–18, 20–23. (NIV) Here we see the Jewish leadership of the nascent Jesus-movement revising their established theological points of reference (initially with reluctance) to accommodate what the God of Israel clearly had done in Christ among the gentiles, through the outpoured eschatological Spirit, outwith Torah.

narrative. Thus, we suggest that Israel's story is both the context in which God's covenantal work in Christ is situated and the means by which it can best be understood. Before and after the Christ-event, there is clear continuity in how atonement is made possible: namely, a covenantal decision in the heart of God, birthed in the grace of God and accessed by responsive faith to his covenantal offer. Along with the other benefits of relationship with God, atonement is accessed not through a transaction (whether effected at the cross or an altar) but in the same way it always has been: through a relational response to God's gracious invitation, on God's covenantal terms. We may call this a *new-covenantal nomism*, informed by Sanders's famous phrase, *covenantal nomism*, to which we shall suggest it bears comparison.

The imagery offered by the traditional Christian metaphors, models, and motifs of atonement continues to have an invaluable role in explaining what Christ has done (at least insofar as they are images that continue to "make sense" within the cultural contexts in which they are used). However, we argue that all such imagery is addressing the *benefits* of atonement, not its *source*; they are implications flowing from and accessed by our response to atonement's *causa proxima*—God's sovereign covenantal decision.

In a similar way to how an illustration such as ransom from slavery communicated effectively in the New Testament period and imagery such as the "satisfaction" theory spoke powerfully in Anselm's day, creative reimagining through the picture-language of metaphor can and should continue to be deployed in new and evolving cultural contexts. However, consistent with the full canonical story of salvation—that begins with (and for its overall coherence depends upon) the relationship of Israel and its God—atonement imagery past, present, and future should be understood as deriving from a first principle that atonement is and has always been to do with a divine covenantal decision. The heart of atonement lies in the heart of God.

CHAPTER ONE

The Doctrine of Atonement

How can a judicial murder be represented as a salvific event? This is the kind of question that has driven the church to seek a theology of atonement. Many such theories have been produced and there is no single one that is universally accepted. At the best, we can only hope to have a number of analogies and metaphors, correcting and supplementing each other but together conveying something of the mystery of the cross as it has been experienced in Christian faith.[1]

1.1 INTRODUCTION

THE CHRISTIAN DOCTRINE OF atonement is attempting to answer the question of how, exactly, humanity is made "at one" with God through the person and work of Christ—or, in the language of Middle English, restored to a state of "at-one-ment."[2] Given its critical importance, it is unsurprising that Leon Morris should describe the atonement as "the central doctrine of Christianity."[3] One might therefore be forgiven for finding it curious that no particular or exclusive understanding of atonement has ever been insisted upon by the church as determining Christian orthodoxy. As J. N. D. Kelly sums it up, "While the conviction of redemption through Christ has always been the motive force of Christian faith, no final and universally accepted definition of the manner of its achievement has been formulated to

---

1. Macquarrie, *Jesus Christ in Modern Thought*, 400.
2. See "Atonement" in *The Concise Oxford Dictionary*, 68.
3. Morris, "Atonement," 57.

this day."[4] Accordingly, one can inhabit the land of Christian orthodoxy, classically defined, without embracing one particular theory of the atonement.[5] Through the centuries, atonement has been explained by reference to sundry analogies and metaphors deriving from biblical imagery, mediated through contemporary thought, each "conveying something"—in John Macquarrie's phrase, quoted above—of how the cross of Christ is salvific.

Theological consideration of atonement has tended to focus either on arguing for a preferred theory or, alternatively, on how the various theories ought to be understood to fit together. A recent example of this is the debate within Evangelicalism concerning the claimed hegemony of the penal substitutionary doctrine (on which, more anon). However, the burden of this particular work lies elsewhere. Perhaps the most curious thing about all of the traditional Christian accounts of atonement is the virtual absence of any meaningful reference to the historic relationship between Israel and its God within which the atoning work of Christ took place. To all intents and purposes, atonement has been abstracted from the religious context in which it was achieved—it has come adrift from its Jewish moorings. It is as if the entire narrative of Israel and its God up until that point has no material bearing on the Christian doctrinal perspective, notwithstanding that Jesus was speaking to Jews from within Judaism and that his immediate followers were all Jews.[6] It seems that a conflation has occurred, in which the fact that Christ's work has universal and timeless significance has been confused with the idea that atonement is to be explained in universalized and dehistoricized terms. The doctrine of atonement exemplifies what Soulen calls an "Israel-forgetfulness"; namely, that

> Christians [. . .] have commonly accounted for [the gospel's] truth by means of a construal of the Bible's narrative unity that [. . .] renders God's identity as the God of Israel and the center of the Hebrew Scriptures almost wholly indecisive for grasping God's antecedent purpose for human creation.[7]

Soulen's insight offers the intriguing idea of looking at the subject of atonement through the opposite end of the telescope—that is to say, with a presumption that God's identity as the God of Israel and the center of the Hebrew Scriptures is actually *decisive* for grasping his antecedent purpose and that accounting for the gospel's truth might somehow *depend* on such

---

4. Kelly, *Early Christian Doctrines*, 163.
5. Green, "Must We Imagine the Atonement in Penal Substitutionary Terms?" 154.
6. Levine, *The Misunderstood Jew*, 216–17.
7. Soulen, *God of Israel*, 49, 156.

a construal. This would be a radical change of direction from the assumption that an old and inferior religion called Judaism is the province of the Old Testament, while a new and better religion called Christianity is the province of the New.[8] It would render null and void any on-going construal of Christian faith that sought to define its own qualities over against Judaism's corresponding failings. It would necessitate reversing the tendencies in Christian history to separate Jesus from his Judaism and to espouse an essentially ahistorical gospel beginning with a decontextualized and universalized Savior.

However, the development of such an account must await chapter three. The purpose of this present chapter is a discussion of the current state-of-play concerning how atonement is and has historically been understood and an analysis of its key themes. We will reflect on the manner in which its theories, models, and metaphors construe the interaction of the "problem" with its corresponding "solution" and the role that is played in that construal by culture and worldview. Given our chosen scholarly context, we will be mostly concerned to consider Evangelicalism's perspective. This will necessitate addressing, in particular, the claims to hegemony of the penal substitutionary doctrine, since Evangelicalism widely perceives this to be "obviously" the principal and necessary biblical understanding.[9] Self-evidently, were this to be the case, there would be no "gap" to fill, whether with reference to the story of Israel or anything else.

The chapter will therefore develop as follows. To begin, we will look at atonement in history. Here, we will firstly note the absence of creedal confessional affirmations concerning the atonement. Secondly, we will briefly review how atonement has been conceived historically, through various "objective" or "subjective" models, metaphors, or theories. Thirdly, we will consider in depth the principal Evangelical idea of the atonement—penal substitution. Finally, we will contrast that approach with the alternative multi-faceted or "kaleidoscopic" understanding that many prefer.

In the second part of the chapter we shall briefly review the work of a few scholars who may be perceived already to have taken some steps along

---

8. We are conscious of the complexities in deploying the word "Judaism" as a simple descriptor of the first-century Jewish religious context, as well as the development that has taken place in Judaism between then and now. For present purposes we are using the term simply to speak in a general sense of the religion of ancient Israel at the time of Christ—the context of religious belief and practice that was the product to date of the history of Israel and the God of Israel.

9. Thomas Schreiner, for example, claims that "penal substitution functions as the anchor and foundation for all other dimensions of the Atonement when the Scriptures are considered as a canonical whole." Schreiner, "Penal Substitution View," 67.

the same path, in offering a contribution to atonement theory drawn from aspects of the biblical story of Israel.

As the chapter develops, we shall see time and again that—whether we are talking about the traditional models or recent thinking—"Israel-forgetfulness" is to the fore. We find this to be so in both parts of the chapter. Even where atonement accounts touch upon Old Testament "themes" it will be evident that they draw no necessary or substantive contribution from the relationship between Israel and its God. This omission is not necessarily through any conscious decision; it simply does not appear to have been a relevant consideration.

We close the chapter by summarizing the current position concerning how atonement is typically conceived and explained, and the weaknesses it displays. In particular, we note once again the supersessionist and dehistoricizing tendency that disallows any meaningful place to the antecedent story of Israel and its God. Finally, we anticipate the potential implications for the traditional models and metaphors of any fresh account of atonement that seeks to redress the balance.

1.2 ATONEMENT IN HISTORICAL PERSPECTIVE

1.2.1 *Atonement in the Creeds*

It is fascinating that though there are numerous references to Christ's work in the Apostolic Fathers, they appear to be concerned more with the benefits imparted by Christ than the manner of atonement. Nowhere, it seems, do the Fathers "co-ordinate their main ideas," or "attempt to sketch a rationale of salvation."[10] Accordingly, Kelly concludes, "It is useless to look for any systematic treatment of the doctrine in the popular Christianity of the second century."[11] Indeed, it appears this was the case for at least the first five centuries of the church's life and confession.

> The manner in which the death of Christ, particularly in relation to the forgiveness of sins, is referred to in the creedal and later confessional statements of the Church and the Churches is singularly frugal, very varied, and nowhere approaches the sophistication which the doctrines of God and of the Person of Christ achieve.[12]

---

10. Kelly, *Early Christian Doctrines*, 163.
11. Ibid., 163.
12. McIntyre, *The Shape of Soteriology*, 1.

Creedal confessional affirmations were originally taught orally and transmitted to catechumens for profession at baptism, long before they were committed to writing. Growing out of baptismal *formulae* and scriptural statements that profess belief—such as Peter's declaration in Matthew 16:16, "You are the Messiah, the Son of the living God"—various "brief and popular" rules of faith developed and were committed to writing for general use.[13] All of the articles ultimately comprising the Apostles' Creed appeared individually in theological *formulae* that were current *c.* 100 CE and were compacted in that form in Rome by *c.* 200 CE.[14] After the fourth century, The Apostles' Creed came to be the prevailing text in the West, alongside The Nicene Creed in the East.[15] Philip Schaff speaks of The Apostles' Creed as "the Creed of creeds," containing "all the fundamental articles of the Christian faith necessary to salvation."[16] The Nicene Creed, meanwhile, enlarges upon those ideas and is more definitive concerning the Trinity and the Holy Spirit.

In neither case, however, do these foundational doctrinal documents provide a "rationale of salvation" through Christ; the statements in the second article of The Apostles' Creed, for example, concerning Christ's birth, death, burial, and resurrection, are presented as straightforward historical statements and "separated from the belief-affirmation in 'the forgiveness of sins' that comes in the third article. In other words, forgiveness of sins would seem to be more associated with the Holy Spirit, and is not explicitly related to the death of Christ."[17] Similarly, "remission of sins" in the Nicene Creed appears only towards the end, where it is conjoined with "one baptism," yet clearly separated from the christological affirmations in the early and middle parts. McIntyre suggests that if anything, salvation is being presented as the objective of the *incarnation* rather than the crucifixion (namely, "For us

---

13. Schaff, *The Creeds of Christendom*, 5. "Creed" comes from the Latin *credo* ("I believe").

14. McIntyre, *Shape of Soteriology*, 2. Also, Leith, *Creeds of the Churches*, 22.

15. Schaff, *Creeds of Christendom*, 6, 14–23.

16. Ibid., 14–15. The title "Apostles' Creed" indicates a popular summary of apostolic teaching derived from the New Testament rather than apostolic authorship, as was once believed—see Schaff, *Creeds of Christendom*, 22–23, and Kelly, *Early Christian Doctrines*, 44–45. On the Apostles' Creed, generally, see Schaff, *Creeds of Christendom*, 14–23, and on The Nicene Creed, 24–29.

17. McIntyre, *Shape of Soteriology*, 2.

and for our salvation he came down from heaven: by the power of the Holy Spirit he became incarnate from the Virgin Mary, and was made man."[18]).[19]

Given the significance of Christ's work at the cross in Western thought—evidenced in our word "crucial," deriving from "cruciform" (pertaining to the cross)[20]—the apparent ambivalence of this creedal background is puzzling. It is a state of affairs that McIntyre regards as being

> so very, very odd as to merit much more consideration than it is traditionally given in histories of soteriology; and, moreover, it has consequences for the later development of the discipline of soteriology which have been too long ignored.[21]

Although Green cautions against reading too much into the lacuna—there may have been no creedal doctrine of atonement in the period, but the creeds do not stand alone[22]—Gustaf Aulén points out that neither the New Testament nor the teaching of the early church provides a developed theological doctrine of the atonement. What we find instead is "an idea or *motif* expressed with many variations of outward form."[23]

How, then, is creedal silence on atonement to be explained? Of the reasons customarily advanced, primacy is usually given to the argument that the creeds were dealing with extant issues of controversy in relation to Christian orthodoxy and the doctrine of atonement was simply "not an issue" in the period up to the fifth century and beyond. Kelly, for example, suggests that "the redemption did not become a battle-ground for rival schools until the twelfth century, when Anselm's *Cur Deus Homo?* (c. 1097) focused attention on it."[24] There is undoubtedly truth in this,[25] but the significance of the creedal materials for early Christian teaching suggests there must surely be rather more to it. After all, even a cursory review of the comprehensive overall content of the creeds obviates the idea that they were only seeking to offer theology "by exception." In fact, if Schaff is right in asserting that "the value of creeds depends upon the measure of their

---

18. This modern language version is available at http://anglicansonline.org/basics/nicene.html (accessed June 1, 2017).

19. Ibid., 3.

20. "Crucial" in *The Concise Oxford Dictionary*, 278.

21. McIntyre, *Shape of Soteriology*, 6.

22. Green, "Must We Imagine," 154.

23. Aulén, *Christus Victor*, 78.

24. *Early Christian Doctrines*, 375.

25. The christological dispute generated by Arius is an example of a doctrinal issue felt to require creedal determination.

agreement with scripture,"[26] then those creeds' failure to offer a scriptural basis for how redemption in Christ is accomplished would seem significantly to undermine their value.

What is equally interesting is that the church's creedal confession is also remarkably silent on God's history with Israel. As Soulen has observed, that history has played a role that has been ultimately indecisive for shaping the canonical narrative's overarching plot:

> Israel's story contributes little or nothing to understanding how God's consummating and redemptive purposes engage human creation in universal and enduring ways. Indeed, the background can be completely omitted from an account of Christian faith without thereby disturbing the overarching logic of salvation history. This omission is reflected in virtually every historic confession of Christian faith from the Creeds of Nicaea and Constantinople to the Augsburg Confession and beyond.[27]

In summary, then, from the earliest times we find the field of Christian doctrinal thought surprisingly lacking in affirming a particular or exclusive "orthodox" statement of atonement. The reasons for this are far from clear. While the basis of atonement could perhaps have been simply "obvious" to the early Christians, that is certainly not obvious from the materials handed down to us and still less is it obvious quite why that should have been the case. Similarly, the creedal affirmations are also astonishingly silent with regard to Israel's story.

Might it perhaps be that there is some relation between these twin silences? Or put more ambitiously, might the introduction of a positive "Israel-recognition" shed some potentially significant light on how we think about the atonement from a doctrinal perspective? Chapter three will explore this further.

1.2.2 Atonement and the Nature of the Human Predicament

As we noted earlier, Christians typically employ imagery drawn or derived from the biblical materials that are variously referred to, amongst other terms, as metaphors, models, or theories of the atonement.[28] The most basic

---

26. Schaff, *Creeds of Christendom*, 7.

27. Soulen, *God of Israel*, 32. He footnotes that until recently the one exception referring in detail to God's history with the Jewish people was the First Scottish Confession (1560).

28. On "models," see McIntyre, *Shape of Soteriology*, 26–87; on "metaphor," see Gunton, *The Actuality of Atonement*, esp. 27–48; on "idea, theory and motif," see Aulén,

division usually drawn between these modes of explanation is whether they address atonement in so-called "objective" or "subjective" terms. In *Christus Victor*, for example, Aulén starts his consideration of the main types of the atonement with precisely that distinction.[29] He explains atonement conceived in "subjective" terms by reference to the power of the cross effecting a change in us, while in "objective" terms it consists in a changed attitude on the part of God.[30] In recent times, however, commentators such as Fiddes have challenged the "either-or" nature of this distinction. Although subjective *versus* objective serves as "a convenient piece of shorthand,"[31] no theory of atonement, he suggests, can be *entirely* objective or subjective; rather, there will be a shifting balance between the two elements in the different understandings.

> The question then is not whether a view of atonement is objective *or* subjective, although much fruitless argument has been spent on this by Christian thinkers in the past; the question to be asked is how well it *integrates* the two elements.[32]

There are of course dangers in an undue emphasis on either dimension in isolation. As Fiddes points out, the more that atonement is stressed in terms of a *past event*, the more danger there is of present experience being seen as "a mere appendix to a completed act"; salvation must include the human response, for "it needs two to make a meeting." On the other hand, the heavier the stress on *present experience*, "the greater the danger becomes of regarding salvation as a merely subjective matter of human feelings."[33]

The "subjective *versus* objective" divide in terms of atonement concepts continues to feature in the present-day atonement debate, but within

---

Christus Victor, esp. 174–75; on "images," see Stott, *The Cross of Christ*, 168; on "picture-words," see Morris, *The Atonement*, 13 onwards; and on "story," see Mann, *Atonement for a "Sinless Society,"* 63–103. Clearly, these terms are not synonymous, but their nuances and distinctions are mostly not material for our purposes and they will be used as if they were synonymous.

29. Aulén, *Christus Victor*, 2–6.

30. Ibid., 2. Fiddes defines the terms slightly differently: an interpretation of atonement is *objective* when it locates salvation in a past event, outside our experience and feelings; it is *subjective* when it describes salvation as a process within present human experience. Fiddes, *Past Event*, 26. The distinction is typically illustrated by contrasting the eleventh-century theories of Anselm of Canterbury ("satisfaction," objective) and Peter Abelard ("moral influence," subjective) and tracing developments from these starting points.

31. Fiddes, *Past Event and Present Salvation*, 26.

32. Ibid., 26.

33. Ibid., 26–27.

Evangelicalism it is now a sub-set of a wider discussion, in which the central issue seems to have become the perceived need to preserve and defend biblical "truth" in the face of the threat posed by contemporary culture—in particular, postmodern relativism, which denies objective truth and any controlling metanarrative. The doctrine of atonement features prominently because it is at the heart of the gospel message, which in turn is at the heart of Evangelicalism. Accordingly, it acts as something of a lightning-rod for the tension within Evangelicalism as to what constitutes its core beliefs—where precisely, in Lloyd-Jones's phrase, the "essential lines" are to be drawn[34]—by touching upon all the key features of Bebbington's quadrilateral of Evangelical distinctives. Evangelicals are concerned that their faith is, at its center, *cruciform*, meaning that it accords central significance to Christ's work on the cross, and for *biblicism*, that Christ's work should be presented in complete faithfulness to the message of the biblical text. At the same time, though, they are concerned for *conversionism*, that people may hear and respond personally to the gospel. This drives them in an *activism* which requires cultural engagement and that the "truth" of the gospel be expressed in culturally-relevant modes of thought that will touch the hearer and evoke a response. A century ago, Princeton Reformed theologian B. B. Warfield articulated this tension in the following terms:

> No one will doubt that Christians of today must state their Christian beliefs in terms of modern thought. Every age has a language of its own and can speak no other. Mischief comes only when, instead of stating Christian belief in terms of modern thought, an effort is made, rather, to state modern thought in terms of Christian belief.[35]

It is self-evident that reasonable people may differ when it comes to deciding which of Warfield's two options is occurring in a particular instance!

The tensions to which Warfield drew attention between holding to a timeless biblical truth and explaining it in a time-bound contemporary culture continue to be the case. In other words, the objective truth of the Bible—"Christian belief," as Warfield puts it—is still perceived by Evangelical conservatives as under attack from modern thought (and more recently, "postmodern thought").[36] To examine more deeply how the doctrine of atonement is playing out in this debate will necessitate further consider-

---

34. Lloyd-Jones, *What is an Evangelical?* 63.

35. Warfield, *The Works of Benjamin B. Warfield, X: Critical Reviews*, 322, as cited in Armstrong (ed.), *The Coming Evangelical Crisis*, 70.

36. See, e.g., Armstrong (ed.), *Coming Evangelical Crisis* and Dockery (ed.), *The Challenge of Postmodernism: An Evangelical Engagement*.

ation of the links between Evangelicalism and the cultural conditions in which the movement developed—specifically, the Enlightenment and the era known as Modernity.

That Christianity might lack a single orthodox position on atonement doctrine does not mean that atonement lacks explanation in scripture, of course. The question has always been how the sundry ways in which scripture engages with atonement themes are to be read, correlated, and culturally translated; this includes whether different ideas should be allowed to peacefully co-exist, or a certain understanding should be granted hegemony. Historically, theologians wanting to articulate a positive account of a particular atonement theory have tended concurrently to advance a negative critique of competing theories they felt the need to depose. This quest for a "winner" leads McIntyre to observe that "most soteriological theories contain a major anti-theory component, as if the positive theory gained strength from the destruction of its counterpart."[37]

The literature on the various historical theories of atonement is plentiful, and the doctrine's most common themes are reasonably well-known. Scot McKnight's succinct summary serves as a useful reminder:

> Abelard contended that the cross was a demonstration of God's love to evoke a change of heart on the part of those who perceive its costly love. In Anselm's view, sin dishonors God; humans can never return the glory lost to God by their sin; someone must stand in between who is both God and human; and Jesus Christ "satisfies" that condition. Incarnationists emphasize God becoming human, God identifying with humans, and God taking on mortality in order to provide life for those destined to death. Penal substitution frames atonement in terms of God's wrath against sin as the holy reaction of an all-holy God; Jesus absorbs that wrath on the cross as propitiation; and God's wrath is pacified in that act of "self-punishment." *Christus Victor* expresses the entrance of Christ into captive territory and his death and resurrection as providing the means of liberating humans from their slavery to sin, self, and Satan. Recapitulation trades on the idea that Jesus Christ recapitulated Adam's life, and therefore the life of every human, and undoes the sin and death Adam handed on to humans. Jesus's identification with humans enables humans to have a perfect redemption.[38]

---

37. McIntyre, *Shape of Soteriology*, 27.
38. McKnight, *A Community Called Atonement*, 161.

This multiplicity of perspectives draws attention to something touched upon earlier—presenting Christ as the *answer* presupposes that there is a *question*, which in turn focuses attention on the nature of that question. No explanation of atonement as the divine solution can be detached from how we understand the predicament to which it corresponds, the so-called "human problem."

The nature of that problem is generally summed up in the concept of "sin." In modern times, sin has tended increasingly to be seen in personal autobiographical terms, as acts of individual human behavior (sins of commission). The roots of such a view are commonly associated with Anselm of Canterbury in the eleventh century. However, the context Anselm had in mind was the proper ordering of cosmic society, in which human sin was seen as disturbing order and beauty in the universe,[39] whereas the perspective of Modern thought in the Reformed and Evangelical tradition centers on a framework of universal moral laws established by a sovereign God within which rebellious human wrongdoing places us in breach. In Wayne Grudem's definition, for example, sin is "any failure to conform to the moral law of God in act, attitude, or nature."[40] For Grudem, the twin *foci* of each individual's account of personal wrongs and a corresponding legal culpability are at the center of what sin is.[41]

But *is* this, in fact, what sin is? Or more particularly, is the imagery of the sinner standing in the dock of the heavenly law-court enough? Does sin, conceived this way, justify being positioned as the central problem to which the biblical explanation of atonement must principally correspond as its solution?

We might firstly note that the problem of "sin" has here become the problem of "sins"—a subtle but significant shift of emphasis—particularly given that the apostle Paul almost always speaks of sin in the singular. Of sixty-two instances in the Pauline *corpus*, only nine are in the plural. According to Stephen Travis, this is because Paul does not understand sin as "a collection of individual acts."[42] Morna Hooker believes the concept has to do with the "power of sin."[43]

A further concern is that Grudem's narrow characterization is woefully inadequate to meet the full range of the meaning of sin as described in

---

39. *Cur Deus Homo?* 1.XV. A "proper ordering of cosmic society" as that was understood in mediæval feudalism, of course.

40. Wayne Grudem, *Systematic Theology*, 490.

41. Ibid., 501.

42. Travis, "Christ as Bearer of Divine Judgment," 345.

43. Hooker, *Not Ashamed of the Gospel*, 21.

the Old Testament. Chris Wright offers multiple facets as to how the human predicament is portrayed, which he summarizes in the following terms:

> Sin, then, in its broad Old Testament perspective, has a devastatingly wide range of effects. It breaks our relationship with God, one another and the earth; it disturbs our peace; it makes us rebels against God's authority; it makes us guilty in God's court; it makes us dirty in God's presence; it brings shame on ourselves and others; it blights us from the past and already poisons the future; it ultimately leads us to destruction and death.[44]

Wright concludes that we should see atonement as far more than the individual sinner gaining judicial forgiveness for personal wrongdoing, though that is also there. Rather than simply something that concerns the individual and his or her personal world, there is a social and, indeed, cosmic significance in the symbolism of atonement—bringing about a restoration of the wholeness, the *shalom*, that God wanted within his creation.

Philip Jenson similarly finds that the central concern in the priestly writings is the creation, maintenance, and restoration of an ordered world. Here, both sin and impurity are understood as generating disorder—a broad category applicable to the personal and the impersonal, the unavoidable and the deliberate, the individual and the corporate.[45] Fiddes, too, echoes Wright and Jenson that sin has to do with "a situation of disorder which runs deeply in human life."[46] Important categories here include human perceptions of alienation from ourselves and the world and the fragmentation of personality and social relations. Thus conceived and applied, Fiddes argues that "ancient images of salvation as victory over hostile powers take on a modern significance."[47]

There is, of course, a conservative counter-assertion that the basic sinful state of humanity has not altered since the disaster in the Garden of Eden, such that the question of sin is one of unchanging, timeless truth centered on disobedience at the individual level and the punishment that it rightly incurs in the divine court. In other words, the nature of sin and human behavior has been—and remains—the same for all time, all people, and all cultural circumstances and a judicial *motif* remains necessary and appropriate. On this view, we have an unchanging question and an unchanging

---

44. "Atonement in the Old Testament," in Tidball, Hilborn and Thacker (eds.), *The Atonement Debate*, 69–71.

45. "The Levitical Sacrificial System," 32.

46. Fiddes, "Salvation," 177.

47. Ibid., 178. On the imagery of salvation as victory over hostile powers, see Aulén, *Christus Victor*.

answer. Many conservative voices within Evangelicalism would argue precisely this, and that any attempt to instill a broader-based understanding of sin is simply evidence that the Evangelical pulpit has, as Gary Johnson puts it, "succumbed to the triumph of the therapeutic."

> This is painfully obvious in the way psychology has captured the evangelical mind. Evangelicals by their vocabulary betray the fact that they have forgotten the language of biblical and systematic theology, while learning instead the balderdash of pop psychology. Across the board, evangelicals virtually revel in terms such as *dysfunctional, codependent, victimization, self-affirming,* and the like, but most haven't a clue about the meaning of God-given words such as *propitiation* and *justification*.[48]

However, for both pastoral and missional reasons we must surely distinguish between the human condition as such and humanity's self-understanding and articulation of that condition. Cultural missiologists have long recognized that such a distinction is critical.[49] Moreover, the historical development of atonement models clearly reflects such lines of thinking. Anselm's honor-based "satisfaction" imagery, for example, was particularly meaningful in mediæval feudalism; similarly, redemption imagery in cultures familiar with the experiences of slavery and oppression (which remains the case in such cultures today). Fiddes sees the reason that the church has failed to exhaust the meaning of the cross in images and concepts as precisely because it makes contact with a human need that is, itself, many-dimensional. It touches human life at many points.[50]

The questions of "what sin is"—and of the problem that atonement is therefore solving—come to a head in the current impasse between those Evangelicals, particularly from the Reformed tradition, who insist on the hegemony of a penal substitutionary understanding *versus* those who advocate a multi-faceted kaleidoscopic view. One might say that the entire atonement debate within the tradition has currently run aground on this particular argument. Let us, therefore, address these two perspectives in turn, giving particular weight to the discussion concerning penal substitution, by virtue of its significance within Reformed Evangelicalism.

---

48. Johnson, "Does Theology Still Matter?" 62.
49. See, e.g., Newbigin, *Foolishness to the Greeks*.
50. Fiddes, *Past Event*, 5.

1.2.3 Penal Substitutionary Atonement, Its Underlying Assumptions and Worldview

If one view of atonement could be said to represent "the norm," certainly in popular Evangelical presentations of the gospel, then penal substitution would be it. As Joel Green has pointed out, it is assumed by many Christians to be the *only* way of understanding the atonement.[51] Thus, if we are to take atonement forward, we cannot skirt around the place of penal substitution along the way. Furthermore, an examination of the issues involved here will reveal just how significantly one's understanding of the influence of culture—or failure to understand it—affects the atonement debate.

Stated simply, in penal substitutionary atonement Christ on the cross takes my place (becomes my personal substitute) and bears the judicial punishment (the penalty) that is rightly due to me for the inventory of sins I have committed and for which I stand guilty before God. This substitution enables me to be forgiven and to be "let off" that judicial penalty, which I would otherwise have to bear.[52] However, the problems emanating from this conceptualization are numerous.

To begin with, penal substitution is questionable based simply on its own internal logic that the principles of law must be upheld. That God, as Judge, cannot simply ignore lawbreaking. Justice must be done and seen to be done and hence a penalty must be exacted. However, for penal substitution to fit this judicial construction requires a concurrent principle that a person can legally bear someone else's penalty. Whilst it may be feasible in civil litigation for a benefactor to pay another person's fine, or an insurer to settle an award of monetary damages on behalf of a policyholder, by no means does this seamlessly translate to criminal penalties, such as imprisonment or execution.[53] Contemporary Western judiciaries would reject out

---

51. Green, "Must We Imagine," 155.

52. Naturally, there are many variations and nuances in how "penal substitution" can be explained. In recent years, the penal substitutionary doctrine has been the subject of extensive and heated debate, in which its critics argue (amongst other things) that it is "unsalable" in popular preaching and teaching, if not also unbiblical, whilst its advocates affirm it to be an essential part of Evangelical Christian truth. Such debate led to the London Symposium on Atonement, the papers from which comprise Tidball, Hilborn and Thacker (eds.), *The Atonement Debate*. For a rigorous defence against its critics, see Jeffery, Ovey, and Sach, *Pierced for our Transgressions*. It is important to note that not all substitutionary understandings of atonement necessarily involve a penal element.

53. In a dialogue with N. T. Wright over the law-court context of justification, Kevin Vanhoozer asks the interesting question as to which kind of court one takes to be the context for God's declaration: *civil*, or *criminal*? "Is God prosecuting a civil case between Israel and the nations over who has legitimate claim to the title 'people of God,' or

of hand that justice could be fulfilled by a criminal penalty being borne by another party. Furthermore, punishing an innocent person—even a willing victim—is inherently *un*just,[54] and even then, it does not change the status of the one substituted for, who remains guilty. Christians are, of course, at liberty to argue that such human logic need not necessarily apply to God's perspective, but that involves advocating a position which stands in direct contradiction to perceptions of justice in our own world.

What penal substitution appears to miss is that if the upholding of justice requires the guilty to be punished then, by deeming that a criminal penalty can legitimately be borne by another, God is already waiving or modifying supposedly immovable judicial principles in order to make the arrangement lawful.[55] The penal substitutionary theory is therefore internally inconsistent—in order to "work," it must subvert the integrity of "immutable" universal legal principles on which it claims to be founded.

However, if God does indeed rewrite the definitions of "justice" and "punishment" through his redemptive acts, perhaps he does not do so in the way that penal substitution supposes. If it is allowed that God could sovereignly adapt inalienable cosmic law in this penal sense—as the penal substitutionary doctrine requires—might it not be that he could equally choose to do so in another sense,[56] such as the unconditional forgiveness shown by the prodigal's father? After all, Grudem makes the point that "God himself is the ultimate standard of what is just and fair in the universe" and that this gives him the right to decree the way in which atonement should take place (though it seems probable that Grudem would not care to see his point being applied in this way!).[57] Nonetheless, it is perhaps what James has in mind in affirming that "mercy has triumphed over judgment" (Jas 2:12–13). In other words, mercy has been shown to be the overarching divine priority, such that "judgment without mercy"—*the apparent irony may be intentional*—will be shown to anyone who has been insufficiently merciful, rather than to anyone who has been insufficiently judicial. James's concern appears to be less that the principle of *divine judgment* is upheld than that the principle of *divine mercy* is upheld—particularly, one might say, if "upholding justice" depends in this instance upon a legal fiction or

---

a criminal case in which all humanity has been charged with 'crimes against divinity'?" Vanhoozer, "Wrighting the Wrongs of the Reformation?" 249–50.

54. Murray-Williams, "On the Lost Message of Jesus," available at http://www.anabaptistnetwork.com/node/233 (accessed March 6, 2016).

55. Smail, *Once and for All*, 97–98. Crisp, "The Logic of Penal Substitution Revisited," 208–27.

56. McFarlane, "Atonement, Creation and Trinity," 204.

57. Grudem, *Systematic Theology*, 574.

contrivance. Perhaps it is less the case that "there must be punishment" than "there must be mercy." What seems to be unacceptable, as James sees it, is the waiving of mercy, not the waiving of punishment.

Penal substitution also struggles to correlate the twin features of divine forgiveness and the payment of a price to enable that forgiveness. If a price is paid—and *must* be paid—then God has not freely forgiven. It seems odd that this requirement for recompense in order to make forgiveness possible, to which God is apparently bound by cosmic judicial principles, should be the prior expectation of a God who, in Christ, exhorts humanity to forgive freely and unconditionally over and over again, e.g., in Matthew 18—"seventy times seven" (a context in which Christ's parable plainly relates the human behavior that God expects to be a characteristic of the heavenly Father).

A further problem is the "saleability" of the penal view; which brings us back to the question of Evangelicalism's interaction with contemporary culture. The notion that criminal justice is satisfied through the public infliction of punitive physical violence is now almost unknown in Western society.[58] In the early-Modern period of the Reformers, however, up to one-in-four of all convicted criminals in England was publicly executed, many for what we would today consider petty crimes. At one time, more than two hundred different crimes were capital offences.[59] The severity of sentencing was driven by all crime being seen as a threat to the hierarchal order of society. Breaking the law that reflected the will of the sovereign was therefore a direct personal attack on sovereignty and authority and so must be dealt with severely.[60] In the Reformers' day, judicial punishment through the infliction of brutal physical violence such as torture, bodily mutilation, burning alive, and drowning was the normal sentence in criminal justice.[61] The idea of the prison sentence as we know it today came into being only around two hundred years ago. Moreover, in most of Europe the establishment of guilt was at the absolute right and exclusive power of the sovereign

---

58. Though not, of course, in all societies. Attitudes to crime and punishment are but one example of the "clash of worldviews" between contemporary thought in the West and continuing pre-Modern thought elsewhere in the world, that each type of society find so hard to understand in the other. One could also ask legitimate questions as to the extent to which the notion of redemptive penal violence underlies Western political thought, as manifest in issues such as the US response to the terrorist attacks of September 11, 2001. See, e.g., Pearse, *Why the Rest Hates the West.*

59. Briggs et al., (eds.), *Crime and Punishment in England*, 77, 73. Foucault, *Discipline and Punish*, 14.

60. Foucault, *Discipline and Punish*, 35–36, 47–50.

61. Ibid., 3–5, 8, 12, 32–35, 54. Briggs et al, *Crime and Punishment*, 23–24, 84.

and his judges.[62] Both secular and religious crimes (as we would distinguish them today) were similarly prosecuted and punished.

A number of assumptions about the nature of crime and the appropriate punishment for crime appear to be embedded in the supposedly "divine view" that penal substitution advances. Neither crime nor punishment, though, is still seen in these terms in the contemporary Western worldview.

How, then, in a world in which retributive physical violence is not regarded as just sentencing—in fact, the court of public opinion would regard it with revulsion—do we explain that on the cross Jesus was absorbing the punishment that each of us is due from God for our sins? Furthermore, when only a small minority of crimes, if any, carry the death penalty in human law courts,[63] is there not a logical problem in explaining how each and every human wrongdoing—even the smallest—carries the full death penalty in the divine law court equivalent? This is even before we attempt to explain, if we are so minded, how eternal conscious torment in hell represents a just sentence.[64] In today's world, of course, it requires some considerable work even to persuade people of God's absolute and exclusive right to establish divine laws to which we are subject, to judge us against those laws and to condemn us for our failure to obey—particularly when such judgment and condemnation is presented as appropriate even for people who do not know they exist.[65]

Unlike today, people at the time of the Reformers readily understood their situation as being sinners under the judgment of a holy, sovereign God, needing their sins to be taken away and dealt with.[66] This perspective is exemplified in Cranmer's Book of Common Prayer (1549):

> [. . .] we acknowledge and bewail our manifold sins and wickedness, which we from time to time, most grievously have

---

62. Foucault, *Discipline and Punish*, 35–38. Weisser, *Crime and Punishment in Early Modern Europe*, 24–26.

63. And even here, there is a concern to ensure execution is swift and humane.

64. This is not to suggest this represents "the Christian view" on the existence (or nature) of hell, but simply to illustrate an area of cultural challenge involving what many would see as a traditional "biblical" position, particularly among Evangelicals. For a useful short treatment of that subject, see Hilborn (ed.), *The Nature of Hell*.

65. Modern hermeneutics recognizes that "what the Bible teaches" in legislating God's expectations for human behavior is not fully self-explanatory. As William Webb points out (in a chapter titled "Welcome to the World of Application"), applying the ancient text to our modern context involves a task in which "we must determine whether we should apply a particular biblical statement in the exact form articulated on the page or whether we should apply only some expression of its underlying principle(s)." Webb, *Slaves, Women & Homosexuals*, 13.

66. Smail, *Once and for All*, 40.

committed, by thought, word and deed, against thy divine majesty, provoking most justly thy wrath and indignation against us [. . .], the remembrance of them is grievous unto us, the burden of them is intolerable.

In today's society, however, the recognition that one is a sinner and the corresponding sense of guilt that framed previous generations' assumptions about atonement no longer apply. As Alan Mann has pointedly observed, "Individuals no longer live with a sense of sin and guilt in the way that evangelists would wish them to."[67] Nor is it the case that a sense of personal guilt is present, yet dormant, as a universal anthropological feature, simply waiting to be awakened by the preaching of a timeless gospel, as popular preaching has tended to assume. All of which, perhaps, underlies Stephen Holmes's insightful observation that

> If the only gospel we've got solves a problem that nobody feels, then it is no wonder our churches are shrinking. There is a lot of work in first explaining to people that they really ought to be feeling guilty, before then solving the problem for them.[68]

Taken together, these are considerable obstacles to surmount if one is to approach atonement though a penal lens. In order to promote the Christian gospel, thus conceived, must we first convince people that contemporary society's judicial framework is seriously flawed and that God's is both different and superior? This implied expectation underlies the penal view. In mounting its argument, it is unfortunate that penal substitution presupposes an appropriate divine punishment for wrongdoing centered in judicial violence which happens to correspond to an ancient-world criminal justice system that people no longer recognize for life today in the West.

Unsurprisingly, its Evangelical adherents propose a counter-argument based in the penal substitutionary doctrine's centrality according to scripture. Limitations of space do not permit an exhaustive critique of this common assumption, but it should be said that the biblical case for the penal view is by no means easily sustained, unless, of course, one begins with an unshakeable conviction that it must be so. Moreover, once we disallow as inappropriate the requisitioning of scriptures that speak of "sacrifice," "ransom," "paying the price," or Passover imagery—none of which embody any

---

67. Mann, "*Sinless*" *Society*, 4.

68. Holmes, *The Wondrous Cross*, 113. Holmes also suggests that "a sense of guilt is making a comeback, not least in the churches" and denies "our society has yet lost its sense of sin completely" (113–14), but the tentative nature of the statements seems to endorse Mann's core point.

necessary reason to attach penal associations[69]—the supposedly scriptural basis for the doctrine recedes at an alarmingly fast rate. As Holmes concedes:

> Much of the language about the atonement in the NT could be understood in penal substitutionary terms if we had good reason to do so, but equally could be understood in other terms. When we read of Jesus "redeeming" us, or "paying the price" for our sin, if we already know from somewhere else that penal substitution is the right way to understand the atonement, then we can read these as different ways of describing penal substitution. When you look at writers arguing that penal substitution is the right way to understand the cross in the Bible, this seems to be what a lot of them do.[70]

To some extent, the objections raised against it can be overcome if penal substitutionary atonement is recognized as but one metaphor amongst many—one that may be effective in "conveying something" about Christ's atoning work in certain eras and cultures but is ineffective in other eras and cultures. However, this would require a willingness by its advocates to concede some of penal substitution's weaknesses; that, like all metaphors, it can be expected to work in part and fail in part. The real problems come when demands are made for the doctrine to be granted primacy as the overarching metanarrative of atonement (for some, even a pre-requisite for Christian fellowship[71]) and when it is presumed to function literally rather than metaphorically.

A further reductionism which is evident in the standard imagery of the sinner standing accused in the heavenly law court is its failure to allow space for the sense in which humanity is the *victim* of sin.[72] Failure to allow for the effects of sin suffered as a victim leaves untouched a vast swathe

---

69. In ransom, for example, Jesus does not take the place of other slaves or bear punishment on their behalf.

70. Holmes, *Wondrous Cross*, 43. Note that he is writing ostensibly in support of the doctrine.

71. "If the attack is simply on a caricature of the doctrine, all is well and good [...]. But if the accusation is indeed an accusation against penal substitution itself, as it surely is, then I fear that we cannot simply carry on as we are. [...] I cannot see how those who disagree can remain allied without placing unity above truths which are undeniably central to the Christian faith." Williams, "Penal Substitution," 188. "We can no more afford to sidestep this issue for the sake of unity than we can lay aside disagreements on the deity of Christ [...]. [D]ifferences over penal substitution ultimately lead us to worship a different God and to believe a different gospel." Jeffery et al., *Pierced for our Transgressions*, 216–17.

72. Wright suggests that, for Paul, "the real culprit" is sin itself: "on the cross God punished (not Jesus but) sin." *The Climax of the Covenant*, 213.

of human experience—something that has rightly been noted in liberation and feminist theologies. It needs to be acknowledged that individually and collectively we experience sin in these twin capacities. At times we are its perpetrators, at times we are its victims, in a complex mix.[73] To conceive sin, therefore, primarily or exclusively as a problem of *perpetration*—as the individual's personal account of wrongful acts committed—will tend to lead to a majoring on a juridically-centered solution in which the metaphor of God as Judge is granted theological priority. Atonement then becomes about escaping judicial punishment for wrongdoings committed, clearing one's way to heaven, through a transaction that took place exclusively within the Godhead.

Similarly overlooked is the ethical dimension. Legal and transactional categories alone will never lead to salvation from sin being conceived as the "flourishing of human life" that God desires through the transforming of persons, communities and institutions, of which David Ford rightly speaks.[74] Equally, the penal view centered on legal guilt seems to have nothing much to say to the concern to which John Howard Yoder draws attention, namely, "what does it mean to be lost, and how does the death of Christ deal with lostness?"[75]

In contrast, a more kaleidoscopic view (that we shall cover shortly) allows ample space to accommodate and address broader questions such as these. It also helps avoid the reductionism in the popular domain to what Dallas Willard calls "gospels of sin management," in which justification—defined as being "let off the divine hook"—takes the place of regeneration and transformative new life.[76]

We would suggest that the very wide concerns to which the penal view gives rise ought not lightly to be dismissed as merely "the balderdash of pop psychology."[77]

1.2.4 Feminist Concerns

It is a commonplace criticism by feminist theologians that the image of Christ suffering on the cross without complaint communicates the notion that suffering is inherently redemptive. Moreover, it acclimates society to

---

73. One of the attractions of a "kaleidoscopic" view is that it allows space for multiple complementary images addressing different dimensions.
74. Ford, *Self and Salvation*. See, e.g., 9–10.
75. Yoder, *Preface to Theology*, 288.
76. Willard, *The Divine Conspiracy*, 42–43. See generally 35–59.
77. Johnson, "Does Theology Still Matter?" 62.

idealizing self-sacrificial suffering in unquestioning obedience as a Christian virtue, not least amongst women—characteristics which, unfortunately, directly mirror those of a victim. Self-evidently, the central place accorded to the cross in the Christian story is problematic in relation to these concerns. However, if the doctrine of redemption does require the suffering and death of Jesus on the cross, it cannot simply be set aside. One would need to focus, instead, on ameliorating the appalling consequences of a wrongful interpretation and application of that imagery in relation to women, children, and other sufferers of abuse.

Joanne Carlson Brown and Rebecca Parker acknowledge that throughout the scriptures is the idea that Jesus suffered and died for our sins but question: "Did he? Is there not another way for sins to be forgiven?"[78]

> Jesus died on the cross to save us from sin. This is what the penal theory of the atonement affirms. [. . .] Without the death of Jesus we would not be saved. Though there are many different interpretations of *how* we are saved by the death of Jesus, there is no classical theory of the atonement that questions the necessity of Jesus' suffering.[79]

To reject the notion of redemptive suffering is not to reject the cross *per se*, but it is to challenge the presumption of the power of let blood. "Why does blood have the power to protect life, establish relationship, restore life, [and] speak with silent eloquence?" they ask.[80]

As we noted earlier, if the elements of penal substitution's imagery are simply metaphorical referents to one way of conceiving the atonement that has worked (and perhaps still works) in certain cultures, then feminist theology is well within its rights and within the bounds of Christian orthodoxy to choose to set aside that imagery in favor of other models. Once more we are reminded of the significance of whether penal substitution is believed to be *more than* metaphorical and, instead, speaks directly of how atonement is *actually* accomplished, in a direct correspondence between the event and its effects.

Rather than God on the cross suffering *for* us, some theologians are now proffering the image and concept of the God who suffers *with* us; who suffers passionately what the world suffers.[81] Carlson Brown and Parker argue that "the emergence of the notion that God suffers with us is theological progress"—"the advent of the Suffering God changes the entire face of

---

78. Brown and Parker, "For God So Loved the World?" 2.
79. Ibid., 4.
80. Ibid., 10.
81. Ibid., 14.

theology."[82] How this operates in an atoning sense is pictured through a deeply relational lens:

> The challenge of how to claim that a suffering God offers not only comfort and companionship but also redemption is perhaps met by the argument that the cross makes relationship where relationship has been lost. It breaks down the dividing wall between suffering humanity and an impassive God and calls disciples to cross the barrier that separates oppressor from oppressed, rich from poor, healthy from sick, into a new humanity in which each takes on the burdens and joys of all in a fellowship of mutual openness and support.[83]

Carlson Brown and Parker maintain that Jesus did not choose the cross *per se* but rather chose integrity and faithfulness, refusing to change course because of threat. The cross is a sign of tragedy in which God's grief is revealed; not just there but everywhere and every time life is thwarted by violence. God's grief is as ultimate as God's love.[84]

Whilst we would agree that this is an important element in apprehending the nature and character of God revealed at the cross, precisely *how it functions redemptively* is unclear; it appears to operate as a subjective theory akin to Abelard's moral influence. Nonetheless, a perspective on atonement located in a "suffering God" suffering *with* us seems qualified to take its place alongside the other images of atonement in a kaleidoscopic view, at least insofar as it enables us to personally identify with Christ and be drawn to him relationally.

However, as we have seen, the fundamental question that feminists raise is not "what traditional doctrine of the atonement can be most successfully adapted to a feminist consciousness?" but "(can) feminists accept an atonement doctrine at all, in view of the disastrous consequences this has had for women?"[85]

Elaine Storkey recognizes the passion underlying the feminist unease over atonement theories but rejects the post-Christian positions of radical feminists such as Mary Daly and Daphne Hampson. For her, the necessity is for Christians to concede there has been a grave imbalance in how we have

---

82. Ibid., 14–15.
83. Ibid., 17.
84. Ibid., 27.
85. Grey, *Redeeming the Dream*, 110, as cited by Storkey, "Atonement and Feminism," 227–35.

represented God, even in the assumptions we have brought to the biblical text.[86]

> It is interesting for example to ask why the *authority of God the Father* has been far more prominent in the church over the centuries than the *relationality of God the Trinity*, when this is a foundational biblical notion. When that same emphasis has been carried into our doctrine of atonement we have often focused exclusively on an authoritative and punitive model. [. . .] We need to develop an emphasis which has been there in evangelical theology from the earliest times, that at its heart atonement speaks about the deep *relationality* of God.[87]

This theme, "that at its heart atonement speaks about the deep relationality of God," identified by Storkey as a foundational biblical notion, is one to which we shall return in chapter three. She helpfully reminds us that our thinking on the atonement will be profoundly shaped by what we consider to be the most foundational characteristics of God.

1.2.5 The Epistemology of Modernity

What, then, would explain the strident insistence within Evangelicalism on penal substitution's primacy amongst atonement theories? We would suggest this is directly related, firstly, to Evangelicalism's origins in the Enlightenment with a corresponding absorption of the epistemology of Modernity and then, in turn, to Evangelicalism's perceived calling to be the defender of a timeless biblical truth (or rather, its own Modern spin on that truth) in the face of an onslaught from subjective postmodern relativism. A failure to recognize the place of culture and worldview in the conception and articulation of Christian faith lies at the heart of the problem.

It is entirely unsurprising that Bebbington should observe that the deepest divisions in the Evangelical world have generally arisen from the impact of "cultural waves."[88] The rift in Evangelical ranks in the early twentieth century, for example, appeared precisely because of different responses to the same cultural mood. Liberals wanted to modify received theology in the light of current thought,[89] while the conservative position had been

---

86. Storkey, "Atonement and Feminism," 233. Perhaps this is a result of the articulation of traditional doctrine having been the exclusive preserve of male theologians for almost two millennia, adopting distinctly male categories of thought.
87. Ibid., 233–34.
88. Bebbington, *Evangelicalism*, 275.
89. Ibid., 183.

summed up by Charles Spurgeon: "There is nothing new in theology except that which is false; and the facts of theology are today what they were eighteen hundred years ago."[90] As the 1982 Chicago Statement on Biblical Hermeneutics expresses it:

> We affirm that the Bible contains teachings and mandates which apply to all cultural and situational contexts [. . .]. We deny that the distinction between the universal and particular mandates of Scripture can be determined by cultural and situational factors.[91]

One Evangelical theologian who has sought to articulate a more nuanced penal substitutionary doctrine, whilst still approaching the subject as one of its ardent defenders,[92] is I. Howard Marshall:

> It is clear that essentially the same basic principle is expressed in each of these different understandings of the death of Jesus. The principle of one person bearing the painful consequences of sin is the *modus operandi* of the different understandings of the cross. There are different nuances in these expressions of the nature of salvation. But the central action, common to them all, is God doing something in Christ that involves the death of Christ, who bears our sins and the painful consequence of them. Christ's sacrifice saves us from exclusion from the kingdom of God. The term "penal substitution" appropriately expresses this process.[93]

A close reading of Marshall, however, shows that while he is offering a valid description of atonement, that which he is describing is actually no longer *penal*, although it remains substitutionary. Atonement is indeed "God doing something in Christ" (note the hint of mystery) that directly relates to sin and its "painful consequences," but to count this as synonymous with penal substitution would be something else entirely. Marshall's attempt to redeploy the term "penal substitution" as an umbrella idea under which all atonement imagery can shelter involves redefining the doctrine

---

90. Spurgeon, *An All-Round Ministry*, 17, as cited by Bebbington, *Evangelicalism*, 146.

91. Available at http://library.dts.edu/Pages/TL/Special/ICBI_2.pdf (accessed July 6, 2013).

92. See e.g., Marshall's surprisingly strong endorsement of Jeffery, Ovey, and Sach, *Pierced for Our Transgressions*, which (he claims) offers "a careful demonstration of the weaknesses of so many of the current criticisms made of the doctrine."

93. Marshall, "The Theology of the Atonement," 61.

to a point where it is no longer recognizable as such.⁹⁴ The whole point is precisely that penal substitution *does not* appropriately express something "common to them all," but only something particular to its own view.

Albert Mohler exhorts Evangelicals to resist "those explicitly calling for a program of theological revisionism to recast evangelicalism in a mode more attractive to twentieth-century secular culture."⁹⁵ For post-conservative Evangelicals such as Stanley Grenz, however, such a quest for a culture-free theology is both ill-founded and unwarranted. Grenz speaks of the task posed by cultural sensitivity in terms of *the translation* of biblical truth in *response* to the culture—as a necessary precursor to its effective communication within the culture—rather than *the determination* of biblical truth that would be a *capitulation* to culture, which appears to be the concern of Spurgeon and Mohler. Grenz puts it this way:

> A theology that is culturally relevant seeks to articulate Christian beliefs in a manner that is understandable to people within the wider society in which the church ministers. Consequently, the theologian draws from the cognitive tools—including language, symbols and thought-forms—by means of which people in the host society view and speak about their world, so as to engage in a kind of "translation" task in which the categories of a society, including its philosophical conceptions, become the vehicles for the expression of the Christian belief-mosaic.⁹⁶

"How to persuade people to respond to God's offer of forgiveness," as Fiddes puts it,⁹⁷ or more formally stated a concern for Christian mission, has always been at the heart of Evangelicalism. If the gospel is to be persuasive, its preaching requires an awareness of and a sensitivity towards the contemporary culture that is inhabited by those who are to be reached. The gospel message must be explained in language and thought-forms that are accessible to the audience. At the same time, though, Evangelical commitment to *biblicism* demands a concurrent faithfulness to scripture. This gives rise to a perceived tension between maintaining an "unchanging" biblical gospel while at the same time explaining that gospel in terms to which people today can relate. The tension works itself out in atonement

---

94. Marshall has subtly shifted the meaning of "sacrifice" to something approaching its contemporary understanding as noble and costly self-giving for the sake of others. Note also an apparent distinction between a *penalty paid* for sin and *bearing the painful consequences* of sin.

95. Mohler, "Evangelical: What's in a Name?" 32.

96. Grenz, "How Do We Know What To Believe?" 31.

97. Fiddes, *Past Event*, 28.

in the following way. Conservatives are suspicious that all understandings based in contemporary thought must, by definition, be "subjective"—therapeutic soteriology tailored to suit current tastes. In order for the gospel to be unchanging therefore (runs the logic), it must continue to be stated in its original biblical form.[98] Thus the atonement gets sucked into a battle for the preservation of Evangelical "truth" in the face of a perceived onslaught from the culture of the day—the *zeitgeist* of "this world" or the "spirit of the age." Successfully to resist these attacks appears to require the defenders to find—and thereafter to mount a stringent, unyielding defence of—an unchanging understanding of the atonement that is "objectively" set forth in scripture and then to articulate that understanding in its original terms. The doctrine's contours therefore become molded by the characteristics that it necessarily must possess in order to be deemed to be "biblical."

This in itself does not tell us why any single understanding of the atonement needs to be granted hegemony, bearing in mind scripture's variegated allusions. For this we need to touch upon the foundationalist epistemology of Modernity as regards its concept of biblical truth. Evangelicalism grew up as a child of the Enlightenment and along with modern Western culture and society generally is permeated with its influences.[99] Evangelical thought is built on the Enlightenment's concept of truth, which for convenience may, as Peter Hicks explains, be simplified to four basic components:

- Objectivity—truth is outside of us and independent of us;
- Universality—truth is the same the world over and for all people, unaffected by cultural differences;
- Eternity—truths remain true forever; and
- Intelligibility—we as human beings are able to discover, comprehend and know the truth.[100]

---

98. "The correspondence or lack of it between a given doctrine and human cultural ideas is entirely irrelevant to the question of whether that doctrine is biblical. What counts is whether it is taught in Scripture." Jeffery et al., *Pierced for our Transgressions*, 221.

99. The emergence of Evangelicalism "was itself an expression of the age of reason." Bebbington, *Evangelicalism*, 19; see also 53, 63, and 74. On the foundational concepts of truth on which evangelicals, consciously or otherwise, have based their beliefs, see Hicks, *Evangelicals and Truth*. For a recent work challenging some of Bebbington's findings and arguing for greater continuity with pre-Enlightenment movements, see Haykin and Stewart (eds.), *The Advent of Evangelicalism*, especially Haykin, "Evangelicalism and the Enlightenment," 37–60. In the judgment of this writer, Bebbington's critics fail to make a persuasive case that his core point concerning the influence of the Enlightenment on Evangelical thought is anything other than entirely valid.

100. Hicks, *Evangelicals and Truth*, 10. Hicks freely concedes that it would be wrong

Accordingly, it is difficult for mystery to feature within this conceptualization. If truth is inherently knowable and certain, then conceding a place for mystery amounts to allowing for doubt and uncertainty. And if truth is timeless and culture-free then its expression in the Bible will be appropriate not only for its authors' time (corresponding to their concepts and thought-forms) but *ad infinitum*, appropriate for explaining that truth in all times and cultures.

Since knowledge must be built on a sure footing, Enlightenment foundationalism borrows from the metaphor of a building, where the "foundation" consists of unquestioned basic beliefs that are supposedly universal and context-free. In approaching theology, conservative Modernists routinely understand knowledge as "the compiling of correct conclusions from a sure foundation."[101] The primary idea of foundationalism is that all knowledge or belief in relation to any given subject must ultimately rest on its one "most basic" foundational truth, which anchors all other beliefs that arise as conclusions from it. Thus, the foundationalist's initial task for the construction of a knowledge edifice on a subject (such as atonement, in our case) is to determine the one foundational belief or principle on which all that subject-knowledge rests. Any other knowledge or belief—such as other theories of atonement—must then be derived from, dependent upon or subsidiary to this most basic foundational one.[102] Thus, it can be seen how Enlightenment rationale underlies Evangelical belief that there is one, winning theory which "must be" the foundational biblical truth about atonement. The implications are obvious: for traditional conservative Evangelicalism a true biblical doctrine of atonement must conform to these rational features.

Lastly, since the Evangelical movement is also deeply committed to remaining true to the principles of the Reformation and especially during

---

to assume that this conceptualization of truth has been monochrome, or the only conception of truth available in the West. "Within its basic parameters, there has been much variety, as different thinkers stressed different aspects, or attempted different tasks, or set themselves to solve problems which arose out of the concept." Nonetheless, he affirms this as "the dominant concept" which, we suggest, suffices to summarize Evangelical thinking with regard to, e.g., scripture and scriptural truth, notwithstanding the risk of oversimplification and hence caricature that it carries. Although penal substitution's claims to hegemony might arguably be premised on such an oversimplification of how truth operates, we would argue that this understanding underlies its proponents' conceptualization of why it is true, at least in the popular domain.

101. Grenz and Franke, *Beyond Foundationalism*, 47, 30.

102. "Far from being viable *alternatives* to penal substitution they [the other aspects of the atonement] are outworkings of it. As the hub from which all of these other doctrines fan out, penal substitution is surely central." Jeffery et al., *Pierced for Our Transgressions*, 211.

times when Christians have looked like losing sight of them,[103] atonement's foundational truth can be expected to be located in the Reformers' insights and it must therefore be defended against any critics for this reason also.

The stage, then, is fully set. Enter, stage right, penal substitution, standing on the shoulders of Enlightenment epistemology embedded in the Modern worldview, which Evangelicalism has unconsciously applied to the task of establishing and articulating biblical "truth." As with worldviews generally, it has done so without even realizing that it is manifesting a worldview at all. Somewhat ironically, Evangelicalism believes itself to be defending a timeless and culture-free biblical understanding *against* Modern thought, which it understands as "liberalism."

> In one sense, it is no surprise that the Bible's teaching [on penal substitution] should be criticized in this way, for foundational truths of the Christian faith have always come under attack from time to time—witness the debates that have raged in the past over the Trinity, the deity of Christ, the bodily resurrection, and so on.[104]

Notwithstanding, therefore, its many problems, the penal substitutionary view comes to be given primacy in modern Evangelicalism. Non-foundational understandings such as the kaleidoscopic view may be granted a subsidiary role but they cannot be allowed on center stage. Equally, an Evangelicalism that is built upon the assumption of certain knowledge that underlies Enlightenment epistemology cannot grant any material significance to the idea of "the mystery of the cross." An element of mystery may perhaps be allowed as a "something more," transcendent beyond the certain truth that we do know, but for apologetic reasons (at least) the mindset of Modernity would struggle to accept that the cross could be something that Christians really may not fully understand![105]

At the same time, the Evangelical commitment to mission—which involves evoking personal commitments in response to hearing the gospel message—inevitably leads to a dilemma of which post-conservative Evangelicals are only too well aware. They realize that the mission of the church is threatened if atonement is explainable only by reference to imagery and

---

103. Hicks, *Evangelicals and Truth*, 12.

104. Jeffery et al., *Pierced for Our Transgressions*, 24. We may note that the other doctrines to which the authors draw comparison are all subjects addressed in the Creeds.

105. That the postmodern mindset finds itself quite at home with the idea of mystery and of truth understood in non-foundational terms simply adds fuel to the fire, of course, for the conservative concern that Christian truth not be compromised by the contemporary cultural mood.

ideas locked in alien cultures or anachronistic worldviews which are inaccessible to contemporary thought, as penal substitution would seem to be. Although receiving and responding to the gospel is not to be reduced to mental assent to a set of cognizable beliefs, the message of atonement must still possess a communicative ability to touch people in the present age in terms that they can understand and to which they can relate in the particular circumstances in which they find themselves.

The inherent flexibility of the alternative "kaleidoscopic" view to which we shall now turn—in which multiple biblical images of atonement may be accessed with little or no hierarchy—has clear missional benefits, therefore, not least in a postmodern world.

1.2.6 The Kaleidoscopic View

We noted earlier that, as McKnight puts it, "the way we define the problem shapes the way we define the solution" and that any discussion of atonement requires we define the problem that atonement remedies.[106] Since perceptions of the human situation shift over time, Fiddes sees a direct correspondence to a multiplicity of perceptions of atonement:

> As the expression of the human predicament alters, so there will likewise be a shift in the way that salvation is expressed. Thus as time passes there develops a whole kaleidoscope of images of atonement, none of which can be complete in itself, each of which remains to overlap with the next, and all of which contribute to the pattern of God's act of reconciliation.[107]

Fiddes hits on a key point: human understanding of "the problem" is unavoidably culturally-situated and hence that understanding will be different in different places and, even in the same place, will evolve over time in line with cultural shifts. For Fiddes, this explains why a kaleidoscope of atonement imagery is necessary and appropriate. The reason different images of atonement have gripped the imagination in different periods of history is undoubtedly because the understanding of the basic human predicament has changed from age to age.[108] McKnight similarly recognizes that

> There are real differences in the big epochs in history when it comes to perceptions of sin. Once we admit that sin defines how we approach atonement, we are driven to the conclusion that

---

106. McKnight, *Community Called Atonement*, 22–23.
107. Fiddes, *Past Event*, 7.
108. Ibid., 5.

atonement is a challenge because of the mind-numbing complexity of sin.[109]

McKnight illustrates his argument in favor of multiple atonement theories by relating them to a dinner-table discussion with a fellow-golfer concerning which golf club was his favorite. McKnight's response was that he had no favorite; he uses all fourteen clubs in his bag, and the one he likes best depends on where he is on the course and what he sees in front of him. This is in contrast to a man he once knew who carried but one club, admitting "I'm too lazy to carry a bag of clubs." In a similar vein, says McKnight:

> Some atonement theories today are "one-club" theories that have to be adjusted each time one plays "the atonement game." This is unfortunate because we have a big bag of images in our Bible and we need to pull each from the bag if we are to play out the fulsomeness of the redemptive work of God. The game of atonement requires that players understand the value of each club as well as the effort needed to carry a bag big enough.[110]

Joel Green founds his own case for the kaleidoscopic view on the observation that the biblical narrative "authorizes an expansive range of images and models for comprehending and articulating the atonement."[111] Because of this, "the church has worked faithfully to embrace the message of the atonement without presuming that one image subsumed or trumped the others."[112] It is notable that as Green articulates this multiple-image perspective, he centers it in the variety of images from Israel's scriptures that he perceives would have been most self-evident to the early church.

> Given the wealth of images for divine-human interactions in the Scriptures of Israel, we might not be surprised that early Christians, returning again and again to search the Scriptures, brought forth treasures both old and new. Reading the death of Jesus in light of Israel's Scriptures, and reading those Scriptures in light of the death of Jesus, they found telling images everywhere: substitution, sacrifice, forgiveness, deliverance and more. Seeking to inscribe new followers of Jesus into Israel's Scriptures, they worked to make those ancient images familiar ones.[113]

109. McKnight, *Community Called Atonement*, 48.

110. Ibid., xiii. In private correspondence with me, Shelton has affirmed McKnight's golfing metaphor with a rider that "covenant-renewal imagery is the golf bag!"

111. "Kaleidoscopic View," 170.

112. Ibid., 170.

113. Ibid., 169.

At first glance, Green's attempt to contextualize atonement within Israel's scriptures in this way appears promising. Examined more closely, however, there is a significant difference between finding aspects of salvific divine action in the scriptures of Israel that may be applied to illustrate the efficacy of Christ's work at the cross and finding a necessary overarching correlation between Christian atonement and the story of Israel within which it was situated. As Yoder astutely observes, the test of a doctrine is not the Hebraic flavor of its vocabulary, but its adequacy in interrelating and synthesizing the exegetical material into an intellectually graspable whole.[114]

Perhaps as a consequence of Green's reading being through a specifically Evangelical lens, his findings tend towards images of atonement that are universalized, dehistoricized, and individualized. The saving significance of Jesus's death is tied to particular conceptions of "the human situation" expressed at the individual level: "People who are blind need illumination. Slaves need liberation. The lost need to be found."[115] Leon Morris similarly finds attractive the kaleidoscopic view of everything Christ has done for us:

> Christ's atoning work is so complex and our minds are so small. We cannot take it all in. We need the positive contributions of all the theories, for each draws attention to some aspect of what Christ has done for us. And though in the end we cannot understand it all, we can thankfully accept so great [a] salvation.[116]

Although, as Green points out, the New Testament authors articulate images drawn from the life worlds of their audiences and relate them to the world of Israel's scriptures, he proposes no necessary role or function for the antecedent relationship of Israel and its God within this way (or ways) of thinking about atonement. Israel's scriptures provide a source-book, but the overarching story itself is set aside in favor of abstracted pictures. Despite Green speaking warmly of a "wealth of images" and "old and new treasures" from the scriptures of Israel, we see Soulen's "Israel-forgetfulness" continuing to influence how the doctrine is conceived and articulated.

While we may agree with the conclusion that "the significance of Jesus' death could not be represented without remainder by any one concept or theory or metaphor,"[117] this does not mean we should assume that there is no aggregating feature or common *nexus* to be found. We can endorse his three reasons for adopting a kaleidoscopic conception of the atonement—

---

114. Yoder, *Preface to Theology*, 312.
115. "Kaleidoscopic View," 167.
116. Morris, "Atonement," 56.
117. Green and Baker, *Recovering the Scandal of the Cross*, 23.

"the universal profundity of Jesus' death as saving event," "the variety of contexts within which Jesus' death required explication" and "the variety of ways in which the human situation can be understood"—without at the same time having to conclude that atonement itself is fragmented.

In sum, the present situation in the atonement debate reflects a stalemate between on the one hand the claims to hegemony by adherents of the penal substitutionary doctrine and on the other, those who affirm a multifaceted, kaleidoscopic view.

In relation to penal substitution, while it may in certain cultural circumstances be entitled to a place at the table, we have shown how it cannot support the scale of its claims to be an overarching metanarrative.

In relation to the kaleidoscopic view, the role of metaphors as explanatory tools is to be encouraged—and, from a missional perspective, multiple metaphors offer a welcome correspondence to postmodern modes of thought—but it surely remains deeply unsatisfactory to leave atonement as little more than "a bit like this, and a bit like that."

In both the penal view and the kaleidoscopic view, however—which right now are broadly speaking the two options on the Evangelical table—we note the virtual absence of a meaningful relationship between *any* of the current conceptualizations of atonement and the story of Israel in which the atoning work of Christ was situated. In relation to the question, "What is the doctrine of the atonement about?" Yoder has rightly identified the importance of identifying the answer that "fits best within the framework of the rest of biblical and historic Christian thought."[118] However, the answers presently on offer effectively exclude any such biblical and historic thought insofar as it depends upon Israel, at least in any positive sense.

1.3 RELATING THE ATONEMENT TO THE STORY OF ISRAEL

In the final section of this chapter, we turn to a short review of the work of some scholars who may be perceived already to have taken some steps along the same path: namely, to identify a continuity in theological thought between what it means to be in an atoned relationship with God in the story of Israel and what it means in Christian articulations. In each case, our goal is neither a comprehensive presentation of each scholar's work nor an exhaustive critique. Our aim is briefly to consider whether, and if so the extent to which, they have identified that which we perceive to be missing—a positive contribution to atonement drawn from the story of God's relationship

---

118. Yoder, *Preface to Theology*, 289.

with Israel. As we have noted previously, there is a substantial difference between simply borrowing cultural imagery (even scriptural imagery) that would have been familiar to a first-century Jewish audience and crafting a systematic theological account that shows any necessary dependency on Israel's then-current relationship with God.

We will firstly look at a suggestion from John Howard Yoder that the redemptive significance of Jesus's death on the cross would have been simply "obvious" in first-century thought. Secondly, we will consider Gustaf Aulén's *Christus Victor*. Aulén is of interest because of his claim to have identified the Christian understanding of atonement prevailing for the first thousand years of the faith. Thirdly, we will review S. Mark Heim's work, *Saved from Sacrifice*. Heim's thesis is based in the scapegoat ritual of the Day of Atonement and thus is rooted in an Old Testament *motif* with clear atoning significance in Israel's relationship with God. Finally, we will consider R. Larry Shelton's *Cross and Covenant*. Shelton proposes a relational understanding of atonement centered in covenantal terms, a theme that quite evidently spans both Testaments.

One scholar who springs to mind, with whom we might have engaged at this point, would of course be N. T. Wright. Instead, we shall discuss Wright—including his take on atonement—in the next chapter, addressing the New Perspective.

1.3.1 *"Redemptive Death"—John Howard Yoder*

We begin with an intriguing suggestion from John Howard Yoder that the idea of a death "for sin"—a death that was inherently redemptive—was so widespread in first-century culture that it was "not a real problem" in that first generation.[119] This could be most instructive, since we are concerned to identify what a first-century understanding of atonement might look like (i.e., what its premises might have been) as a potential interpretive lens for understanding atonement in Christ. Unfortunately, he offers little by way of support for the idea, which lays it open to the accusation of an argument from silence. Were he still with us, Yoder might respond, not unreasonably, that a classic feature of a worldview is that certain shared understandings of author and audience are so obviously the case that they are taken as read. Such a possibility cannot be ruled out—indeed, a somewhat comparable lacuna is identifiable in relation to how, exactly, sacrifice was understood to "work" in the ancient world. However, the shortcoming of Yoder's idea is

---

119. Yoder, *Preface to Theology*, 133. Yoder here cites an earlier work of Taylor, *The Names of Jesus*.

that it fails to tell us quite *why* the idea of a redemptive death should have been obvious and why that in turn has significance in our quest to better understand the atonement today. Yoder's point is interesting, but it is not developed into a systematic theological account of the atonement. It may hint in the direction of a continuity with Israel's pre-existing relationship with God, but no more than that. In terms of helping us with the "how?" question of atonement, it contributes nothing.

Yoder makes a slightly different yet closely-related proposal that initially the New Testament church did not give any real thought as to *why* Jesus's suffering and death was necessary to salvation—something that was left to the later church to address.

> It was because of their faith that they were talking about redemptive suffering or redemptive death, but the New Testament church did not have to get around very soon to thinking just why his death was saving, why his death was "for sin." The New Testament is clear on his motive, on his obedience. But it does not answer the question, "Why did the Son of God have to die?" This is the question with which the later doctrine of atonement deals. These questions are not dealt with in any clarity of consciousness in the early church.[120]

Again, however, his observation offers no constructive account of atonement berthed in the early church's understanding.

One could of course speculate that the concept of an atoning death for sin would have been centered in Jewish familiarity with the Levitical sacrifices, but the idea that one simply switches a sacrificed Messiah for a sacrificed animal—and in particular, a Messiah now understood to be in some sense divine—hardly seems so "obvious" as to require no further comment. Could the idea of a redemptive human sacrifice really have been, as Yoder put it, "not a real problem"? Surely there is a very particular problem, when texts such as Deuteronomy 12:31, 18:9–12, and Jeremiah 19:4–5 expressly condemn human sacrifice.[121]

It has been noted that the nobility of redemptive suffering and faithful self-sacrifice was to some extent a recognized feature of first-century Israel's

---

120. Ibid., 133.

121. Discussion about human sacrifice within ancient Near Eastern religions (e.g., as a framework for understanding the story of Abraham and Isaac) and even potentially amongst the early Israelites need not distract us here. It suffices for now that the Old Testament neither prescribes nor permits—indeed, it condemns—the practice of human sacrifice. One might further add that not all sacrifices, even for sin, necessarily involved sacrifice of a living creature (special provisions existed for the poor to offer grain, for example).

consciousness; not least perhaps because of its value in inspiring the Jewish people in enduring their own sufferings under Roman occupation. The narratives of the Suffering Servant (Isaiah 53) and the Maccabean Martyrs (2 Macc 7:37–38) would have been familiar texts and so too the book of Daniel.[122] However, one must question whether any one or a combination of these background ideas in themselves would have gone so far as to make atonement through sacrificial human death simply "obvious" to an early Jewish-Christian understanding (let alone to gentiles) in the absence of any available evidence. As N. T. Wright puts it, it seems very unlikely that there was "a well-known pre-Christian belief, based on Isaiah 53, in a coming redeemer who would die for the sins of Israel and/or the world, such that Paul could simply slot Jesus into a ready-made framework."[123]

1.3.2 *"The Classic Understanding"—Gustaf Aulén*

Aulén's *Christus Victor* idea of the atonement lays claim that for the first thousand years of Christianity there was a dominant teaching he dubs the "dramatic" or "classic" idea, within which the central theme is the idea of the atonement as a divine conflict and victory. Since the earliest part of that first thousand years would self-evidently have been the first century CE, we might reasonably expect Aulén's proposal to be securely anchored in Jewish thought, in direct continuity with the Judaism within which early Christianity was incubated. Aulén sees this as preceding the traditional accounts of atonement that feature the two poles of so-called "objective" and "subjective" thought with which the names of Anselm and Abelard are commonly associated and which historically have framed the discussion of atonement.

In his short but influential work Aulén explains how the victorious Christ—*Christus Victor*—fights against and triumphs over the evil powers of the world, the "tyrants" under which mankind is in bondage and suffering, and how in Christ God reconciles the world to himself.[124] Aulén argues that this is the typical view of the atonement found in both the New Testament and the Greek and Latin church fathers, revived in the theology

---

122. Dan 7; 11:35; and 12:2–3 give an indication that the death of martyrs can atone and do so within a "son of man" context. Scot McKnight offers evidence that Jesus "thought of his death in terms of a divinely destined martyr for his prophetic calling": as a prophet, "he would have pondered over Scriptures that might shed light on his destiny—and at least one place he might look to see his life inscripturated would be Daniel 7." McKnight, *Jesus and his Death*, 155.

123. Wright, *Climax*, 60.

124. Aulén, *Christus Victor*, 4.

of Luther, but later falling into neglect. This classic idea "has a clear and distinct character of its own, quite different from the other two types."[125]

Aulén's strong claims for its primacy may be summed up as follows:[126]

> The classic idea has in reality held a place in the history of Christian doctrine whose importance it would not be easy to exaggerate. Though it is expressed in a variety of forms, not all of which are equally fruitful, there can be no dispute that it is the dominant idea of the Atonement throughout the early church period. It is also in reality, as I shall hope to show, the dominant idea in the New Testament; for it did not suddenly spring into being in the early church, or arrive as an importation from some outside source. It was, in fact, the ruling idea of the Atonement for the first thousand years of Christian history. [. . .] It therefore has every right to claim the title of *the classic Christian idea of the Atonement*.[127]

Aulén's work has taken its rightful place in the atonement debate and his ideas continue to have influence. J. Denny Weaver, for example, accepts Aulén's view of *Christus Victor* as the predominant image of the early church and has developed what he calls a "narrative Christus Victor" theory as a non-violent approach to the atonement.[128] Rather than being another of the "different versions of the Father who arranges the death of the Son for the sake of the Father's other children," in Weaver's narrative Christus Victor Jesus carries out a mission to make the rule of God present and visible; a mission to bring and to give life.

> When this mission threatens the forces of evil, they retaliate with violence, killing Jesus. This suffering is not something willed by nor needed by God and it is not directed Godward. To the contrary, the killing of Jesus is the ultimate contrast between the nonviolent reign of God and the rule of evil.[129]

McIntyre concedes that Aulén's idea reflects much that is said in the New Testament about the death of Christ, but he believes it to be inaccurate

---

125. Ibid., 6.

126. Aulén declines to characterize *Christus Victor* as a "doctrine" or "theory." Ibid., 157–58.

127. Ibid., 6–7, emphasis original.

128. For Weaver, all of the traditional ideas exhibit or accommodate violence, displayed in one form or another. Weaver, "Violence in Christian Theology."

129. Ibid. For a fuller treatment of the same themes, see Weaver, *The Nonviolent Atonement*.

to give it such prominence. It is "a case of a brilliant idea being overstated."[130] The same conclusion is reached by Gunton, whose principal critiques are firstly, an understating of the continuing ethical dimension ("talk of a past victory is not to be isolated from matters of present practice") and secondly, that it is not merely a *divine* victory: the victory is at once human and divine—a divine victory only because it is a human one (and of course, *vice versa*).[131]

It is clearly the case that Aulén's idea has biblical support and there is every reason why it should be placed alongside other *motifs* of what Christ has done. For our purposes, however, its most notable feature—which is also the case in Weaver's reworking—is the absence of any necessary connection to the story of Israel. His theory draws no obvious insights from it and neither McIntyre nor Gunton see any reason to criticize that omission; their theological concerns lie elsewhere. Aulén's consideration of atonement begins with a pristine New Testament and develops through the early church fathers and the mediæval theologians. The reason for this omission becomes somewhat obvious, however, when we come upon Aulén's summary of "the contrast between the New Testament and the Old":[132]

> It is Law—the Law—that says the final and decisive word in the Old Testament view of man's relation to God. Man's way to God is first and last the way of duty, of obedience to Law; and this in increasing degree as time goes on. It is, however, exactly at this point that the emergence of the classic idea of redemption in the New Testament shows how radical the breach between Judaism and Christianity is.[133]

If one begins one's inquiries from the standpoint that a "radical breach" between Judaism and Christianity is extant in the pages of the New Testament, as Aulén clearly does, a continuity in atonement thought that accords a high value to the former is not likely to be found. Indeed, Aulén argues that "the New Testament idea of redemption constitutes in fact a veritable revolution; for it declares that sovereign Divine Love has taken the initiative, broken through the order of justice and merit, triumphed over the powers of evil, and created a new relation between the world and God."[134] Thus we find both supersessionism and theological anti-Judaism embedded in Aulén's assumptions. Whatever may have been the ruling idea of the atone-

130. McIntyre, *Shape of Soteriology*, 43.
131. Gunton, *Actuality of Atonement*, 54–59.
132. Aulén, *Christus Victor*, vi.
133. Ibid., 79.
134. Ibid.

ment in the *first* thousand years of Christian history, the ruling ideas from the *preceding* thousand years—rooted in Israel's relationship with the God of Israel—appear in Aulén's perspective to offer only a negative contribution. No wonder, then, that he finds an atonement theory that comports with that belief: namely, a "new relation between the world and God"—a "veritable revolution"—which reflects a "radical breach" with Judaism.

Unless one begins with negative presuppositions, however, it is hard to see how a theory that has no apparent connectivity to Torah preceding could suddenly have become the dominant atonement idea in the early New Testament era. This absence of continuity passes unnoticed in the discussion and debate of atonement models, perhaps because (as Aulén exemplifies) a negative view of the preceding relationship in Torah is so often the express or implied starting point.

We are forced to conclude that Aulén's theory fails to offer a logical coherence in the nature of God's atoning actions pre- and post-Christ. Specifically, it is a dehistoricized Christian articulation of salvation that has wholly bypassed Israel (indeed, one that reflects a "radical breach" with Judaism).

1.3.3 *"The Scapegoat"—S. Mark Heim*

In contrast to the very real questions concerning the provenance of Aulén's theory vis-à-vis Israel, Heim's work is unquestionably engaging with an established Old Testament *motif*, rooted in Torah—the "scapegoat" found in the rituals of the Day of Atonement. This seems promising because it would appear to be built directly on a *praxis* of Israel that has deep significance in relation to atonement.

Heim argues that Jesus is the innocent scapegoat who is the victim of the human community rather than a redemptive sacrifice offered to God to save humanity from sin—scapegoating sacrifice is the fundamental human sin that causes Jesus's death.[135] We humans took a terrible thing—scapegoating violence against the innocent—and made it into a good thing on the grounds that it "brings us together, stops escalating conflict among us, and unites us against a common enemy."[136] The practice of scapegoating is therefore part of our broken human condition. Importantly, in Heim's proposal, it is *our* practice, not God's.[137] The need for Christ's work arises because all of us are too fully immersed in the scapegoating process to be able to break its spell. "Only one whose innocence can be undeniably vindicated may, by

---

135. Heim, *Saved from Sacrifice*, 214.
136. Ibid., xi.
137. Ibid., 9.

suffering this sacrifice, reverse it."[138] Thus, Christ's sacrifice saves humanity from the sin of sacrifice itself—"sacrifice is the disease we have."[139]

Heim therefore builds a theory on the biblical concept of sacrifice, yet he radically redefines its meaning. Rather than a divine provision that has to do with the amelioration of sin and its effects, sacrifice becomes a human mechanism in which to appease its own aggression the community heaps violence on an innocent victim who takes the blame. The church has therefore been right to understand Jesus's death as a sacrifice, according to Heim, but wrong in its basis for understanding what it was doing; namely, to end sacrifice.[140] "Christ died for us, to save us from what killed him. And what killed him was not God's justice but our redemptive violence."[141]

> Blood is not acceptable to God as a means of uniting human community or a price for God's favor. Christ sheds his own blood to end that way of trying to mend our divisions. Jesus's death isn't necessary because God has to have innocent blood to solve the guilt equation. Redemptive violence is our equation. Jesus didn't volunteer to get into God's justice machine. God volunteered to get into ours. God used our own sin to save us.[142]

In developing his argument concerning the scapegoat, Heim is building on the foundational work of René Girard.[143] In its biblical context, the scapegoat originates in Israel's Day of Atonement rituals. However, Heim argues that rather than authorizing and endorsing the practice of what he calls "scapegoating sacrifice" (a questionable linkage, which we shall address in a moment), the overall trajectory of scripture is actually to expose and subvert it.[144] We may wonder, though, whether in building on Girard's theories of mimetic desire and mimetic violence Heim is reading rather more into the texts than he is reading out of them. Scapegoating is clearly a disquieting feature of human nature. That is not in doubt. The question is whether it can lay claim to major salvific relevance in the Christian idea of atonement, especially when viewed through an Evangelical lens. Was the cross really no

---

138. Ibid., 196–97.
139. Ibid., xii.
140. Ibid., 294.
141. Ibid., 306.
142. Ibid., xi.

143. The title of Part One of *Saved From Sacrifice*, "Things Hidden From The Foundation Of The World," consciously echoes Girard's *Des Choses Cachées Depuis la Fondation du Monde*. For another perspective applying Girard's ideas, see Bartlett, *Cross Purposes*.

144. Girard, *I See Satan Fall Like Lightning*, 154–60.

more than "an occasion of overcoming scapegoating violence"?[145] Moreover, it is highly questionable whether this is an appropriate reading of the Old Testament.

Heim rightly identifies that human beings are shaped and defined by three dimensions of relation—with God, with others and with created nature; furthermore, that the biblical story highlights each such dimension and describes how it has gone astray. This is helpful insofar as it identifies aspects of a more holistic view of God's salvific purposes, which are often ignored in individualistic presentations of the gospel. However, Heim then limits his hypothesis to how the cross pertains to "the dimension of interpersonal evil": "We are concerned almost entirely with the way the cross might bear on one crucial and specific type of social evil, sacrificial scapegoating."[146] To leave aside human relations with God—which Evangelicalism, at least, would expect to see receiving primary consideration within any discussion of the cross—seems surprising. Might the obvious difficulties in applying the scapegoating theory to our relationship with God explain Heim's overlooking of it? The practice of sacrificial scapegoating may, indeed, be part of our broken human condition,[147] but our broken human condition is surely much more than that. Christ's atoning work must be broader and deeper than God's vindication of scapegoats—which one reviewer dismisses as "solely a moral influence theory, and a relatively weak one at that."[148] Shelton, too, concludes that Girard's theory is a creative form of moral influence.[149] Perceiving Christ's work as an unmasking of the mimetic scapegoat process in human behavior does not in itself constitute a theory of how salvation is thereby achieved.

Heim's idea is disappointing at a number of other points, many of which are rooted in the weaknesses in its assumptions concerning sacrifice.

Firstly, there is a problem of anachronism. Israel's understanding of the cultic ritual of the Day of Atonement, from which "scapegoating" derives its name, is not synonymous with the modern idea of scapegoating by the community.[150] It is basic to hermeneutics that today's understanding of

---

145. Heim, *Saved from Sacrifice*, xii.
146. Ibid., 8–9.
147. Ibid., 9.
148. Merrick, "Review Article" 887.
149. Shelton, *Cross and Covenant*, 212–13.
150. Girard himself concedes that, "the arguments I make are based [. . .] in the modern sense of 'scapegoat.'" He anticipates the critique, but addresses it only by resorting to a "must be" presupposition: "The similarities are great between phenomena of attenuated expulsion that we observe every day in our world and ancient scapegoat rituals . . . *so great that they must be real*." Girard, *Satan Fall*, 154 and 160, emphasis added.

a word or concept—the horizon of the contemporary reader—should not be superimposed on its original understanding—the horizon of the author and his audience.[151]

Secondly, there is the problem of the place that the theory attributes to violence. The expelling of the goat on the Day of Atonement was not a punishment ritual, nor was the goat subjected to violence. Granted, it may reasonably be presumed that the goat was being sent to its death by virtue of being driven into the wilderness, but that is simply a presumption—the text itself is silent on the matter and such a death has no stated ritual role. Heim's general supposition that violence is unveiled in scripture as "the operative element" inherent in sacrifice is both highly questionable in itself and, once again, imposes a modern value system on the text.[152] Heim is uncritically appropriating "Girard's tendency to see sacrifice as simply violence,"[153] which is to seriously misread what is taking place:

> In a sacrifice, the animal is *made sacred* and is given to God as a sacred gift or returned to the offerer as a sacred meal. That sense of sacrifice should never be confused with *suffering* or *substitution*. [. . .] Offerers never thought that the point of the sacrifice was to make the animal suffer, or that the greatest sacrifice was one in which the animal suffered lengthily or terribly.[154]

Rather than being to do with violence or punishment, the original scapegoat functioned as a ritual expulsion, to carry away from the community the polluting effects of sin, to "outside the camp." It parallels the idea of removing our sins as far away from us as the east is from the west.[155] Not only was the scapegoat not situated in a context of (judicial) violence as Heim either believes or imposes on the text, this was not even the case with sacrifice generally.[156] Sacrifice appears to have "worked" simply because God said it would.[157] Indeed, as Gordon Wenham explains, the hermeneutical

---

151. On the "two horizons" of hermeneutics, see Thiselton, *The Two Horizons*.

152. Heim, *Saved from Sacrifice*, 17. Heim claims that "(1) violence and (2) ritual cultic practice, the center of which is ritual sacrifice [. . .], are actually one connected topic" (93). This entirely fails to take account of the wider covenantal context, as a practice ordained by God, over-stresses one aspect of it and links that to an anachronistic reading-in of the feature of violence.

153. Shelton, *Cross and Covenant*, 215.

154. Borg and Crossan, *The Last Week*, 37.

155. Ps 103:12.

156. We note that sacrifices were not limited to the slaying of animals.

157. "At times [. . .] it seems to have no meaning or context at all, except the command of God." Holmes, *Wondrous Cross*, 22.

key to the efficacy of sacrifice almost certainly lies in the offeror's penitent participation and identification.[158]

Thirdly, Heim conflates "scapegoat" and "sacrifice" into one idea, in which the terms effectively become interchangeable; he does the same with "offering" and "victim." Biblical sacrifices, however, were made not just for sin, but for a variety of purposes, including sealing a covenant, thanksgiving, remembrance of a historic salvation, communion with God, or simply a gift to God in response to God's goodness.[159] Sacrifice "is a grander idea and does not in itself require a narrative of God's judicial wrath needing to be satisfied."[160] Moreover, sacrifice was a continuous practice in Israel's community life, whereas the scapegoat ritual was a once-a-year event.

Fourthly, nowhere does the New Testament speak explicitly of Jesus as the scapegoat and associate his death with the rituals of the Day of Atonement.[161] On the contrary, Jesus's death is clearly presented as occurring within the context of—and hence, is surely to be more strongly identified with—the Passover, in which "the paschal lamb of Passover indicates celebration over deliverance from bondage rather than an appeasement for sin."[162] The imagery is of divine liberation in Exodus, rather than the sacrifices in Leviticus.

Girard's own solution to this problem is imaginative, if unconvincing—not least because it requires a reconfiguration of the biblical references to lamb and goat:

> [The New Testament] use[s] an expression equal and even superior to "scapegoat," and this is *lamb of God*. It eliminates the negative attributes and unsympathetic connotations of the goat. Thereby it better corresponds to the idea of an innocent victim sacrificed unjustly.[163]

For Girard's purposes "lamb of God" may indeed better correspond to the idea of an innocent victim sacrificed unjustly, but it does so at the cost of less-well corresponding to the actual Day of Atonement ritual that his theory is built upon! No doubt the New Testament could have spoken of Jesus as the "goat of God" too, had it wished. The fact that the lamb draws

---

158. Wenham, "The Theology of Old Testament Sacrifice," 79–80.

159. Gunton, *Actuality of Atonement*, 120.

160. Motyer, "The Atonement in Hebrews," 137.

161. Perhaps John 1:29 is a reference (though note the problem of "lamb" *versus* "goat" discussed below).

162. Shelton, "Relational Atonement," 14.

163. Girard, *Satan Fall*, 155.

us back towards Passover, meanwhile, simply adds a further—and perhaps fatal—hurdle for Girard's hermeneutical creativity.

Finally, the Old Testament texts would tell us that sacrifice was initiated and ordained by YHWH. Even allowing for development over time in Israel's understanding of God's nature, character, and purposes as the biblical story unfolds—including the prophets' later denunciations of sacrificial ritual absent the heart's involvement—to suggest that sacrifice lacks divine mandate within God's gift of Torah involves quite a step.[164] Like it or not from a modern liberal perspective that tends to view salvation history through the lens of contemporary sensibilities, Israel understood sacrifice to be divinely instituted and somehow efficacious in, amongst other things, restoring fractured covenantal relations.

We are compelled to agree with James Merrick, therefore, that "quite often Heim appears too eager to find that for which he is looking."[165] If one is seeking genuine continuity in God's salvific actions across Old and New Testaments, the linkage between Heim's ideas concerning scapegoating and Israel's praxis within Torah is at best tenuous. Heim's interpretation bears only superficial resemblance to the original context and has negligible, if any, dependence on it.

In conclusion, Heim offers no material contribution to an "Israel-remembered" account of the atonement. Indeed, he is explicitly critical of "scapegoating" in its original context within Israel's story, seeing it as a flawed, human idea. He simply borrows an Old Testament image—the scapegoat—extracts it from its context and makes it totemic for his concerns over a feature of human nature that manifests in tendencies towards violence, exclusion, and blame. Insofar as Israel is concerned, Heim's theory operates as a deeply negative critique—the atoning significance of the ritual in the eyes of Israel, in obedience to God's command, and their obedient trust in its covenantal efficacy, is treated with disdain.

1.3.4 "Covenant"—R. Larry Shelton

Last but by no means least, Larry Shelton is particularly interesting among this small group, in terms of the potential for us to build further upon his insights later in the book. Like Shelton, we too will be exploring a continuing covenantal theme throughout God's salvific dealings with humanity in both Israel and Christ—the idea that covenant relationship and atonement are directly and profoundly linked.

164. On "development" in the Bible, see Ward, *The Word of God*.
165. "Review Article."

A foundational concern that underlies Shelton's work is one that we share—the lack of persuasiveness for a postmodern world of the penal substitutionary doctrine and the consequent missional implications for an Evangelicalism characterized by conversionism.[166] As the title *Cross and Covenant* suggests, with considerable promise, he proposes "an embracing integrative motif of covenant renewal for a biblical concept of atonement."[167] Shelton's perspective can be summarized thus:

> The key issue and divine objective in the biblical teaching on salvation is the restoration of covenant fellowship, not simply the removal of guilt. The disposition of guilt and sin is part of the salvation process, but not the entire issue. Covenant fellowship with God is the goal for which humanity was created and which it has lost as a result of its fallenness. The key question for all atonement theories, then, is how this alienation from God can be overcome and the covenant relationship restored.[168]

Shelton argues that "The biblical covenant idea may most effectively be used to serve as a hermeneutic that evaluates all the atonement metaphors."[169] The covenant, he suggests, "was the primary contextual framework God used to communicate and interpret divine love to an alienated humanity in terms they could understand."[170] Thus, the biblical writers contextualized God's message into the cultural thought forms of the ancient world.[171] This is the cultural context within which the biblical atonement concept is developed.[172]

The specific covenants of which we read in the Old Testament were made between God and certain persons for particular purposes but operated within the overall context of a general covenant relationship between YHWH and creation. The reality of covenantal relationship is present even where the word itself does not specifically appear; for example, in the story of the Garden of Eden. "The foundation of this general covenant relationship and what it reveals about God [. . .] gives authenticity to the specific covenants, such as those with Abraham and David."[173] Sin, meanwhile, is

---

166. Reflected in his sub-title: *Interpreting the Atonement for 21st Century Mission*.
167. Shelton, "Relational Atonement," 1.
168. Shelton, *Cross and Covenant*, 20.
169. Ibid., 20–21.
170. Ibid., 21.
171. Ibid., 37.
172. Ibid., 37.
173. Ibid., 38.

relationally-centered as a moral transgression, not a legal one; it requires a moral rather than legal antidote.[174]

Shelton does not treat distinctives and differences between the various Old Testament covenants in any depth or detail.[175] "The major concern here is the theological concept of covenant that is formally expressed in the Old Testament covenants *such as* those with Abraham and Moses."[176] Accordingly, he somewhat glosses over the polarity between covenants of law (Mosaic) and covenants of promise (Abrahamic) that features centrally in Reformed covenant theology.[177]

Thus far, Shelton has set the stage for a potentially significant contribution from God's covenantal relationship with Israel to the Christian idea of atonement. From this point on, we might expect him to develop a continuous covenantal narrative in which the salvific relationship between Israel and the God of Israel retains center stage—but this does not happen.

Shelton's thesis begins well enough: with reference to Romans 11, "the relationship Christians now have with God is not a brand-new covenant, but an old one *into which* they [Christians] have been grafted."[178] Paul is speaking of a singular covenant which Judaism and Christianity share.

In order to appreciate the relevance of the covenant motif for communicating the gospel to contemporary culture, it is important to see that Christianity shares the same covenant as Judaism. The purpose of the law,

---

174. Ibid., 49.

175. Ibid., 37. "A significant body of [other] literature deals with the historical and critical sources of the various covenants reflected in the Hebrew Bible." For a recent example, see Hahn, *Kinship by Covenant*.

176. Shelton, *Cross and Covenant*, 37. Emphasis added.

177. Reformed covenant theology is sometimes known as "federal" theology (from *foedus*, the Latin for "contract"). For a useful primer, see Horton, *Introducing Covenant Theology*. Reformed doctrine asserts that all of the covenants found in scripture can be grouped around one or other of two kinds of arrangement: conditional covenants that impose obligations, and unconditional covenants based on divine promise. Salvation through the covenant of works requires absolute obedience, in which human efforts are doomed to fail—contrasted with God's covenant of promise in which trusting faith is all that is required. At the heart of federal thought lies a sharp distinction between the two types, corresponding to general lines of Reformed thought concerning "law" and "grace," which we shall discuss further in chapter two. However, as Chris Wright presciently observes, "The covenants are all "unconditional" in the sense that they issue from the redemptive intention of God to act in blessing for human beings, who neither deserve such action, nor could fulfill any condition to deserve it. They call for human response, but they are not based on it, nor motivated by it. Yet, in another sense, they are all "conditional" in that some clear stipulations are laid down for those who are to benefit from the covenant relationship." *Knowing Jesus Through The Old Testament*, 79. We shall say more on Reformed covenant theology in chapter three.

178. Shelton, *Cross and Covenant*, 42. Emphasis added.

the epitome of Judaism, is also the purpose of Christianity. The prime directive under the Mosaic covenant is the same as that under Jesus: love God with all your being by obeying his commands in an attitude of covenant love.[179]

In *what sense*, though, is this a singular covenant that is shared? "The 'new' covenant in Christ is *related* to those of the community of Israel" in that "they *share the same family tree*."[180] One might quibble with Shelton that while both of his statements apply a horticultural metaphor, "grafting in" is not synonymous with "sharing the same family tree." The former is indicative of synthesis within one on-going entity, whereas the latter simply indicates an antecedent parent, common to parties who are otherwise distinct.

A further concern then arises in Shelton's apparently innocuous—and some would say incontrovertible—statement that "the previous covenants are not abolished with the new covenant in Christ, but have come to their fullest purpose and significance."[181] What might Shelton mean by this turn of phrase? A plain meaning of "not abolished" would suggest they continue—and if they continue, that they remain valid. However, the "but" here appears to bear some considerable weight. The "new covenant in Christ" has caused these previous covenants to have "come to their fullest purpose and significance." Again, what does this mean? The phraseology implies that the previous covenants have only benefitted—in terms of gaining a fuller purpose and greater significance—*with nothing forfeited*. And yet it appears that the process of acquiring these benefits actually involves *so much change* to the covenants that they become unrecognizable in terms of their original features. To gain a "fuller purpose and significance" is surely not synonymous with the idea of being rendered effective for the very first time by Christ's coming; so does he mean rendered *more* effective? The problem here is not so much with the statement itself as the implications. "Not abolished" does not appear to imply having prior and continuing validity separate and apart from Christ.

For example, Shelton quotes from an article by C. E. B. Cranfield, that without the Spirit the law remains only an external letter rendered ineffective by human sinfulness.[182] But it hardly seems logical that Torah was rendered ineffective by human sinfulness when by divine design it included provisions to address that—hence the prospect of human sinfulness affecting the covenant could hardly be said to have caught God unawares. And in

179. Ibid., 42.
180. Ibid., 42. Emphases added.
181. Ibid., 42.
182. Ibid., 89.

what sense could a divinely-authored Torah be said to be *without the Spirit*? Shelton does not explain, but Cranfield's logic can be found elsewhere in that same article and it derives from an embedded theological anti-Judaism: the *"legalistic relation of the Jews of Paul's time* to God and to His law" sits in contrast to "the new relation to God and to His law established by the Holy Spirit and resulting from Christ's work." Furthermore, "the literal observance of circumcision and other ceremonies of the law was valuable and significant as "a shadow of the things to come," a pointer forward to Christ; but *to regard such things as having an independent value in themselves* quite apart from Him is to be left with a mere empty 'shadow.'"[183]

The presuppositions of both Cranfield and Shelton contain these anti-Judaic theological assumptions. Shelton, for example, fails to see any contradiction in saying on the one hand that "the Law provided the ceremonial rituals as a means by which a sinful people could maintain the covenant relationship"—which appears to be granting an effective, relational role for Torah—yet on the other hand, "at best [. . .] even with the Day of Atonement ritual that covered all sins for all the people, the sacrificial system only *represented* the deliverance from sins; it did not actually eliminate them (Hebrews 10:1–14)."[184] This begs the question once again—was Torah efficacious or not, within its own terms of reference, temporally prior to the birth of Jesus of Nazareth (not to mention, subsequently)?[185] If, as Shelton says, "the purpose of the Law" is also "the purpose of Christianity"—which in itself sounds affirming—did the law *fail* in that purpose or *succeed* in it? If it failed, at what point did it fail? If it succeeded, at what point did it stop succeeding? After all, Cranfield himself rightly makes the point that "the view that the law was an unsuccessful first attempt on God's part at dealing with man's unhappy state, which had to be followed later by a second (more successful) attempt," is "a view that is theologically grotesque, for the God of the unsuccessful first attempt is hardly a God to be taken seriously."[186] Both he and Shelton, however, fail to follow through on the obvious implications of that statement.

183. "St. Paul and the Law," 53, 57. Emphases added.

184. Shelton, *Cross and Covenant*, 42, 138.

185. This is not, of course, to imply that affirming Torah in its own terms amounts to a dismissal of all need to consider relationship in Torah in the light of Christ. Nor is it to suggest that the God of Israel and Torah was not always and everywhere the Triune God, eternally active by Word and Spirit. Rather, our concern is firstly to highlight the tendency to treat the validity of God's relationship with Israel (particularly as that relationship is framed in Torah) with an express or implied disdain, and then secondly to explore the implications of a repristinated understanding of that relationship for Christian doctrinal thought, specifically in relation to the atonement.

186. Cranfield, "St. Paul and the Law," 68.

And this brings us to the crux of the problem concerning Shelton's account: it does appear that soteriologically one can leapfrog the "previous covenants" completely: "The covenant relationship with God [that was] *lost* with Adam's fall is *recovered* with Christ's incarnational atonement."[187] From Adam to Christ in a single bound is a small step linguistically but a giant leap theologically, since it renders the post-fall story of Israel and its covenants ultimately irrelevant.

It is almost as if a dim view of Israel and its relationship with God, notably through Torah, is so deeply ingrained that such questions are not even noticed. A further example arises in Shelton's statement that the new covenant is to be favorably contrasted with the old covenant (*singular* at this point—presumably the Sinaitic covenant) because it is not "a new code of laws that are out of reach of fallen humanity,"[188] with the obvious implication that Torah was an *old* code of laws out of reach of fallen humanity. Hence, suggests Shelton, we are not to understand the two versions of covenant the same way.

> The Old Testament covenant does provide the foundation for understanding the New Testament message of Christ's incarnation and atoning death, but there are significant differences between the two versions of covenant understanding [. . .]. Just as the Mosaic covenant established a new Israel, so Christ's sacrifice of death and his resurrection delivers humanity from sin and establishes a new covenant with God and a new people of God.[189]

Shelton's concept that "the Old Testament covenant" provides a "foundation for understanding" the new covenant in Christ is, of course, promising. However, there appears to be a distinct contrast between its value as a foundation for understanding the new and attributing value to it in its own right. Moreover, we see a continuing embedded supersessionism—Christ has established "a new people of God"—and anti-Judaic contrasts.

In presenting some genuine and meaningful insight focused on covenant, it is disappointing that Shelton appears to have settled slightly too early in the development of his account for two findings (important though they are):

---

187. Ibid., 86. Emphasis added.
188. Ibid., 89.
189. Shelton, *Cross and Covenant*, 83. Note that "Old Testament covenant" has become singular. Shelton uses singular and plural almost interchangeably, further reinforcing the view that it is (or they are) simply an "idea" to help us understand the message of the New Testament.

1. That covenant is of fundamental significance for understanding the atonement; and
2. That atonement is relationally-based.

We can warmly endorse both. Unfortunately, he has stopped short of engaging with the many implications for the "previous covenants" that are center stage in the story of Israel. In fairness, Shelton is writing from an Evangelical perspective within which much of the traditional language we are questioning here is common currency and yet to his considerable credit he raises questions that begin to challenge some traditional Reformed thought.

Shelton is clearly aware of the work of E. P. Sanders,[190] and he speaks supportively of Sanders's core perspective on first-century Judaism—e.g., that the "Law [was] based on grace and given to assist Israel in maintaining its personal relationship with God"[191]—but he really does not identify the questions for atonement doctrine that derive from such a statement. Namely, in what ways does a personal relationship with God through a Torah based in grace, given to Israel by God himself, say something enduring concerning God's salvific actions pre- and post-Christ? And, specifically, what might a presumption of radical continuity—instead of one of radical discontinuity—tell us about the nature of God's covenantal initiative in Christ?

Shelton is right to identify a "spiritual thread that runs through both testaments [which] concludes with Christ's revelation as the last phase of God's faithfulness to his covenant commitments of salvation to Israel, and through that nation to the entire world,"[192] but he could surely go further to address in what sense the *previous* phase or phases were necessary and efficacious in their own terms (if indeed, it is his view that they were) and how, exactly, it is *one* thread rather than two.

It appears that for Shelton the principal value of Israel's own covenantal story is to offer an illustrative background for better understanding the Christian one. We see a persistent contrasting of a favorable and effective "new" with an unfavorable and ineffective "old." For example, Shelton says that "while the law by continued repetition enabled the sinner by continued repentance and obedience to remain in the covenant community, *it did not justify and set the sinner right with God*."[193] Apparently, it "lacked spiritual

---

190. *Cross and Covenant*, 44, 48, 66, etc.
191. Ibid., 47.
192. Ibid., 28.
193. Ibid., 139. Emphasis added.

50　Atonement and the New Perspective

power," which is "where Christ fits in."[194] In statements such as these, he defaults to the tendency of theological anti-Judaism to deploy negative assertions concerning the old to more powerfully present the new.

It has not been our intention to be unduly harsh in critiquing Shelton's work, which offers considerable opportunity for further development of the themes he identifies. Indeed, it is because of a high regard that we are led to interrogate some of the detail so closely. Shelton's covenantal understanding holds significant potential for both continuity and confluence between the Christian story and the story of Israel. Nonetheless, *Cross and Covenant* leaves scope for further consideration of exactly how the "old" and "new" aspects of covenant interface.[195]

1.4 THE QUESTIONS OUTSTANDING

At the close of this chapter, we may sum up the largely unsatisfactory state of play in contemporary atonement thought as follows. Within the Evangelical context, the atonement is typically conceived and explained by reference to one or more of the following assumptions:

1. Penal substitutionary atonement is either *the* way to understand the Christian gospel, synonymous with it and inseparable from it, or at the very least is the foundational truth on which all else depends or is derived.[196]

2. In the alternative, atonement encompasses many different things and is necessarily to be explained in many different ways.[197] The reason we have only metaphors, models, and images of atonement—and so many of them—is because atonement is, at heart, simply a mystery, the full wonders of which we shall never fully grasp.

3. Atonement deals with a universal human problem that requires no particular historical rooting, for what is true now of humanity and its

---

194. Ibid., 139.

195. Other works by the same author concerning covenantal atonement themes treat Israel and the Old Testament covenants similarly. See Shelton, "A Covenantal Concept of Atonement."

196. "Penal substitution functions as the anchor and foundation for all other dimensions of the Atonement when the Scriptures are considered as a canonical whole." Schreiner, "Penal Substitution View," 67.

197. Notwithstanding that some would still argue for prominence to be given to a particular understanding (which may or may not include a penal element).

condition has always been so. In that sense, Christ's work could have been "anywhere, anytime."

4. The relationship between Israel and its God into which Jesus entered performs no explanatory role in relation to atonement, save insofar as it (a) enables the positivity of the "new" covenant of Christianity to be favorably contrasted with the negativity of the "old" covenant of Judaism, and (b) offers an Old Testament treasure chest that can be raided for stories, images and metaphors to help illustrate Jesus's work (e.g., sacrifice, exodus, etc.).

These commonplace assumptions about atonement have to a greater or lesser extent become institutionalized within both popular and academic Christian theological thought, either because their shortcomings have not been fully perceived or because no more-compelling options have been proposed.

Concerning point one, we have suggested that penal substitution can be allowed a seat at the table, but it cannot be a table for one, nor can it be head of the table. Concerning point two, the extant theories, models, and metaphors of atonement are not so much wrong in what they tell us about atonement as in their apparent comfort with leaving things fragmented and atomized. Moreover, we question whether celebrating "mystery" as a virtue, as if it were the biblical writers' intention, is entirely legitimate, however amenable that approach may be to postmodern thought.[198] Points three and four, meanwhile, illustrate the extent to which atonement theology has become entirely ahistorical. If nothing else, its detachment from any concrete historical context is surely inconsistent with Paul's claim in Romans 5:6 that Christ died "just at the right time." Based upon the current thought lines of atonement theology it appears that it could have been at any time and any place. The only truly necessary historical events would appear to be Adam's fall, giving rise to a universal human plight, and Christ's death to resolve it.

At the close of our survey of the current state of play with respect to the atonement debate we can clearly see two features emerging. One is that—save for some limited references to Old Testament themes—no current conception of the atonement in Christian thought appears to invoke any positive salvific correspondence to or dependence upon the story of

---

198. With but a couple of possible exceptions (Eph 5:32; 1 Tim 3:16), instances of the word "mystery" (*mystērion*) in the New Testament seem to concern what was previously a mystery now having been revealed in Christ. See e.g., Rom 16:25; Eph 1:9; and Col 1:26–27. The references are not to a permanent, on-going state of mystery, nor is their focus the atonement *per se*. On "mystery," see e.g., Walls, "Mystery, Mysteries." Walls notes Moffat's translation of *mystērion*, in Eph 1:9 and Col 1:26; 2:2 and 4:3, as an "open secret"!

the Israel of God's relationship with the God of Israel. All of the theories are ahistorical and "Israel-forgetful." It is as if the salvation history of Israel recounted in the Hebrew scriptures had never happened or need never have happened. The second feature that emerges is founded in a theological anti-Judaism. To the extent that Israel appears at all for the purposes of understanding Christ's work, it is almost entirely by way of its usefulness as a *negative* foil—law *versus* grace, faith *versus* works, carnal *versus* spiritual, etc.—to provide the dark background against which the light of Christ is enabled to shine all the more brightly.

CHAPTER TWO

New Perspectives on First-Century Judaism

It appears that a Jew, so strong in his Jewish faith that he persecutes Christians, himself becomes a Christian through a sudden and overwhelming experience. Yet a closer reading of these accounts, both those in Acts and those by Paul himself, reveals a greater continuity between "before" and "after." Here is not that change of "religion" that we commonly associate with the word *conversion*.[1]

2.1 INTRODUCTION

THE TITLE OF THIS chapter consciously echoes the "New Perspective on Paul," which has justifiably been likened to "a Copernican revolution" in Pauline studies.[2] Indeed, such is the NPP's influence that it is inconceivable today to think of embarking on any serious consideration of Paul's theology absent engagement with it. In the words of Don Garlington, "Pauline exegesis will never be the same again."[3] That said, the term itself is something of a misnomer. To begin with, what we have grown accustomed to calling *the* NPP is not a single perspective at all, but rather a "bundle of interpretive approaches to Paul, some of which are mere differences in emphasis, and

---

1. Stendahl, *Paul Among Jews and Gentiles and Other Essays*, 7. The essay is based on lectures delivered in 1963 and 1964.

2. Hagner, "Paul and Judaism," 111–30. Terence Donaldson and Magnus Zetterholm are among those who recognize it as a paradigm shift of worldview, in the idea developed by Thomas Kuhn, *The Structure of Scientific Revolutions*.

3. Garlington, *In Defense of the New Perspective on Paul*, 19.

others of which compete rather antagonistically."[4] The NPP is more properly characterized as "variations on a theme";[5] clustered round what Moisés Silva has dubbed the "Sanders/Dunn trajectory."[6] Taken together, though,

> [These various approaches] belong to the "new perspective" in that they share certain things in common, not least a more-or-less common reading of the documents of Second Temple Judaism, and a conviction that earlier readings of Paul, not least from the Protestant camp, and especially from the German Lutheran camp, with lines going back to the Reformation, are at least partly mistaken, and perhaps profoundly mistaken. [Their] interpretive grids share enough in common that together they have generated a reigning paradigm that to some extent controls contemporary discussion on Paul, the genesis of early Christianity, justification, grace, the identity and boundaries of the people of God, Torah, and a host of related themes.[7]

As well as not being a single perspective, the NPP is really a new perspective on "Paul" only in a secondary, or derivative, sense. As Stephen Westerholm observes, "The conviction most central to the 'new perspective on Paul' pertains in the first place to Judaism, not Paul."[8] Indeed, one might say that it is impossible properly to understand Paul unless and until one has properly understood the Judaism in which he was inculcated. Here, of course, lies the crux of the debate—*Paul's relation to Judaism*. The two are unavoidably conjoined.

And lastly, the NPP is really not that "new" anymore. Four decades have now passed since the publication of E. P. Sanders's landmark book, *Paul and Palestinian Judaism*, which "lit the blue touch-paper," so to speak. Moreover, we have recently witnessed the emergence of a "Post-'New Perspective' Perspective."[9] Magnus Zetterholm identifies, in broad terms, three different contemporary schools in Pauline scholarship: those scholars who basically work from a traditional, Reformation perspective; those

---

4. Carson, "Introduction," 1.
5. Garlington, *In Defense*, 1.
6. Silva, "The Law and Christianity," 339–53.
7. Carson, *Complexities*, 1. Carson rightly identifies the breadth of the theological subject-matter that is impacted by what we call the NPP.
8. Westerholm, "The 'New Perspective' at Twenty-Five," 2. Similarly, "The fundamental point of the new perspective on Paul has to do not with Paul himself, but with the nature of first-century Judaism." Hagner, "Paul and Judaism," 111.
9. Byrne, "Interpreting Romans Theologically," 227–41.

who would define themselves as adherents of the NPP; and those who have moved beyond, into a "radical new perspective."[10]

2.2 APPLICATION OF THE NEW PERSPECTIVE TO ATONEMENT DEBATE

In recent decades, a whole body of new literature on the true characteristics of first-century Jewish faith has been developed, bringing with it radical implications for Christian doctrine. In relation to that which interests us here, the scholarship of the NPP has been contemporaneous to the atonement debate, but without the insights of the one having yet been meaningfully applied to the other. Despite the NPP's considerable body of literature and the different streams that Zetterholm identifies, it has had little if any discernible impact to date on how the atonement is conceived. Our intention, therefore, is to draw from the well of New Perspective scholarship in order to initiate a dialogue between the two. This will provide us with the basis to develop a new perspective on atonement itself.

In this process, we are not looking to break new ground in relation to the NPP or to engage with its scholars on their own historical-critical terms. Our concern is simply to sift and assemble—in order later to bring to bear on our subject—the implications of some of the core findings of those operating within the field (the "more-or-less common reading" of first-century Judaism that Carson identified). In other words, we shall be taking as a basic premise that the general findings of the NPP are valid in exposing an historic Christian misreading of the Judaism of Jesus and Paul. However, in the process of reviewing their work we shall be raising questions on systematic theological grounds—in particular, the extent to which (a) these scholars have failed to address the "Israel-forgetfulness" identified by Soulen and (b) they continue to reflect supersessionist and/or anti-Judaic theological presuppositions.

Since our interest is atonement viewed from the perspective of the Evangelical tradition, we shall specifically be looking for how these scholars' work can help us in developing a new way of thinking about the atonement that is still recognizably Evangelical. For example, we shall challenge elements of the more "radical" new perspective that downgrade or marginalize Christ's atoning role and hence violate two of Bebbington's quadrilateral of key elements of Evangelicalism: crucicentrism and conversionism. At the same time, however, we shall be challenging elements of Evangelical

---

10. Zetterholm, *Approaches to Paul*, 231.

thinking within the NPP that continue to presuppose or perpetuate supersessionism and theological anti-Judaism.

The very idea of a new perspective, of course, presupposes an old perspective that preceded it. Hence we will begin this chapter with the Reformation roots of the "old" perspective, followed by the anti-Judaic developments that set the tone for the standard canonical narrative, and then the emergence of new perspectives in the twentieth century up to and including the pivotal work of E. P. Sanders. After this, we will consider the work of the two most prominent scholars in the wake of Sanders, N. T. Wright and James Dunn. Then we will look at how those early insights have since been built upon in further engaging with the world of first-century Judaism, all of which will contribute to the picture we shall ultimately paint in chapter three. There we will seek to build an alternative account of atonement that is predicated upon a positive (rather than negative) role for the antecedent story of Israel and its God into which Jesus was born and within which his salvific work took place, which we will suggest can only properly be understood through the lens of God's relationship with Israel, informed by the recent scholarship. This will be an account that looks to continuity rather than contrast to explain the efficacy of God's atoning actions;[11] one that is, so far as possible, free of supersessionism and theological anti-Judaism.

This current chapter will not be treating atonement as such to any great extent. Our concern here is to establish relevant features of a rehabilitated view of the first-century Judaism within which one would expect the soteriological thought of that period to have been founded. Once those features are identified and assembled, we can move on in chapter three to propose a way of thinking about the atonement to which they might lead us.

2.3 THE BASIS OF THE "OLD" PERSPECTIVE

At the heart of the debate about first-century Judaism and Pauline theology rests the question of the law.[12] In the period from the Reformation through

---

11. This is not intended to mean a denial of all possible elements of discontinuity when Torah is seen in the light of Christ. It is, rather, a very deliberate shift in focus away from the customary assumptions of stark contrast that cloud the theological lens.

12. We shall have cause to consider later what, precisely, is meant by "law." Suffice to say that it is not an entirely helpful rendition of "Torah." Illustrative of the implications to which notions of law give rise is C. K. Barrett's matter-of-fact assumption that "it is very difficult (perhaps not in the end impossible) to have a law without legalism, and legalism in religion is sin because it magnifies the human ego." Barrett, *Paul*, 82. Similarly, Thomas Schreiner's reading (or reading-in?) that "although the term *works of law* does not denote legalism, Paul condemns legalism when he says that righteousness

to the early part of the twentieth century, the Protestant understanding was dominated by the insights of Luther and the Reformers. The NPP critiques Protestantism for misreading Paul, in its traditional assumption that both apostle and reformer were engaging in passionate arguments for the same truth: that salvation does not come by fulfilling the law, the performance of meritorious human acts as each of those religions assumed, but rather by the "passive" righteousness of faith in Christ, God's work alone, apart from any human effort. Grappling with the excesses of mediæval Catholicism and the burden of his own conscience ("How do I find a gracious God?"), Luther, as the NPP sees him, inappropriately universalized the role and function of law, finding common ground between his own struggle and that of the apostle in Pauline passages such as Galatians 2:16–21: "Namely, that both were confronting a religion of works-righteousness, exemplified in the one case by certain tendencies of late-mediæval Catholicism and in the other by Judaism."[13]

Frank Thielman helpfully summarizes the problems accruing from Luther's presupposition that his own, contemporary religious context directly correlated with that experienced by Paul.

> It is easy, when reading Luther, to concentrate on the theological argument with the Roman Catholic Church in which he is so energetically engaged and to miss a subtle hermeneutical impropriety in which the great Reformer and theologian has indulged. [. . .] Luther assumes that the Jews, against whose view of the Law Paul was arguing, held the same theology of justification as the medieval Roman Catholic Church. This hermeneutical error would be perpetuated over the next four centuries and eventually serve as the organizing principle for mountains of Protestant scholarship on the OT and ancient Judaism.[14]

The problem as James Dunn puts it is that "Luther's fundamental distinction between gospel and law was too completely focused on the danger of self-achieved works-righteousness and too quickly transposed into an antithesis between Christianity and Judaism."[15] Accordingly, "the Luther of the NPP" was *creating theology* in his reading of Paul, rather than engaging in an authentic historical reconstruction of Paul's situation.

---

is not by works of the law." Schreiner, *The Law and Its Fulfillment*, 94.

13. Byrne, "Interpreting Romans Theologically," 227.

14. Thielman, "Law," 530.

15. Dunn, *New Perspective*, 22.

It is easy to see how this theology affected the view of Judaism. As even the mere thought of relating to God by means of the law by definition represents a hopeless endeavor, Luther's doctrine of grace and atonement implied the complete rejection of Judaism. The law is unable to bring forth any good deeds and can only provide knowledge of the sin that finally will result in damnation. As will be evident, this is exactly the conclusion Luther himself arrived at regarding Judaism.[16]

Thus Paul's Jewish adversaries became coterminous with Luther's own opponents, the Catholic theologians, while Luther identified with Paul in their common struggle against human religious legalism. "We have here the retrojection of the Protestant-Catholic debate into ancient history, with Judaism taking the role of Catholicism and Christianity the role of Lutheranism."[17] In the process, Luther's hermeneutical method unwittingly succumbed to a "blurring of the distinctions between historical and dogmatic perspectives."[18] From that time on, argues the NPP, the tendency was to read and interpret Paul and the Judaism of his day through the lens of Luther and the Catholicism of his day,[19] with more than unfortunate consequences for Jewish-Christian relations.

A further thread in the characterization of Judaism as antithetical to Christian faith developed in the period from the seventeenth century onwards, as thinkers in a line beginning with John Locke sought to protect the uniqueness of Christianity against the threat posed by religious relativization in Enlightenment thought. Jeremy Worthen describes the path marked by Locke, in which the classic New Testament claim of prophetic fulfillment in Christ is now "re-conceived as the assertion that the New Testament provides evidence for the historical superiority of Jesus and the religion he founded":

> This signals the replacement for some leading Christian thinkers of newness as prophetic fulfilment by newness as the summit

---

16. Zetterholm, *Approaches to Paul*, 61.
17. Sanders, *Paul and Palestinian Judaism*, 57.
18. Peter Stuhlmacher, *Revisiting Paul's Doctrine of Justification*, 35.
19. Morna Hooker has proposed Luther may not have been wrong to interpret Paul in the way he did, "given the situation at the time." Might it not be an "interpretation of the Spirit," she says, in which the gospel is "reapplied to the situation of the day" to give life? The Spirit "takes the words of scripture and reapplies them to new circumstances." However, the corollary, as Hooker immediately recognizes, is that "though Luther's interpretation of Paul's words may have brought the gospel to medieval Europe, it may itself become a 'veil' which conceals the meaning of the gospel in the twentieth century." Hooker, *From Adam to Christ*, 10.

of gradual revelation through history. What had been a *subordinate* strand in the theological understanding of Christian newness in medieval thinking [. . .] now becomes the *dominant* one. [. . .] Indeed, Christianity now understood as the decisive culmination of a historical process needed to keep proving that Judaism's place in history was finished.[20]

In this recasting of Christian newness, it was necessary that the appeal to the Jewish scriptures as prophecy be "displaced by a form of theological argument that relies on a historical narrative including Jewish decline and intrinsic limitation in order to legitimate Christianity."[21] Once this shift takes place in how that which is "new" in the Christian gospel is articulated, Christianity is subtly uprooted from its historic embedding in the Jewish scriptures and the historical superiority argument leads ultimately to "the absence of any mention of the Old Testament as scripture in Locke's summary of God's purpose in sending Jesus."[22]

> With that ancient anchorage of Christianity in the text of the Hebrew scriptures cut away, voices openly advocating the Old Testament's relegation from or at least demotion within the canon of Christian scripture begin to be heard for the first time since the early centuries, voices that would ultimately include two of the most influential figures for nineteenth- and earlier twentieth-century theology, Kant and Schleiermacher.[23]

The decision to deploy this argument in contending with the threat posed by liberal thinking "virtually required the defenders of Christianity's historical superiority to minimize Christian debts to Judaism, especially first-century Judaism, and to portray it in the blackest colours possible, so that the brightness of the Christian *novum* could shine and avoid being obscured in the mists of historical relativism."[24]

---

20. Worthen, *The Internal Foe*, 108. Emphasis added. Worthen's study traces the articulation of Christian doctrine in relation to Israel through the past two thousand years. The title "Internal Foe" is drawn from correspondence during WWI between Jewish writer Franz Rosenzweig and his Christian (convert) friend, Eugene Rosenstock-Huessy: "We are the internal foe; don't mix us up with the external one!" Quoted by Worthen, xiii.

21. Worthen, *Internal Foe*, 139.

22. Ibid., 139.

23. Ibid., 149.

24. Ibid.

Worthen notes that the influential figure of Adolf von Harnack "brought to a kind of culmination" this path of historical superiority.[25] For Harnack, "Jesus' 'newness' is to be located in an activity strangely akin to that of a nineteenth-century religious liberal, who seeks to purify religion by stripping away the accretions of tradition and returning to the purity of origins."[26] Unsurprisingly, this involved painting a deeply negative picture of ancient Judaism—and by implication, contemporary Judaism—exemplified in what Worthen calls a "purple passage" in which Harnack contrasts first-century Jews with his Jesus:

> They [first-century Jews] thought of God as a despot guarding the ceremonial observances in His household; he [Jesus] breathed in the presence of God. They saw Him only in His law, which they had converted into a labyrinth of dark defiles, blind alleys and secret passages; he saw and felt Him everywhere. They were in possession of a thousand of His commandments, and thought, therefore, they knew Him; he had one only, and that is why he knew Him. They had made this religion into an earthly trade, than which there is nothing more detestable; he proclaimed the living God and the soul's nobility.[27]

The apostle Paul is of particular significance for Harnack:

> It was Paul who, in the guiding metaphor of Harnack's book, stripped the "husk" of Judaism away from the "kernel" of Jesus' message. Judaism was a stage in history that history left behind in the first Christian century.[28]

Accordingly, "It was Paul who delivered the Christian religion from Judaism."[29] In Christianity, "The last and highest stage of humanity had been reached."[30]

A dehistoricization and universalization of Christ and his message thus became somewhat inevitable. As recently as 1969, Ernst Käsemann continued to reflect this same view of Paul's perspective on Judaism: "It has rightly been repeatedly noticed that the apostle's message of justification is a fighting doctrine, directed against Judaism."[31] "Seeking for one's own

---

25. Ibid., 163.
26. Ibid., 162.
27. Harnack, *What is Christianity?* 163.
28. Worthen, *Internal Foe*, 163.
29. Harnack, *What is Christianity?* 130–32, as cited by Worthen, *Internal Foe*, 163.
30. Ibid., 204.
31. Käsemann, *Perspectives on Paul*, 70.

righteousness, which is the mark of the ancient people of God according to [Romans] 10.3, no longer has any place."[32] Käsemann summarizes Paul's contention with Judaism thus: "As the law-giver with his demand for works, Moses stands over against the righteousness conferred by faith."[33] This being the case, one can quite understand how David Novak concludes that some form of supersessionism is simply intrinsic to Christian belief: that after Jesus, Judaism simply has nothing to say to the Christian church.[34]

The nineteenth century also saw the beginnings of Jewish study of Christianity, though in its early stages no "school of thought" developed; it remained the work of isolated individuals.[35] Most Jewish scholars devoted only a portion of their effort to this field.[36] Consequently, and notwithstanding that writers such as Samuel Hirsch had long appealed that the traditional Christian understanding of Paul was, at best, inconsistent with the Judaism that they recognized,[37] Walter Jacob was able to say as late as the mid-1970s that "the influence of the earlier Jewish writers on Christian thought was almost nonexistent; only the more recent writers have aroused some interest and a response from the Christian community."[38]

In the late nineteenth century, Ferdinand Weber published a work that became highly influential for New Testament research: *The Theological System of the Ancient Palestinian Synagogue Based on the Targum, Midrash, and Talmud* (1880). Weber was attempting to present a systematic "Jewish theology" compiled from the Mishnah and related rabbinic writings from a later era—an idea that Zetterholm has described as "patently absurd," referencing "Jewish sources that in no way were suitable for the purpose" and predicated upon "a selection of texts, which in many cases were misread."[39] Long before

---

32. Käsemann, *Perspectives*, 156.

33. Ibid., 157.

34. Novak, *Talking with Christians*, 41 and 164, as cited by Worthen, *Internal Foe*, 259.

35. Jacob, *Christianity Through Jewish Eyes*, 5.

36. Jacob identifies notable exceptions as Claude Montefiore, Hans Joachim Schoeps and Samuel Sandmel. Ibid., 5.

37. Contrary to Christian assumptions that presumed Paul's expert status, Hirsch concluded that Paul had been a young and immature student of Judaism when he left it, and was therefore critiquing something he did not fully understand: "Paul carried on a sharp and violent polemic against Judaism, and he was correct about the Judaism which he attacked, but unfortunately, the Judaism he attacked was and is only the Judaism of Paul and his followers; it is not the Judaism of the Jews." Samuel Hirsch, *Die Religionsphilosophie der Juden* (Leipzig, 1842), 726f., as cited by Jacob, *Jewish Eyes*, 54–55.

38. Ibid., 54–55.

39. Zetterholm, *Approaches to Paul*, 64–65. "Jewish law, ritual, and observance, were ordered and codified in the Mishna and kindred works; but the Jews did nothing

Zetterholm, George Foot Moore was similarly critical of Weber, whom he took to task for the assertion that Judaism's fundamental conception was of an inaccessible God, to be unfavorably contrasted with the Christian conception of Jesus. Moore describes Weber's "material principle" as the belief that "legalism is the sum and substance of religion, and is, in Jewish apprehension, the only form of religion."[40] However, Moore asserted that Weber was working from an entirely false assumption:

> He deceives himself; the necessity is purely apologetic. The motive and method of the volume are in fact apologetic throughout; the author, like so many of his predecessors, sets himself to prove the superiority of Christianity to Judaism.[41]

Unsurprisingly, then, working backwards from an apologetic starting point, Weber's research affirmed his *a priori* conclusion.

> Keeping the many and peculiar commands of the Law, said Weber, was the means by which the rabbis believed salvation was earned. The ordinary rabbi, therefore, believed that the goal of rabbinic religion was the search for reward on the basis of merit, that God was a stern judge, and that approaching death brought with it the fear of losing salvation due to a lack of merit.[42]

Moore blamed Weber for a fundamental change that took place in the nineteenth century in works by Christian authors about Judaism.[43]

> Through the eighteenth century Christian literature had primarily tried to show the *agreement* of Jewish views with Christian theology. To be sure, Judaism had been attacked—often viciously—but the overall intent was to convict Jews out of their own mouths: to show, for example, that their statements about

---

of the kind for the religious and moral teaching of the school and synagogue. No one even thought of extracting a theology from the utterances of the rabbis in Midrash and Haggada, to say nothing of organizing the theology in a system. [. . .] The fundamental criticism to be made of Weber's 'System' is precisely that it *is* a system of theology, and not an ancient Jewish system but a modern German system." Moore, "Christian Writers on Judaism," 230. Sanders bluntly describes the Weber view as "Based on a massive perversion and misunderstanding of the material" (*Paul and Palestinian Judaism*, 59).

40. Moore, "Christian Writers," 229.

41. Ibid., 230. Moore attributed this to Weber's original idea of becoming a missionary to the Jews. "Weber never succeeded in getting into the missionary calling, but the 'system' on which he spent the last years of his life was the outcome of studies undertaken to that end." Ibid., 228.

42. Thielman, "Law," 530.

43. Moore, "Christian Writers," 228–33. See Sanders, *Paul and Palestinian Judaism*, 33.

intermediaries (*logos, memra*) proved the truth of Christian dogma. With F. Weber, however, everything changed.[44]

Weber's picture of Judaism as the antithesis of Christianity, "now clad in the impressive robes of scholarship,"[45] provided the source material for several subsequent and influential works such as: W. Sanday and A. C. Headlam's ICC *Commentary on the Epistle to the Romans* (first published 1895, and reprinted seventeen times through to 1952);[46] Emil Schürer, *The History of the Jewish People in the Age of Christ*, in three volumes (1866-90); and Wilhelm Bousset, *The Judaic Religion in the New Testament Era* (1903). Bousset is of particular interest because "Bousset's view, which depended on Weber, was [. . .] appropriated and disseminated to generations of New Testament scholars by his student, Rudolph Bultmann." In turn, Bultmann supervised the doctoral thesis of Ernst Käsemann. "Bultmann is significant because he lent his enormous prestige to Bousset's work in particular and thus made it acceptable for New Testament scholarship to overlook, for example, Moore's evaluation of Bousset and the arguments of such scholars as Büchler and Schechter."[47]

One particularly glowing review, at the time, succinctly summarized Weber's influence on then-current New Testament scholarship:

> No one can rise from the reading of Dr. Weber's book without feelings of the profoundest gratitude to God, through Christ, for redemption, not only from Sin and Death, but from "Legality." It shines with sunlight clearness, that the whole difference between the Christian and Jewish Soteriology is that between

---

44. Sanders, *Paul and Palestinian Judaism*, 33.
45. Thielman, "Law," 530.
46. Described by Cranfield (in his successor ICC publication) as "this most distinguished work"; "anyone who has worked with it for many years is likely to have become more and more grateful for its thoroughness and exactness, its massive learning and sound judgment." Cranfield, *A Critical and Exegetical Commentary on the Epistle to the Romans*, 41.
47. Sanders, *Paul and Palestinian Judaism*, 39 and 47, emphasis original. Büchler, for example, slates Bousset for having "managed to dispose of the Jewish concepts of sin and atonement in a few incidental remarks, based mainly on the Apocrypha and the Apocalypses; without considering the religious effects of sin and atonement upon the Jew and his life as reflected mainly and characteristically in rabbinic statements of the first century. This fundamental mistake was due to the author's ignorance of the undoubtedly peculiar and difficult rabbinic literature, and to the absence of any preparatory or systematic theological work of scientific value on the problem." Büchler, *Studies in Sin and Atonement in the Rabbinic Literature of the First Century*, xiii.

Grace and Law. And, in the sphere of Anthropology, how deep Israel's apostasy has been.[48]

At the end of the nineteenth century, then, and stretching well into the twentieth, Weber's "distorted picture of Jewish legalism was the standard interpretation among New Testament scholars. Christianity had acquired a perfectly dark background against which it could shine all the more brilliantly."[49] Such a picture continues to this day to provide the controlling paradigm for most Evangelical and Reformed thinking about first-century Judaism, Jesus, and Pauline theology, at the popular level.

2.4 THE DAWNING OF THE NEW PERSPECTIVE—INITIAL PIONEERS

While it is commonplace for the emergence of a new perspective in the twentieth century to be credited to E. P. Sanders—and in many respects rightly so, for it was he who "addressed pointedly and exhaustively the distorted view of Judaism which Lutheran scholarship, and those under its influence, had produced"[50]—Sanders was building on the largely unrecognized groundwork of a number of others: in particular, Claude Montefiore,[51] George Foot Moore,[52] and in the post-War years, W. D. Davies[53] and Krister Stendahl.[54] With direct reference to "the still too habitual use of the one-sided and biased book of Ferdinand Weber's *Jüdische Theologie*," Montefiore drew attention to the methodological inadequacy underlying Christian

---

48. West, "The Old Hebrew Theology," 14–19.

49. Zetterholm, *Approaches to Paul*, 65. In the early 1920s, George Foot Moore disapprovingly identified Weber's *System* as "the book that has for forty years been the chief resource of Christian writers who have dealt *ex professo* or incidentally with Judaism at the beginning of the Christian era" ("Christian Writers," 230). Although most of the main proponents of Weber's view had been Lutheran German scholars, with the best constructive accounts that differed from Weber being in English, Sanders makes clear that "in speaking of the continuation of Weber's view we are not describing an isolated phenomenon in Germany" (*Paul and Palestinian Judaism*, 55).

50. Thielman, "Law," 531.

51. Montefiore, *Judaism and St. Paul*.

52. Especially, "Christian Writers on Judaism"—described by E. P. Sanders as "an article which should be required reading for any Christian scholar who writes about Judaism" (*Paul and Palestinian Judaism*, 33).

53. Davies, *Paul and Rabbinic Judaism*.

54. In his 1963 *Harvard Theological Review* article, "The Apostle Paul and the Introspective Conscience of the West," now available as the second essay in *Paul Among Jews*.

treatment of rabbinic Judaism, not least because of an absence of first-hand knowledge:

> Rabbinic Judaism seems to be the one department of learning about which many great scholars have been willing to make assertions without being able to read the original authorities, or to test the references and statements of the writers whom they quote.[55]

Montefiore has been described as the first Jew to view Christianity entirely sympathetically—succeeding, in Jacob's eyes, to a fault: "A sympathetic understanding of the New Testament was needed, but not the exaggerated enthusiasm to which Montefiore was inclined."[56] Montefiore was also prepared to acknowledge weaknesses in first-century Judaism.[57] Nonetheless, he still spoke of the gulf between rabbinic Judaism and Paul as being "gigantic." Montefiore identified a critical need to "gain some sort of an idea of what Paul's religion was before his conversion," for which "we should have to start with a description of Rabbinic Judaism as it existed about the year 30 or 50 A.D."[58] However, this highlighted the problem of a lack of source material from the relevant period. Accordingly, Montefiore's assessment presupposed a commonality with the rabbinic Judaism of several centuries later, about which a great deal more is known.[59] Subject to this important caveat—which in fairness, he freely acknowledged—Montefiore's conclusion was that:

> Paul must have been less than a Rabbinic Jew, and more. To explain him are needed: (1) a Judaism which was other than

---

55. Montefiore, "The Genesis of the Religion of St. Paul," 7, 8n1.

56. Jacob, *Jewish Eyes*, 93, 98.

57. E.g. "Here we draw near to the one really sore point, the one grave deficiency of the Rabbinic religion. It cannot truthfully be ignored or denied that the great outstanding fault of Rabbinic Judaism was its particularism. [. . .] The general line of Rabbinic Judaism towards the "nations" was distinctly hostile and bitter. [. . .] Rabbinic Judaism [. . .] did not greatly worry its head over the future lot of the Gentiles." Similarly, "some bad Jews in every generation may have thought that the ceremonial laws were more important than the moral laws. But the average Rabbinic Jew did not think so." Montefiore, "Religion of St. Paul," 53–55, 33.

58. Montefiore, "Religion of St. Paul," 14.

59. One cannot overstate the significance of this assumption, which W. D. Davies was later to reject as a "convenient identification": "We cannot, without extreme caution, use the Rabbinic sources as evidence for first-century Judaism. Especially it is important to realize that our Rabbinic sources represent the triumph of the Pharisean party, and moreover as a 'party' within the Pharisean party as it were, that of Johanan ben Zakkai. Pharisean opinions alone are recorded; parties, movements and opinions contrary to these were naturally excluded" (*Paul and Rabbinic Judaism*, 3–4).

Rabbinic; (2) religious influences, conceptions and practices which were not Jewish at all.[60]

Along with Hirsch, Montefiore believed that Paul knew only a different and inferior Judaism, one "more anxious and pessimistic, more sombre and perplexed," which he put down to Hellenistic and apocalyptic influences in the Diaspora, together with outside influences that were not Jewish at all.[61] Judaism was not "obsessed by the sense of human frailty and sinfulness" in which Paul "had discovered no remedy strong enough to cope with the [. . .] evil impulse, the wicked promptings of the heart."[62] If that was the case in Paul's experience of his religion then the rabbinic Judaism of 50 CE must have been very different from the rabbinic Judaism of 500 CE.[63]

Rabbinic Judaism did not, as is still too commonly believed, produce a regular crop of proud and self-righteous Jews, upon the one hand, and a regular crop of anxious, scrupulous, timid and despairing Jews upon the other.[64]

> Pauline soteriology seems to me impossible upon a purely Rabbinic basis [. . .]. The excellence of faith was not unknown to, or uncelebrated by, Rabbinic Judaism, but it was never opposed to works. If one had faith in God, one naturally tried to fulfill his commands. Faith and works were parts of a single whole.[65]

Montefiore therefore found no trace of the particular points of Pauline theology concerning this "inadequate Judaism" that formed the dominant assumptions of Christian scholars of his day.

60. Montefiore, "Religion of St. Paul," 66.

61. As with Hirsch, it is interesting that Montefiore accepted Paul's negative statements as accurately representing the Judaism that Paul knew, focusing his objection on the fact that this was not *main-line* rabbinic Judaism. See Sanders, *Paul and Palestinian Judaism*, 4.

62. Montefiore, "Religion of St. Paul," 114.

63. Ibid., 18. Whilst eminently useful as a standpoint from which to refute negative views on Judaism, Montefiore's assumption that later rabbinic Judaism was in direct continuity with a singular first-century forebear is widely challenged. See e.g., "The rabbinic literature is not the timeless and universal summary of Jewish belief that it was once taken to be, and it does not adequately reflect the time period in which the New Testament arose." Elliott, *The Survivors of Israel*, 2–4. Even the commonplace assumption of later Judaism's continuity with the Pharisees is challenged: "Although rabbinic Judaism claims the Pharisees as forebears, the differences between the rabbis and the Pharisees are great." Alan Segal, *Paul the Convert*, xiv.

64. Montefiore, "Religion of St. Paul," 34.

65. Ibid., 77. It would be more than a half-century before E. P. Sanders made a similar observation concerning the relationship of faith and works, which he was to dub "covenantal nomism."

However, the critique by writers such as Montefiore, Hirsch, and Moore had little impact. Their voice "was drowned out by the emerging Protestant biblical scholarship and the distorted picture of Paul as the definite opposite of Judaism continued to dominate."[66] Already, however, "those who knew rabbinic Judaism did not feel at home with the traditional view of the religion Paul was supposed to have abandoned."[67] But for Christianity to be willing to revisit this traditional view would inevitably require a willingness to call into question a number of core premises that had become embedded in the Christian understanding.

2.4.1 W. D. Davies

In the aftermath of World War II, scholarship found good reason to reflect on the historical sources of the Holocaust and, in particular, the role played by Christian religion and its prevailing theology. This inevitably brought customary assumptions about Judaism into sharp focus, not least because of the establishment of the modern political state of Israel. Judaism had not conveniently gone away over the past nineteen hundred years and nor was a nation called Israel any longer merely an artefact of ancient world history.

In the early post-war years, W. D. Davies's work was pioneering in re-examining Paul's relation to the Judaism of his day.[68] First published in 1948, *Paul and Rabbinic Judaism* was, as he put it, an "attempt to set certain pivotal aspects of Paul's life and thought against the background of the contemporary Rabbinic Judaism."[69] Notably, Davies maintained that Paul belonged to what he called "the main stream of first-century Judaism."[70] This was significant in that, up until then, most scholars had been influenced by Albert Schweitzer's proposal that a clear distinction had existed between Semitic or Palestinian Judaism and its Hellenistic or Diaspora counterpart,

---

66. Zetterholm, *Approaches to Paul*, 92.

67. Ibid.

68. Sanders acclaimed Davies's *Paul and Rabbinic Judaism* as "a watershed in the history of scholarship on Paul and Judaism" (*Paul and Palestinian Judaism*, 7). The influences of Davies, who supervised Sanders's doctoral thesis, are discernible in *Paul and Palestinian Judaism* from the title onwards. Davies returns the honor in the Preface to the fourth edition of *Paul and Rabbinic Judaism* (1981), xxix–xxx, describing *Paul and Palestinian Judaism* as "a work of immense learning and penetration, a major milestone in Pauline scholarship [. . .] of potentially immense significance for the interpretation of Paul"—as it has, indeed, turned out to be.

69. Davies, *Paul and Rabbinic Judaism*, xvii.

70. Ibid., 1.

and further between apocalyptic Judaism and Pharisaism.[71] Davies, however, argued that these were false dichotomies, because "in the fusions of the first century we cannot split Hellenistic, Jewish and other factors." Without denying that there was *any* Greek influence upon Paul, Davies nonetheless sought to prove that "elements in his thought, which are often labelled as Hellenistic, might well be derived from Judaism."[72] Radically for his time, Davies made the case that "in the central points of his interpretation of the Christian dispensation Paul is grounded in an essentially Rabbinic world of thought, that the apostle was, in short, a Rabbi become Christian and was therefore primarily governed both in life and thought by Pharisaic concepts, which he had baptized 'unto Christ.'"[73] Despite his apostleship to the gentiles, Paul remained "as far as was possible, a Hebrew of the Hebrews."[74]

Already, then, we see developing a number of themes that have come to the fore in the NPP. A further observation of Davies is also important: he saw that the effect of Schweitzer's insistence on the eschatological content and context of Paul's thought was to relegate justification by faith to a secondary position. In so doing, Schweitzer "inevitably introduced a new perspective," setting a hare running which would carry profound consequences for Pauline studies:

> To root Paul seriously in Jewish eschatology, as did Schweitzer, was to remove the centre of gravity of Paulinism from justification by faith to a cosmic act involving the destiny of the totality of nature and of man: it was to shift the essential direction of the Pauline salvation from being primarily the alleviation of the pangs of conscience (a term not found in the OT and borrowed in the NT from popular Hellenistic "philosophy") to being the redirection of the cosmos.[75]

2.4.2 Krister Stendahl

Moving into the 1960s, the assumption that "Paul had wrestled with the pangs of a troubled conscience, just like Luther" and that his "conversion"

---

71. Schweitzer placed Paul in the Palestinian category and isolated him, as he had previously with Jesus, in an aberrational apocalyptic Judaism that was alien to and divorced from Pharisaism. See *Paul and His Interpreters* and *The Quest of the Historical Jesus*.

72. Davies, *Paul and Rabbinic Judaism*, 1.

73. Ibid., 16.

74. Ibid., xvii.

75. Ibid., xviii.

marked the end of a "long, inward spiritual struggle"[76] was dramatically and effectively challenged by Krister Stendahl in his short but influential *Harvard Theological Review* essay of 1963.[77] The cracks first began to appear in relation to Luther's correlation of first-century Judaism with the conditions of sixteenth-century Catholicism. Now they began to show in relation to Luther's belief in the centrality of justification by faith as the universalized Pauline answer that enables individuals—like their antecedents, Paul and Luther—to find peace with God through Christ. Stendahl pointedly observed that in all the places where Paul expressly describes his own pre-conversion religion, he makes no suggestion of living under the burden of an agonized conscience. The famous question—"How can I find a gracious God?"—may have been Luther's burden, but it did not seem to have been Paul's. Hence, this also brought into fresh question the reigning paradigm that Judaism—as Christianity's antithesis—was what Paul had been saved from in his conversion experience. In Philippians 3, where Paul speaks most fully about his life before his Christian calling, Stendahl noted "there is no indication that he had any difficulty in fulfilling the Law."[78] On the contrary, the apostle is able to say that as to the righteousness required by the law he had been "blameless" (ESV) or "faultless" (NIV). Whatever the phenomena of Paul's Damascene conversion, "it was not to him a restoration of a plagued conscience" since "he does not think about the shortcomings in his obedience to the law, but about his glorious achievements as a righteous Jew."[79] That Paul may now have learned to consider these achievements as but "rubbish" in the light of his experience of Jesus the Messiah (Phil 3:8) does not change the fact. What is more, Paul never urges Jews to find in Christ the answer to the anguish of a plagued conscience. Stendahl identifies the origins of such thought in Augustine, "one of the first to express the dilemma of the introspective conscience."[80] By Luther's time, "penetrating self-examination" had "reached a hitherto unknown intensity" as the "theological and practical center of Penance shifted from Baptism, administered once and for all, to the ever repeated Mass, and already this subtle change in the architecture of the Christian life contributed to a more acute introspection."[81]

76. Dunn, *New Perspective*, 195.
77. Stendahl, "Introspective Conscience."
78. Ibid., 80.
79. Ibid., 80.
80. Ibid., 81. Dunn, *New Perspective*, 195, describes Augustine's Confessions 8:5 as "the classic example of reading pre-conversion experience in the light of Rom. 7." For an interesting recent work on Augustine, see Fredriksen's *Augustine and the Jews*.
81. Stendahl, "Introspective Conscience," 82–83. Stendahl notes that Luther's

> For those who took this practice seriously [...] the pressure was great. It is as one of those—and for them—that Luther carries out his mission as a great pioneer. It is in response to *their* question, "How can I find a gracious God?" that Paul's words about a justification in Christ by faith, and without the works of the Law, appears as the liberating and saving answer [...]. In these matters, Luther was a truly Augustinian monk.[82]

What then of Paul's "conversion"? In Stendahl's view, this was not a change of religion such as we commonly associate with the word.[83] The usual conversion model of Paul the Jew who gives up his former faith to become a Christian is not Paul's model but ours.[84]

> Rather, his call brings him to a new understanding of his mission, a new understanding of the law which is otherwise an obstacle to the Gentiles. His ministry is based on the specific conviction that the Gentiles will become part of the people of God without having to pass through the law. This is Paul's secret revelation and knowledge.[85]

Instead of experiencing "some conversion from the hopeless works righteousness of Judaism into a happy justified status as a Christian,"[86] Paul has experienced a *call* to be the apostle to the gentiles. Assignment, rather than conversion in the modern sense, is always the emphasis in the accounts that describe it. Accordingly, Stendahl argues that "a doctrine of justification by faith was hammered out by Paul for the very specific and limited purpose of defending the rights of Gentile converts to be full and genuine heirs to the promises of God to Israel."[87] To take Paul's answer to *this* question and apply it as a response to Luther's pangs of conscience, says Stendahl, is to take it out of its original context. Paul did not speak about justification by faith as a universal principle, using the gentiles' and Jews' common situation as an *example*. Rather, it was in the context of his soteriological concern for the

---

famous 95 theses "take their point of departure from the problem of forgiveness of sins as seen within the framework of Penance."

82. Stendahl, "Introspective Conscience," 83.
83. Stendahl, *Paul Among Jews and Gentiles*, 7.
84. Ibid., 9. *Contra* Stendahl, Segal argues in *Paul the Convert*, esp. 285–300, that Paul's experience *can* be described as a conversion in modern psychological terms. Paul's conversion involved a "disaffiliation from Pharisaism" and a "change in religious community" (299–300).
85. Stendahl, *Paul Among Jews and Gentiles*, 9.
86. Ibid., 15.
87. Ibid., 2.

relation of gentiles and Jews that he deployed justification by faith as one of his *arguments*.

2.5 E. P. Sanders

James Dunn cites Stendahl as having "cracked the mould" of twentieth-century reconstructions of Paul's theological context by showing how much it had been determined by Luther's quest for a gracious God, but he credits E. P. Sanders with having "broken it altogether" in showing how different these reconstructions are from what we know of first-century Judaism from other sources. Sanders offered us "an unrivalled opportunity [. . .] to shift our perspective back from the 16th century to the first century."[88]

The first part of Sanders's landmark work, *Paul and Palestinian Judaism*, is a comparison of the various forms of Judaism in and around the first century CE, concluding with his hypothesis concerning the nature of Palestinian Judaism. The second part involves a comparison between the religion of Paul and Palestinian Judaism, again with Sanders's own hypothesis as its conclusion. Unlike many prior studies, Sanders attempted to compare Judaism understood on its own terms with Paul understood on his own terms. This stands in sharp contrast to earlier works in which Paul's apparent polemic against Judaism served to define the Judaism against which Paul's thought was then contrasted![89] From the early stages, Sanders does not conceal that his chief aims unashamedly include "to *destroy* the view of Rabbinic Judaism which is still prevalent in much, perhaps most, New Testament scholarship" and "to establish a different view."[90]

Methodologically, Sanders's work involved a thoroughgoing examination of Palestinian Jewish literature from around 200 BCE to 200 CE by which he sought to draw conclusions about Judaism in Palestine in the

---

88. Dunn, *New Perspective*, 103.

89. Sanders, *Paul and Palestinian Judaism*, 4.

90. Ibid., xii and 59, emphasis added. Sanders was determined that his polemic stance against the traditional mischaracterization of Judaism would be "up-front" and unmistakable, to avoid the problem experienced by George Foot Moore, whose protest in *Judaism* had been "hidden" and explicit only in his 1921 article, "Christian Writers." See Dunn, *New Perspective*, 5–6n20. In Sanders's words: "Bultmann cited Moore as if he only gave additional details about the rabbis to flesh out the portrait in Bousset's book. I was not going to let that happen again, and so I decided to make it clear that some scholars were wrong and that the rabbis had been misrepresented. Thus the polemics of the book when it finally appeared" (Sanders, "Comparing Judaism and Christianity," 22). Moore "in a way, permitted his work to be used as a source book" for the very views that he opposed. "The impact of his work would have been greater had the article [. . .] been attached to the book" (Sanders, *Paul and Palestinian Judaism*, 59; also, xiii).

first century and some of its characteristics at the time of Paul in order to "answer the question of the basic relationship between Paul's religion and the forms of religion reflected in Palestinian Jewish literature."[91] Sanders's basis of comparison is what he dubbed their respective *patterns* of religion, by which he meant something quite different from the more commonplace comparison of reduced, one-line *essences* (such as "faith *versus* works," or "law *versus* liberty") or searching in Judaism for the origin of individual Pauline *motifs*. For this purpose, "Paulinism" is a religion. A pattern of religion does not include its every theological proposition or religious concept but deals with "the question of how one moves from the logical starting point to the logical conclusion of the religion."[92] Since this term is a key idea in Sanders's work, an extended quotation is in order:

> A pattern of religion, defined positively, is the description of how a religion is perceived by its adherents to *function*. "Perceived to function" has the sense not of what an adherent does on a day-to-day basis, but of *how getting in and staying in are understood*: the way in which a religion is understood to admit and retain members is considered to be the way it "functions." This may involve daily activities, such as prayers, washing and the like, but we are interested not so much in the detail of these activities as in their role and significance in the "pattern": on what principles they are based, what happens if they are not observed and the like. A pattern of religion thus has largely to do with the items which a systematic theology classifies under "soteriology." "Patterns of religion" is a more satisfactory term for what we are going to describe, however, than "soteriology." For one thing, it includes more than soteriology usually does: it includes the logical beginning-point of the religious life as well as its end, and it includes the steps in between.[93]

As is now well known, Sanders concluded that the common pattern of religion in Second Temple Judaism was "covenantal nomism." The basis of "getting in" to the people of God was understood to be fundamentally *covenantal*, through God's mercy in electing Israel. Israel's appropriate *response*

---

91. Sanders, *Paul and Palestinian Judaism*, 18–19. Segal observes that the reconstructive task is complicated by Paul being one of only two Pharisees to have left any personal writings from the period, the other being Josephus, though whether Josephus was really a Pharisee, rather than one who had merely "tailored his life to Pharisaism," is debatable. *Paul the Convert*, 307n1. This leaves us only with Paul. For a critical evaluation of Sanders's reading of the literature of Second Temple Judaism, see Carson, O'Brien, and Seifrid (eds.), *Complexities*.

92. Sanders, *Paul and Palestinian Judaism*, 12–18.

93. Ibid., 17, emphases original.

to that gracious election—or the means of "staying in"—was faithful obedience to God's gracious gift of Torah and hence, *nomism*. Notwithstanding the many streams, branches, or emphases in diverse first-century Judaism—the presence of which Sanders did not deny[94]—"covenantal nomism" was the right way to understand the "normal" or "common" Judaism of the period. In another memorable Sanders phrase,[95] this was simply "what the priests and the people agreed on."[96] In general, the same common Judaism was recognized by Diaspora Jews, who shared a worldwide feeling of solidarity. Notwithstanding numerous differences within it, this normal Judaism was, to a limited degree, also *normative* in that "it established a standard by which loyalty to Israel and to the God of Israel was measured."[97]

The existence and extent of a "normal" Judaism in the relevant period, of the character Sanders describes, is one of the major issues of contention for his critics. Carson complains of "the straitjacket [Sanders] imposed on the apostle Paul by appealing to a highly unified vision of what the first-century 'pattern of religion' was really like."[98] He argues that "nomism" in early Judaism is "far more variegated than Sanders allows [and] even covenantal nomism itself is best understood to have various shapes."[99] However, Carson seems to be rejecting an assertion that Sanders does not make. Sanders takes numerous opportunities to acknowledge that there existed both diversity *and* a common *nexus* of core features, not least among the ordinary "people of the land." Carson may be right that the literature of Second Temple Judaism "reflects patterns of belief and religion too diverse to subsume under one label,"[100] but Sanders does not appear to be arguing against that in the way he uses the term "covenantal nomism." There were "numerous differences within 'normal Judaism' [. . .]"—his emphasis was

---

94. "Palestinian Judaism was a rich, diverse, multifaceted society, with a good deal of restless change [. . .] different individuals and groups had different degrees of influence at various times and on various issues. Who ran what? It varied" (Sanders, *Judaism*, 490).

95. Sanders concedes the phrase owes much to Morton Smith, who was his "strongest single influence" on how to define common Judaism. Smith had said that "normative Judaism should be defined as whatever the Pentateuch, the ordinary priests, and the common people agreed upon" (Sanders, "Comparing," 29).

96. Sanders, *Judaism*, 47.

97. Ibid., 47-48.

98. Carson, O'Brien and Seifrid (eds.), *Complexities*, 5.

99. Ibid.

100. Ibid.

on what was common.[101] In striving to explain the point, Sanders alludes to contemporary Western Protestant denominationalism:

> We shall see in first-century Judaism fairly small but significant groups, which had special practices and beliefs, and thus a sort of separate "constitution," and the majority, who accepted widespread and common religious practices, especially as taught and administered by the priesthood, with no denominational tag and no membership in a group other than the people of Israel. Their only constitution was the Bible as commonly interpreted. All who were Jewish were members of "Judaism"; very few belonged to a sub-group.[102]

It is precisely *because* Sanders agrees that no single party was able "to coerce the general populace into adopting its platform" that he seeks to uncover what was basic common ground in the sense of "agreed on among the parties, agreed on by the populace as a whole."[103] We might state this simply as being what "living Jewishly" meant to most Israelites.[104]

When Carson still insists that the interpreter of Paul must be "freed up from the restraints imposed by a too narrowly defined and controlled 'background,'"[105] one suspects an apologetic concern operating beneath the surface; a foreseeing of the significant theological consequences to which Sanders's perspective inexorably leads: namely, an undermining of the traditional Reformed interpretation of Pauline theology. For that theology not to completely collapse under the weight of the NPP would appear to require *some element* of the "old" perspective on Judaism still to be identifiable in a first-century context.[106] The NPP may have consigned to the theological

---

101. Sanders, *Judaism*, 48.

102. Ibid. 19–20. The hazards of anachronism here are obvious, but the analogy is not unreasonable in making his point. With minor variations, Sanders might be describing popular Evangelical Protestantism today.

103. Ibid., 11–12.

104. Sanders thought of it as a "lowest common denominator" of many types of Judaism but chose not to use that phrase. Sanders, "Comparing," 37n39.

105. Carson et al., *Justification and Variegated Nomism*, v.

106. Something rather more than simply Montefiore's acknowledgment that "some bad Jews in every generation may have pretended to believe, and may have acted upon the belief, that the strict observance of the Sabbath and the dietary laws made an observance of the moral laws—of justice, charity, compassion—unnecessary and superfluous. Some bad Jews in every generation may have thought that the ceremonial laws were more important than the moral laws. But the average Rabbinic Jew did not think so. The bad Jews did not conform to type. They were the excrescence; they were not the usual and regular product. They did not represent the 'spirit' of the Rabbinic creed." Montefiore, "Religion of St. Paul," 33–34.

dustbin the exaggerated Weberian portrait of Judaism, but in the eyes of the NPP's critics, Judaism's *complete* rehabilitation still threatens the Pauline gospel as traditionally understood in Reformed circles. As Michael Horton sums it up, what is "at stake" here is "nothing less than our definition of the gospel itself."[107] In other words, the Reformers' reading of a Pauline soteriology drawn from scripture that sets its face against the law—and/or Jewish legalism—must still be found to be *essentially* correct, since it sits at the very heart of the Reformed articulation of the gospel. This is well-illustrated in the following example from a popular commentary (referencing Galatians 5):

> To live "under the law" (v.18) is to live under the crushing expectation of fulfilling God's moral standards through one's own human ability. People who try to live that way are likely to end up in misery because sooner or later they are bound to fail (Rom. 7:7–24). Rather than experiencing the joy of a clean conscience, they feel enslaved to legalism and guilt.[108]

This brings us to the question: Why did Paul apparently reject Judaism? According to Sanders—in what Stephen Westerholm calls Sanders's best known epigram[109]—what Paul finds wrong in Judaism is that it is "not Christianity";[110] albeit, as he subsequently clarified, "that is *all* that he found wrong, not that he saw Christianity as being entirely discontinuous with Judaism."[111] Sanders concluded that Paul's "Christian" pattern of religious thought is basically different from anything known from Palestinian Judaism; it was *not* a covenantal nomism.[112] But as Morna Hooker points out, this comes as something of a surprise—one might have expected something quite different based on Sanders's argument up to this point.

> No doubt many will have thought that they recognized Paul in the pages of the first part of Sanders's book, and will have concluded, as they turned to part 2: "so Paul is thoroughly Jewish after all." Yet it is at this point that Sanders springs his surprise, and argues that the pattern of Paul's religion, also, is quite different from what we had imagined: we end with Paul and Palestinian Judaism as far apart as they have ever been.[113]

107. Michael Horton, "Déjà vu All Over Again," 23–30.
108. *The Word in Life Study Bible*, 654.
109. Westerholm, "Twenty-Five," 3.
110. Sanders, *Paul and Palestinian Judaism*, 552.
111. Sanders, *Paul, the Law and the Jewish People*, 165n38.
112. *Paul and Palestinian Judaism*, 552.
113. Hooker, *Adam to Christ*, 155. Sanders describes Paul's type of religion as a

How then does Sanders see Paul arriving at this view? In another famous Sanders phrase that challenged the received wisdom of the time, "Paul's thought did not run from plight to solution, but rather from solution to plight."[114] In other words, traditional Pauline theology had assumed that Paul was preoccupied with the plight of sinful man, reading Romans 7:24 as autobiographical,[115] a reference to his former Pharisaic life under the law. Hence, it was to this grievous problem that Paul had discovered Christ as the divine solution: "I thank God through Jesus Christ our Lord" (Rom 7:25). Rudolf Bultmann, for example, had viewed Romans as structured in precisely this way, with Paul's discussion of sin preceding his solution to it:

> In Romans [... Paul] begins by exposing the plight of mankind, so that then the proclamation of God's salvation-deed becomes a decision-question [...] after man-under-the-law has been made to see his situation under it as that of the "miserable wretch" groaning for deliverance from the "body of death," he can then see the salvation-occurrence as salvation-bringing.[116]

Sanders, however, argued that Paul-under-the-law—the Paul we see in Philippians 3—did not at the time see himself as having a plight from which he needed saving. Accordingly, Paul's logic "did not start from man's need but from God's deed."[117]

> It appears that the conclusion that all the world—both Jew and Greek—equally stands in need of a saviour *springs from* the prior conviction that God had provided such a saviour. If he did so, it follows that such a saviour *must* have been needed, and then only consequently that all other possible ways of salvation are wrong [...]. If his death was *necessary* for man's salvation, it follows that salvation cannot come in any other way and consequently that all were, prior to the death and resurrection, in need of a saviour. There is no reason to think that Paul felt the need of a universal saviour prior to his conviction that Jesus was such.[118]

"participationist eschatology," which is essentially "transfer terminology." *Paul and Palestinian Judaism*, 549, 463–72. On this, see Hooker, *Adam to Christ*, 155–64.

114. Sanders, *Paul and Palestinian Judaism*, 443.

115. "O wretched man that I am! Who shall deliver me from the body of this death?" (KJV).

116. Bultmann, *Theology of the New Testament*, 301, as cited by Sanders, *Paul and Palestinian Judaism*, 442.

117. Sanders, *Paul and Palestinian Judaism*, 444.

118. Ibid., 443.

For Sanders's Paul, the conviction that God had provided a universal solution in Christ preceded—and directly led him to—the conviction that mankind faced a universal plight.[119] Paul's rationale was that if God had provided Christ as a universal savior then, universally, humanity must have needed saving. Moreover, since God had already provided the law, it must be the case that the law had been ineffectual.

We will complete this review of Sanders by noting how, in his view, inclusion within the group that is being saved comes about.

In the concluding section of *Paul and Palestinian Judaism*, Sanders states that one of the reasons Pauline thought is sharply distinguished from anything found in Judaism is that Paul's formulation of being among the saved is different.[120] He acknowledges there is similarity too, in that both Judaism and Paul "take full account" of the individual *and* the group, but the process is quite different. In Judaism, God's covenant is with Israel; hence the prior existence of that covenant seems to place the individual's focus on what is required for "staying in" the group. In Sanders's Paulinism, however, the focus would seem to be on the individual's initial "getting in"—the actions required of the individual to come into the group. And once "in," Sanders also sees the nature of the *group identity* as different.

> However close the feeling of corporate unity in Judaism, there are no expressions parallel to Paul's statement that Christians become one person in Christ (Gal. 3:28), just as one could not imagine a parallel formula to "Christ is in you" ("Israel is in you"?) [. . .]. The body of Christ is not analogous to Israel, and being in Christ is not formally the same as being in the covenant between God and Israel.[121]

Sanders argues that in Paul's thought both Jew and gentile must "transfer" from the group of those who are perishing to the group of those who are being saved, and the way in which that group is constituted follows a different pattern to Judaism. In Paul, a person is saved (or "gets in" to the group) by an act of faith in Christ that results in participation in one body. In Judaism, however, a person is saved (or "in" the group) already, by virtue of being in Israel (i.e., within the covenant with Israel), albeit that this "in no way removes the individual's personal relation with God. He must be pious before God, remain right with God, and thus retain his membership in the group of the saved."[122] Thus, for Sanders, "righteousness terminol-

---

119. Ibid., 474.
120. See ibid., 543–56.
121. Ibid., 547.
122. Ibid.

ogy" is used in Judaism and Paul in different ways. In Judaism, it refers to maintenance of status, or "staying in"—a person is righteous if they obey the Torah and repent of transgressions. The covenant *puts* one in, and commitment to that covenant, manifest through obedience, is the righteousness that *keeps* one in. This pattern is what he dubs covenantal nomism.

> Paul is obsessed with getting people into the new movement, and his discussions of correct behaviour, once in, are rather cursory. The rabbis were concerned with correct behaviour by the in-group and seldom had occasion to mention "getting in"—but, of course, concern over the behaviour of the in-group implies that it existed.[123]

However, being made righteous (or, justified) in Paul is a term indicating "getting in" to the body of the saved, not staying in. According to Sanders, this is why Paul says that one cannot be made righteous by the works of the law: he means that one cannot by works of the law "transfer to the body of the saved."[124] Thus, "Paulinism"—Paul's pattern of religious thought—is, for Sanders, a participationist eschatology that is basically different from Judaism.

The significance of Sanders's achievements is evidenced by the fact that the field continues largely to be defined by where scholars stand in relation to him. Greatly to his credit, Sanders pretty much set the agenda for all future discussion of Paul and Judaism. Virtually no scholar can credibly address Pauline theology today without engaging with the NPP in general and Sanders in particular.

As we now turn to the post-Sanders world, limitations of space will not permit us to review all those who have followed in his wake. Numerous scholars could bear mention, with a wide range of angles and ideas.[125] Equally, we shall not significantly engage with those who critique the NPP from more-traditional perspectives.[126]

It is a measure of how much has changed in Pauline studies that already we should feel the need to categorise the two scholars who have most

---

123. Sanders, "Comparing," 23.

124. Accordingly, the debate about righteousness by faith or by works of law turns out to result from the different usage of the "righteous" word-group. Sanders, *Paul and Palestinian Judaism*, 544.

125. The literature on Paul and Pauline theology, old and new, is, of course, almost endless. See, for example: Yinger, *The New Perspective on Paul*; Zetterholm, *Approaches to Paul*; and, Westerholm, "Twenty-Five," which appears in a longer and more detailed version in his *Perspectives Old and New on Paul*, 101–258.

126. For a thoughtful and detailed critique of the NPP, see Carson et al., *Justification and Variegated Nomism*.

frequently been identified with the NPP as now reflecting an "Early" New Perspective which should be distinguished from a more recent "Radical" New Perspective that we shall touch upon in a moment. These are of course N. T. Wright, whom Michael Thompson has described as the most influential popular writer who advocates a New Perspective reading,[127] and James D. G. Dunn, who is widely credited with inventing the term.

2.6 THE EARLY NEW PERSPECTIVE POST-SANDERS

2.6.1 N. T. Wright

Wright's literary output, not least in relation to Pauline theology, is prodigious. A particular interest for our purposes arises out of his stated endeavor to identify the "theological 'deep structure' of Paul's thought" instead of the issues dealt with on the surface of his letters.[128]

> The right approach will, rather, grapple with the task of understanding Paul's own thought-forms and thought-patterns, as a Pharisee and then as a Christian, and attempt to restate them coherently in such a way as to show their proper interrelation, within his total worldview, without doing them violence en-route.[129]

Compared to much modern scholarship in which the subjects tend to be discussed "in separate and isolated boxes," Wright argues that "Israel and the law, on the one hand, and christology and pneumatology on the other, are locked together in Paul." Unfortunately for the interpreter, he says, they are locked together in "what often seems a very ambiguous set of relationships."[130]

Wright endorses the NPP's critique of "the traditional and false picture of Judaism" which was "the manufacture of an imaginary apostle, attenuated and demythologized to suit the limited needs and desires of certain periods and groups, an apostle who must be made to oppose sixteenth- or

---

127. *The New Perspective on Paul*, 11.

128. Wright, *Climax*, 16. Wright is alluding to structuralism, which claims that to understand the surface structure of language, one has to understand the deep structure and how that influences the surface structure. For a short summary, see Mark Glazer, "Structuralism," 1994, available at http://www.utpa.edu/faculty/mglazer/theory/structuralism.htm (accessed February 23, 2012).

129. Wright, *Climax*, 17.

130. Ibid., 16.

twentieth-century enemies of which the Paul of history was unaware."[131] However, this is not to say that the Judaism known to Paul is thereby endorsed. On the contrary, says Wright, Paul "mounts a detailed and sensitive critique of Judaism as its advocates present it."[132]

While "the traditional view has been to maintain that Paul attacked Israel for following the law, showed that the law was abolished by Christ, and set up a new way of salvation, that of faith,"[133] Wright denies that Paul is saying anything against the law itself. Israel's fault is not in fact "legalism," he says, but "national righteousness" in making claim for "permanent and automatic Jewish privilege" and "boasting" by claiming God as the God of the Jews but not of the gentiles.[134] Wright claims support from Sanders's accounts of "Jewish attitudes to the Gentiles" to conclude that Paul's criticism of Judaism "was on target."[135]

Contrary to Sanders, Wright takes it that Paul *does* argue from "plight" to "solution," but the nature of that plight is not the individualized dilemma of a burdened conscience asking "How can I be saved?" Indeed, it is not primarily based in a concern for the individual's standing at all. The plight is that, notwithstanding Israel's physical presence in the land, "at least some Jews in this period" understood the exile to be continuing;[136] Roman occupation was simply the mode that Israel's continuing exile had now taken.[137] The plight was to do with the life of the nation as a whole.

> Israel had been called to be the covenant people of the creator God, to be the light that would lighten the dark world, the people through whom God would undo the sin of Adam and its effects. But Israel had become sinful, and as a result had gone into exile, away from her own land. Although she had returned geographically from her exile, the real exile condition was not yet finished. The promises had not yet been fulfilled. The Temple had not yet been rebuilt. The Messiah had not yet come.[138]

---

131. Wright, "The Paul of History and the Apostle of Faith," 80.
132. Ibid., 82.
133. Ibid., 82–83.
134. Ibid., 82.
135. Ibid., 83.

136. Wright, *Climax*, 141. In the almost contemporaneous *The New Testament and the People of God*, 269, Wright upgrades his claim from "some" Jews to "most" Jews: "This perception of Israel's present condition [that the exile is not yet really over] was shared by writers across the board in second-temple Judaism." That "we are still in exile" was the belief of "most Jews of the period." Ibid., 268.

137. Wright, *Climax*, 141.
138. Wright, *What Saint Paul Really Said*, 30–31.

Paul saw Israel's history set forth in the Jewish scriptures as a story in search of an ending—a story in which they were still living. The scriptures spoke of that future time when God himself would intervene in the story and put everything right. This was to be understood in a concrete way; it had nothing to do in the first instance with spiritual bliss in the afterlife. Wright agrees with Sanders that we have misunderstood Judaism, but sees him as wrong to conceive it in de-politicized terms, which reflects non-political religious thought derived from the later Mishnah. Paul was not interested in questions of "getting in" or "staying in" any system of religion—he was looking for the redemption of Israel from its exiled state. The problem *was* to do with "sin"; but "not so much the question of what happens *when this or that individual sins*, but the question of what happens when *the nation as a whole fails to keep the Torah as a whole*."[139]

> This is not, then, to say that the Torah is bad; merely that, in the face of divine covenantal judgment on Israel, one cannot say that the Torah, and the attempt to keep it, provide the way to life.[140]

What was evident was "the inability of the Torah to give the blessing which had been promised."[141]

For Wright's Paul, the moment of time for exile to end and restoration to begin had been reached. And this was a restoration in which the gentiles were, quite properly, being invited to share, as the great prophets believed would happen. However, it had not turned out as Saul the Pharisee had expected. What God had done for Jesus of Nazareth, in the *middle* of time, was what Saul had thought he was going to do for Israel at the *end* of time; rather than God vindicating Israel after *her* suffering at the hands of the pagans, God had instead vindicated Jesus the Messiah after *his* suffering at the hands of the pagans. Saul realized, says Wright, that his whole perspective on the way in which God was going to act to unveil his plan of salvation had to be drastically rethought.[142]

> Saul had imagined that the great reversal, the great apocalyptic event, would take place all at once, inaugurating the kingdom of God with a flourish of trumpets, setting all wrongs to right, defeating evil once and for all, and ushering in the age to come.

---

139. Wright, *Climax*, 146, emphasis original.
140. Ibid., 150.
141. Ibid., 147.
142. Wright, *Really Said*, 36–37.

> Instead, the great reversal, the great resurrection, had happened to one man, all by himself. What could this possibly mean?[143]

What it means for Wright is that Israel's future—its eschatological vindication, the fulfillment of its promises—now comes exclusively through Jesus as its Messiah and the "new world" that he had inaugurated.

Wright is well-known for seeing the *motif* of exile as a central concern for both Paul and first-century Judaism, but others question its significance. Douglas Moo, for example, wonders "whether the wholesale application of the 'Israel in exile' background to the New Testament runs the risk of imposing a category on the material that the material itself does not clearly support."[144] Moo accepts that the express *language* of exile need not be present to justify the *concept*, and further that Jesus often uses language and concepts drawn from Old Testament expectations of national deliverance. Nevertheless, he questions whether "still in exile" is really a dominant category in Second Temple Jewish eschatological consciousness. Carson calls it a sweeping exegetical conclusion.[145] Wright, however, argues that the cross serves as the climax of Israel's exile:

> For Paul, the death of Jesus, precisely on a Roman cross which symbolized so clearly the continuing subjugation of the people of God, brought the exile to a climax. The King of the Jews took the brunt of the exile on himself.[146]

A further criticism can be levelled at Wright for in effect "switching categories" on Paul's behalf: what he first identifies as Israel's longing for restoration from exile understood in a concrete way then shifts to a spiritual solution fulfilled, through Jesus, in the church. Harink critiques this in strident terms:

> Wright's suggestion that in Jesus Christ Israel's exile has ended, that its hopes for a new exodus and return to the land (rooted in this text) are fully summed up and achieved in Jesus alone, appears to render this text a cruel joke. That the people of Israel, Jews, Abraham's descendants after the flesh, should take this text [Deut 30:1–5] seriously as a promise of their own destiny simply confirms for Wright that they have a sense of "effortless racial

---

143. Ibid., 36.

144. "Israel and the Law in Romans 5–11," in Carson, O'Brien and Seifrid (eds.), *Complexities*, 202.

145. 'Summaries and Conclusions," in Carson, O'Brien and Seifrid (eds.), *Complexities*, 546n158.

146. Wright, *Climax*, 146.

superiority" and an "identity marked out by blood and soil, by ancestry and territory." The God of whom the text speaks would appear, in Wright's reading, as a capricious character who can, with a turn of the face, simply abandon the people to whom this promise of fidelity and restoration is made and in their place put a predominantly Gentile church, accompanied by those few Jews who "choose" to put their faith in Jesus.[147]

Harink argues that "Wright is one of the most able, unapologetic and forceful contemporary proponents" of supersessionism.[148] He renders Paul "a supersessionist of the most rigorous kind" such that, if Wright is correct, "Paul is indeed the most significant enemy of Judaism in the history of Christianity."[149]

In a forthright review of Wright's recent *summa theologica* (as she calls it), *Paul and the Faithfulness of God*, Paula Fredriksen is in no doubt:

> Is this not classic, indeed deeply traditional supersessionism? Wright swats the term around ("I suspect that the 's'-word will retain its pejorative overtones" [p. 1,412, n10]), disowning it, embracing it, telling misty-eyed post-Holocaust—thus "pro-Jewish"—softies like Krister Stendahl to just deal with it (p. 1129). At one point he ingeniously legitimates it (after all, these are Paul's views) as "*Jewish* supersessionism" (p. 810, referring as well to Qumran). At the end of the day, stuck between denial ("this is *not* supersessionism") and rehabilitation ("this is *Jewish* supersessionism"), Wright settles on rehabilitation, insisting that what was superseded was actually "fulfilled."[150]

In Wright's interpretation of Paul, it certainly does appear that Israel's failings are considerable. Though he says the Torah itself is good, affirmed as the covenant-document, "Israel's fault is not that she pursued it but that, pursuing it in the wrong way, she did not attain to it." "Israel's fault was her rejection of God's plan; which manifested itself in her 'national righteousness' (which was invalidated by her Adamic sin); which expresses itself in her rejection of the crucified Messiah." Paul has "made it clear beyond any doubt" that "there is no covenant membership for Israel on the basis of racial or 'fleshly' identity."[151]

---

147. Harink, *Postliberals*, 165. For his extended critique of Wright, see esp. 152–84.
148. Ibid., 184.
149. Ibid., 153.
150. Fredricksen, "Review of NT Wright, *Paul and the Faithfulness of God*," 387–91.
151. Wright, *Climax*, 244–46.

> Israel's rejection of Jesus as Messiah simply *is* the logical outworking of her misuse of the Torah, her attempt to treat it as a charter of automatic national privilege.
>
> Israel is now shown to be guilty of a kind of meta-sin, the attempt to confine grace to one race. The result of this idolatry of national privilege is that Israel clings on to the terrible destiny—of being the place where sin was concentrated—which she was meant to allow her Messiah to bear on her behalf.
>
> The Messiah is the fulfilment of the long purposes of Israel's God. It was for this that Torah was given in the first place *as a deliberately temporary mode of administration*. In the Messiah are fulfilled the creator's paradoxical purposes for Israel and hence for the world. He is the climax of the covenant.[152]

According to Wright, however, there is no reason why Israel should not be saved, and every reason that she should: "*All she has to do is relinquish her frantic grip on the Torah.*"[153] The Torah was holy, just, and good, given for a purpose, for a time, but "with the Messiah, the time was up. All that was there in Torah that God intended to be of permanent value and intention had been transformed into the life of Messiah and Spirit."[154]

Despite the supersessionist language in these passages, however, not all agree with Harink's charge that Wright is supersessionist. Richard Hays, for example, thinks that Harink has got Wright wrong.[155] He quotes Wright's commentary on Romans:

> Abraham's family, Israel, the Jews, the circumcision, are neither reaffirmed as they stand, nor "superseded" by a superior group, nor "replaced" with someone else—that is what he [Paul] is arguing against in 11:13–24—but transformed, through the death and resurrection of Israel's own Messiah and the Spirit of Israel's own God, so that Israel is now, as was always promised, both

---

152. Ibid., 240–41, emphasis added. Whilst it may not be intrinsically supersessionist to suggest "Torah was given in the first place as a deliberately temporary mode of administration," it is questionable whether the idea of its "temporariness" is notably evident within Israel's scriptures.

153. Ibid., 248, emphasis added.

154. N. T. Wright, "Whence and Whither Pauline Studies in the Life of the Church," 265.

155. "It is at least uncharitable, and at worst intellectually dishonest, for Harink to bludgeon Wright with the epithet of 'supersessionist' without giving any indication of how he would read texts such as these [Rom 9:6–8; 10:1–13; 11:23, Phil 3:2–11] which are the basis for Wright's position." Richard Hays, Review of *Paul among the Postliberals*."

less and more than the physical family of Abraham: less, as in 9:6–13; more, as in 4:13–25.[156]

We should also note that Wright has himself denied supersessionism, albeit without offering a fully-developed response.[157] Clearly, supersessionism is an emotive word, and it can be defined in different ways, with different emphases.[158] We have already noted how Soulen, for example, distinguishes between punitive, economic, and structural supersessionism.[159] Others prefer to speak in terms of a "fulfillment," believing this "softens" the idea (or, "softens the blow," perhaps?). Nor need supersessionism even be necessarily *anti-Judaic*, some would say—Boyarin, for example, notes a supersessionist dimension in Paul's thinking but insists that rather than being anti-Judaic, Paul's discourse is "indigenously Jewish."[160]

One difficulty in pinning down Wright's position with regard to supersessionism is that—due to the sheer volume of his works and the repetitive nature of much of his writing within them[161]—they inevitably include potentially contradictory statements from time-to-time; or, at least, statements that allow "wriggle-room," to be understood in different ways. For example, does it evade the supersessionist tag to speak of Israel being "transformed"?[162] Similarly, are we right to see supersessionism in the following description of the church as a continuation of Israel, whose history has reached its intended fulfillment?

> Those who now belonged to Jesus's people were not identical with ethnic Israel, since Israel's history had reached its intended fulfilment: they claimed to be the continuation of Israel in a new

---

156. Wright, "The Letter to the Romans: Introduction, Commentary and Reflections," 690.

157. Wright, "Whence and Whither," 275–76. "These days, if you get anywhere near what I've just said, someone will use the S word: Supersession. 'The church has superseded Israel'; that's what people will say I am saying. Actually, this is completely wrong." Wright's (brief) defence is based on Jesus being the Jewish Messiah: "How can it be anti-Jewish to celebrate the coming of Messiah at the climax of Israel's long history and the fulfilment of its ancient prophecies?" However, one might say that Wright has subtly changed the question here; or perhaps he has answered a different one entirely.

158. A leading work is Soulen, *God of Israel*. For a useful short summary and critique of the arguments, see Vlach, "Replacement Theology."

159. See General Introduction, page xvii.

160. Boyarin, *A Radical Jew*, 205.

161. Tilling expresses it nicely in reviewing Wright's voluminous recent tome, *Paul and the Faithfulness of God*: "When the word 'concise' has nightmares, it's dreaming of PFG"! "*Paul and the Faithfulness of God*. A Review Essay (Parts 1 & 2)."

162. See e.g., "Whence and Whither," 265.

situation, able to draw freely on Israel-images to express their new situation.[163]

Wright can of course be commended for an Evangelical desire to look for what Longenecker characterizes as the "exegetically superior reading" rather than being intimidated by contemporary scholarship into settling for "the morally superior reading of Paul in today's complex world" (to which a two ways of salvation reading that Wright rejects can so easily lay claim).[164] Furthermore, we share his desire to situate Jesus and his first interpreters within their first-century Jewish context and try to understand how they and their audiences would have thought. Wright speaks, for example, of an "overarching first-century Jewish worldview," which has echoes of Sanders's concept of a *common Judaism*. Indeed, Wright makes the valid point that for there to be *many* "Judaisms" there must still be something common, however generalized, that one can call "Judaism" in the first instance; although first-century Judaism is a "complex and pluriform entity," it still possesses "an overall worldview which distinguishes it from first-century paganism."[165]

Although Wright makes numerous references to OT themes, and to established first-century Jewish concepts such as covenant's centrality, we see these being significantly reworked. When speaking of Israel and Torah, he habitually defaults to traditional Christian language, such as an "intended fulfilment," a "completion," and a "failure to attain," that at the very least border on supersessionism. As we have previously suggested, these phrases do not seem to be notably signposted in the Old Testament concerning God's plans and purposes, including its prophetic expectations in relation to the Messiah and/or the age to come. While the prophets may have passionately railed against Israel when delivering warnings about the dire consequences of apostasy and disobedience to Torah, there seems little suggestion that they felt it to be beyond attainment or in need of being completed or fulfilled. Still less are there obvious signposts to Israel and its Torah being replaced by something else. Even the prophetic promise of Jeremiah 31:33—"I will put my law in their minds and write it on their hearts"—appears to affirm a continuing Torah. A plain reading of the text suggests that the content of the law will remain valid, it will simply be written on minds and hearts in a (presumably) more efficacious way.

---

163. Wright, *People of God*, 457.

164. Longenecker, "On Israel's God and God's Israel," 2.

165. Wright, *Jesus and the Victory of God*, 11n22. See also Wright, *People of God*, 118–19.

Our principal interest has been Wright's general perspective on Paul and first-century Judaism, but what of his take on the atonement? Wright appears to advocate a *Christus Victor*-based reading, in which "in and through the cross of King Jesus the one true God has dealt decisively with evil."[166]

> The cross is for Paul the symbol, as it was the means, of the liberating victory of the one true God, the creator of the world, over all the enslaving powers that have usurped his authority. That is why it is at the heart of "the gospel."[167]

> For this reason I suggest that we give priority—a priority among equals, perhaps, but still a priority—to those Pauline expressions of the crucifixion of Jesus which describe it as the decisive victory over the "principalities and powers." Nothing in the many other expressions of the meaning of the cross is lost if we put this in the centre.[168]

"In Jesus of Nazareth," Wright declares, "specifically in his cross, the decisive victory has been won over all the powers of evil, including sin and death themselves."[169] "'The gospel' is the announcement of a royal victory."[170]

> When we ask how it was that Jesus' cruel death was the decisive victory over the powers, sin and death included, Paul at once replies: because it was the fulfilment of God's promises that through Abraham and his seed he would undo the evil in the world. God established his covenant with Abraham in the first place for this precise purpose.[171]

Wright interprets this victory in terms of a victory over sin, upon which a sentence of death has been passed and carried out at the cross. Its deadly force or power having been broken paves the way for God to give the life that sin would otherwise thwart. Wright concurrently makes clear that he does not endorse a penal substitutionary understanding (whether a caricature of it or otherwise). Yes, sin was condemned in the flesh of Jesus, *per* Romans 8:3, but Jesus himself was not punished on our behalf and nor was the cross simply a judicial transaction to provide individuals with salvation. An extended quotation is in order:

166. Wright, *What Saint Paul Really Said*, 52.
167. Ibid., 47.
168. Ibid.
169. Ibid., 60.
170. Ibid., 47.
171. Ibid., 48.

> God, says Paul, condemned sin. Paul does not, unlike some, say that God condemned Jesus. True, God condemned sin in the flesh of Jesus; but this is some way from saying, as many have, that God desired to punish someone and decided to punish Jesus on everyone else's behalf. Paul's statement is more subtle than that. It is not merely about a judicial exchange, the justice of which might then be questioned (and indeed has been questioned). It is about sentence of death being passed on "sin" itself, sin as a force or power capable of deceiving human beings, taking up residence within them, and so causing their death (Romans 7:7–25). To reduce Paul's thinking about the cross to terms of a law-court exchange is to diminish and distort it theologically and to truncate it exegetically. For Paul, what was at stake was not simply God's judicial honor, in some Anselmic sense, but the mysterious power called sin, at large and destructive within God's world, needing to be brought to book, to have sentence passed and executed upon it, so that, with its power broken, God could then give the life sin would otherwise prevent. That is what happened on the cross.[172]

For Wright, the cross is "evil doing its worst to Jesus"—taking upon himself the weight of evil, so that we would not have to bear it ourselves. It was time for evil "to gather into one great tidal wave of evil that would crash with full force over his head."[173]

Unsurprisingly, Wright has been criticized in Reformed quarters for advocating a non-penal model—interpreting Christ's work as *breaking the power of* sin and evil that leads to death, rather than *taking our punishment for* the sin and evil that leads to death. Alan Spence, for example, complains that Wright uses the victory model of salvation to expound the soteriological themes of Romans, consistently interpreting its central concepts within the framework of that theory, and thereby undermining Reformed emphases such as justification by faith:

> The fact that mediatorial ideas such as enmity, guilt, reconciliation, forgiveness and mercy are almost wholly absent in his interpretation is an indication of the determinative and exclusive nature of the model. There is in it no need for forgiveness, because the predicament facing us has to do not with the person of God, but a consortium of external powers; Christ has come

---

172. Wright, "Letter to the Romans," 578.

173. Wright, *Simply Christian*, 110. This is consistent with chapter 12 of *Jesus and the Victory of God* ("The Reasons for Jesus' Crucifixion"). See e.g., 610–11.

then not to make peace with God, but to overcome these alien forces.[174]

We earlier observed in relation to Aulén that a *Christus Victor* theory of the atonement offers no intrinsic connection or continuity with Israel; we must conclude the same concerning Wright's version. In *Christus Victor*, the story of the human problem and its divine solution leapfrogs effortlessly over Israel, going directly from Adam's sin to Christ's work. Israel, in-between, contributes nothing of substance or significance in salvific terms. As an atonement model, *Christus Victor* is entirely ahistorical and universalized—it could have happened any place and any time. Israel and its place in the story may safely be excised, with nothing lost as a result.

Wright's extensive deployment, by way of a "re-reading," of "Israel's symbols and stories" and "tradition" may appear to integrate Israel, but in reality it simply offers illustrative pictures of Christ's work, rather than contributing anything of structural necessity in relation to that work in its own right.[175] Wright's soteriology still works perfectly well if Israel is taken out.

Thus, while Wright's atonement model may not initially present as supersessionist, effectively it becomes so as a result of rendering Israel irrelevant. Israel makes no appearance, soteriologically-speaking, in *Christus Victor* and may be disposed of without any damage being done to the model. Although Wright is a NPP scholar—perhaps, for many, the most well-known NPP scholar—his brand of "new perspective" is distinctly "old perspective" insofar as its theological anti-Judaism is concerned.[176]

There is, however, something more that should be said concerning Wright's negative view of Torah. Another theme he identifies in Paul is that through the cross God has "fulfilled the promises" to Abraham.[177] Wright sees a concern of Paul in Galatians 3:10–14 that "the works of Torah" not only fail to provide blessing, they "hold out curse instead"—what happens to the promises to Abraham, Wright has Paul asking, "granted the plight of the Jews *which is brought about by the Torah?*"[178]

> How could the promises, the blessings promised to Abraham, now reach their intended destination? The Torah looks as

---

174. Spence, *The Promise of Peace*, 14.
175. See e.g., *Jesus and the Victory of God*, 591, 597.
176. Although Wright is not strictly guilty of "Israel-forgetfulness" (given his core theme of exile) the manner in which Israel is remembered is almost entirely negative.
177. Wright, *Really Said*, 46.
178. Wright, *Climax*, 142. Emphasis added.

though it might render the promise to Abraham, and to his worldwide family, null and void.[179]

A soteriological consequence of the death of Christ, therefore, is that "now the blessing of Abraham can come upon the Gentiles."[180] According to Wright, Torah placed a "valid interdict" on those promises, but now "the problem has been dealt with" in the death of the Messiah.[181]

It is hard to read Wright's articulation of the necessity of the role of Christ's death in delivering the promises of Abraham to the gentiles as anything other than a denunciation of the efficacy of Torah preceding it. How else should we read that the works of Torah hold out curse? Or that the plight of the Jews is brought about by the Torah?—a Torah that looks as though it might render the promise to Abraham, and to his worldwide family, null and void? Harink draws attention to the stark conclusion implied in Wright's analysis, that if Torah was temporary so too was Israel; the end of Torah amounts *de facto* to the end of Israel:

> If the actual Gospel narratives of Jesus depict him "fulfilling" that story in some way, if Israel's calling and destiny so construed is in some manner completed in Jesus, as Wright argues it is, it can only be in some highly "interpreted" sense: Jesus sums up, indeed *is himself* Israel, land, king, and temple. There is nothing left of a calling and destiny for Israel as an historical people. The meaning of "Israel" as a people is now thoroughly absorbed into the doctrine of Christ and the church.[182]

However, Wright is a master of the nuanced ambiguity—in an "on the one hand, on the other hand" style of writing—which leaves porous borders around apparently straightforward statements.[183] For example, in spite of the damning criticisms noted above, Paul is apparently *not* "saying that the Torah is somehow in itself evil" (which in itself is interesting . . . *did someone say Paul was?*) and, in Paul's writings Wright claims that we see a "balance between the relativization and reaffirmation of Torah."[184]

---

179. Ibid., 142.
180. Ibid., 143.
181. Ibid.
182. Harink, *Postliberals*, 199.

183. Even a critic such as Spence feels the need, in discussing Wright on justification—a subject on which one would think Wright's distinctive views had frequently been made clear enough—to footnote as follows: "There are times when Wright's interpretation of justification appears far closer to the Reformed tradition than is suggested by this quotation from *What St. Paul Really Said*." Spence, *The Promise of Peace*, 11n4.

184. Wright, *Climax*, 143.

> This is not, then, to say that the Torah is bad; merely that in the face of divine covenantal judgement on Israel, one cannot say that the Torah, and the attempt to keep it, provide the way to life. Nor therefore is this to deny, what Paul will later argue in both Galatians and Romans, that there is a true fulfilment of the law—actually, that there are various true fulfilments of the law—which come about through faith. This passage [Gal 3:10–14] simply asserts that the Torah *as it stands* is not the means of faith, since it speaks of "doing," which is best taken in the sense of "doing the things that mark Israel out," and hence cannot be as it stands the boundary-marker of the covenant family promised to Abraham.[185]

Notwithstanding some of these more positive-sounding remarks, just a little further on in the same passage it would appear that Torah is actually quite bad after all:

> The immediate problem was: granted the covenant promises to Abraham, what will happen to those promises in the light of Torah? There are many reasons why Torah would come between the promises and their fulfilment [. . .] here he concentrates simply on the fact that the law brings curse, not blessing [. . .]. It cannot of itself produce the faith which, according to Genesis and Habakkuk, is the true demarcation of the covenant people, Abraham's family. How then is the blessing of Abraham to come on either Jew (enclosed and threatened by Torah) or Gentile (whose promised blessing will thus never reach him)?[186]

Nuances aside, then, it seems reasonable to conclude that Wright's core position is supersessionist. Whatever we may say to the claim that Paul's writings show a "balance between the relativization and reaffirmation of Torah," very little affirmation of Torah is apparent. Israel's "chair at the table" has clearly been "taken by another." Wright follows the conventional trajectory of pitting old "Judaism" against new "Christianity," with the failings of the old providing the rationale for the necessity of the new. Christ, in sum, took upon himself "the curse which hung over Israel and which on the one hand prevented her enjoying full membership in Abraham's family and thereby on the other hand prevented the blessing of Abraham from flowing out to the Gentiles."[187] Thus, Israel bears the blame for the plight of the gentiles.

185. Ibid., 150.
186. Ibid., 151.
187. Ibid., 151.

Finally, although Wright states that Paul "is expounding covenantal theology, from Abraham, through Deuteronomy and Leviticus, through Habakkuk, to Jesus the Messiah," he argues that Paul also "is showing, albeit paradoxically, that the Torah *per se* rules itself out from positive participation in this sequence."[188] However, we would argue that the very opposite of this should be the case. A new perspective on Paul—with correspondingly, a positive perspective towards first-century Judaism—should lead us to inquire what covenantal theology would look like if a rehabilitated view of Torah was instead very much ruled in, with a positive role to play in that covenantal theological sequence. This we shall be exploring in chapter three.

2.6.2 James D. G. Dunn

Arguably as prolific as N. T. Wright—and perhaps more so, in relation to Paul and the NPP—is James Dunn. There is considerable common ground between Wright and Dunn and their differences often seem more in the nature of nuances or shades of emphasis. While Dunn speaks of the *motif* of covenant within Judaism, for example, Wright speaks of covenant as the "grand narrative."[189] Similarly, while Wright speaks of how the "entire scriptural story, the great drama of God's dealings with Israel, came together when the young Jew from Nazareth was nailed up by the Romans and left to die,"[190] Dunn speaks of the "two stories" of Israel and Christ that in Pauline theology have "a symbiotic relationship."[191]

A distinctive of Dunn's understanding, which he himself has described as being at the heart of his contribution to the NPP debate,[192] is the "works of the law." For Dunn, Paul clearly distinguishes "works of the law" from the idea of good works in general. The two ideas "operated within different substructures of his thought."[193] Hence, to commend good works while railing against works of the law was no inconsistency—after all, no-one doubted that everyone was required to do good. In passages such as Galatians 3:10,[194]

---

188. Wright, *Climax*, 150, emphasis added.

189. For a flavor of their similarities, from which this example is drawn, see Wright and Dunn, "An Evening Conversation on Jesus and Paul: James Dunn and N. T. Wright," 2004, available at http://www.ntwrightpage.com/Dunn_Wright_Conversation.pdf, accessed February 26, 2012.

190. Wright, *Really Said*, 49.

191. Dunn, *Theology of Paul*, 726.

192. Ibid., 340n23.

193. Ibid., 365–66.

194. "For all who rely on the works of the law are under a curse, as it is written: 'Cursed is everyone who does not continue to do everything written in the Book of the

Dunn sees Paul referring to something quite different. Interpreters tend to assume a hidden premise that the law requires our perfect obedience, i.e., we have "to do everything written in the Book" but—since that is an impossibility—everyone is under a curse thanks to the law. However, Dunn points out that there is no evidence that the law expected perfection in that sense; clearly evidenced by the fact that the law provided for atonement.[195] The obedience being called for was within the terms of the covenant and such obedience was considered practicable.[196] Works of the law has something else in mind and in Paul's terminology "justification by works of the law" had nothing to do with a scheme of salvation by human efforts. Rather, it has to do with the terms upon which someone is or is not admitted to the people of God.

> "Works of the law" are what distinguish Jew from Gentile. To affirm justification by works of the law is to affirm that justification is for Jews only, is to require that Gentile believers take on the persona and practices of the Jewish people.[197]

In Dunn's understanding, the *works of the law* are in general terms all of the practices required by Torah. Practically-speaking, though, the term refers to the principal "boundary-markers" that most visibly marked out Jewish lifestyle from its gentile neighbors: circumcision, Sabbath, and purity/food laws. Paul realized that these were of secondary importance (given to regulate life within the people of God), whereas justification by faith, as exemplified in Abraham and the Abrahamic covenant, was the primary, more fundamental identity marker. It is not a criticism of the law to say that it is not from faith, simply an assertion that they have different functions within the divine dispensation.[198] The crux of the issue, for Paul, was the place and role of Jewish identity markers for gentiles, now that the Messiah had come. The law of Moses had served as a barrier between Jew and gentile and had served its purpose in its time, but (as Wright puts it) its time was up.[199] To continue to insist on works of the law as the distinctives for defining who was (and was not) within the covenant was to argue for the

---

law.'" (Deut 27:26).

195. We might add that to do what the law required in relation to atonement is just as much an act of obedience to the law as any other of its requirements. "Human failure" was expressly provided for *in the law itself.*

196. In support, Dunn cites Phil 3:6; Rom 8:4; 13:8–10; and Gal 5:14. Dunn, *Theology of Paul*, 361.

197. Ibid., 363–64.

198. Ibid., 153.

199. Wright, "Whence and Whither," 265.

"presumption of privileged status before God by virtue of race, culture or nationality"—an illegitimate attempt to preserve "spurious distinctions by practices that exclude and divide,"[200] against which Paul's argument of justification by faith was raised as a banner. The "works" that Paul consistently warned against were therefore a misunderstanding on the part of Israel as to what her covenant law required, a misunderstanding of God's universal purposes and indeed, a misunderstanding of God himself:

> That misunderstanding focused most sharply on Jewish attempts to maintain their covenant distinctiveness from Gentiles and on Christian Jews' attempts to require Christian Gentiles to adopt such covenantal distinctives. Furthermore, that misunderstanding meant a misunderstanding of God and of God's promised (covenantal) intention to bless also the nations.[201]

For Dunn, the works of the law were "a Jewish assumption of 'favoured nation' status, and the corollary assumption that even when Jews sin it is not so serious as Gentile sin"; it is "*this* attitude and misapprehension" that is summed up by Paul as "the confidence of justification by works of the law" and which in turn "give the 'Jew' his false confidence and which cloak the seriousness of his sin."[202] Hence, works of the law "had become a badge not of Abraham's faith but of Israel's boast."[203] We note how Wright speaks in similar terms of the works of the law as "badges of membership" by which some Jews had sought to demarcate themselves as "covenant-keepers, as true Israel," whereas the true badge of membership was faith, and now, *faith in Christ*.[204]

> [Dunn's] proposal about the meaning of "works of the law" in Paul—that they are not the moral works through which one gains merit but the works through which the Jew is defined over against the pagan—I regard as exactly right.[205]

In Dunn's eyes, then, this is what constitutes Jewish "boasting in the law," and it is clearly antithetical to the gospel. Israel's failing was "treating the realm of righteousness as exclusively Jewish territory (marked out by

---

200. Dunn, *New Perspective*, 205.
201. Dunn, *Theology of Paul*, 366.
202. Dunn, "Yet Once More," 109.
203. Dunn, *New Perspective*, 119.
204. Wright, *What Saint Paul Really Said*, 132.
205. Wright, "New Perspectives on Paul," Paper delivered at the 10th Edinburgh Dogmatics Conference, 2003, available at http://www.ntwrightpage.com/Wright_New_Perspectives.htm, accessed February 26, 2012.

works of the law),"²⁰⁶ which blinded them to the seriousness of their own sin and to a false confidence that Paul calls "trusting in the flesh" (Gal 3:3, etc.). They had failed to see that the role of the law was a *temporary* one, featuring commands that served to restrict Israel's contact with the surrounding pagan nations. This, in turn, protected the people of Israel (who were "like a child growing up in an evil world") from the "idolatry and the lower moral standards prevalent in the Gentile world."²⁰⁷ However, one of the unfortunate consequences of this had been to prevent the blessing of Abraham reaching the gentiles,²⁰⁸ the same critique of Israel that we have seen articulated by Wright.²⁰⁹

Once the promises to Abraham came to fulfillment in Christ, however, all this was swept away. Jewish distinctives were no longer necessary in demarcating the people of God and indeed they operated as a barrier. There was a failure to grasp what Dunn calls "the limited and temporary scope of the epoch represented by Moses."²¹⁰ In clinging on to it, they were behind the times—it was "passé."²¹¹

In summary, then, while the "new perspective" on first-century Judaism has disavowed the old caricatures by which it was negatively equated with a religion of works-righteousness, of "good works" that qualify one for heaven, this by no means leads to a positive view. Israel's failings were still manifold—Paul was correct in his condemnation—but the grounds are different to those previously supposed:

- Dunn's Paul criticizes a misplaced Jewish emphasis "on the outward and physical, their claim to an exclusive Jewish righteousness [. . .] an attitude which is at odds with the faith of Abraham and the faith through which the Gentiles entered into the blessing promised to Abraham."²¹²

- The point of Jesus's death on the cross was to "remove the boundary of the law and its consequent curse, to liberate the blessing promised to Abraham for all to enjoy."²¹³ And

---

206. Dunn, "Yet Once More," 116.
207. Dunn, *The Epistle to the Galatians*, 199.
208. Ibid., 169.
209. Wright, *Climax*, 142.
210. Dunn, *Theology of Paul*, 149.
211. Ibid., 145–46, 160.
212. Dunn, *New Perspective*, 139–40.
213. Ibid., 140.

- Paul's concern was to break down the presupposition on the part of his fellow Jews that their privileged position before God involved some sort of restriction of God's grace to Israel, a restrictiveness implicit in Jewish "counter emphasis" on the works of the law.[214] Herein, for Dunn, lies the central point with regard to justification and to atonement itself:

> Just as we now recognize that Paul's teaching on justification by faith was directed to the specific issue of how the righteousness of God might be known by Gentile as well as Jew, however justified later systematic reflection on the doctrine was in enlarging and extending it, so now we need to recognize that his initial teaching on the cross was also specifically directed to the same problem, however justified later Christian reflection was in enlarging and extending the doctrine of the atonement.[215]

Although Dunn shares the same conclusion as Wright, that in works of the law Paul does not have in mind meritorious human works in the general sense but rather those practices that define the Jew over against the pagan, a number of fundamental questions still arise. As we saw with Wright, Dunn finds in his christological re-casting of Israel's story not only that Christ is the Jewish Messiah but also that the Messiah's role was self-evidently to complete the Judaism defined by Torah (complete in the sense of end it, in its current form and content). A "new" covenant has unilaterally replaced an "old" covenant, and with it "Jewish identity markers" have now inevitably been swept away. They no longer hold any soteriological or relational relevance. The use of positively-nuanced language of "fulfillment" or "completion" should not blind us to this being the reality.

It seems impossible to argue for a setting aside of the more visible features of the works of the law—such as circumcision, Sabbath, and purity/food laws—that served to separate Jews from gentiles without at the same time concluding that the covenant that required them is now to be set aside as well. There is an assertion that Israel inappropriately pursued the practice of these visible features; and yet surely the whole point of Israel's calling was precisely to be a distinctive people of God, living in accordance with (all of) the features of the Torah that God had given them to define that distinctiveness. Dunn himself concedes that although the visible identity markers come more into focus than other features, the observation applies in principle to the whole of Torah.[216] Thus, a new covenant inaugurating a

---

214. Ibid., 372–73.
215. Ibid., 140.
216. Dunn, *Theology of Paul*, 354–66, esp. 358: "The phrase 'the works of the law,'

new people of God exclusive of Torah does mean for all practical purposes the end of Israel.

Rather than self-evidently "good news" for Jews, this sounds at best to be the classic "good news, bad news" scenario. The *bad news* is that the longstanding relationship and identity that God graciously gifted to Israel in Torah has now suddenly ended ... with no prior warning.[217] The *good news*, however, is that Israel is being invited to share in a brand new relationship and identity—which incidentally, bears no apparent resemblance to the features of the old one that it has (foolishly?) relied upon for many centuries. The lacuna that would otherwise result from Torah's supposed fulfillment is addressed by the offer of inclusion in a new "spiritual" Israel that supersedes old "carnal" Israel.

Assuming for a moment that Dunn is correct concerning the way Paul's fellow Jews were improperly appropriating God's gift of Torah in terms of national righteousness, ethnic exclusivity and privileged status before God, this begs further questions. Was that something that was true of all Jews, all those of Paul's acquaintance, or only of some? It seems unlikely that Paul would speak of all Jews in this way;[218] which suggests he was criticizing the error of some Jews (even if that may have meant *many* Jews) and their practices as a *contingent* critique rather than the error of all Jews and all Jewish practices as a *universal* critique.[219] In which case, what was Paul's view of the Jewish faith properly understood and practiced by those Jews who were correctly appropriating Torah? Might that view have been a positive one? Would God have dispensed with the covenant for all because of the failings of a few—or even of a majority? Dunn has rather closed off the option of a positive viewpoint, though, in his further claim that Torah's role was only temporary; and moreover, a childish way to relate to God.[220] Torah was akin

---

does, of course, refer to all or whatever the law requires, covenantal nomism as a whole. But in a context where the relationship of Israel with other nations is at issue, certain laws would naturally come more into focus than others. We have instanced circumcision and food laws in particular." In a footnote, Dunn complains of "repeated misunderstanding of my initial essay on this subject."

217. Of course, if one assumes that "the old plan" was never effective in the first place—something that Israel needed saving from—one would inevitably fail to see any "bad news" element.

218. If only because of Jews such as himself, whom he clearly considered part of a faithful remnant of "true Israel."

219. However, perhaps Dunn does have in mind "all Jews." Already we have seen Wright's description of the problem, as "what happens when the nation as a whole fails to keep the Torah as a whole" (see page 81).

220. Dunn, *Galatians*, 199.

to the rules and restrictions one places around a child who is too immature to look after herself.[221]

One wonders which parts of all of this should have been "obvious" to Israel at the time. What was there, inherent in its texts and *praxis*, that ought to have flagged to them that this was the case? Surely these sad truths about Torah's temporary status, its ineffectuality and Israel's inability to "fulfill" or "complete" it could not be features that the God of Israel had intentionally concealed from them, until the time of Christ's coming.

In short, Dunn subscribes to a traditional Christian denigration of Torah's value. In relation to soteriology, it was providing Israel with only an "interim measure" to deal with the problem of transgression "until it could be dealt with definitively and finally in the cross of Christ."[222] Again we see the tendency to affirm the definitive and final nature of the cross through a concurrent denial that Torah preceding it had any true efficacy of its own until its soteriological efficacy was retrospectively validated by the cross (whereupon, somewhat curiously, Torah then immediately ceases to have any future efficacy).

Dunn credits Christ's work at a cross as the means by which the righteousness of God might be known by gentiles—with the death of the divine Son serving to "remove the boundary of the law and its consequent curse, to liberate the blessing promised to Abraham for all to enjoy."[223] And yet it seems odd, if such a momentous event was necessary to liberate the blessing for all to enjoy, that no such event appears to have been needed to establish that blessing for Israel to enjoy in the first instance. That being so, why would such an event now be required to extend its scope from "Israel" to "all"? It can only be because Christian thought ascribes a low view to Israel enjoying that blessing to begin with. And the very term "liberate" indicates a belief that that blessing had been somehow held in captivity by Israel and its Torah.

And finally, we must question the reductionism implicit in treating the law as little more than a catalogue of legalistic human practices. Dunn's analysis fails to do justice to a fuller and richer meaning. Torah was, at a minimum, a framework for understanding the proper response to God of the nation and of each faithful Jew within it—a framework graciously given by God himself as a "light to the path" of his people as to how to walk with him.[224] Was the Psalmist therefore guilty of "national righteousness"

---

221. Gal 3:24–25.
222. Dunn, *Galatians*, 190.
223. Dunn, *New Perspective*, 140.
224. E.g., Ps 119:105, 130.

or "Jewish exclusivity" in believing that "The law of the LORD is perfect, reviving the soul. The statutes of the LORD are trustworthy, making wise the simple" (Ps 19:7)? To question the appropriateness of God's people practicing the *nomism* that he himself had asked of them—their proper covenantal response[225]—is to question the terms established by God for the covenant itself. It questions the trustworthiness of a divine covenant-maker who would provide them with what appears to have been an inherently flawed (or unfulfillable) basis for relationship in the first place. If Torah was God-given, then faithfully to follow it cannot fairly be criticized as inappropriate human legalism, or ethnocentric cultural elitism.

In sum, it is unsurprising that Westerholm sees considerable common ground between Dunn and a traditional "Lutheran" reading of Paul.[226] Although in Dunn's new perspective the common Christian assumption of a Judaism based in salvation by good works has been comprehensively rejected, fatal flaws still persist; just as the Lutheran reading criticized Jewish *legalism*, so now Dunn criticizes Jewish *nationalism*. In both the traditional reading and Dunn's new-perspective reading, Torah is negative and has to go. Both Wright and Dunn find fault with Israel for its "national righteousness" and "Jewish exclusivity." However, if Israel's calling and destiny was to be a distinctive people of God defined by Torah vis-à-vis other nations and empires, then, as Harink points out, it is truly harsh to condemn them as ethnocentric nationalists for actually pursuing that option.[227]

Having reviewed Wright and Dunn at some length, as representative of the "Early" New Perspective following on from Sanders, we may summarize our findings as follows. On the one hand, the "old" perspective of Judaism as a religion of legalism and works-righteousness has been substantially consigned to the theological dustbin. On the other, it has been succeeded by a Paul who is still set against the Judaism of his day because he finds fundamental flaws in it. Their views continue to remain distinctly old perspective insofar as an embedded supersessionism and theological anti-Judaism is concerned. "Judaism" is still problematic and lacking, just on different bases. Israel is still at fault and its covenant remains flawed. Thus, the old contrasts persist, even though they are articulated differently. The traditional Reformed thought that defaults towards positive *versus* negative theological contrasts in Torah *versus* Christ, pitching them as competing opposites, is perpetuated.

---

225. Always assuming, of course, that the *nomism* is being understood and practiced as God intended, with "clean hands and a pure heart" (Ps 24:4).

226. Westerholm, *Perspectives Old and New*, 188, 190.

227. Harink, *Postliberals*, 199.

As to the implications for atonement, we are so far seeing little to identify any meaningful connectivity between Torah and Christ and Jew and gentile in salvific terms—in other words, how they are able to be brought together in a wholly-positive way. Thus, in figure 1 below, we struggle to draw a circle around all of the ingredients such that they can be seen as constituting one comprehensive salvific *schema* that finds a coherent place for all of the aspects: Torah, Christ, Jew, and gentile. As we know, the ingredient that always gets "left out" in the Christian explanation is Torah. The "Early" NPP, at least, has not articulated any rehabilitated view of Torah absent Christ to the extent that it can be granted an efficacious, complementary role within the salvific circle. In fact, the very opposite prevails—Torah and Christ continue to be seen in a "winner takes all" competition—in which (naturally) the new covenant in Christ triumphs and the old covenant in Torah is the loser. These questions therefore continue to concern us.

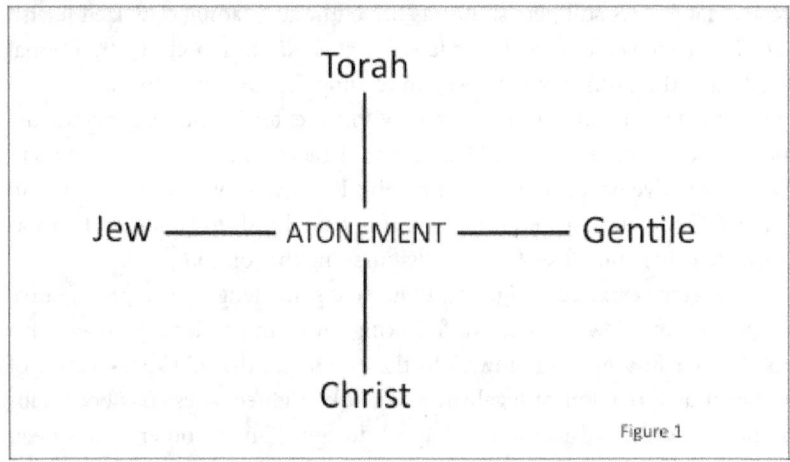

Figure 1

2.7 THE CONTINUING DEVELOPMENT OF NEW PERSPECTIVES

We turn now to developments since the "Early" New Perspective and it is at this point that classifications get a bit messy. For example, a number of scholars from both Christian and Jewish backgrounds would now place themselves within a so-called "Radical" New Perspective (sometimes known as the "Paul within Judaism" movement) that is not simply critical of the "old" perspective but equally critical of the "Early" NPP:

> These Jewish and Christian interpreters of Paul argue that the new perspective on Paul has simply replaced one negative stereotype of Judaism—that of legalism—with a different negative stereotype, that of exclusivism or ethnocentrism. Their

alternative argument is that Paul's negative rhetoric about the Torah was intended only for Gentiles, not for Jews.[228]

Scholars who have been identified as "Radical" NPP include Lloyd Gaston, John Gager, Mark Nanos, Paula Fredriksen, Amy-Jill Levine, Pamela Eisenbaum, Neil Elliott, Anders Runesson, William Campbell, Kathy Ehrensperger, and Stanley Stowers, although Nanos has described this as "an informal categorical affiliation" with no "confession for admission,"[229] which makes generalizations invidious. What is notable, however, is a clear endeavor to move beyond an embedded supersessionism and theological anti-Judaism and to apply the implications. One proposal that is identified by some (but by no means all) sees a "two-track" Pauline soteriology at work, in which Christ now enables gentiles to be included in God's people, whilst Torah remains valid and appropriate for Jews. Other scholars are not identified with a categorical affiliation but also offer helpful contributions—new perspectives—concerning the world of first-century Judaism and/or to the theological reimagining of Christian doctrine post-supersessionism, notwithstanding the extent to which they address Paul *per se*.

Necessarily, we can include contributions from only a selected few whose particular insights we believe will further aid in clarifying the issues and help to build a reconstructed view later in the book.

2.7.1 Lloyd Gaston

Lloyd Gaston begins from the standpoint that Paul stands in clear continuity with Judaism (rather than representing its antithesis) and that he is to be interpreted from within a context of covenantal nomism:

> Unless there are clear indications to the contrary, I shall assume that Paul understood "covenantal nomism" very well indeed and that he is to be interpreted within the context of early Judaism rather than that the Christian concept of Judaism is to be derived from what Paul denies. It may well be that when Paul says something seemingly quite different, it is because he is asking a different question, or even more because he is addressing a different audience.[230]

---

228. See *The Paul Page*: http://www.thepaulpage.com/paul-within-judaism/ (accessed 19 April, 2017).

229. Nanos, "Locating Paul on a Map of First-Century Judaism," paper presented at the SBL Annual Meeting, Atlanta, November 22, 2010.

230. Gaston, *Paul and the Torah*, 5.

The question of Paul's audience is, of course, a critical one in Pauline interpretation, and particularly in relation to passages dealing with Israel and the law, such as Galatians and Romans. While some element of contingency is clearly recognizable in his writings, the epistle to the Romans is one that more than any other has tended to be viewed as closest to a systematic Pauline theology. An interpretive assumption has prevailed that he writes here primarily as a dogmatic rather than pastoral theologian, dispensing universal timeless truths about God and the world, rather than simply what he feels needs to be said in a concrete situation. However, this assumption has been challenged. If Paul knew some of the Roman Christians and the circumstances of the church there, as suggested by Romans 16, then his letter cannot be read solely as a general theological treatise.[231] Stowers, Harink, and Nanos are among those who along with Gaston see Romans as instruction addressed to a wholly-gentile audience, at least insofar as its implied or encoded audience is concerned. Understanding the situation addressed as a gentile one is very crucial to Gaston's understanding of Paul.[232] Its importance comes not only in relation to what Paul is saying to gentiles but also in what he is therefore not saying to Jews. Donaldson suggests that "everything Paul has to say about Jews and Judaism is in letters addressed to Gentile churches."[233]

The idea that Paul is writing to gentiles can be seen to affirm a conclusion that Paul has no problem with Judaism and Torah *so far as Jews are concerned*. In other words, in God's purposes as understood by Paul there exists a "two-track" plan of salvation involving two distinct and separate paths, in which Christ provides a way of salvation for gentiles alone:[234]

---

231. "While it is true that Romans is the most systematic of Paul's letters, its occasional nature cannot be denied." Mark Reasoner, "Rome and Roman Christianity" in Hawthorne et al., (eds.) *Dictionary of Paul and his Letters*, 854. Barrett observes that the length of the letter may be explained by Paul having little precise knowledge of the form that Christianity had taken in Rome: hence, Paul had to cover a good deal of ground, and to write to some extent in abstract terms, in order to make sure of touching on every relevant point. *Introduction*, 42–43.

232. Gaston, *Paul and the Torah*, 9.

233. *Jews and Anti-Judaism in the New Testament*, 136.

234. Gager, *Reinventing Paul*, 146. Other terms that are deployed to discuss "two-track" soteriology—referencing distinct covenants that God has, on the one hand, with the Jewish people (through the Old Testament covenants including Torah) and, on the other, with the church (through Christ)—include "dual-covenant theology," "Bi-covenantalism," the "two-covenant approach," or simply, "the two ways." The German term *Sonderweg*, or "special way," is also used, with reference to the Jews being saved through faith in Christ at the *Parousia*. See Vanlaningham, *Christ, the Savior of Israel: An Evaluation of the Dual Covenant and Sonderweg Interpretations of Paul's Letters*.

> Had all Israel followed Paul's example, we could have had an Israel loyal to the righteousness of God expressed in the Torah alongside a gentile church loyal to the righteousness of God expressed in Jesus Christ and his fulfilment of the promises to Abraham.[235]

Stress on Paul's gospel being for gentiles is consonant with a particular view of "the gentile problem": namely, that Israel always had a relationship with God through the law, but being outside the law gentiles were without hope. Accordingly, as Stowers puts it, "God's justice seems to require a further act of mercy toward the gentiles if the overall course of the world's history is not to seem unfair toward the non-Jewish peoples."[236] Thus, in a letter like Galatians where he also deals at length with the supposed "problem" of the law, the situation of the gentiles is, once again, what Paul has in mind.

> When Paul writes about Torah, he is writing about it to Gentiles in relation to Gentiles, not to and in relation to humanity in general or to Jews. It is important to keep the implied audience in mind especially when reading Galatians, or one easily slips into thinking that what Paul writes there is a letter to "humanity" or to "Jews and Gentiles" or a critique of "Judaism," when in fact it is a letter to Gentiles critical of an attempt (by Jews? "Christian" Jews? Christian Gentile proselytes to Judaism?) to require full Jewish practice from the Gentile believers in Galatia and their seeming willingness to accept this imposition.[237]

The benefits of such a conclusion are considerable, of course, not least for Jewish-Christian relations in the post-Holocaust world. At a stroke, it abolishes the idea that Paul was espousing a new and better religion called Christianity over against an old and defunct religion called Judaism, and hence, it removes any continuing rationale for Christian anti-Judaism. The flip side, of course, is that it means the Son of God came into the world and died on the cross to save *gentile* sinners alone. The "us" of Romans 5:8—"God demonstrates his own love for us in this: While we were still sinners, Christ died for us"—must now be read as meaning "us gentiles," which presumably includes Paul himself in some self-identifying sense.

However, one is tempted to ask whether it would not have been easier—if all else was well—for God simply to tinker with the entry requirements of the law. Rather than create a parallel track, with wholly separate

---

235. Gaston, *Paul and the Torah*, 33. The citation is from Gaston's essay in its earlier, 1979 form, which was slightly reworded in the later book.

236. Stowers, *A Rereading of Romans*, 106.

237. Harink, *Paul among the Postliberals*, 39n30.

soteriological provisions for Jew and gentile, would it not make more sense to expand the scope of the existing Judaic covenant in some way?

Evangelical thought concerning the gospel, in which crucicentrism is paramount, would struggle to accept that Christ's mission should be limited to gentile salvation; that Christ has no salvific relevance for Jews.[238] The problem can be resolved, of course, if Jesus is not the Jewish Messiah; which is precisely what Gaston proposes:

> Jesus is then for Paul not the Messiah. He is neither the climax of the history of Israel nor the fulfillment of the covenant, and therefore Jesus is not seen in relation to David or Moses. For Paul, Jesus is the new act of the righteousness of God in the inclusion of the Gentiles, and therefore he is seen in negative relationship with Adam and positive relationship with Abraham.[239]

Not everyone sympathetic to Gaston's general proposition is quite so convinced of this, however, and hence some speak more tentatively. Stowers, for example, suggests that language such as Romans 3:30 ("there is only one God, who will justify the circumcised by faith and the uncircumcised through that same faith") reveals that the ways of Jews and gentiles are separate but related—Paul assumes that Israel continues to live by the law, but righteous life in that law "*also somehow* seems to proceed out of Christ's faithfulness." "Evidently [. . .] Israel does have a relation to Christ's faithfulness, although Paul speaks as if it differs from that of the gentiles."[240] Of that relation, however, Stowers finds that Paul's letters provide only hints, which he puts down to the fact that the audience was gentiles and Paul was writing about the gentile situation. The reason that it differs therefore remains

---

238. The notion of distinct salvific categories does not seem to make much sense of Galatians 3:28: "There is neither Jew nor Greek [. . .] for you are all one in Christ Jesus."

239. Gaston, *Paul and the Torah*, 7. Gaston claims to be following the conclusions of Dahl and Kramer that for Paul *Christos* is a proper name and not to be translated Messiah. See "The Messiahship of Jesus in Paul," in Dahl, *The Crucified Messiah and Other Essays*, 37–47; Kramer, *Christ, Lord, Son of God*. However, John Knox suggests Gaston has not fully reflected Dahl's view: "The Messiahship of Jesus in Paul" makes principally two points: (1) that although the word *Christos* in Paul is already surprisingly far on the way to becoming a second proper name for Jesus and is apparently often used by Paul as such, nevertheless, the theological meaning of the term as designating an office is very much present to him; (2) that what provides this meaning of the word for him is "less Paul's pre-Christian messianic concept than the pre-Pauline Christology of the church. These claims, as well as Dahl's conception of the theological meaning itself, are supported by impressive arguments, philological, historical, and exegetical." John Knox, *Theology Today*, October 1975, Vol. 32–33. Available at http://theologytoday.ptsem.edu/oct1975/v32-3-bookreview4.htm, accessed March 16, 2012.

240. Stowers, *Rereading of Romans*, 205, emphasis added.

unclear—somehow there is a relation between Christ's relevance for Jew and his relevance for gentile, but the nature of that relation has yet to be determined.

Most obviously problematic for the Gastonian two-track thesis, though, is that Paul himself fails to fit the mold. As Donaldson rightly asks, if all Israel had responded to Christ as Paul did, would we not have had a company of Israelites who, whatever their on-going relation to Torah, would have joined him in serving Christ too?[241]

> Gaston's argument is that if all Israel had followed Paul's teaching or his intention, we would have had distinct bodies of Torah-loyal Jews and Christ-loyal Gentiles. But this is to highlight the anomaly. In a two-covenant reading of Paul, what is to be done with that category of people for which Paul is the prime example, namely, Jews who are also "loyal to the righteousness of God expressed in Jesus Christ"?[242]

All of which suggests that the paradox of Paul and the law is not to be so easily resolved by the simple idea that Paul finds no flaw in Judaism *for Jews*, as some within the "Radical" NPP seek to argue. We continue to grapple with the question of how loyalty to the righteousness of God expressed in the Torah sits with loyalty to the righteousness of God expressed in Christ, for Jew and gentile (per the conundrum of figure 1).

2.7.2 Daniel Boyarin

The second contribution we have chosen is from Daniel Boyarin, who follows Sanders in an unashamed objective "to thoroughly discredit the Reformation interpretation of Paul and particularly the description of Judaism on which it is based."[243] Boyarin is of particular interest because he writes as an Orthodox Jew who affirms a high regard for Christianity and treats Pauline themes at some length.

Of special interest is Boyarin's view that prior to his conversion Saul the Pharisee already sensed that something was "not quite right" in his historic faith. However, this had nothing to do with an anguished conscience, or legalistic works-righteousness. It was, instead, a tension perceived by

---

241. Donaldson, "Jewish Christianity, Israel's Stumbling, and the *Sonderweg* Reading of Paul."

242. Ibid., 30.

243. Boyarin, *Border Lines*, ix–xi. In the present chapter, we shall be focusing on Boyarin's earlier work, *Radical Jew*, returning to *Border Lines* in chapter three.

Paul to be inherent within Judaism, between the particularity of Torah in relation to the one tribe or people Israel and the God of Israel's universal concerns for the world:

> The Torah, in which he so firmly believes, claims to be the text of the One True God of all the world, who created heaven and earth and all humanity, and yet its primary content is the history of one particular People—almost one family—and the practices that it prescribes are many of them practices which mark off the particularity of that tribe, his tribe. In his very commitment to the truth of the gospel of that Torah and its claim to universal validity lies the source of Paul's trouble.[244]

It was a tension between "narrow ethnocentrism and universalist monotheism,"[245] which Boyarin suggests was sensed by many Jews of the first century.[246] This idea is hinted at by Sanders:

> We can never exclude with certainty the possibility that Paul was secretly dissatisfied with the law before his conversion/call. If one is to look for secret dissatisfaction, however, it might be better to look to his stance toward the Gentiles than to his possible frustration with his own situation under the law, or to his analysis of the situation of Jews under the law. It is by no means inconceivable that he had native sympathy for the Gentiles and chafed at the Jewish exclusivism which either ignored them or which relegated them to second place in God's plan.[247]

Unlike Sanders, Boyarin believes that Paul *did* work from plight to solution.[248] However, the nature of that plight was not a *personal* one but a *theological* one. What troubled him was the unequal status of Jew and gentile before the one God of all. Hence, Boyarin's Paul was motivated by a critique of Judaism, but for different reasons from those traditionally assumed. Paul's Damascene experience is therefore to be read against this background. Boyarin sees it as "a moment of *blinding insight*, so rich and revealing that he *understands it to have been*, in fact, an apocalypse."[249] Paul's insight was that Christ is the solution to this plight of unequal status

---

244. Boyarin, *Radical Jew*, 39.
245. Ibid., 52.
246. Ibid., 39.
247. Sanders, *Jewish People*, 152–53.
248. Boyarin, *Radical Jew*, 206.
249. Ibid., 39, emphasis added.

by virtue of being "the way to render Torah salvation for all"[250] (which is broadly consonant with Sanders's proposal that Paul relegated the Mosaic dispensation to a less glorious place because he found something more glorious[251]—in Boyarin's phrase, a contrast between good and greater good). For Boyarin, however, Paul's revelation is to do with a less-glorious *particularism* and a more-glorious *universalism*. He perceives this to be part of a broader Pauline scheme of dualism of physical and spiritual, of signifier and signified, that begins with Christ himself:

> The coming of Christ is, in fact, the perfect model for Paul's ontology, for just as Christ had a physical nature and a spiritual nature (Romans 9:5), and both are valuable, though the former is subordinated to the latter, so also the physical observances of the Torah and the people of Israel.[252]

In other words, the dual nature of Christ becomes a kind of hermeneutical key to resolving the tension Paul perceived between the universalism of the Torah's content and the particular ethnicity of its form. There was a Christ according to the flesh—the literal, historical Jesus—and a Christ according to the spirit, an allegorical, risen Christ.[253] Boyarin sees this as corresponding in Paul's thought to Israel and its physical practices of the law, as carnal, physical and literal—Israel according to the flesh—being transcended by (and subordinated to) an Israel according to the spirit, that is spiritual and universal.

> The birth of Christ as a human being and a Jew, his death and his resurrection *as* spiritual and universal was the model and the apocalypse of the transcendence of the physical and particular Torah for Jews alone by its spiritual and universal referent for all.[254]

The "lesser glory of the Torah"—centered in the flesh and applicable to physical Israel—becomes apparent when it is "read as a signifier for that which it truly signifies": a universal Israel centered in the spirit.[255]

Boyarin sees dualistic contrasts driving Paul's entire thought and modes of expression: Paul's hermeneutic finds two meanings in the historical texts, a literal and a spiritual. Examples of these "sets of oppositions"

250. Ibid., 45.
251. Sanders, *Jewish People*, 138.
252. Boyarin, *Radical Jew*, 29.
253. Ibid.
254. Ibid., 39.
255. Ibid., 45.

or "analogical ratios" can be gleaned from various places in his writings: flesh-spirit, body-soul, literal-figurative, Israel-church, works-faith, circumcision-baptism, earthly Jerusalem-heavenly Jerusalem, and genealogy-promise.[256] Rather than being supersessionist, though,[257] the nature of this dualistic relation is found in a hierarchy of signifier and signified. It is not a Pauline rejection of Israel so much as a way of understanding Israel and its vocation—Paul was engaging in a cultural critique of Judaism *from within*: "I treat Paul's discourse as indigenously Jewish. [. . .] This is an inner-Jewish discourse and an inner-Jewish controversy."[258] It is analogous to our own times, Boyarin argues, in which Reform Jews argue that the Torah intended itself to change with the times, Orthodox Jews totally disagree, and yet no-one doubts the Jewishness of either group.

Paul's understanding is therefore allegorical, one in which the particular signifies the universal. Because the present Christian situation was to be interpreted spiritually, allegory was the appropriate mode for understanding it.[259]

> Accordingly, interpretations of Paul which focus on his apocalypticism, understanding it as only a version of the general Palestinian Jewish apocalyptic, have also seriously mistaken the thrust of his gospel; it is not only that the fulfillment of time has come but more to the point that Paul understands it in a certain, specific way, as the revelation of the inner meaning of outward signs, an inner meaning which is always already there, whether the outward signs are the flesh, the Jews, the Law, or the historical Jesus.[260]

In summary, Boyarin's fundamental idea is that what motivated Paul ultimately was "a profound concern for the one-ness of humanity," a concern "motivated both by certain universalistic tendencies within biblical Israelite religion and even more by the reinterpretation of those tendencies in the light of Hellenistic notions of universalism."[261] In line with Dunn, Boyarin's Paul opposes "works of the law" because it refers to Jewish cultural practices that were thought by Jew and gentile alike to be divisive in marking the special status of the Jews.

---

256. Ibid., 31.
257. Ibid., 205.
258. Ibid., 205, also 52.
259. Ibid., 34.
260. Ibid., 35.
261. Ibid., 52.

N. T. Wright takes issue with Boyarin on a number of levels, beginning with method.[262] He accuses Boyarin of doing to Paul precisely what Boyarin claims Paul has done to Judaism: abstracting certain sets of ideas out of their historical context, reading between the lines, and producing an *allegorized Paul*.

> Paul's own very specific and concrete mission, suffering, writing, preaching, plans, hopes—*and* his personal pre-history as a zealous Pharisee—are here treated as *signifiers* for the real thing, the *signified*—which is "Paul," seen as a critical moment in an essentially Platonic scheme, a history of ideas.[263]

As a result, says Wright, Boyarin has produced an allegorized and ahistorical reading. Everything has been shifted onto the plane of the spirit, away from the letter. This contrasts sharply with Wright's own belief that uppermost in Paul's mind (and for the Jews of his day) was the actual history of Israel. Paul thought he belonged within that history which, for him, was both reality and still in process: the real flesh-and-blood story of God and God's people: "It was not a code, a mere signifier for something else, for a timeless, ahistorical or static scheme."[264] For Wright, Paul's concern for the gentile mission is to be understood eschatologically: when Israel is redeemed, the nations will come to share in that blessing.

Wright is also critical of Boyarin's interpretation of Paul's "conversion": the pre-Christian Paul was not "an ideas man" who had a revelation of a big new idea on the Damascus road. Paul did not have an intellectual problem before his conversion any more than he had a moral problem. As we have seen, for Wright Paul's concern was liberation and the end of exodus, understood concretely: how and when the true God would vindicate his name and manifest his righteousness. As well as allegorizing Paul and Israel, Boyarin has done the same to Jesus. Rather than a bodily resurrection according to the flesh, we have an "allegorical, risen Christ," according to the Spirit.[265] This, Wright argues, would be entirely inconsistent with a first-century understanding of resurrection-language, which was about "bodies coming out of tombs."

The biggest single weakness that Wright sees, however, is Boyarin's failure to explain what the cross meant to Paul, or how it features in his

---

262. Wright, "Two Radical Jews."
263. Ibid. (no pagination).
264. Ibid. (no pagination).
265. Boyarin, *Radical Jew*, 29.

theology, "let alone his life." Moreover, the person of Jesus has been de-historicized into a "Christ-figure," a Christian-idea.

> I suggest that at the heart of Paul's theology, and of his Damascus Road experience, there lay not an idea, but a person; that the historical human being Jesus, not merely some abstract Christian idea, was what grasped the historical Paul and set him about a historical task; that this task was, as far as Paul was concerned, to establish and maintain not philosophical academies but historical communities in which love would be historically lived out.[266]

Boyarin argues that "Paul was *not* anti-Judaic" but he agrees with Sanders that Paul "did undermine *any* traditionally understood notions of what being Jewish meant."[267] However, such an argument seems contradictory. It seems illogical that the Paul of the New Perspective—with his newly-restored "Jewishness"—would have allegorized his core Jewish practices, identity and explanatory framework out of the picture.[268] It is surely more likely that the Paul of Philippians 3:4–6 would have sought and found a theological explanation of his encounter with the resurrected Jesus that far from undermining the traditional notions of what being Jewish meant was, in fact, wholly consonant with them. An overnight shift on Paul's part into a wholly allegorical new religious framework that saw no validity in Israel's carnal religious practices—save in the sense of offering a "picture language" to help explain new, spiritual things—seems inconsistent with a Paul who is comfortable and confident in his Jewishness. Rather, it bears more than a passing resemblance to the Paul of the "old" perspective.

Notwithstanding these critiques, three aspects of Boyarin's account are notable for our purposes. The first is that he affirms Paul's thinking as coming entirely from within Judaism and based in Jewish categories (albeit featuring a significant allegorization as part of the package). The second is that although he shares with Wright and Dunn the view that Paul had nagging concerns about the status of the gentiles, unlike them he sees Paul as having no essential difficulty with the law itself. The third aspect builds upon this, in that in Christ there is a "something more" which is to do with "the way to render Torah salvation for all."[269] Boyarin concludes that for Paul there is a correspondence between the good news of Torah and the good news of

---

266. Wright, "Two Radical Jews." (no pagination).

267. Boyarin, *Radical Jew*, 273n9.

268. Notwithstanding that Boyarin notes, in Philo, that allegorization was already an established Jewish interpretive practice. *Radical Jew*, 14–15, 96.

269. Boyarin, *Radical Jew*, 45.

Christ (which he characterizes as a "signifier" and "signified" relationship). We shall return to these aspects in the following chapter.

2.7.3 Mark Adam Elliott

Although he is not writing from a specifically Pauline perspective, Mark Adam Elliott offers some valuable insights on the Jewish background to the New Testament, particularly in relation to covenant. He seeks to establish a "systematic theology" of Judaism in the first century as represented by the Pseudepigrapha and the Dead Sea Scrolls.[270] In a substantial volume developed from his doctoral thesis,[271] Elliott argues that the concerns of that literature are of critical importance to the illumination of the message of the New Testament, reminding us of the relatively late provenance of the rabbinic literature that he argues to be too late—and therefore too historically and ideologically distant—for satisfactory comparison with the New Testament.[272] The rabbinic literature is simply not "the timeless and universal summary of Jewish belief that it was once taken to be, and it does not adequately reflect the time period in which the New Testament arose."[273] Not only was the Talmud the product of a particular viewpoint within Judaism, historical events (not least, the destruction of Jerusalem in 70 CE) had exercised a profound influence, effectively distinguishing it from the Judaism that went before. Elliott argues that "a literature that reacts against the milieu in which the New Testament arose can hardly provide a balanced, let alone sympathetic, portrait of the Judaism with which the New Testament had so many features in common."[274] Elliott criticizes scholarly tendencies to (i) draw on modern Jewish belief for purposes of systematizing ancient doctrine, and (ii) treat Judaism as timeless and, therefore, as largely unconditioned by development.[275] In contrast, the literature in Elliott's purview can be dated to "what is rightly called the formative period of Christianity,"[276] c. 200 BCE to 100 CE.

Working from the representative view of Joseph Bonsirven—that notwithstanding "the Jews of Palestine were divided into various sects:

---

270. Elliott, *Survivors of Israel*, 4.

271. To my knowledge, *Survivors of Israel* was Elliott's only published book before his untimely death in 2007.

272. Ibid., 3.

273. Ibid., 4.

274. Ibid.

275. Ibid., 31.

276. Ibid., 3.

Pharisees, Sadducees, Essenes, popular and apocalyptic groups" with differences that were in some cases profound and in others superficial, the sects "were united by a common fund of beliefs and practices derived directly from the Bible and from revered and universally accepted traditions"[277]—Elliott focuses on one of the principal pillars of that view: "the doctrine, widely assumed to belong *universally* to Judaism, of the *irrevocable national election of Israel*."[278] The view he challenges is the conventional assumption that

> Israel is the people of God, different from all peoples, and as such the *focus* of God's redemptive work; the individual Israelite is secure in the knowledge that redemption is assured for the individual member of the nation.[279]

"Normative Judaism" (Moore's term) has perpetuated a "conventional view of national election theology."[280] Nationalism "is not only a political concept" argues Elliott, "it is also a *theological* concept, especially as it embraces a particular view of God's relations and intentions with respect to the nation Israel, and especially as it is reflected in the doctrine of the *election of Israel*."[281]

Of particular interest are the implications concerning the status of the *nation*, or of a faithful group within the nation, versus the *individual*: obedience to the law as an "individual" concern and the election of Israel as a "corporate" matter.[282] Elliott cites a "glaring contradiction" of which the writer was presumably oblivious in the following statement: "The ultimate reward of a conscientious observance of Torah will be the participation in the world to come which *awaits every Israelite*."[283] What is it to be, asks Elliott—the reward of the conscientious observer or the reward of every Israelite? Or was every Israelite *automatically* a conscientious observer? For Elliott, this illustrates "how the conventional nationalistic view can only be sustained in the face of real tensions with other ideas that may have been emerging within the Jewish world."[284]

---

277. Bonsirven, *Palestinian Judaism in the Time of Jesus Christ*, vi, as cited by Elliott, *Survivors of Israel*, 28.

278. Elliott, *Survivors of Israel*, 28.

279. Ibid., 28.

280. Ibid., 32, 39.

281. Ibid., 33.

282. Ibid., 41–43.

283. Helfgott, *The Doctrine of Election in Tannaitic Literature*, 128, as cited by Elliott, *Survivors of Israel*, 42 (emphasis added by Elliott).

284. Elliott, *Survivors of Israel*, 43.

> The important feature of a basically nationalistic theology, in the sense intended here, is that its *chief focus* is the life and ideals of the *nation*, in contrast to a theology that focuses on any other group or on the individual.[285]

Elliott's proposal in contrast is that the various sects in first-century Israel each saw themselves through the lens of "the remnant"—the "true" people of God—in which God's purposes for the larger nation were being enacted by a relatively small number.

Elliott finds that during the course of the Second Temple period the written Torah gained ever-increasing importance within Judaism, eventually displacing all other institutions—including temple and priesthood—as its chief authority. Once deprived of its ancient social institutions and scattered throughout the world, Judaism necessarily became a religion of the Book and a people of the Book. The resultant enhanced focus on attention to the requirements of the law for the individual at a personal level could be said to result in a more legalistic (law-oriented) religion, and an inevitable tension between obedience to the law as an "individual" concern and the election of Israel as a "corporate" concern. Elliott suggests that "all truly individualistic systems will eventually tend towards a downplaying of national ideas."[286] Elliott sees the formation during this period of a movement or movements of protest—a variety of groups expressing dissatisfaction with the *status quo*. This included both strongly nationalistic reactions and groups who rejected the nationalistic response, even to the point of becoming *non*nationalistic or even *anti*nationalistic in posture—"those who resigned themselves to the failure of the national model would have reacted by condemning that national vision." It is the latter whom Elliott finds of particular interest: "The groups we are concerned with here opted for a clean break with nationalistic Judaism." Interestingly, these groups' alienation was directed against the masses as much as the establishment. When it comes to the conservatives of the late Second Temple period, he argues, one is dealing with a reaction of the pietistic to the perceived apostasy within Israel.[287]

This in turn leads to a further anxiety in relation to the understanding of covenant. There has always been a tension inherent in the aspects of covenant as *gift* (given by God's grace) and of covenant as *demand* (the requirement for obedience). All Jewish theologies embraced both aspects to some extent. However, not all Jewish groups would have felt the same way

---

285. Ibid., 34.
286. Ibid., 41.
287. Ibid., 236–42.

about covenant.[288] At one extreme was the unconditional view of covenant, emphasizing it as inviolable or undefilable, since no sin could break it.

> As there could accordingly never be an occasion for another covenant to displace this covenant, it would make the covenant *permanent* and virtually irreplaceable [...]. This leads logically to the idea of *irrevocability*. One can see how this view of covenant would breed a certain kind of conservatism or traditionalism [...]. In short, this would result in a *static* view of covenant, as every and all change would be avoided.[289]

At the other extreme was the view of covenant that emphasizes its *demands*. Such an approach sees covenant as *conditional*, dependent upon performance; in which failure can, indeed, invalidate the covenant. Hence, importance is necessarily placed on the *legal* aspects of the covenant and the behavioral choices of the individual.[290]

> Since particular requirements involve the cooperation of the individual, the covenant would also tend to be interpreted *individualistically*. In its extreme form, the corporate notion of election would be entirely subjugated to the individual's acceptance or rejection of the terms of the covenant and mechanisms would be put in place by which either to judge the individual or to facilitate the continued participation of the individual within the covenant (such as atonement rituals, feasts and regular sacrifices).[291]

Owing to the uncertainty inherent in a conditional covenant, a means of renewing the covenant—and even, if necessary, the possibility of a new covenant to take the place of one that had failed—would become at least desirable, if not absolutely necessary as well. Rather than the *static* view of covenant, this would give rise to a more *dynamic* view, open to change and improvement. Within *this* scheme of thought, then,

---

288. Elliott cites this as a reason that Sanders's attempt to define all Judaism uniformly under the rubric of "covenantal nomism" is especially rash. Ibid., 247.

289. Ibid., 247.

290. By way of example, in the words of Moses to the people of Israel in Deuteronomy 30:15 & 19–20—"See, I set before you today life and prosperity, death and destruction. [...] Now choose life, so that you and your children may live and that you may love the Lord your God, listen to his voice, and hold fast to him. For the Lord is your life." "What may originally have been a corporate warning to all Israel [...] is now interpreted as an individual choice between two ways." Elliott, *Survivors of Israel*, 278.

291. Ibid., 248.

While former covenants might be considered paradigmatic, no covenant would be considered sufficient in itself, including either the Abrahamic or Mosaic covenants. Many covenants are therefore possible and different ones would come into prominence from time to time. Such a view of covenant would tend to be more tolerant of *innovative revelation*, which might involve either significant advances in doctrine, or merely clarifications. It would demand a less nationalistic orientation, inasmuch as God judges individuals, and could easily lead to various cosmic and universalistic applications.[292]

Elliott cautions that neither of these views of covenant is ever likely to have existed in its extreme: "Jewish groups would have synthesized and combined the aspects of both, producing a variety of final products that nevertheless would be all *well within the spectrum of possibilities of what one would expect for covenantal thought.*"[293]

Elliott then offers further consideration of the implications. The first would be expectations about the nature of the coming Messiah: instead of questions about a material, earthly figure in contrast to an apocalyptic, heavenly figure, the distinction focused upon would become between "*a nationalistic view of the messiah's role in contrast to the view of the messiah in these groups as messiah-of-the-elect.*"[294] The Messiah was not so much coming for the nation as for the particular sect in question—the remnant that comprises the elect. Second would be a distinction introduced not simply between Israelite and gentile, but also between Israelite and fellow Israelite. And thirdly, there would be implications for soteriology:

> On the soteriological level, one also witnesses a move away from a national "soteriology" (better: covenantal nationalism), an increased attention to individual categories, and, finally, the emergence of a soteriology based on a renewed (but entirely redirected) experience of corporate consciousness. This last stage of the development is the important one, inasmuch as soteriology is no longer centered on the nation, nor has it become entirely individual, but through an emerging "corporate identity" stimulated by shared experiences of crisis has become *ipso facto* a *corporate soteriology* focused on a remnant of Israelites.[295]

---

292. Ibid., 249.
293. Ibid.
294. Ibid., 513.
295. Ibid., 354.

There are clear soteriological implications here concerning the status in first-century Judaism of the "individual" *versus* the "remnant" *versus* the "nation." In other words, whether one's salvific status was derived from participation in the covenant (a) at a national level, collectively, through election, (b) nomistic faithfulness at an individual level, or (c) some combination of those aspects within a remnant that constituted true Israel. Within the same mix are the implications of the tension between "covenant as gift" (with its inferred inviolability) and "covenant as demand" (with its inferred conditionality)—two different directions from which one can look through the covenantal telescope—and how the nomistic response (or failure) of an individual or a number of individuals affects it.

Unlike most of the writers we are reviewing, Elliott does not seek to draw out the implications for interpreting Paul. However, the fact that these various understandings co-existed (if not also contested) within the milieu of first-century Judaism has considerable relevance for how covenant operates—and so too, how it may potentially be reflected in the perspectives of the New Testament authors. In particular, it has a bearing on the irrevocability of the covenant with Israel and on the *modus operandi* of the new covenant in Christ.

From an Evangelical perspective, of course, salvation has tended to be treated fundamentally as an individual matter—or better stated, a personal matter (although in modernity and postmodernity the two can easily become confused). This is, in part at least, a reaction against the notion that one is passively "born Christian" by virtue of being a citizen of a "Christian country"; in Evangelicalism, one must actively make a "decision for Christ." However, this appropriate personalization of the gospel and relationship with God through Christ can result in the covenantal framework within which the salvific relationship comes about being conceived as a "one-on-one covenant" with the individual. This, in turn, can lead to an assumption that each individual begins by being "out" until he or she responds to the gospel by making a personal decision to come "in" (which gives rise to further questions about what constitutes "staying in").

Although the focus of verses 31–33 in Jeremiah 31 is generally directed to the nature of the promised *new* covenant, a feature of the *present* covenant in Torah can be clearly identified within verse 34 that pertains to the place of the individual. The writer appears to treat this as something that is self-evidently the case, rather than some fresh revelation: within the present covenant, the members urge one another to individually "know the LORD."[296] Hence, in some sense, the nature of the covenant relationship

---

296. "No longer will they teach their neighbor, or say to one another, "Know the

is "both-and," with corporate *and* individual features. One enters into the covenant relationship by virtue of one's inclusion with the group God has graciously elected, but the community recognizes that there is also an individual relational element to be pursued.

Elliott offers some fascinating observations concerning how covenants operate at individual, remnant and group level and we shall draw further from them in relation to the new covenantal understanding developed in chapter three.

2.7.4 Alan Segal

Graydon Snyder has cited Alan Segal's work as an example of a Jewish response to New Perspective writers.[297] Segal is of particular interest due to the significance he finds in Paul's so-called "conversion" on the Damascus road and the implications he sees for Paul in his experience of Christ *versus* his experience of Torah.

Writing concurrently with the "Early" NPP, Segal is another scholar who has argued that Paul and his so-called "Christian" thought should be firmly situated within the world of first-century Judaism rather than as one sitting outside of it, as a critic, looking in.

> Jewish Christianity probably continued to be the dominant form of Christianity for at least two generations and maybe for several generations after Paul. Even Acts, written in an environment of a more confident gentile mission, claims to be written from within Judaism.[298]

For Segal, Paul thought and wrote as a Jew, rather than in some antithetical "Christian" capacity. He notes that Paul is a trained Pharisee and his Judaism is Pharisaic. In fact, he is one of only two Pharisees to have left us any personal writings.[299] Contrary to many customary understandings of Paul, his own self-description as a Pharisee does not allow much room for guilt feelings or lack of self-esteem[300] (Phil 3:4-6). Paul obviously thought himself to be guilty of no infraction of Torah before he became a Christian. Furthermore, Segal argues, Paul did not repudiate his Jewish background

---

Lord," because they will all know me, from the least of them to the greatest."

297. Snyder, "Major Motifs in the Interpretation of Paul's Letter to the Romans," 63.

298. Segal, *Paul the Convert*, 275. Segal has a particular interest in how the NT, and Paul in particular, can inform Jews about first-century Judaism.

299. See ibid., n.331.

300. As Stendahl had recognized, in "Introspective Conscience."

when he did so—in fact, since he does not use the word "Christian" and he lacks a specific term to refer to Christianity, there is no evidence of any desire to describe something called Christianity as a completely different phenomenon from something called Judaism.[301]

> [Paul] began as a Pharisee and became a convert *from* Pharisaism. He spent the rest of life trying to express what he converted *to*. He never gave it a single name. Whatever it was, he never felt that he had left Judaism.[302]

Accordingly, "The issue is not so much whether Paul was a Pharisee, which seems beyond rational dispute, but what his Pharisaism tells us about him and Judaism"[303]—to which, we might add, what Paul's Pharisaism can tell us about what we commonly speak of as Christianity.

> History after Paul has judged Christianity to be different from Judaism. That fact seems undeniable today, but it was hardly evident in the first century. Paul would have objected strenuously against any distinction between his faith and his Judaism [. . .].[304]

Segal emphasizes the necessity of understanding Paul as writing from within and informed by the Judaism of his day, and addressing issues pertinent to that context.[305] He sees the keys to understanding Paul's advocacy of Christianity as located in two features: (i) "his Jewish past," and (ii) "the terms of his conversion."[306]

It is Segal's perceptions of this second element on which we need now to focus. What precisely happened in that "conversion"?—assuming, for the moment, that conversion is an appropriate description, not least because Paul himself does not use it and nor does he discuss the event directly,[307] so we have only Luke's accounts to work from. Notwithstanding the discrepancies between those accounts,[308] Segal works with the Lucan portrayal of a

---

301. Segal, *Paul the Convert*, xi–xii, 5, 262, 283–84.
302. Ibid., 283–84, emphases original.
303. Segal, "Paul's Jewish Presuppositions," 162.
304. Segal, *Paul the Convert*, xiv.
305. "Paul was not writing to the church of Augustine in the fourth century, or to the Protestant Reformers of the sixteenth century, or to post-Holocaust Christians in the twentieth century. This sounds silly. Yet this is precisely how the apostle to the Gentiles has been read throughout Christian history." Gager, *Reinventing Paul*, 66.
306. Segal, *Paul the Convert*, xiv.
307. Paul's brief allusions appear in 1 Cor 9:1; 15:8; and Gal 1:15–16.
308. Acts 9:1–19; 22:3–21; and 26:12–18. "The disagreement in detail between the

decisive and sudden ecstatic event, at least insofar as he finds support for it in Pauline texts.[309] Segal differs from those such as Stendahl who identify Paul's conversion solely in terms of a prophetic calling. He agrees that from the viewpoint of mission Paul is commissioned, but from the viewpoint of religious experience he is converted. What's more, Paul is a convert in the modern sense of the word.[310]

All of which might lead one to assume that Segal is affirming the widespread assumption that "Paul's name leads the list of converts [. . .] and certainly the most famous one. In the West, Paul typifies conversion."[311] However, this is not the case. Whatever it was that happened to Paul, it is inappropriate to treat this conversion as paradigmatic for "non-believers becoming Christians." Elsewhere, says Segal, Paul does make use of the Greek words *epistrepho* and *metanoia*, which normally imply conversion, but never to describe his own experience. Most likely this is because the terms signify *repentance* (which Paul found inappropriate to his own circumstances, according to Philippians 3:4–6), rather than that which Paul experienced, which was *transformation*.[312] Accordingly, Segal concludes that Paul's conversion involved "a radical change in a person's experience."[313] Experience, for him, is the key to understanding the event: "My purpose is to show that Paul's writing, thought, and theology are shaped by his personal, religious experience."[314]

If Paul's "conversion" is to be identified as (and understood in terms of) an "experience," why has the notion not received greater scholarly attention? Segal is probably right in suggesting that "scholarly reticence to ascribe spiritual experience to Paul may be rooted in theological embarrassment with

---

three versions is less significant than what the repetition tells us about Luke's perception of the event." Johnson, *The Acts of the Apostles*, 166.

309. Segal maintains a scholarly skepticism over the historicity of Acts—"Methodologically, we can be sure of Luke's portrayal of Paul only when Paul's own letters confirm them [sic]"—whilst still, in effect, accepting the account (or something very like it) in his analysis. Segal, *Paul the Convert*, 12. Elsewhere, though, he questions Luke's portrayal: "The account of Paul's ecstatic conversion in Acts is a product of Luke's literary genius." Segal, *Paul the Convert*, 35.

310. Ibid., 6, 21. Much of Segal's book deals with the concept of conversion, with particular reference to modern studies of the phenomenon, and even ends with a psychological study as an Appendix. For a radical dismantling of the core assumptions of conversion within the traditional Justification theory, see Campbell, *The Deliverance of God*, 125–65.

311. Segal, *Paul the Convert*, 3.

312. Ibid., 19–22.

313. Ibid., 6.

314. Ibid., 6.

the nonrational aspects of the human soul."[315] Paul is also a mystic, in Segal's view, so it is a combination of Paul's conversion experience and his mystical ascension that forms the basis of his theology.[316] Paul's "conversion" is not to be explained in intellectual categories alone, as the exchange of one set of religious facts and information for another: "Paul is not converted by Jesus' teachings, but rather by an experience, a revelation of Christ, which radically reorients his life."[317] None of this, of course, is to suggest that Paul abandoned his Pharisaic learning and traditions in favor of a theology derived solely or even primarily from ecstatic experience. Rather, as Segal says, "He was trying to understand the meaning of events in the way that any pious Jew of his day would have done: by consulting scripture and comparing it with his experience."[318] He did not suddenly receive a brand new systematic theology that simply dropped into his mind from heaven on the Damascus road. As John Gager points out, "Paul remained a Jew throughout his life; we should always read him within the context of traditional Jewish thought, not against it."[319]

Intriguingly, Segal observes that there is a vital connection *of some sort* between Paul's conversion experience of the risen Christ and his prior experience of Torah, albeit that the nature of that experience was in some way different too:

> [Paul] had to work out for himself what the conversion meant for his understanding of Torah. Perhaps something important in the law had to be transmuted, as Paul himself had been transformed by his conversion.[320]

Segal thus offers a tantalizing suggestion that Paul's conversion involved a transformed understanding of Torah—indeed, that some sort of transformation had taken place in Torah itself. Hence while we may agree with Segal that Paul's conversion experience was not paradigmatic of "becoming a Christian" in the sense traditionally understood in Evangelicalism, it opens up the possibility that it may be paradigmatic in another way.

---

315. Ibid., 12. A reticence that Paul would not appear to have shared; see e.g., his writings on spiritual gifts. It would not seem unreasonable to assume that his writings were influenced by both his personal experiences and his observations of the Spirit at work in his communities.

316. Ibid., 69.

317. Ibid., 3.

318. Ibid., 282–83.

319. Gager, *Reinventing Paul*, 46.

320. Segal, *Paul the Convert*, 205.

In due course, we shall make the proposal that this transmutation of Torah is precisely what happened in Christ—in whom the Word became flesh and dwelt among us (John 1:14). It had something to do with a transformed way in which Torah could be experienced.

2.7.5 R. Kendall Soulen

Our final contribution to this chapter comes from R. Kendall Soulen, who has been pivotal from the outset in framing this study theologically through his explicit highlighting of embedded supersessionism and theological anti-Judaism in the church's doctrinal formulations. As Soulen rightly observes, "the rejection of supersessionism is fraught with profound implications for the whole range of Christian theological reflection, and the full extent of these implications is still far from fully clear."[321] In a post-Holocaust world, Soulen proposes that

> The integrity of Christian theology after Christendom requires a renewed conversion of basic Christian forms of thought towards the God of Israel. Such a conversion is necessary, I argue, because Christian theology in its dominant classical and modern forms embodies what is in effect an incomplete conversion towards the living God, the God of Abraham, Isaac and Jacob.[322]

By an "incomplete conversion," Soulen has in mind that if the gospel about Jesus is credible only insofar as it is predicated of the God of Israel, then traditional forms of Christian thought must be brought into a further degree of congruence with that God. A key element of Soulen's presentation is calling into question the church's "standard canonical narrative"—meaning, how Christians have understood the theological and narrative unity of the Christian Bible as a whole. Canonical *narrative* is not the same thing as *canon*, though, as Soulen explains.

> A canonical narrative is to be clearly distinguished from the biblical canon itself. The biblical canon is the collection of texts that constitute the sacred writings of the church. In contrast, a canonical narrative is a framework for interpreting the biblical canon. Arising from the biblical canon, but not simply identical with it, a canonical narrative reflects a fundamental decision about how the Bible "hangs together" as a whole.[323]

---

321. Soulen, *God of Israel*, x.
322. Ibid.
323. Ibid., 13.

A canonical narrative is therefore the explanatory story that is drawn from the canon's materials. This is of particular relevance with regard to how the Old and New Testaments cohere in their telling of the story and come together in Jesus Christ. As the fruit of this bringing together, the canonical narrative establishes the hermeneutical foundation of Christian theology and doctrine.[324] Alternatively put, the canonical narrative weaves together the scriptural events and developments into a story that forms the Christian explanation of salvation-history. The church's standard canonical narrative, however, embodies structural supersessionism in the way that it construes (or, "structures") this narrative unity. In the *foreground*, says Soulen, are the perceived key events of creation, fall, Christ's incarnation, the inauguration of the church, and final consummation—what he calls the "four key episodes." What is noticeable here, though, is that God's engagement with the human story is being told in cosmic, universal terms: the Hebrew scriptures are almost completely omitted, save for Genesis 1–3. The God of Israel's history with the Israel of God recedes into the *background* of the story and "God's history with Israel plays a role that is ultimately indecisive for shaping the canonical narrative's overarching plot."[325] Soulen notes that this omission is reflected in virtually every historic confession of Christian faith from the creeds of Nicaea and Constantinople to the Augsburg Confession and beyond.[326] David Fox Sandmel makes the same observation: "Noticeably missing from this rehearsal of the Christian sacred story is any mention of what we Jews would consider the core of our history."[327] Effectively, therefore, this background can be completely omitted from the Christian account without disturbing the essential logic of salvation-history.

Since "supersessionism has shaped the narrative and doctrinal structure of classical Christian theology in fundamental and systematic ways," in Soulen's argument it follows that "the rejection of supersessionism entails the reevaluation of the whole body of classical Christian divinity."[328] This gives rise to profound implications for the integrity of Christian theology. As a prime example, the church's standard canonical narrative involves a *soteriological* foreshortening of Israel's scriptures, by which "the vast panorama of the Hebrew Scriptures is made to unfold within the basic antithesis of

---

324. Ibid., 14.
325. Ibid., 32.
326. Ibid.
327. Sandmel, "Israel, Judaism and Christianity," 165.

328. Soulen, *God of Israel*, xi, 3. Re-evaluation need not necessarily result in rejection of that classical Christian divinity, of course, but the point is that a rigorous process is called for.

Adam's sin and redemption in Christ."[329] Necessarily, this seriously impacts Christian perceptions of what the story is all about and its key theological features.

> This soteriological framework foreshortens the Hebrew Scriptures both thematically and temporally. Thematically, because the Scriptures are thought to relate a story whose fundamental presupposition is the catastrophe of sin and whose goal is therefore deliverance from the negative conditions of existence. This perspective obscures the possibility that the Hebrew Scriptures are not solely or even primarily concerned with the antithesis of sin and redemption but much rather with the God of Israel's passionate engagement with the mundane affairs of Israel and the nations.[330]

In what Soulen dubs the "standard model," Israel's involvement in the story effectively ceases with Christ. The vocation of the people Israel has reached its foreordained goal and comes to an end, a passing stage on the way to God's truly abiding commitment—to Christ and the community of salvation in its spiritual rather than fleshly form. Humanity is redeemed not so much *in* history as *from* history.[331]

> Taken as a whole, the standard model embodies a vision of Christian faith that seeks to reconcile the *affirmation* of the God of Israel's passionate and enduring engagement with creation with the *denial* of God's equally passionate and enduring engagement with the people Israel. The result is an evisceration of the God of Israel in Christian theology. When the question is put: is the God of Israel irrevocably bound to creation, Christians have traditionally answered with a resounding yes. But when the question is put: is the God of Israel irrevocably bound to the people Israel, Christians have equivocated.[332]

The upshot of this, says Soulen, is a Christian "vision of the God of Israel that is internally ordered to the disappearance of the Jewish people." Their history—whilst not denied—can be ignored as largely irrelevant for deciphering God's enduring purposes for creation as a whole. The Israel of the flesh can be by-passed in favor of an Israel of the spirit.[333]

---

329. Ibid., 53.
330. Ibid.
331. Ibid., 54–55.
332. Ibid., 55.
333. Ibid.

The presentation of this argument fills part one of Soulen's book, which in summary argues that Christianity's standard model of the story has rendered God's identity as the God of Israel practically irrelevant in shaping Christian theological conclusions about God's works in bringing about redemption and consummation in universal terms.

What then, for Soulen, would an alternative way of conceiving the narrative unity of the Christian Bible look like?—one that positively addresses the weaknesses inherent in the "standard model" vis-à-vis God's history with Israel? Part two offers Soulen's answer. It requires that "Christians should acknowledge that God's history with Israel and the nations is the permanent and enduring medium of God's work as the Consummator of human creation, and therefore it is also the permanent and enduring context of the gospel about Jesus."[334] This is in contrast to Christian thought that has collapsed the covenant with Israel into a universalized scheme in which Israel's place has been both subjugated and completed.

In the process of redeeming the story from supersessionism, therefore, we arrive at the idea of one story, in which Israel and the nations share a relationship of *both* distinction *and* mutual dependence—God's economy of mutual blessing between those who are and remain different:

> As attested by the Scriptures, God's work as Consummator engages the human family in a historically decisive way in God's election of Israel as a blessing to the nations. The resulting distinction and mutual dependence of Israel and the nations is the fundamental form of the economy of consumption through which God initiates, sustains, and ultimately fulfills the one human family's destiny for life with God. So conceived, God's economy of consummation is essentially constituted as *an economy of mutual blessing* between those who are and remain different.[335]

In referring to an "historically decisive" engagement, Soulen means one that does not simply peter out at the dawn of the Christian era. The fulfillment in universal terms is "ultimate," meaning still to come. God's plan as consummator of the human story is constituted around two groups—Israel and the nations—who have been, are now and will remain different. This serves, for Soulen, as an essential feature of the divine plan.

As can be seen, an important emphasis for Soulen is prioritizing God's work as consummator over above that of simply redeemer. Christian thought has tended to collapse the story into one that is primarily about dealing with

---

334. Ibid., 110.
335. Ibid., 111.

sin on a universal scale rather than the eschatological restoration of *shalom* to the entire created order in a reign of wholeness, righteousness, and peace. In other words, there is a greater divine goal than Christian thought has allowed for, one that includes redemption but does not stop at redemption.

What then is the precise role of Christ? For Soulen, *"the gospel is good news about the God of Israel's coming reign, which proclaims in Jesus' life, death, and resurrection the victorious guarantee of God's fidelity to the work of consummation."*[336] Jesus's life is therefore seen primarily through the lens of God's work as consummator rather than that of redeemer (redemption is present, but subordinated). Jesus's resurrection from the dead, meanwhile, proclaims the *guarantee* of God's eschatological reign; however, "Jesus himself is not that reign in its fullness," only the first-fruits (1 Cor 15:20).[337] Soulen argues that "Paul does not say that in Christ all of God's promises are fulfilled but rather that they are confirmed."[338] It is somewhat unclear whether, rather than Christ's work being *decisive* in soteriological terms, Soulen sees it as simply *anticipatory*. If so, he appears to be countenancing something that falls short of simply an "already, but not yet" eschatology of the kingdom.[339]

In Soulen's view, then, the God of Israel has made a decisive statement in Jesus—demonstrating his commitment(s) to Israel and the nations—in which the victory of Jesus's life, death and resurrection is offered up as a guarantee and reminder of what he will ultimately do for the whole world.

> Jesus's resurrection from the dead anticipates a future event whose character as victorious fidelity can no longer be in doubt. That event is God's intervention on behalf of all Israel in keeping with God's promises, such that God's final act of covenant faithfulness toward Israel redounds not only to the blessing of Israel but also to the blessing of the nations and all of creation [. . .]. It is certain not only that God will intervene on behalf of the whole body of Israel at the close of covenant history but also that by this very act God will consummate the world.[340]

In relation to the implications for Christianity and Judaism in the present day, Soulen suggests that Christians should not seek to proselytize

336. Ibid., 157, emphasis original.
337. Ibid., 165.
338. Ibid., 165.
339. In which the kingdom is ("already") inaugurated in Jesus's first coming but also still to come in all its fullness, in his future return ("not yet"). See e.g., George Eldon Ladd, *The Presence of the Future*.
340. Ibid., 166.

Jews to become Christians,[341] and he sees the nature of the church as "a table fellowship that is open to all persons *as* Jews and *as* Gentiles," in which difference is preserved rather than overcome; "The church's fundamental character is revealed in the fact that it is the place where Jews and Gentiles, with equal right, are together with one another."[342] However, this does raise questions as to (a) what this type of shared faith within the church would look like in practice and (b) the degree to which the person and/or role of Christ is thereby downgraded or subordinated within Jewish thought that continues to be centered on Torah (the christological weakness in the "two-track" way of thinking that we have previously noted).

Soulen grounds his view of the appropriate relationship between Jews and gentiles within the church upon his reading of the so-called Council of Jerusalem's decision (Acts 15:1-21; Gal 2:1-10):

> In back of this decision is the belief that what God has done in Jesus engages Jews as Jews and Gentiles as Gentiles. Hence obedience to Jesus is equally possible from either of two vantage points. It is possible from the vantage point of Jews, who continue to observe the Mosaic law in light of Jesus' messianic interpretation of the same. And it is possible from the vantage point of Gentiles, who, without first becoming Jews and hence without incurring obligation to the Torah, nevertheless live in obedience to Jesus as Gentiles.[343]

It is slightly unclear, in this fascinating passage, whether Soulen is proposing a nuanced variation on a two-track theory for Jews and gentiles, in which Jews and gentiles both engage with Christ, yet separately. What would "obedience to Jesus" look like, exactly—how would it differ—from each vantage point? For example, how would "Jesus' messianic interpretation" of the Mosaic law impact on Jewish practice of that law, compared to what would have been the case in the absence of Jesus? Alternatively, are Jews impacted at all by what obedience to Christ looks like from "the Gentile vantage point," and if so, how? And all of this still begs the question of how Christ's life, death and resurrection are efficacious for Jews.

Katherine Sonderegger questions whether it is right for Christianity to refashion its claims to finality and universality as the price of achieving Soulen's aims of repudiating supersessionism in all its forms and affirming the Pauline claim that "God has not abandoned his people." She argues

---

341. Ibid., 173.
342. Ibid., 173, 171, 169.
343. Ibid., 170-71.

that "a stronger case for such radical reshaping should be made,"³⁴⁴ and asks whether there is not a degree of anachronism here.

> We should not overlook, I believe, a form of supersessionism that Judaism and Christianity both share: as systems of thought and practice they supersede their biblical origins. Judaism has a complex relation to its biblical past, as does Christianity. Christianity can no more address Judaism, a system of Torah and Talmud, through discussion of biblical Israel, than can Judaism address Christianity, a system of Church and doctrine, through discussion of the Apostles.³⁴⁵

2.8 "Judaism" and "Christianity" in the First Century

Already we have had opportunity to see the inadequacy of the terms "Christianity" and "Judaism" to describe distinct religious categories prevailing in first-century Israel and it is now appropriate to look at this further. This is an important consideration, because it is extremely difficult for the contemporary reader to set aside her awareness of today's two fully-formed and distinct religions called "Christianity" and "Judaism" and to conceive that a different state of affairs could have pertained in the New Testament period (not least because Christians routinely use those terms when discussing it).³⁴⁶ The tendency is for what we know of today's Christianity, refined and defined by two thousand years of theological reflection and development, to be read-into what we find in the pages of the New Testament. As a result, its stories, characters, and theological statements are typically viewed through a grid of meaning that takes the theology of modern-day creedal Christianity as its points of reference.

At the popular level of Evangelicalism, it is generally taken for granted that two different religions were in evidence from the time of Christ onwards (or very shortly thereafter—certainly from the day of Pentecost), outworked in distinct entities called "the church" and "the synagogue"— churches for Christians practising their new religion of Christianity, alongside synagogues for Jews practising their old religion of Judaism.³⁴⁷ The text

---

344. Sonderegger, Review of *The God of Israel and Christian Theology*, 454–56.

345. Ibid., 455.

346. Equally, of course, the same reader is likely to assume that the nature of Judaism today corresponds to that of the New Testament era (which Jesus, Paul and their Christian contemporaries apparently judged and rejected).

347. To take an example from the popular domain, *The Word in Life Study Bible*, xv, summarizes the message of Galatians: "The transition from Judaism had been an

is assumed to be telling the story of the successful rise of the new and living faith launched by Jesus and the corresponding demise of the old, ineffectual religion of Judaism, and that this was generally obvious to the characters of the time. The statements, events, and dialogue recorded in the New Testament are assumed to reflect the same meaning, then, that they would bear now; what we know today about Christian doctrine is broadly what they knew.[348]

In this, of course, we remind ourselves of Thiselton's "two horizons" in hermeneutics—the horizon of the text and the horizon of the present—in the fusion of which is to be found meaning. To avoid crass anachronism in biblical interpretation, that two horizons exist must be recognized. In popular assumptions about "Christianity" *versus* "Judaism" in the New Testament period, however, the near-horizon of the present has superimposed itself.

A further problem is that today's Christian reader has a rather better understanding of her own religion than she has of Judaism—then, or now. Compounding the problem is that the principal source for what she thinks she *does* know about Judaism will be what she thinks she finds in the pages of the New Testament (which, as we know, is typically seen as an unflattering portrait). She is unaware of any alternative perspective on the nature of first-century Judaism beyond what, on a plain reading, those biblical texts seem to be telling her.[349] Evangelical Christians hold the veracity of "what the Bible says"—and, the reliability of a plain reading of it—in the highest regard, and the Bible appears to have much to say about the nature of Judaism. To seem to be challenging "what the Bible says," therefore, risks raising questions about one's Evangelical commitment to the Bible as the word of God.[350]

---

uneasy one for some early believers, resulting in attempts to 'add on' to the simple, pure gospel of Christ. But this letter urges believers to hold on to Christ alone so their faith and the church can grow."

348. One may say, "Does it matter?" in relation to what an uninformed reader may think. However, Joel Green makes the point (in relation to the widespread misunderstandings and caricatures generated by the penal substitutionary doctrine) that theologians must bear some responsibility for what is understood at the popular level and to correct serious errors. Green, "Must We Imagine," 160.

349. The New Perspective appears to have made limited inroads into popular Christianity's perceptions (perhaps because, as we have shown, scholars such as Wright who cross over into the popular domain remain supersessionist).

350. The conservative Reformed approach, for example, which tends to set the agenda within Evangelicalism, speaks of the "entire perfection," "infallible truth" and "divine authority thereof" (Westminster Confession, chapter 1). If, as is further claimed, "The whole counsel of God concerning all things necessary for His own glory, man's salvation, faith and life, is either expressly set down in Scripture, or by good and necessary consequence may be deduced from Scripture: unto which nothing at any

The consequences of these interpretive presuppositions are profound insofar as they form a hermeneutical lens or filter through which scripture is read and understood; the New Testament in particular.[351] Whether express or implied, the paradigm develops along the following lines:[352]

- Jesus was the first Christian. His arguments with the Jews arose in teaching the people the errors of Judaism and exposing the hypocrisy of Jewish religious leaders.[353] Those who accepted his message were set free into a new and living faith—open not just to Jewish exclusivists who sought to keep God for themselves, but to all.

- In the New Testament, therefore, Jesus is speaking from the perspective of Christianity into—and indeed, against—the prevailing religion of Judaism.

- Paul's perspective is, unsurprisingly, the same as that of Jesus, and forms the backdrop to his writings subsequent to coming to faith—i.e., being converted to Christianity from Judaism—on the Damascus road.

- Upon becoming a Christian, Paul repented of Jewish practices and thereafter opposed them in favor of a new life of faith, released from the petty ceremonialism of the law. In writing to the churches in Galatia, for example, he was promoting Christianity against Judaism, which was trying to steal the fledgling Christians' new-found freedom in Christ by burdening them with the self-same Jewish legalism from which Christ had come to set them free.

---

time is to be added, whether by new revelations of the Spirit, or traditions of men," then to suggest that the plain reading biblical portrait of "Judaism" and "the Jews" is either an incomplete or misleading picture may appear to be challenging that. What we are really saying, however, is that the biblical portrait of "Judaism" and "the Jews" has been subject to a mis-reading and hence, one needs to look to the very next statement in the Confession: "Nevertheless, we acknowledge the inward illumination of the Spirit of God to be necessary for the saving understanding of such things as are revealed in the Word." It is bringing the illumination of the Spirit to bear on precisely those things that *appear to be revealed* in the Word about "Judaism" and "the Jews" which concerns us and of course, given our context, "the saving understanding."

351. Somehow, the Old Testament escapes some of these problems and remains useful for examples and inspiration of Christian life and practice. That might not be the case, of course, if persons called Pharisees appeared in its pages.

352. We are both over-simplifying and exaggerating to make the point . . . though perhaps not as much as one might at first suppose!

353. Of course, not all "Jewish religious leaders," or all Jews for that matter, then or now, are presumed by our generic modern reader to be hypocrites, but a religious system based on pernickety law-keeping is often thought to tend naturally towards a prioritization of form over substance, and external compliance over internal piety.

- Human nature is to be legalistically religious, of which Judaism is a prime example; it features, as a recurring warning to us, in the pages of the New Testament. Legalism is completely antithetical to believing faith, and so too therefore is Judaism and its practices.
- The narratives in Acts contrast the early church inaugurated at Pentecost with the temple and synagogue, and contrast the first Christians with the disbelieving Jewish persecutors against whom they were striving for the sake of the gospel. The outpouring of the Spirit on the Christian communities in a new and unprecedented way affirms God's endorsement of Christianity over Judaism.

One has only to listen to a typical Bible study or Sunday sermon to be aware that this way of thinking more or less reflects the commonplace understanding within popular Evangelicalism. That it appears to correspond to the biblical text, on a plain reading, provides confirmation; or put another way, if one already knows this was the situation, it is easy to find that scripture confirms it.

Since the circumstances of first-century Israel are the critical context for this book, we must now spend some further time on it. If the New Testament is not the story of "Christianity *versus* Judaism"—two systems of religion, church versus synagogue, concurrently battling for the hearts and minds of the people—then how are we to understand what was happening in that period?

Jacob Neusner has drawn attention to "the theological error" within modern-day Judaism in making the same assumptions of Judaism that Christians tend to do in relation to Christianity: namely, "that there was, is, and can forever be only one Judaism, the orthodox one," and that this was the same Judaism that prevailed in first-century Palestine. The assumption that the Judaism of the first century is an exact representation of that which was to emerge in the Talmud of Babylonia some seven hundred years later is false, he argues. We cannot simply consult the later writings in which Judaism came to its full and complete expression to find out what Judaism ("the one, orthodox Judaism") was in the first century.[354] The names "Christianity" and "Judaism" themselves are both "utterly post facto."[355]

> Can we identify one Judaism in the first centuries B.C.E and C.E.?
> Only if we can treat as a single coherent statement everything all

---

354. Neusner, *Jews and Christians*, 21–22.

355. Ibid., 27. In the first century, "Judaism" is "a word that can stand for just about anything" and hence is to be distinguished from the later Judaism—drawing heavily upon the system and method of the Pharisees—that became normative. At the time, the Pharisees were but one group among first-century Judaisms, plural. Ibid., 3.

Jews wrote. That requires us to harmonize the Essene writings of the Dead Sea, Philo, the Mishnah, the variety of scriptures collected in our century as the apocrypha and pseudepigrapha of the Old Testament, not to mention the Gospels! [. . .] The writings attest to diverse religious systems, and in the setting of which we speak, to diverse Judaisms. There was no one orthodoxy, no Orthodox Judaism. There were various Judaisms.[356]

As Judith Lieu observes, though it is theologically less satisfying, it may be sociologically more persuasive to picture the first century situation as "a criss-crossing of muddy tracks."[357] Rowan Williams describes it as similarly unstructured when he speaks of a people "whose corporate life significantly involves some shared myths, texts and rituals, not necessarily consistent or systematized, but loosely intermeshed, sometimes in conflict."[358]

Given the diversity in the situation, choosing meaningful terminology for the collective whole (or the component parts) is therefore no easy task, not least because any proposed phrase brings with it its own challenges in meaning. For example, to speak instead of "Israelite religion" or "the ancient religion of Israel,"[359] simply raises questions such as what we mean by "Israel" and the potential anachronism of "a religion."[360] James McGrath observes that "this field is in desperate need of new terminology that can be used to speak of the beliefs people held in this period without reading back into the ancient world our modern concepts and assumptions."[361] However, even the concept of "beliefs" is problematic; Lieu has noted that at the time of Ignatius, in the late first century CE, "Judaism" indicated "not a belief system but a total pattern of practice and adherence."[362] Far from there being but one mode of thought in first-century Judaism, and perhaps surprisingly to our contemporary ways of thinking, it could tolerate "the widest varieties and even contradictions of beliefs."[363] As we have already seen in the work of Sanders and others, it is now well established that there were a

---

356. Neusner, *Jews and Christians*, 25–26.

357. Lieu, *Neither Jew Nor Greek?* 29.

358. Williams, *On Christian Theology*, 96.

359. We would need to take account of the history and development in "Yahwism" (from the Late Bronze Age/Iron Age onwards) preceding our first century context. On this, see Patrick Miller, *The Religion of Ancient Israel*.

360. As Williams puts it, "The very concept of a religion is anachronistic here—a unified system of beliefs and rituals with its own frame of reference over against other forms of thinking and behaving." *Christian Theology*, 96.

361. McGrath, *The Only True God*, 3.

362. Lieu, *Neither Jew*, 24.

363. Davies, *Torah in the Messianic Age and/or the Age to Come*, 53.

number of identifiable groups holding passionate yet somewhat divergent views on what constituted "authentic" Judaism—each group being one of the various "Judaisms," plural, of the period—while sharing what was basic common ground, in the sense of "agreed on among the parties, agreed on by the populace as a whole."[364] Sanders, we recall, thought of this as the "lowest common denominator" of these many types of Judaism (while choosing not to use that phrase).[365] It is precisely as one of the diverse streams recognizing themselves as Judaism, says Neusner, that we must classify "Christianity"—"The earliest Christians were Jews, who saw their religion, Judaism, as normative and authoritative."[366]

Neusner explains the process of development by which Israel's symbols and *praxis* were re-worked into Christianity and Judaism as we know them today.

> Christianity and Judaism each took over the inherited symbolic structure of Israel's religion. Each, in fact, did work with the same categories as the other. But in the hands of each, the available and encompassing classification-system found wholly new meaning. The upshot was two religions out of one, each speaking within precisely the same categories but so radically redefining the substance of these categories that conversation with the other became impossible.[367]

The categories within which the piety of the people was defined—namely, priest, scribe, and messiah—were carried forward in different approaches: both Christians and Pharisees radically revised the principal existing categories of the inherited Israelite religion and culture.[368] In expounding the categories more fully,[369] Neusner explains that the organization of Jewish society and the interpretation of its history were founded on three symbols: "temple altar," "sacred scroll," and "victory wreath for the head of the King-Messiah":

> Ancient Israel's heritage yielded the cult with its priests, the Torah with its scribes and teachers, and the prophetic and apocalyptic hope for meaning in history and an eschaton mediated by messiahs and generals. From these derive Temple, school

---

364. Ibid. 11–12.
365. Sanders, "Comparing," 37n39.
366. Neusner, *Jews and Christians*, 27–28.
367. Ibid., 5.
368. Ibid., 6.
369. The expansion that follows is drawn from Ibid., 1–15, with only the lengthier citations specifically footnoted.

and (in the apocalyptic expectation) battlefield on earth and in heaven.[370]

The generative symbols of each respective mode—the sacrificial altar, the scroll of scripture and Israel's messianic freedom—framed the ways in which people understood their world. Each focused on a particular aspect of national existence:

- For the priest, Israel's history was an account of what happened in (and on occasions to) the Temple.
- For the scribe, or sage, the life of society required wise guidance in how to live by the revealed laws of Torah, as interpreted by the scribes. Thus, they saw "the sage, the master of the rules" standing at society's head.
- The Messiah's kingship, meanwhile, "would resolve the issue of Israel's subordinate relationship to other nations and empires, establishing once and for all the desirable, correct context for priest and sage alike."[371] In the first century, in particular, "we come to a turning point in the messianic hope"—an "intense, vivid, prevailing expectation among some groups that the Messiah was coming soon."[372]

Interestingly, the messianic framework carried within it a perspective on the world beyond Israel—for which, Neusner argues, priest and sage cared not at all:

> The priest perceived the Temple as the center of the world: beyond it he saw in widening circles the less holy, then the unholy, and further still, the unclean. All lands outside the Land of Israel were unclean with corpse uncleanness; all other peoples were unclean. Accordingly, in the world, life abided within Israel; and in Israel, within the Temple. [. . .] From such a perspective, no teaching about Israel among the nations, no interest in the history of Israel and its meaning, was apt to emerge.[373]

This symbolic system of temple cult, Torah, and Messiah demanded choices. The particular way in which symbols were arranged, rearranged, and bonded—the relative importance of each and their proper interpretation and application—became definitive to a Judaism (i.e., to what really mattered

370. Ibid., 6.
371. Ibid., 8.
372. Ibid., 10.
373. Ibid., 8.

within what a particular group considered to be authentic Judaism).[374] The various sects were all reflecting the different aspects of Israel's piety in their own way, even though (at the same time) "all stood together with the Jewish people along the same continuum of faith and culture":

> Each expressed in a particular and intense way one mode of the piety that the people as a whole understood and shared. That is why we can move from the particular to the general in our description of the common faith in first-century Israel. That common faith, we hardly need argue, distinguished Israel from all other peoples of the age, whatever the measure of "hellenization" in the country's life.[375]

Neusner, then, offers evidence that supports Sanders's notion of "common Judaism"—in Neusner's phrase, the "common faith" of the people in general—within which multiple sectarian groups were nonetheless to be found vying for what really constituted "Judaism." These groups included the holiness sects such as Pharisees and Essenes, professions such as the scribes, the radical nationalist Zealots, and the followers of messiahs, not least the Jesus-followers.[376] Each was experiencing and understanding events within the same symbolic framework, yet ascribing different weight and interpretive meaning to each of its modes. Each was a "Judaism" within the framework of belief of Israelite religion. Each believed themselves to be living out authentic Judaism.

Luke Timothy Johnson suggests we can define Judaism in the first century as "an adherence to certain central symbols such as Torah and Temple"; but even then, "the most cursory review of the extant literature reveals that these symbols in particular were open for debate"—"the messianist claims about the way to read Torah and the proper understanding of God's Temple

---

374. Neusner sees the history of the piety of Judaism as being a story of successive rearrangements and revisioning of symbols. Ibid., 14.

375. Ibid., 13.

376. Paul never uses the term "Christianity" in any form, which leads Gager to ask, "is it too much to insist that since he failed to use the term he may not have had any notion of a new religion which the term Christianity implies?" Gager, *Reinventing Paul*, 23. According to Acts, the early Jesus-following movement was first known as "the Way" or "this Way" (Acts 9:2; 22:4; etc.), meaning, no doubt, the/this way of conceiving and living out authentic Judaism, which would explain the pre-Damascene Saul's opposition to it. After all, if Judaism was uninvolved, why would that trouble him? Ben Witherington believes these references show that at the time Luke writes ("the 70s or early 80s") "the Jews" are distinguishable from "the Way" (i.e., Christianity). However, this seems to be overreaching—a self-description of "the Way" was concurrently in use by the Qumran sect. Ben Witherington III, *The Acts of the Apostles*, 322, 316. See I. H. Marshall, *Acts*, 169.

represented only one more voice among many loud and clamoring ones in that period."[377]

Judaism as we know it today is largely the product of "the winners" after 70 CE—or perhaps one should say, the survivors—namely the Pharisees,[378] and in fact, of one stream within Pharisaism, that of Rabbi Johanan ben Zakkai.[379] With the destruction of the temple by the Roman legions, the role of the priests and their claims to community leadership effectively ceased. The inability to practice temple sacrifices led to the place of the priestly cult being subsumed by a focus on the inner person through prayer and the study of Torah.[380] This was consistent with scriptures such as "the sacrifices of God are a broken spirit; a broken and contrite heart, O God, you will not despise" (Ps 51:17) and prophecies that, in the new era, all would be priests of the Lord, in a nation of priests.[381] This development left the Pharisees particularly well-positioned to represent the natural successors of the religion of ancient Israel:

> The Pharisees were a sect which had developed a peculiar perception of how to live and interpret life: they acted in their homes as if they were priests in the Temple. Theirs was an "as if" way. They lived "as if" they were priests, "as if" they had to obey at home the laws that applied to the Temple. When the Temple was destroyed in 70 CE, the Pharisees were prepared. They continued to live "as if" there were a new Temple composed of the Jewish people.[382]

Clearly, the implications are already profound for how, in a first-century context, we think of and speak of nascent "Christianity" since it was, from its adherents' perspective, simply "authentic Judaism." If this seems surprising to the modern reader, particularly given Christianity's longstanding focus on correct *versus* heretical beliefs, we must remember that Judaism at this time never possessed the institutional basis for determining "orthodoxy," as we would now call it. The temple was the central authority against which

---

377. L. T. Johnson, "The New Testament's Anti-Jewish Slander," 427.

378. On the development of Pharisaism, see e.g., Rifkin, "Pharisaism and the Crisis of the Individual in the Greco-Roman World." Interestingly, Rifkin sees Christianity as emerging from Pharisaism.

379. Davies, *Messianic Age*, 53.

380. "After 70 CE, study of Torah and obedience to it became a temporary substitute for the Temple and its sacrifice" (Neusner, *Jews and Christians*, 14).

381. Isa 61:6; Exod 19:6.

382. Neusner, *Jews and Christians*, 12. We see this same theme of the temple being the people of God reflected, of course, in the NT, e.g., 1 Cor 3:16–17; Eph 2:21.

the sects defined themselves, but the high priests lacked sufficient power to be able to state which forms of Judaism were "orthodox"—assuming they even thought in those categories—or to exclude from the temple those Jews whose practices they condemned.[383] What might, from later Judaism's perspective, seem obvious "heresies" in Christian beliefs would therefore have been far less obvious at the time. A similar observation can be made about the emerging "Christian" faith: for at least the first fifty years of its existence, there was no one thing that could be called "Christianity" as a standard by which to measure deviance: "The mission was not centrally controlled with respect either to structure or to ideology."[384]

The religions that we now know as "Christianity" and "Judaism" were therefore unknown as such in the first century context. Each developed as a new mode of defining Jewish piety, while remaining true in its own terms to the inherited categories of the religion of Israel within which that piety was defined. Each took over the established classifications—priest, scribe, and Messiah—but infused them with new meaning. "Though in categories nothing changed, in substance nothing remained what it had been."[385] As Neusner puts it, "Judaism and Christianity as they would live together in the West met for the first time in the fourth century."[386]

Now of course, not all Jews were part of one or other of the sectarian groups. The majority comprised the "common people," the *am ha-aretz* (or, people of the land). Much of Jesus's ministry appears to have been conducted amongst them—"the poor"—and a good deal of his clashes with scribes and Pharisees seem to have been to do with the right attitude to take toward them. This, in turn, was largely dependent on where one saw them standing, as regards righteousness or unrighteousness, in the sight of God.

> Most Jews were not members of any sect. They observed the Sabbath and the holidays, heard the scriptural lessons in synagogue on Sabbath, abstained from forbidden foods, purified themselves before entering the temple precincts, circumcised

---

383. Cohen, *From the Maccabees to the Mishnah*, 136. The rabbis were never united enough to elect a "pope," and nor did they convene synods. Rabbinic literature "lacks the coherent self-definition so abundantly attested in the Christian literature of the fourth century."

384. "It was "a loose network of assemblies on the fringe of synagogues and in lecture halls down the street, whose boundaries of self-definition were vigorously debated." L. T. Johnson, "Anti-Jewish Slander," 423–24.

385. Neusner, *Jews and Christians*, 13.

386. Neusner, *Judaism and Christianity in the Age of Constantine*, ix. "Judaism as we have known it was born in the matrix of triumphant Christianity as the West would define that faith."

their sons on the eighth day, and adhered to the "ethical norms" of folk piety. Whatever they may have thought of the priests and the temple, they went on pilgrimage to the temple a few times a year and probably relied on the priesthood to propitiate the deity through a constant and well-maintained sacrificial cult.[387]

Hence, whilst they did what they could to practice "common Judaism," the main preoccupation of the *am ha-aretz* was most probably pure survival—bearing in mind that up to 90% of the population of first-century Palestine lived in poverty—and staying out of trouble. The principal religious sects tended to be found in urban rather than rural areas, Jerusalem in particular, and "the people of the land" would scarcely have had the opportunity, let alone the time or energy, to join in such a luxury pastime. The Gospels portray Jesus as having a particular affinity for the poor, as being "on their side" (and hence, that God was "on their side"), in contrast to a harsher stance on the part of his religious contemporaries.

2.9 The Parting of the Ways

At what point, then, can it be said that "everything changed" and an identifiable "Christianity" becomes separate and distinct from an identifiable "Judaism"? When did the "parting of the ways" come about and in particular, did it occur during the period during which the New Testament was written?[388] This has particular relevance in relation to how we read the NT on the subjects that concern us here.

Today, of course, belief in the divinity of Jesus is central to Christianity and one might expect that belief, in particular, to have separated it from the rest of "Judaism," on the grounds of "heresy," very early on. The NT witness to that divinity has amongst other things been taken to imply an early dating of the divide. However, the recent work of Daniel Boyarin, *Border Lines: The Partition of Judeo-Christianity*, sheds considerable light on these questions.[389] Of particular interest is the material in Part II, "The Crucifixion of the Logos: How Logos Theology Became Christian."[390]

---

387. Cohen, *From the Maccabees*, 172.

388. Generally reckoned as having a span of composition between 50 CE and 100+ CE, with an outer boundary of around 140–50 CE. However, John Robinson has persuasively argued for an early dating. Robinson, *Redating the New Testament*.

389. Boyarin, *Border Lines*. See also, Becker and Reed, *The Ways That Never Parted*.

390. After its Preface and Introduction, Part I considers second and third-century texts, such as Justin Martyr and early rabbinic writings, and attempts to demonstrate how they engaged in creating a difference between Judaism and Christianity, a process

Like Neusner, Boyarin "refuses the option of seeing Christian and Jew, Christianity and Judaism, as fully formed, bounded, and separate entities and identities in late antiquity."[391] He argues that the demarcation was generated sometime in the second century through the idea of "orthodoxy," involving a group of Christian writers called "heresiologists" and their Jewish counterparts, the Rabbis. Early Christian heresiology was "largely the work of those who wished to eradicate the fuzziness of the borders [. . .] and thus produce Judaism and Christianity as fully separate (and opposed) entities."[392]

Rather than coming about as a natural-sounding "parting of the ways," Boyarin demonstrates that the border between Christianity and Judaism was "an imposed *partitioning* of what was once a territory without border lines"; hence, the border was "constructed," "imposed," "artificial" and "political."[393]

Interestingly, Boyarin does not find this partitioning to be an exclusively Jewish *or* Christian enterprise. The redistribution of modes of identity was "the net result of [a] virtual conspiracy between Christian and Jewish would-be orthodoxies."[394] What occurred was two parallel heresiological projects, mutually convenient to their practitioners, forming "a perfect mirror in which the Rabbis construct (as it were) Christianity, while the Christian writers [. . .] construct (as it were) Judaism."[395] By the end of the process, which did not conclude until the fourth century, "Judaism and Christianity had been more or less definitively divided on theological grounds."[396] However,

> In the earliest stages of their development—indeed I suggest until the end of the fourth century [. . .]—Judaism and Christianity were *phenomenologically indistinguishable* as entities, not

---

"intimately connected with and implicated in the invention of the notion of heresy during these centuries" (27–28). Part III looks at what happens in the "two new entities thus formed (especially in Judaism)" (32) following the consolidation of Orthodox Christian theology in the fourth and fifth centuries. By "crucifying the Logos" Boyarin is referring to the Rabbis' giving it up to the Christians—i.e., ceding to Christianity traditional Jewish Logos theology—"in an interesting kind of complicity" with Christian heresiologists "who regard belief in the Logos as the very touchstone of Christian orthodoxy" (31).

391. Boyarin, *Border Lines*, 7.

392. Ibid., 2. Skarsaune, however, believes Boyarin has overstated the case. *Shadow of the Temple*, 260n1.

393. Boyarin, *Border Lines*, 1, emphasis original. The concern of Boyarin's book, in large part, is how and why that border was written and who wrote it.

394. Ibid., 32.

395. Ibid., 31.

396. Ibid., 32.

merely in the conventionally accepted sense, that Christianity was a Judaism, but also in the sense that differences that were in the fullness of time to constitute the very basis for the distinction between the "two religions" ran *through* and not *between* the nascent groups of Jesus-following Jews and Jews who did not follow Jesus.[397]

Accordingly, Boyarin situates the separation far later than would usually be assumed. This lack of early distinction has profound ramifications for New Testament hermeneutics, he argues, since much traditional Christian dogma has been founded on the supposition that the two "religions" were separate and distinct from a very early date situated well within the first century.[398] Bruce Chilton and Jacob Neusner identify some of the implications:

> The superiority that is alleged for this Christianity against Judaism then derives from the flaws imputed to the old religion. Since the (single, uniform) new religion so markedly transcended the (single, uniform) old religion, we explain the advent of the new by appeal to the inferior qualities of the old; and, in the nature of things, a complex and diverse set of religious systems, all of them passing among their faithful for Judaism, hardly serves the requirement of argument in such a context.[399]

If we do not have a single, uniform Judaism in the first century against which something called Christianity was railing, then some significant reformulation of traditional Christian thought may be required.

At this point, Boyarin's perspective on the treatment of God's Logos is worthy of some extended consideration,[400] since he uses "Logos theology" as "a general term for various closely related binitarian theologies."[401] Hence it also sheds light on the supposed early "heresy" of the incarnation. His findings may be summarized thus:

[397]. Ibid., 89, emphases added. The process by which these differences *within* became reconstituted as differences *between* is a key concern of the book.

[398]. H. L. Ellison, for example: "By AD 90, the rabbinic leaders felt strong enough to exclude those they considered heretics (the *mînîm*), including Hebrew Christians, from the synagogue." "Judaism," in *Wycliffe Dictionary of Theology*, 300.

[399]. Chilton and Neusner, *Judaism in the New Testament*, 21. The title consciously mimics Sanders's work, which they criticize for fabricating a "single common-denominator Judaism" (10-11).

[400]. For his core discussion of Logos theology and related subjects, see *Border Lines*, 90-147. On the Logos, see Tobin, "Logos," in John Collins and Daniel Harlow (eds.), *The Eerdmans Dictionary of Early Judaism*, 894-96.

[401]. Boyarin, *Border Lines*, 126. See also Hurtado, "Mediator Figures" and *Lord Jesus Christ*.

Part A: Belief in (or rejection of) the concept of God's Logos was a distinction that once did not divide followers of Jesus from Jews who were not;

Part B: Originally, the doctrine was shared, "but finally became central to opposing self-definitions on either side."[402] It was eventually chosen as the most significant of indicia—"the touchstone of orthodoxy"[403]—for both Christian and Jewish separate religious identity; at which point, Jews who continued to believe in the Logos (or Christians who denied it) were categorized as heretics by their respective legislative bodies;

Part C: However, groups congealed into Christianity and Judaism only gradually; not until the mobilization of temporal power in the fourth century can this process be said to have formed "religions."[404]

Boyarin's evidence shows that belief in "two powers in heaven" or "Logos theology" was a vital form of Judaism and that some Jews—perhaps even most Jews—resisted efforts by heresiologists on both sides to appropriate the Logos exclusively for Christianity. "For those Jews, even in Palestine, the Logos (named *memra* "word" in their spoken Aramaic) remained a pivotally important theological being."[405] Boyarin describes the Logos as an ancient Jewish doctrine; indeed, there is significant evidence that in the first century many—perhaps most—Jews held a binitarian doctrine of God.[406]

> Thus, the theology of Two Powers in Heaven [. . .] was once, at least, an acceptable theological current within the circles from which the Rabbis and their theologies grew, but was offered up, as it were, in the dual production of rabbinic Judaism as Judaism and patristic Christianity as Christianity.[407]

---

402. Boyarin, *Border Lines*, 90.

403. Ibid., 89.

404. Ibid., 21. In proposing that Judaism and Christianity were not separate entities "until very late in late antiquity," Boyarin does not claim "that it is impossible to discern separate social groups that are, in an important sense, Christian/not-Jewish or Jewish/not-Christian from fairly early on" (by which he means the mid-second century). To illustrate the "fuzziness" of the categories, though, Boyarin cites Jerome's observation that the sect of the Nazoreans are to be found "in all of the synagogues of the East among the Jews" and that they consider themselves both Christians and Jews but are really "neither Christians nor Jews." Accordingly, Boyarin suggests "that *Jew* and *Christian* are both categories with gradation of membership" (25). See also, Johnson, "Anti-Jewish Slander," 427: "The messianist claims about the way to read Torah and the proper understanding of God's Temple represented only one more voice among many loud and clamoring ones in that period."

405. Boyarin, *Border Lines*, 89.

406. Ibid., 131.

407. Ibid., 145.

Boyarin provides considerable support for the idea that a binitarian doctrine of God was widespread in Jewish religious tradition: "the beginning of trinitarian reflection was in pre-Christian Jewish accounts of the second and visible God, variously, the Logos (*Memra*),[408] Wisdom, or even perhaps the Son of God."[409] He cites other biblical references to the notion of a "second and independent divine agent": the Exodus angel; the two descriptions of the Son of Man and the Ancient of Days in Daniel (a "Father-person" and a "son-person"); the identification of the Son of Man with the Messiah; and, Metatron/Enoch—1 Enoch 71.[410] Equally, the Logos is the linchpin of the religious thought of Philo, who was "clearly writing for an audience of Jews devoted to the Bible"; it is thus apparent that for at least "one branch of pre-Christian Judaism" there was nothing strange about a doctrine of a *deuteros theos*, a "second God" and "nothing in that doctrine that precluded monotheism." In fact, "it can hardly be doubted that, for Philo, the Logos is both a part of God and a separate being, the Word that God created in the beginning in order to create everything else, the Word that both is God, therefore, and is with God."[411] Echoes here of the Johannine Prologue are striking; indeed, the Johannine Prologue is "a continuation of "Jewish" interpretation, no more, no less."[412]

> The earliest Christian groups (including, or even specifically, the Johannine one) distinguished themselves from non-Christian Jews not theologically, but only in their association of various Jewish theologoumena and mythologoumena with this particular Jew, Jesus of Nazareth. The characteristic move that constructs what will become orthodox Christianity is, I think, the combination of Jewish messianic soteriology with equally Jewish Logos theology in the figure of Jesus.[413]

The Christian application of Logos theology to the person of Jesus stands in contrast with the efforts of the Rabbis "to transfer all Logos and Sophia talk to the Torah alone"—thus, in Johannine terms, "if for John the

---

408. Memra is "the leading candidate for the Semitic Logos" as it appears in "synagogal, pararabbinical Aramaic translations of the Bible, in textual contexts that are frequently identical to ones where the Logos hermeneutic has its home among Jews who speak Greek." Ibid., 116. "The strongest reading of the Memra is that it is not a mere name, but an actual divine entity, or mediator." (117).

409. Ibid., 113.

410. Ibid., 134, 135, and 136, 141.

411. Ibid., 114.

412. Ibid., 107.

413. Ibid., 105.

Logos Incarnate in Jesus replaces the Logos revealed in the Book, for the Rabbis the Logos Incarnate in the Book displaces the Logos that subsists anywhere else *but* in the Book."[414]

We find evidence of a first-century Jewish perspective on the incarnation of the Logos that is potentially harmonious with Christianity in Boyarin's recounting of the tradition of Wisdom's attempts to enter the world: the Johannine Prologue, he suggests, presents a clear account of the pre-existent Jewish Logos upon which the Fourth Gospel is founded and the reason for the incarnation on a theological level.[415] John 1 offers a specifically Johannine midrash on the story of Wisdom's failure to be comprehended in the world and frustrated attempts to enter the world as the *Logos Asarkos* (i.e., without flesh) prior to the incarnation.[416] The second of those attempts comprises the giving of the Torah to Israel and the failure of that instrument as a means of bringing the Logos into the world, because Israel did not understand. His own people received him not, though some, such as Abraham, did and are called "children of God" (John 1:12). This reading "provides a retort" to the interpretation of the Wisdom myth in Ben Sira 24, where Wisdom finally finds a home in Israel in the form of the Torah.[417] Instead, "God performed the extraordinary act of incarnating the Logos in flesh and blood, coming into the world as an avatar and teacher of the Word, not the words."[418] Jesus comes to fulfill the mission of Moses, not to displace it—the Torah simply needed a better exegete: the *Logos Ensarkos* (i.e., made flesh). God first tried the text, then sent his voice, incarnated in the voice of Jesus: when the incarnate Logos speaks, he speaks Torah.[419]

Richard Bauckham arrives at similar conclusions to Boyarin, albeit through a somewhat different route. He argues, firstly, that efforts to find a model for christology in semi-divine intermediary figures in early Judaism, such as principal angels and exalted patriarchs, are largely mistaken.[420] Nonetheless, there is a "second category" of intermediary figures consisting of "personifications or hypostatizations of aspects of God himself, such as his Spirit, his Word and his Wisdom."[421] Bauckham argues that the Jewish

---

414. Ibid., 129.

415. Ibid., 100–107.

416. Note in this reading that the incarnation itself is not narrated until verse 14.

417. Cf. 1 Enoch 42:1–2, where Wisdom is driven back to heaven, having found no place on earth she could dwell.

418. Ibid., 104.

419. Ibid., 104.

420. Bauckham, *God Crucified*, vii.

421. Ibid., 17.

literature unequivocally includes these figures in the unique identity of God (thus remaining resolutely within Jewish monotheism).

> In general, the personifications of God's Word and God's Wisdom in the literature are not parallel to the depictions of exalted angels as God's servants. The personifications have been developed precisely out of the ideas of God's own Wisdom and God's own Word, that is, aspects of God's own identity. In a variety of ways they *express* God, his mind and his will, in relation to the world. They are not created beings, but nor are they semi-divine entities occupying some ambiguous status between the one God and the rest of reality. They belong to the unique divine identity.[422]

The concept of "divine identity" here is critical, and so too in christology. In relation to Jesus, Bauckham argues we should be thinking in terms of divine identity rather than divine essence or nature, which are not the primary categories for Jewish theology.[423] The continuity between Jewish monotheism and New Testament christology is not to be found in intermediary figures, but "by identifying Jesus directly with the one God of Israel, including Jesus in the unique identity of this one God."[424]

> While this was a radically novel development, almost unprecedented in Jewish theology, the character of Jewish monotheism was such that this development did not require any repudiation of the ways in which Jewish monotheism understood the uniqueness of God. [. . .] What the New Testament texts in general do is take up the well-known Jewish monotheistic ways of distinguishing the one God from all other reality and use these precisely as ways of including Jesus in the unique identity of the one God as commonly understood in Second Temple Judaism.[425]

Similarly to Bauckham, Larry Hurtado affirms a strict monotheism for first-century Jewish devotional practices, wherein refusal to worship divine personifications (*versus* simple reverence) is the critical distinction. It was "the incorporation of Christ into the devotional pattern of early Christian groups [that had] no real analogy in the Jewish traditions of that period."[426]

---

422. Ibid., 21.
423. Ibid., x.
424. Ibid., 4.
425. Ibid., 4.
426. Hurtado, *Lord Jesus Christ*, 31.

> The Jewish resistance to worshiping any figure but the one God of Israel was manifested not only against the deities of other peoples and traditions but also with reference to figures that we might term "divine agents" of the God of Israel. [...] The refusal to give worship to any other extended to members of the "home team" too.[427]

The question of Jewish monotheism and Christian claims for the divinity of Christ has, of course, always been a core issue. Boyarin's argument in *Border Lines* for a late divergence between Christianity and Judaism is in part a response to Alan Segal's claim,[428] that the "two powers" heresy was "a very early category of heresy, earlier than Jesus"[429] that provides the background context for the writings of the New Testament and "must certainly refer to Christian beliefs, among others."[430] Segal maintains that a clear orthodoxy had emerged in first-century Judaism, within which Christian thought concerning the person of Jesus was already condemned as heretical. The main conceptual difficulty, however, with this proposal—that Segal himself admits—is that "the very category of heresy did not exist in Judaism before the rabbinic formulation," which must therefore date it far later.[431] Hence, rather than a category of heresy, "two powers" must have been one of the options for Jewish belief at the time.[432]

Other scholars reach similar conclusions to Boyarin on this point. James McGrath, for example, affirms that the textual evidence "makes it reasonable to date the origins of the two powers heresy to the end of the second century at the very earliest, and more likely the first half of the third."[433] There are no references within rabbinic literature linking the two powers debate with any of the first-century rabbis.[434] In fact, the material

---

427. Ibid., 31. Hurtado's main point is that it was the inclusion of Christ into exclusively monotheistic *Jewish devotional practices* that was the "most unusual and significant step that cannot be easily accounted for on the basis of any tendencies in Roman-era Jewish religion."

428. In particular, Segal, *Two Powers*. See e.g., Boyarin, *Border Lines*, 130–31, 136–37, 140–42, 43–45.

429. Boyarin, *Border Lines*, 131, and Segal, *Two Powers*, ix.

430. Segal, *Paul the Convert*, 274.

431. Segal, *Two Powers*, 5–6. Whilst generously describing Segal's work as "an otherwise excellent book," Boyarin also asserts that Segal "consistently confounds his own project and mislays, as it were, his best insights"! *Border Lines*, 298n20.

432. Ibid., 131.

433. McGrath, *Only True God*, 93. For a useful short summary and critique of Segal's position, see 81–96.

434. Ibid., 84.

"gives no support for dating the origins of the controversy even to the second century."^435 Any suggestion that it was already underway in the second century, he argues, must remain at best hypothetical. McGrath accepts, of course, that an absence of evidence is not evidence of its absence, but "in view of the clear polemic against two powers in later writings, the complete absence of such polemic in earlier writings at least strongly suggests that two powers only became an issue, for whatever reason, in the period after these documents were put in their present form."[436]

> In the first century at least, monotheism was felt to be compatible with the idea of a divine agent or viceroy who represented God and acted on his behalf. This does not appear to have entirely ceased to be the case even later on. [...] The idea that there was such a principal agent of God does not appear to have been an issue in and of itself even in this later period [second-third century CE]; rather, it was *some specific aspect of the content of the belief* that was in dispute.[437]

Only when Gnosticism brought issues relating to monotheism into focus in the third century were there "the beginnings of polemic against exalted mediator figures"—until this time, "the widespread ideas regarding personified divine attributes and other mediator figures" had been "an acceptable part of Judeo-Christian monotheism."[438]

It is interesting also to note McGrath's proposal that it was the identified need of later Christian theologians to draw a clear dividing line (not previously drawn) between God and creation as part of the development of the doctrine of "creation out of nothing," which necessitated it fall "on one side or the other of the Logos." Hence, Arius and other non-Nicenes drew the line between God and the Logos, whereas Athanasius and the Nicenes drew the line between the Logos and the creation.[439]

2.10 Jesus and "the Jews"

With the benefit of this background we can now move on to interrogate the Gospels' apparently strident critique of "the Jews" and Jesus's vehement condemnation of scribes, Pharisees and their practices. The explanation as to

---

435. Ibid., 93.
436. Ibid., 90.
437. Ibid., emphasis original.
438. Ibid., 92.
439. Ibid., 92, 69.

what is going on in these exchanges is to be derived from the multi-faceted backdrop we have already established, namely:

- Multiple, competing, sectarian views as to what constituted "Judaism" (in which, "Christianity" itself was "a Judaism"), within which there was a vacuum of authority on "orthodoxy";
- Continuing intra-Jewish debate as to the interpretation and weighting of the Israelite religion's key symbols and *praxis*;
- The common people as a target audience—and perhaps in some cases, as a target[440]—for the sectarians.

Jesus's clashes with scribes and Pharisees generally concerned what it meant to "live Jewishly," consistent with the Israelite tradition, in a manner pleasing to God in day-to-day *praxis*. Their debates are often reported as taking place in the open hearing of, and/or to have been specifically directed to, an audience of the common people. The major points under discussion are purity laws, Sabbath observance, the significance of the temple *cultus*, table-fellowship, and interpretations of Torah in and for the present socio-political conditions, enmeshed with the overarching question of the appropriate conception of the nature and character of God and what is of greater and lesser importance in his relationship to his people. We see instances in, for example, Jesus taking a position on Pharisaic ritual purity (Mark 7); on what is appropriate and inappropriate to do on the Sabbath (Mark 1 & 2); on the role of the temple, seen primarily or exclusively as a house of prayer (rather than sacrifice, Mark 11); on table-fellowship (Mark 2); and, in endorsing Torah's validity whilst at the same time offering his own radical interpretations (Matt 5:17–19).

It should not be supposed that each sect had already fully-formed internal uniformity on these subjects and that no intra-sect debate took place. If, for example, the houses of Hillel and Shammai were wings or factions of the Pharisees (or, at a minimum, if their well-attested disagreements are typical of the prevailing environment)[441] then similarly strident internal debates within variegated streams of Pharisaism are only to be expected. Accordingly, we should allow for the possibility, not least because most of Jesus's recorded debates appear to have taken place with Pharisees rather than

---

440. With Israel's woes wholly or partially attributed to the common people's sinfulness.

441. As Cohen observes, "if the House of Shammai says 'impure' or 'forbidden,' the house of Hillel can be counted on to say 'pure' or 'permitted'" (*From the Maccabees*, 157).

other factions,[442] that Jesus himself may have been a Pharisee (as, of course, was Paul), or that he was at least debating primarily within the movement of Pharisaism.[443] David Flusser has expressed the view that most of Jesus's debates with Pharisees were intra-Pharisaic debates, in which the position taken by Jesus can be shown to square with known Pharisaic positions on the same issues.[444] Flusser concludes that "It would not be wrong to describe Jesus as a Pharisee in the *broad* sense," notwithstanding that he did not identify himself as one, as such; moreover, Flusser argues, the tension between Jesus and the Pharisees "never implied negation, nor were the views of Jesus and the Pharisees contrary or ever degenerated into enmity."[445]

> Most difficult is the task of describing in a precise way his relationship with the Pharisees. With no one else did he discuss more intensely; that in itself may be an indication of closeness: *you debate most vehemently with those closest to you.*[446]

Catholic theologians note the same point: "If Jesus shows himself severe towards the Pharisees, it is because he is closer to them than to other contemporary Jewish groups."[447] They note also that criticisms of various types of Pharisees are also not lacking in rabbinical sources.

In relation to this vehement debate, the rhetoric of the New Testament has to be considered within its social context and with due regard to the polemic conventions of the day. As Johnson points out, the way it

---

442. His only recorded direct encounter with the Sadducees, for example, is abruptly dismissive: "You are in error because you do not know the Scriptures or the power of God" (Matt 22:29; cf. Mark 12:24).

443. After all, we know from the Gospels that by no means all Pharisees were hostile towards him.

444. Flusser, *The Sage from Galilee*. Although Flusser sees Jesus as also indirectly influenced by Essenism, "he was basically rooted in universal non-sectarian Judaism. The philosophy and practice of this Judaism was the Pharisees" (47). Flusser is of course affirming the commonplace Jewish assumption that rabbinic Judaism is the direct continuation of a "non-sectarian, universal Judaism" represented by the Pharisees—the Pharisees and the later rabbis "may, in practice, be regarded as forming a unity" (44), a view which we have seen refuted by Neusner.

445. Ibid., 47.

446. Skarsaune, *In the Shadow of the Temple*, 141, emphasis added. Skarsaune also speculates whether Jesus should be seen as a representative of a "distinctively Galilean type of Judaism," but since we know little or nothing of any such stream, the idea can be taken no further. However, if the Pharisees (and Sadducees) were found primarily in and around Jerusalem, this would diminish the likelihood of Jesus being formally counted within their number.

447. Commission for Religious Relations with the Jews, *Guidelines and Suggestions for Implementing the Conciliar Declaration "Nostra Aetate."*

talks about Jews "is just about the way all opponents talked about each other back then."[448] The underlying purpose is not so much the rebuttal of the opponent as the edification of one's own school: "Polemic was primarily for internal consumption."[449] Johnson shows that in the diaspora, "the language was rough both ways, and thoroughly within the conventions of Hellenistic slander"; this was how Jews talked about each other when they disagreed.[450] Readers today hear the New Testament's polemic as inappropriate only because the other voices are silent. In fact, Johnson argues, its slander against fellow Jews is actually remarkably mild; the polemic signifies simply that these are opponents and such things should be said about them.[451] Knowing that all parties to a debate spoke in a certain way, then, forces us to relativize our party's version.[452]

Of particular note in the New Testament is the apparent polemic against "the Jews" in the Fourth Gospel (a term which occurs seventy times in John as compared with five or six occurrences in each of the Synoptics[453]). However, Raymond Brown has shown that rather than a reference to ethnic, geographic or even religious differentiation—setting up a contrast between Christian and Jew—it uses "the Jews" as almost a technical term for the religious authorities who are opposed to Jesus.[454] "John is not anti-Semitic; the evangelist is condemning not race or people but opposition to Jesus."[455]

---

448. Johnson, "Anti-Jewish Slander," 429. For more on literary conventions in Judaism, see Johnson, *Acts of the Apostles*, 161–70.

449. Johnson, "Anti-Jewish Slander," 433.

450. Ibid., 436.

451. Ibid., 441.

452. Ibid. Even with regard to the most hurtful example: "We cannot view with the same seriousness the 'curse' laid on Jews by Matthew's Gospel when we recognize that curses were common coinage in those fights, and there were not many Jews or Gentiles who did not have at least one curse to deal with."

453. Brown, *The Gospel According to John, Vol. 1*, lxxi.

454. Ibid., lxx–lxxi.

455. Ibid., lxxii. Brown says that in the term "the Jews," John is indicating that "the Jews of his own time are the spiritual descendants of the Jewish authorities who were hostile to Jesus during the ministry." The dating of "his own time," however, is particularly difficult. Brown argues that the consensus opinion fixes 100–110 CE as the latest plausible date, rejecting previous datings of as late as H. Delafosse's 170 CE (see *Gospel According to John*, lxxx). On the potential for earlier dating, see Burge, *John*, 28–29. Note 1 of the *Guidelines and Suggestions for implementing the conciliar declaration Nostra Aetate* states simply that "the formula 'the Jews' sometimes, according to the context, means 'the leaders of the Jews' or 'the adversaria of Jesus,' terms which express better the thought of the evangelist and avoid appearing to arraign the Jewish people as such."

All this suggests that Jesus's argument with the Pharisees was a debate happening within the family, as it were, about what it meant to be and to live as the people of the God of Israel in the prevailing times. Whether or not Jesus was engaging in intra-Pharisaic debate *per se*, he was certainly conducting it *within* Judaism and *about* Judaism, rather than speaking from outside, into and against Judaism, as is normally assumed. Moreover, since sectarian alienation generally expressed itself in polemics against the central institutions of Israel's society (notably the temple), its authority figures (notably the priests) and its religious practices (notably purity, Sabbath and marriage laws),[456] we should scarcely be surprised to find that many of Jesus's arguments concerned the same subject-matter. These were, after all, the modalities of Israel's faith.

> It is therefore neither unusual nor surprising to find in the teachings of Jesus (and in the gospel narratives) polemic statements directed against most of the prestigious and ambitious Jewish power blocs of the time (Sadducees, scribes, and Pharisees). As a growing number of scholars are beginning to concede, this has nothing to do with "anti-Semitism" but rather emphasizes that the early Christian movement was an *inner-Jewish* phenomenon (and as such participated fully in inner-Jewish polemics).[457]

Jesus's critique, then, was not an external Christian condemnation of an apostate Judaism, but one Jew contesting with others, internally within Judaism, in the polemic of the day, over the correct understanding of God's nature, character, and purposes within the story, scriptures, and traditions of the Israelite religion. The Gospels' rhetoric and clashes must be seen through this lens. What Jesus objected to was not Judaism or Jews; rather, he was engaging in a passionate intra-Jewish debate concerning how their beloved religion should properly be understood and lived. It was exclusively an *internal argument*.[458] Jesus lived, spoke, and debated from within Judaism—almost entirely with other Jewish people who lived, spoke, and

---

456. Skarsaune, *Shadow of the Temple*, 168.

457. Mendenhall and Herion, "Covenant," in *The Anchor Yale Bible Dictionary*, 1200.

458. Johnson reminds us how small and powerless was the messianic community at the time: a persecuted sect—a "David," to the non-messianists' "Goliath." Compared to nearly seven million Jews in the empire were fewer than one hundred thousand messianists. Unsurprisingly, therefore, it is written defensively: "The symbols of Torah it had appropriated were so much more self-evidently in the control of the dominant group." The experience of suffering deeply influences all the New Testament rhetoric. "Abuse tends to gain in volume when it is powerless" (Johnson, "Anti-Jewish Slander," 423–24).

debated within Judaism. He was raised in, believed in, and lived a life of perfect faithfulness to the religion of Israel. Jesus can only properly be understood—as he would have understood himself—within that framework. Indeed, on no other basis would his message have made any sense to a first-century Jewish audience. He came into the world of the Judaism of his time, within the existing covenantal commitment from the God of Israel to the Israel of God. That Jesus's coming should be understood by his followers as initiating a promised new covenant does not change this. After all, the promise of a future "new covenant" in Jeremiah 31:31 appears to make clear that this will take place within the existing framework:

> "The time is coming," declares the LORD, "when I will make a new covenant *with the house of Israel and with the house of Judah.*"

Simply put, if there is no "new covenant" with Israel, then there would seem to be no basis for a new covenant at all. This is one reason why the "two-tracks" theory does not hold water. We cannot have a new covenant for gentiles alone if that new covenant is a progeny of Israel.

> The phrase "new covenant" has been taken to refer to God's new gift in Jesus Christ (Heb. 8:8–12; 10:16–17). Such an interpretation of the text, however, is a quite secondary matter. What is in fact promised is a renewed relation of fidelity between Yahweh and Yahweh's people Israel, a relation now in good faith and trusting obedience.[459]

We cannot therefore excise Israel from the new covenant without in the process making it void for gentiles. That its reach should be extended *beyond* the house of Israel does not change the context in which, and from which, that extension takes place.[460]

2.11 Overall Conclusions and Next Steps

A short review of scholarship in the wake of E. P. Sanders is illuminating. Despite the meaningful steps that the NPP has taken to reintroduce to Christian theological thought a more positive view of first-century Judaism, its earliest expressions (exemplified by Wright and Dunn) still default towards the "old model," which perceives the soteriology of Israel to contribute

---

459. Birch and others, *Theological Introduction to the Old Testament*, 356.

460. See Luke 24:47, where the risen Jesus says that "repentance for the forgiveness of sins will be preached in [the Messiah's] name to all nations, *beginning at Jerusalem*"; cf. Acts 1:8.

nothing positive to our understanding of soteriology in Christ. Wright and Dunn are, of course, simply repeating a standard assumption of the church's traditional canonical narrative according to Soulen: namely, that "the Old Testament dispensation has *redemptive power solely by virtue of its reference to the future coming of Christ*."[461] This suggests that a rehabilitation of the Mosaic covenant in Christian thought still has some considerable way to go, since it remains characterized at best as temporary and at worst as inadequate as a basis for relationship with God. The New Testament in general and Paul in particular is still seen as providing the theological justification for a continuing supersessionism, nuanced or otherwise, in which Israel provides the negative foil for the truths of Christianity.

Within the diverse group of scholars that has followed in the wake of the "Early" NPP, including those who would self-identify as part of a "Radical" NPP and those who would place themselves outside of any such category, we see a struggle to affirm both Torah and Christ at the same time. Hence we see some scholars attempting to square the circle by creating a soteriological division between Jew and gentile—a "two-track" theory—in which Christ is for gentiles and Torah is for Jews. However, the critical weakness of this approach (at least to the Evangelical mind) is that the necessary *quid pro quo* for Torah's validation is the denial of a universal salvific significance for Christ. One way or another, the cost of Torah's rehabilitation is that something important is being lost in relation to Christ.

Generalizations are always invidious, but there does seem to be an assumption that Christ must be pitted against Torah, as soteriological rivals, such that if both are somehow to "win" in this competition (or alternatively, if neither is to lose), a divide along Jew and gentile lines is the only possible solution. A theological explanation that legitimates and integrates *both* Torah and Christ within a single unchanging and universal divine plan for Israel and the nations therefore remains elusive.

In graphical terms, this is to ask how all of the elements shown earlier in figure 1 (page 100) can be brought together—encompassed within the same circle.

As illustrated below, it is easy to identify an atoning connectivity in Jewish thought between Torah and the Jew (figure 2).

---

461. Soulen, *God of Israel*, 27.

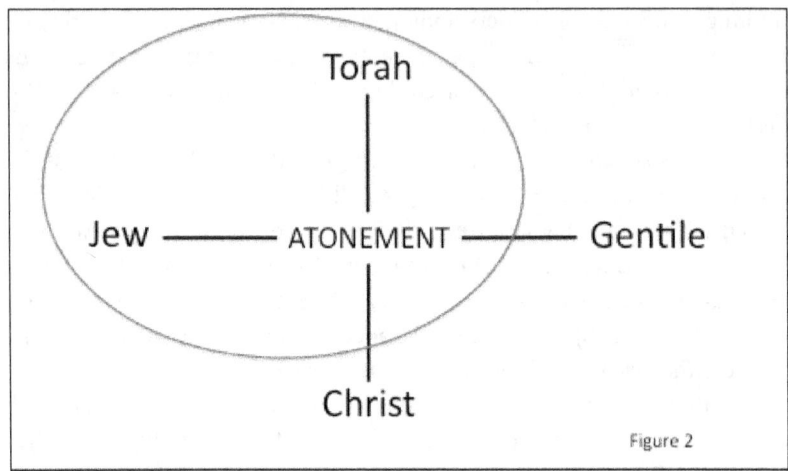

Figure 2

It is also easy to identify an atoning connectivity in Christian thought between Christ, gentile, and Jew (figure 3).

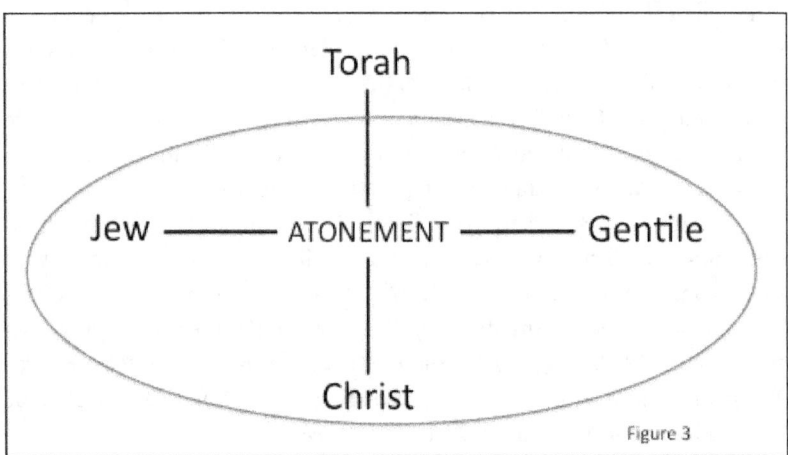

Figure 3

What is altogether more difficult is to see how Torah and Christ have any atoning connectivity (figure 4).

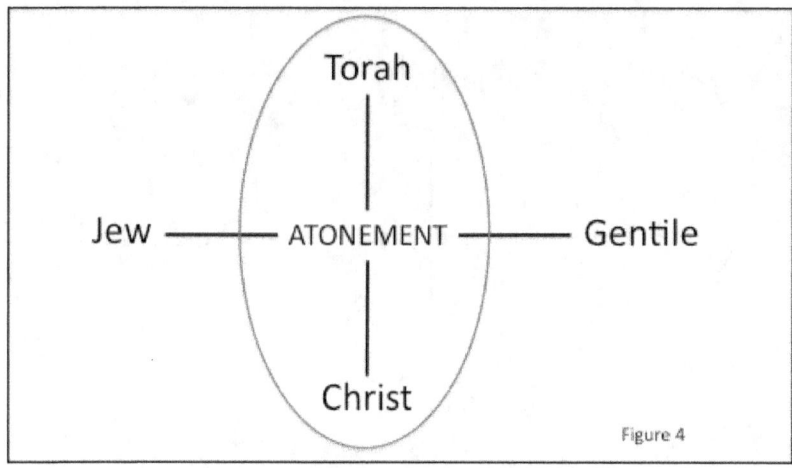

Figure 4

This is the conundrum that has not, so far, been satisfactorily resolved in the NPP. We suggest that until a positive theological relationship between Torah and Christ has been articulated, it will not be possible to draw the circle as shown in figure 5.

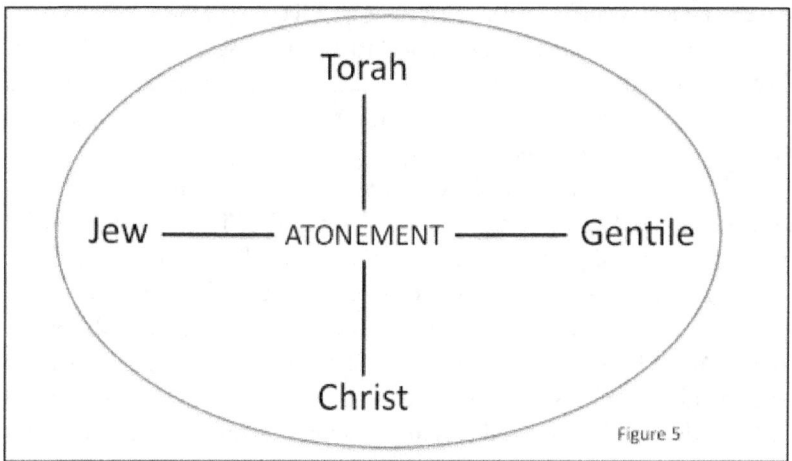

Figure 5

And this, of course, is why some scholars look for that solution through some form of "two-track" version, such as in figure 6, in which atonement is "divided," or shared between different soteriological systems. Already we have noted significant conceptual difficulties with this and there remains the problem of what happens in the space where both circles overlap.

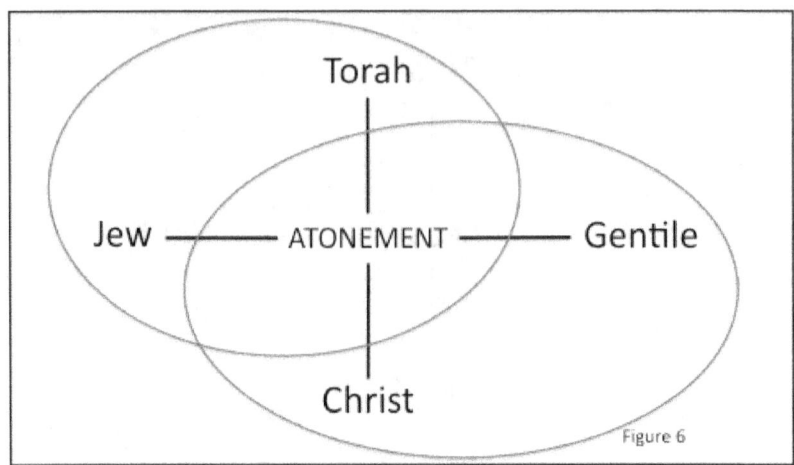

Figure 6

The question therefore remains: how to validate God's relationship to Israel at the same time as validating the person and role of Jesus Christ with respect to both Jew and gentile. The particular problems are how Torah and Christ relate to each other and, how each relates—separately, or together—to Jew and gentile. This brings us full circle to the supersessionist question as to whether, in the light of Christ, Torah has any continuing role, because—if it does not—then surely a question mark must also be placed over its efficacy *ab initio*. Moreover, if Torah is temporary, then so too must be Israel, the people defined by Torah.

In short, the challenge is to determine how the plans and purposes of God for Israel in its election and the divine gift of Torah are in harmony with his plans and purposes for the nations (including Israel) through the divine gift of Christ. How can these be seen as part of one integrated, singular and continuous plan and purpose, as one would expect of the divine mind? At the heart of these questions, of course, the doctrine of atonement is embedded: the basis upon which both Israel and the nations are enabled to be made "at one" with God. It is to the exploration of this concern that we shall turn in the next chapter.

The problem for Reformed Evangelicalism is that the more Judaism is affirmed as a religion of grace through faith after all—and even more so, if by logical deduction the efficacy of its covenant in Torah must be affirmed—the harder it will be for the uniqueness and necessity of Christianity's soteriology to be argued apologetically. There is an inevitable "pushmi-pullyu" effect at work here;[462] which some might prefer to characterize as the pro-

---

462. Doctor Dolittle's gazelle/unicorn-like creature, having a head at each end of its body—to be making forward progress seen from one perspective is to be going backwards from the other!

verbial slippery-slope. It is perhaps this very realization that gives rise to at least a *mild* form of supersessionism in many scholars' positions. After all, as Donald Macleod rightly concludes: "If Stendahl, Dunn and Wright are correct, Luther and Calvin were profoundly wrong."[463] For the traditional reading of Paul within Reformed Evangelicalism, Judaic legalism "must have been" a live issue for Paul that he saw exemplified in at least some Jews of his acquaintance. *Some form of* the Judaism that Paul attacked "must have" existed because he attacked it; even if it was in a milder or less pervasive form than Weber's exaggerated description suggested.

No wonder, then, that the implications in these new perspectives are decidedly inconvenient for Reformed theology. One commentator has lambasted it as a "massive amount of literature aimed at destroying two millennia of clarity regarding the relationships of works, righteousness, faith, and salvation,'" 277. ."[464] To restore this supposed clarity, there must at least be, in human nature, a universal tendency towards legalism and works-righteousness, even if Judaism can no longer be said to exemplify that tendency as readily as had been thought. The Christian message must be offering *something* that Judaism could not and cannot: a new and effective answer to the otherwise unsolvable problem of human sin. In short, the edifice of Weber and his heirs may have fallen, but for the sake of the gospel an essential Pauline contrast between law and grace, works and promise, must be rescued from the rubble. Alan Spence, for example, pleads that Paul's argument in Romans reflects universal human tendencies that Paul is concerned with, even if they ought not to be reckoned to all Jews:

> First-century Judaism as a theological system might well have had important gracious features, but there is no reason why it, along with many Christian theological traditions with tendencies towards self-righteousness or legalism, did not need to be confronted with the argument that "all of our best deeds will not of themselves earn God's approval." The interpretation of "works of the law" as a summary of all that leads to the presumption to righteousness and more that is suggested in the second and third chapters of Romans, cannot simply be thrown out on the basis that it is an inappropriate message to the Jews of that time. Human nature being what it is, they are unlikely to have been very different from us.[465]

---

463. Macleod, "The New Perspective: Paul, Luther and Judaism," 4–5.
464. Barrick, "The New Perspective and 'Works of the Law.'"
465. Spence, *Promise of Peace*, 13.

However, this still does not offer any validation of Torah *approached properly* (as God no doubt would have intended when he gave it!).

How, then, might we draw these threads together? Most of the scholars we have reviewed are at one in seeking to some degree to affirm the continuity of the entire salvation story, beginning with the Hebrew scriptures, and Israel's particular place within it. However, they offer very different views as to where the story goes from there, so far as Israel's place is concerned.

Wright strongly emphasizes the significance of Israel's story, but understood in his own particular terms;[466] moreover, his perspective on Torah is one of temporariness and replacement:

> It was holy, just and good, given for a purpose, for a time; and with the Messiah the time was up. All that was there in Torah that God intended to be of permanent value and intention had been transformed into the life of Messiah and Spirit.[467]

Alongside this supposedly divinely-intended temporariness of Torah, we have seen what Wright identifies as the sundry failings of Israel—such as its misuse of the Torah; pursuing it in the wrong way and hence failing to attain it; attempts to confine grace to one race, and so on. Despite Wright's attempts to disavow a tag of supersessionism and theological anti-Judaism, he seems to have qualified for it on multiple counts. Similar questions must be asked concerning Dunn's treatment, where we have already noted considerable common ground with a traditional "Lutheran" reading of Paul.[468]

Meanwhile, Gaston and other advocates of a "two-track" soteriology avoid disenfranchising Torah, but at the cost of downgrading Christ's person and work to a point where Christ died for the sins of gentiles alone. Evangelicals would surely not be alone in feeling that the divine mission cannot properly be read as simply a solution to the lesser problem of gentile inclusion—especially since, if that were the extent of it, a "tweaking" of Torah would suffice.

Thus, we remain in search of a soteriological account drawing from this new research that achieves the twin objectives of reaffirming a divinely-granted efficacy in the God of Israel's antecedent relationship with the Israel of God in Torah but that at the same time gives full assent to the traditional Evangelical understanding of Christ having a unique, indispensable and pivotal role in enabling relationship with God—for both Jews and

---

466. Fredriksen, for example, observes that "his interpretive context is generated not by a critical sifting of primary evidence but by the requirements of his master narrative's plot." "Review of N. T. Wright," 390.

467. Wright, "Whence and Whither," 265.

468. Westerholm, *Perspectives Old and New*, 188, 190.

gentiles—without resorting to the supersessionism and theological anti-Judaism which have so often been part of the package.

Finally, to revert back to Sanders, who sees Paul as running into difficulties over the conundrum that God gave the law but sent Christ to save humanity apart from the law. Sanders sees Paul struggling to hold these ideas together and explain them harmoniously. He "kept searching for a formulation which was satisfactory," a dilemma that resulted in "tortured explanations."[469] Not least because

> There lurks not very far behind that question the criticism of God to which we earlier pointed. How could God, who all along intended to save on the basis of faith, have given a law which does not save, which first produces and then condemns sin, or which at best does not help?[470]

However, if Sanders has *misperceived* a dissonance that does not in fact exist between Paul's central convictions—namely, Christ and Torah—then Sanders is identifying a problem that does not arise.

---

469. *Jewish People*, 79–81. Also, 76.
470. Ibid., 79.

CHAPTER THREE

Atonement in New Perspective

Since the second century CE mainstream Christianity has been resolutely anti-Jewish. The form in which this bias first appears is the supersession thesis, according to which Christians have replaced the Jews as the people holding the right understanding of the Abrahamic and Mosaic heritage and as the bearers of the salvation history. Already within the apostolic writings an argument is going on about how properly to understand the Hebrew Scriptures and the fulfillment of their promises. Yet when these documents were written, the debate was taking place within Judaism, according to the rules for Jewish debate.[1]

3.1 INTRODUCTION

CHAPTER THREE PRESENTS THE opportunity to construct a narrative that addresses the outstanding questions about atonement in chapter one, by drawing on the insights in chapter two.

In chapter one we noted the current state of the atonement debate in the Evangelical world, which is dominated by arguments about the hegemony of the penal substitutionary model *versus* a kaleidoscopic, multi-model view. We saw how worldviews feature in that discussion and the impact of conservative Evangelical concerns for the dilution of biblical truth in an era of postmodern relativism.

We also saw how the established models and metaphors lack any inherent cohesion among themselves—the view of the atonement that they

---

1. Yoder, *The Jewish-Christian Schism Revisited*, 147.

offer is fragmented and atomized. Although this provides the satisfaction of being able to point to atonement's multiple benefits, it disguises the unsatisfactory absence of any common *nexus* in the church's atonement narrative, leaving it "a bit like this" and "a bit like that."

We further noted that the one thing these customary models and metaphors *do* have in common is that they are wholly "Israel-forgetful." This seems odd, given that Jesus came into the concrete historical setting of the existing story of the God of Israel and the people-group, Israel, that God called and chose as his own. We made the point that although the imagery of atonement has mostly been borrowed from biblical pictures such as sacrifice, or facets of first-century Mediterranean society such as slavery/ransom, none of them shows any necessary dependency upon or continuity with Israel's pre-existing relationship with God. To all intents and purposes, atonement has been abstracted from the historical context in which it was achieved—it has come adrift from its Jewish moorings. We suggested that an inappropriate conflation has occurred, in which a universal and timeless significance for Christ's work has been confused with explaining it in universalized and dehistoricized terms. Moreover, we have seen how the church's traditional narrative of the gospel has found strength and foundation in a negative critique of the features of Judaism as a perceived religion of legalism and works-righteousness, asserting contrasts between "grace, by faith" (Christianity) and "law and works" (Judaism).

We drew attention to the critique of Soulen, who has pointed to the church's historical "Israel-forgetfulness" in its formulations of creed and doctrine, of which atonement would appear to be a clear example. Soulen has shown that the background of Israel's story can be completely omitted from the standard Christian account of God's consummating and redemptive purposes in creation without disturbing the overarching logic of salvation history.[2] The root of this omission is supersessionism, which has "shaped the narrative and doctrinal structure of classical Christian theology in fundamental and systematic ways."[3] Soulen argues that the integrity of Christian theology today requires "a renewed conversion of basic Christian forms of thought towards the God of Israel."[4] He forewarns that the consequences may be profound: "the rejection of supersessionism entails the reevaluation of the whole body of classical Christian divinity."[5] In our case, that includes the re-evaluation of classic Christian thinking on the atone-

---

2. Soulen, *God of Israel*, 32.
3. Ibid., xi.
4. Ibid., x.
5. Ibid., 3.

ment. This comports with Robert Jenson's belief that "Christianity needs a theological interpretation of Judaism, and not a supersessionist one."[6]

In chapter two, we reviewed the historical circumstances by which supersessionism and theological anti-Judaism became embedded in Christian thought, not least in relation to the soteriology of the gospel. However, we then noted the beginnings of a radically different perspective on the circumstances of first-century Judaism, in the latter part of the twentieth century, that has now made it both possible and productive to pursue Soulen and Jenson's proposals, albeit that a legacy of supersessionism and/or theological anti-Judaism still lingers in some of the well-known recent scholarship.

We observed that, to this point in time, the unanswered questions concerning the doctrine of atonement have not been brought into conversation with the new scholarship. In this chapter three we shall therefore look to do that by advancing a constructive alternative reading which offers a "new perspective on atonement" informed by a positive understanding of first-century Judaism. We shall be asking how things might look if theological anti-Judaism and supersessionism are eliminated from our grid of assumptions and instead we assume that Israel's relationship with its God has a vital role to play in helping us understand atonement in Christ.

As we do so, a particular challenge has already been identified in figures 4 and 5 (page 153)—namely, how to articulate a positive relationship between Torah and Christ in the context of atonement. Christian thought has perceived there to be an irreconcilability between the two, in that they represent different (even, competing) approaches to salvation, crudely summed up as "faith *versus* works." This is inseparable from the related problem of how each relates to Jews and gentiles (who feature on the horizontal plane of those diagrams) without dividing along two-track "Torah for Jews" and "Christ for gentiles" lines, as some have proposed. Can we construct a perspective on atonement that continues to hold the person and work of Christ in the highest regard and yet at the same time affirms Torah? We have seen how asserting a central and universal salvific significance for Christ has tended to be at the cost of Israel and Torah, in a "zero-sum game"—the more christocentric one is, the more supersessionist one inevitably becomes. Conversely, scholars who have sought to affirm Israel and Torah and reject supersessionism have tended to do so at the cost of Christ's necessity and universality. Must Torah and Christ forever be seen to be in competition? Can this apparently "either-or" choice be replaced by some form of "both-and" solution, in which Torah and Christ are related *non-competitively*?

---

6. R. Jenson, "Toward a Christian Theology," 6.

Turning specifically to the challenge of constructing an alternative reading within the boundaries of Evangelicalism, how do we deal with the concern that a rehabilitated view of the Judaism of the first-century—if not also, by extension, the Judaism of today—threatens the classic gospel message of *crucicentrism*? If the removal of supersessionism and theological anti-Judaism from the church's armory means that it is denied the option of a failed Judaism to use as a convenient and apparently biblically-sourced whipping boy, how will a gospel of "salvation by grace through faith and not by works" be made distinctive? Already we have seen some prominent NPP scholars wanting to maintain certain supposed failings of first-century Judaism, such as arrogant nationalism, even at the same time as their historical research leads them to conclude that the crude old caricatures of salvation by works and a religion of legalism must be abandoned. Must one therefore include at least some form of "soft" supersessionism or critique of first-century Judaism within the narrative, in order to remain conservative Evangelicals, sufficiently close to Reformed roots? And how exactly—in an "Israel-remembered" account of the atonement—will the cross feature? Evangelical *crucicentrism* holds Christ's work at the cross in the highest possible regard. Are its claims to offer a unique, universal soteriological pathway under threat, if Judaism-absent-Christ also offers some sort of pathway as well?

Then there is the challenge of the traditional ways in which the church has articulated the atonement in models, metaphors, and images. What are the implications for those theories? Do they lose their previous validity? Has the church up to now "missed the point"? Or, conversely, do they find a new place—a new "position"—within the soteriological narrative? And finally, will we be able to identify a coherence and common *nexus* that the traditional models and metaphors have previously appeared to lack?

3.2 TOWARDS A NON-SUPERSESSIONIST COVENANTAL UNDERSTANDING

An appropriate starting point to build an alternative account is a theological feature that Torah and Christ incontrovertibly have in common—that each is based in the notion of covenant. One might reasonably have imagined that covenant in itself ought to draw Torah and Christ together, but if anything it has traditionally provided a theological basis to keep them apart! And that is because of the radically different way that Christian thought has perceived the "two types" of covenant involved—crudely, the "old" and the "new." This difference is particularly visible within the Reformed tradition underlying Evangelicalism, in its so-called "covenant theology" or "federal theology," which we briefly touched upon earlier.[7] Since the doctrine is so important to Reformed thinking, it is appropriate to review it at somewhat greater length before we go any further. In doing so, we will need to bear in mind that the precepts on which the theology relies predate the New Perspective.

3.2.1 Covenant in the Reformed Perspective

The important place that covenant theology holds within the Reformed tradition is clearly articulated by Mark Karlberg:

> The relationship between God and humanity is, in a word, covenantal. God does not deal with his creation apart from covenant.[8]

> Explicitly or implicitly, the doctrine of the covenants provides the organizational structure for the entire Reformed theological system.[9]

B. B. Warfield spoke of the covenant doctrine as the "architectonic principle" of the Westminster Confession.[10] According to John Hesselink, "Reformed theology is simply covenant theology."[11] Given this significance, it is hardly surprising that a vast body of literature exists and that there is some variation in the manner in which the various covenants appearing in biblical history are conceived and described by Reformed scholars. The complexities and nuances in its internal debates need not concern us, however, since the questions we will be asking of the doctrine ultimately boil down to a few core matters. In particular, these relate to the degree of continuity *versus* discontinuity in the covenants pre- and post-Christ.

In simple terms, Reformed doctrine sees a covenant of redemption antecedent to and overarching the scriptural story. This *pactum salutis*, or covenant of peace, was a covenant entered into by the persons of the Trinity "in the councils of eternity." It is the basis for all God's purposes in nature and history and the foundation and efficacy of the covenant of grace (see

---

7. See chapter one, n.177.
8. Karlberg, *Covenant Theology in Reformed Perspective*, 11.
9. Ibid., 12.
10. Ibid.
11. I. John Hesselink, *On Being Reformed*, 57. Cited by Horton, *Introducing Covenant Theology*, 11.

below).[12] Against this backdrop, a "covenant of creation" (also known as a covenant of works, or covenant of nature) was entered into with Adam as the federal head of humanity, its covenantal representative. This was a covenant that man proved incapable of keeping. The consequence of man's disobedience—the stipulation for breach of the covenant conditions—was death. Accordingly, after the fall a subsequent covenant of "grace" was entered into by God with his church, with Christ as its federal representative head and mediator.[13] This covenant of grace is said to be a continuing covenant throughout biblical history, beginning with God's promise of salvation to Adam and Eve, running through to Christ and within which history the covenants along the way (such as with Noah, Abraham, and at Sinai) are to be located.

Although, at first glance, the inclusion of the covenant at Sinai as "a covenant of grace" might appear to be endorsing Torah as a "grace-through-faith-based" covenant, such an assumption would be misleading. One of the key statements in the Westminster Confession of Faith (1647) explains that there are different *administrations* of this one covenant.

> This covenant [of grace] was differently administered in the time of the law, and in the time of the Gospel: under the law it was administered by promises, prophecies, sacrifices, circumcision, the paschal lamb, and other types and ordinances delivered to the people of the Jews, all foresignifying Christ to come; which were, for that time, sufficient and efficacious, through the operation of the Spirit, to instruct and build up the elect in faith in the promised Messiah, by whom they had full remission of sins, and eternal salvation; and is called the Old Testament.[14]

It continues:

> There are not therefore two covenants of grace, differing in substance, but one and the same, under various dispensations.[15]

The Reformed tradition sees the features of the covenant of grace's administration "in the time of the law" operating only typologically—"foresignifying Christ to come." Though it speaks of its features being "for that time, sufficient and efficacious," the reality appears to be that they were only efficacious at the time in some forward-looking sense, insofar as they

---

12. Horton, *The Christian Faith*, 45, 993.
13. Ibid., 45, 992–93.
14. Section V of chapter VII, entitled *Of God's Covenant with Man*.
15. Section VI.

served "to instruct and build up the elect in faith in the promised Messiah, by whom they had full remission of sins, and eternal salvation."

In his *Commentary on the Confession of Faith*, A. A. Hodge says that "the covenant of grace has from the beginning remained *in all essential respects* the same, in spite of all outward changes in the mode of its administration."[16] But this begs the question as to which aspects of the Sinaitic administration of the covenant of grace were "essential." It would be entirely reasonable to suppose that Israel saw the intrinsic efficacy of Torah (purely on its own terms) as something essential. Nor does it appear that a future Messiah was perceived as a necessary condition of the effectiveness of that covenant—a Messiah who would give Torah a retrospective effect that it presently lacked.

Although Reformed scholars wish to say there is just one continuing covenant, the weight being placed on the role and function of "administrations" and "dispensations" in qualifying that statement appears to be rather more substantial. What might from a *Reformed perspective* be characterized as merely a change in "the mode of administration" looks suspiciously like a fundamental change in the covenant itself from an *Israel-centered perspective*. Reformed doctrine appears to be working backwards from a confessional position that sees so little value in that Sinaitic covenant *on its own terms* that, to have any efficacy at all, it must be subsumed into Christ's later work. While this attributes a commendably high value to Christ, it does precisely the opposite for Torah. The Reformed tradition would therefore tell us that rather than an *efficacious* covenant at Sinai—one that was effective on its own terms in its own time—Israel was experiencing a form of covenant that merely foresignified the cross of Christ to come, from which event (and only from which) it derives any power.[17] At Sinai, in other words, Israel received an otherwise *ineffectual* covenant that totally depended on the Messiah's later coming for its benefits, which accrued only retroactively.[18]

---

16. *A Commentary on the Confession of Faith*, originally published Philadelphia: Presbyterian Board of Publication, 1869, 179–81. Emphasis added.

17. One might even question whether, if it truly did operate on that basis, the Mosaic—or any other Old Testament covenant, for that matter—could properly be called a covenant at all, given this apparent lack of contemporary efficacy on its own terms. Would that not make it technically "counterfeit" (i.e., an imitation of something that appeared to be authentic, but in fact was not)?

18. Might not the christology of Heb 2:14–18 and 4:14–16 concerning Jesus's genuine humanity, including his susceptibility to temptation and human free will—leading us to believe that Jesus's victory could never be certain until finally won at the cross—suggest that there *could* be no efficacy for the Mosaic covenant through *foresignifying* in the period between Sinai and Calvary?

Here we must note that *foresignifying* is different from *foreshadowing*. A *foreshadowing* would "hint at" the new messianic covenant to come through its types and symbols; in other words, the "picture-language" of the first covenant would be valuable in helping us to grasp (and perhaps even to anticipate the nature of) the later one. In contrast, a *foresignifying* is showing in advance something that only occurs later. It is simply foreseeing a later event, without which it has no present effect.

Terminology such as "dispensations" or "modes of administration" should not blind us to the reality that, contrary to what the Reformed tradition would ask us to accept, the covenant at Sinai centered in Torah is far from being "in all essential respects the same." It cannot be the same if, from the very outset, the Sinaitic covenant required the Messiah's subsequent coming in order to be effective; or at least, not if the divine gift of Torah is to be taken seriously, on its own terms, in its own time. The faith that Israel placed in the belief that the Sinaitic covenant in Torah "worked"—that it "does exactly what it says on the tin"[19]—is surely an "essential respect."

Hodge asserts that "the new dispensation of this covenant is characterized by its superior simplicity, clearness, fullness, certainty, spiritual power and range of application."[20] Again, these characterizations appear to be rooted in confessional presuppositions. Would not Israel's perspective have been that Torah already possessed those qualities? The possibility that some individuals or sectarian groups within first-century Judaism may have complicated it, or missed the "heart" of it, or applied it at times incorrectly, is hardly the point. After all, the same problems occur in sectors of modern Christianity, too.

Rather than it being *Torah* that self-evidently lacked simplicity and clarity, surely the more likely concern of the early Jewish followers of Jesus would be a lack of simplicity and clarity concerning the person and role of *Christ*—in particular, how Christ simply and clearly related to Torah. Hodge's perspective on what is and isn't in the category of simple, clear, and certain—not to mention, characterized by "spiritual power"—would appear to be purely confessional. This is further indicated by his blatantly supersessionist accusation that the former dispensation "was so encumbered with ceremonies as to be comparatively carnal" and in contrast to which, "the present dispensation is spiritual."[21] Does Hodge mean encumbered by ceremonies through a process by which an initially "perfect" and

---

19. An idiom popularized in a series of UK television commercials by the wood treatments manufacturer Ronseal, that began in 1994 and was still being broadcast in 2016.

20. Hodge, *Commentary*, 179.

21. Ibid., 181.

"spiritual" Torah—as Question 99 of *The Larger Catechism* describes it—was inappropriately added to (by "the traditions of the elders," perhaps[22])? Or is Hodge referring to ceremonies that were *always* intrinsic to practicing Torah? If so, that would surely mean it was God himself who had "encumbered" Israel at the outset and is an implied criticism of the God of Israel for designing it that way.

Reformed theology wants to hold in balance some potentially conflicting ideas:

> On the one hand, it recognizes the unity and continuity of the Old and New Covenants (or Testaments), while maintaining the difference and discontinuity between them. On the other hand, it affirms the ultimate unity of the many and varied covenants in the mind of God.[23]

This question of unity and continuity *versus* difference and discontinuity is a major concern of this book, especially insofar as soteriology is concerned. However, it ought not to be assumed that all Reformed thought holds to precisely the same view as to how the various covenants are to be grouped and how they should be styled or thought to function. Within the movement, there is a genuine question as to the basis of "the fundamental unity among all the individual covenants brought under the overarching Covenant of Grace."[24] Our conclusion will be that a *far greater* fundamental unity exists than Reformed tradition recognizes.

Meredith Kline argues that the question is not whether one should systematically organize the various covenants to identify their overall unity under a term such as "the Covenant of Grace" but rather the proper procedure by which one goes about identifying the levels of unity.[25] The biblical authors themselves already did that kind of systematizing of the covenants:

> For example, in Psalm 105:9,10 (cf. 2 Kgs 13:23; 1 Chr 16:16,17) there is a virtual identifying of God's separate covenantal transactions with Abraham, Isaac and Jacob. And the separate covenants enacted by Moses at Sinai and in Moab and the later renewals of this arrangement in Joshua 24 and elsewhere in the Old Testament are repeatedly spoken of by later Old Testament authors and by New Testament authors as one covenant

---

22. See, for example, Matthew Henry's *Concise Commentary on the Bible*: "One great design of Christ's coming was, to set aside the ceremonial law; and to make way for this, he rejects the ceremonies men added to the law of God's making."

23. Karlberg, *Reformed Theology*, 11–12.

24. Kline, *Kingdom Prologue*, 6.

25. Ibid.

of the Lord with Israel, which the Book of Hebrews refers to as the "first" over against the "new" or "second" covenant (Heb 8:6–8).[26]

A particular debate is the precise nature of the Mosaic covenant. As Jonathan Edwards observed, "there is perhaps no part of divinity attended with so much intricacy, and wherein orthodox divines do so much differ, as stating the precise agreement and difference between the two dispensations of Moses and of Christ."[27] This has also been a central issue in Reformed theology more recently; specifically, whether the Mosaic covenant is to be viewed in some sense as a covenant of works.[28]

> The resolution of the two antithetical elements—law and grace (works and faith)—within the Mosaic economy of redemption has been one of the greatest challenges facing Reformed interpreters of the Bible. [. . .] Not until recent times—notably, the late twentieth century—has the orthodox biblical teaching on law and gospel been vigorously challenged.[29]

This "vigorous challenge" to what Karlberg takes to be "the orthodox biblical teaching" arises not least from the direction of the NPP. The stridency of his language is reflective of what he identifies to be at stake:

> One of the most important aspects of the traditional Calvinist teaching on the covenant is the use of the law-gospel distinction. The antithesis between law and gospel denotes two opposing principles of inheritance, appropriate to the Pauline teaching on the two Adams in Romans 5. [. . .] Repudiation of the law-gospel antithesis, however, immediately registers itself in other critical and related areas of Reformed exposition, particularly that of justification by faith and the atonement of Christ.[30]

Whatever element of "grace" is theoretically involved in the Mosaic covenant—supposedly as part of one covenant of grace, differently administered—it seems that when the stakes get high enough, for all practical purposes the grace goes out the window, as these passages make clear:

---

26. Ibid.

27. *The Works of Jonathan Edwards*, Vol. 1, 465. Available at https://books.google.co.uk/books (accessed 8 January, 2015).

28. Karlberg, *Covenant Theology*, 18. This was, he says, "the conviction of the vast majority of Reformed theologians in the early history of feudalism (up to 1648)."

29. Karlberg, *Covenant Theology*, 15.

30. Ibid., 17–18.

> The biblical-theological exposition of the OT, in order to be authentically christocentric, must do justice to the operation of the works-law-principle in the Mosaic Covenant. Only in this way can one arrive at a proper conception of OT typology. Failure to recognize this feature of OT christology will eventually militate against the NT doctrine of the atonement.[31]
>
> The description of the Mosaic Covenant as one of bondage, death and condemnation (2 Corinthians 3) is appropriate to the symbolic-typical aspect of the OT economy, and is not to be explained away in terms of the popular misinterpretation view, which defines the legal characteristic in terms of the Judaistic perversion of the law.[32]
>
> The law was *not* offered as a means of justification, but served rather to convict Israel of sin and to point her to Christ.[33]
>
> The sacrificial system of the old covenant never did take away sins but only reminded worshipers of their transgressions.[34]

We should finally comment briefly on the importance of the distinction between so-called conditional and unconditional covenants. It does seem that Reformed thought is keen to continue to emphasize the conditional side of the "old" covenant and its consequent demise as the result of human (aka Israel's) inability to perform it (another instance, perhaps, of a perceived need for the old covenant to provide a dark background against which the new covenant can shine all the more brightly?). It is precisely on this ground that Horton mounts a defence against theological anti-Judaism:

> It is hardly anti-Semitic to observe that the covenant with Israel as a national entity in league with God was conditional and that the nation had so thoroughly violated that covenant that its theocratic status was revoked.[35]

However, this seems incongruous on a number of levels. Firstly, the Mosaic covenant always had provisions for atonement (covenant restoration) in the event of human failure; hence to conclude that Israel had "so thoroughly violated" their covenant as to cause it to be revoked is a severe conclusion. Secondly, there seems to be an underlying inconsistency of

---

31. Ibid., 48.
32. Ibid.
33. Ibid.
34. Horton, *Introducing Covenant*, 59.
35. Ibid., 47.

thought in relation to the covenant's corporate application *versus* its individual application. What degree of "corporate" failure by some constitutes a failure by all, causing the covenant to be revoked for all? Or is there the implication of a "representative failure" and if so, by whom or by how many? Conversely, if the covenant is effective at an individual rather than corporate level—in the same manner that, at least in Evangelical thought, the new covenant in Christ is generally treated as being—why would the unfaithful actions of some infringe upon its continuing efficacy for the remainder? Who is the "they," who so thoroughly violated it, causing it to be revoked for all?

Kline observes that in contrast to Adam, where apparently "flawless obedience was the condition," Israel's side of the covenant

> was contingent on the maintenance of a measure of religious loyalty which needed not to be comprehensive of all Israel nor to be perfect even in those who were the true Israel. There was a freedom in God's exercise or restraint of judgment, a freedom originating in the underlying principle of sovereign grace in his rule over Israel.[36]

Horton agrees that it "was always up to God . . . what degree of disobedience God could put up with"; he acknowledges that "after the fall, a covenant of works arrangement—even for a national covenant rather than individual salvation, cannot really get off the ground if absolutely perfect obedience is the condition."[37] This would appear to explain the stridency and vehemence with which Reformed theology characterizes the scale of Israel's covenantal unfaithfulness. Only failure on Israel's part on a massive scale would substantiate the covenant's withdrawal. Whatever the degree of disobedience God could put up with, clearly Israel managed comfortably to exceed it (or the divine bar was set extremely low for Israel in the first place).

In conclusion, it is unsurprising that Reformed theology is inherently supersessionist. Although Horton wants to say "it is not that the church supersedes Israel," the ground on which he makes the claim is that, instead, "Israel widens to include Gentiles."[38] It is hard to see how this is a fair representation of what is happening from a Jewish perspective—it seems that the name "Israel" has simply been requisitioned and applied to something entirely different, namely "the church." Moreover, if as he says, "the New

---

36. Kline, *Treaty of the Great King*, 65, as cited by Karlberg, *Covenant Theology*, 43.
37. *Introducing Covenant*, 32.
38. Ibid., 196–97.

Testament makes clear that the new covenant renders the old obsolete,"[39] what is there to widen in the first place?

The Reformed argument that there is a thoroughgoing continuity in the covenantal biblical story is further undermined by a presupposition that the old covenant is—and always was?—temporary in nature. Horton, for example, says that

> The New Testament treats the old covenant (largely identified with the Sinaitic pact) as obsolete, having fulfilled its temporary function of providing the scaffolding for the building of the true and everlasting temple.[40]

Once again, in the standard canonical narrative we see the assumption that the "old" is there merely to provide a favorable contrast for the "new." "Once Messiah does appear, the old covenant (Sinai) is no longer necessary, as the reality displaces its types and shadows."[41] It is hard to avoid the conclusion that if Torah is temporary and faces obsolescence in the light of Christ then so too does Israel.

Reformed covenant theology seems to build its case on three main premises. Firstly, that the old covenant was revoked because Israel so thoroughly violated it (a punitive supersessionism). Secondly, the old covenant was in any event only ever temporary. Thirdly, the efficacy of the old covenant was not actually as Israel took it to be, at face value; rather than *dealing with* Israel's transgression (as its practitioners would quite reasonably have supposed at the time) it was instead to *remind her* of her transgressions and point her to Christ to come. These seem to be distinct arguments, with no necessary or apparent coherence save for theological anti-Judaism. They are simply multiple separate grounds upon which to deny the effectiveness of Israel's covenant so as, in contrast, to appear to more fully affirm the uniqueness, necessity and sole-sufficiency of Christ's work.

3.2.2 Covenant in the Light of The New Perspective

We recall from chapter one the work of Larry Shelton, who has identified a continuing covenantal theme throughout God's salvific dealings with humanity in both Israel and Christ. Shelton advocates "an embracing integrative motif of covenant renewal for a biblical concept of atonement,"[42] and

39. Ibid., 196.
40. Ibid., 47.
41. Ibid., 55.
42. Shelton, "Relational Atonement," 1.

that "the biblical covenant idea may most effectively be used to serve as a hermeneutic that evaluates all the atonement metaphors."[43] Shelton argues that Christianity "shares the same covenant as Judaism";[44] thus they are not merely connected in series, but in some way shared. He identifies a "spiritual thread that runs through both testaments [which] concludes with Christ's revelation as the last phase of God's faithfulness to his covenant commitments of salvation to Israel, and through that nation to the entire world."[45]

Of particular interest is Shelton's insight that something fundamentally to do with covenant underlies atonement and that it is relational in nature:

> The key issue and divine objective in the biblical teaching on salvation is the restoration of covenant fellowship, not simply the removal of guilt. The disposition of guilt and sin is part of the salvation process, but not the entire issue. Covenant fellowship with God is the goal for which humanity was created and which it has lost as a result of its fallenness. The key question for all atonement theories, then, is how this alienation from God can be overcome and the covenant relationship restored.[46]

However, we have seen Shelton stop short of a non-supersessionist affirmation of Israel's covenants. On the one hand, he affirms that the "Law [was] based on grace and given to assist Israel in maintaining its personal relationship with God."[47] On the other, he draws from the well of traditional Reformed thinking in saying that "while the law by continued repetition enabled the sinner by continued repentance and obedience to remain in the covenant community, *it did not justify and set the sinner right with God.*"[48] It "lacked spiritual power," which is "where Christ fits in."[49] Hence, although "the Old Testament covenant" (singular—presumable the Mosaic covenant) provides a *"foundation for understanding* the New Testament message of Christ's incarnation and atoning death,"[50] once again we see an unwillingness to affirm its validity in its own terms. We have observed similarly in respect of Wright. Though he states that the apostle Paul "is expounding covenantal theology, from Abraham, through Deuteronomy and Leviticus,

43. Ibid., 20–21.
44. Shelton, *Cross and Covenant*, 42.
45. Ibid., 28.
46. Ibid., 20.
47. Ibid., 47.
48. Ibid., 139. Emphasis added. Note the implication of a difference between being enabled to remain in the covenant community and being set right with God.
49. Ibid., 139.
50. Shelton, *Cross and Covenant*, 83, emphasis added.

through Habakkuk, to Jesus the Messiah," he also argues that Paul "is showing, albeit paradoxically, that the Torah *per se* rules itself out from positive participation in this sequence."[51]

One would think that the NPP should give cause to reconsider this default tendency. Davies, for example, made the case early on that "in the central points of his interpretation of the Christian dispensation Paul is grounded in an essentially Rabbinic world of thought, that the Apostle was, in short, a Rabbi become Christian and was therefore primarily governed both in life and thought by Pharisaic concepts, which he had baptized 'unto Christ.'"[52] It seems reasonable to suppose that one—if not the key one—of those Pharisaic concepts in which Paul's life and thought was grounded and governed would be a covenantal framework for Israel's relationship with God—specifically that of the Mosaic covenant in Torah—and that this, in turn, would be one of those "central points." We have already seen that one of the earliest recognitions of the NPP is Stendahl's refutation of the hitherto reigning paradigm that Judaism as Christianity's antithesis was what Paul had been saved from in his conversion experience. In Philippians 3, for example, Stendahl noted "there is no indication that he had any difficulty in fulfilling the Law."[53] On the contrary, the apostle is able to say that as to the righteousness required by the law he had been "blameless" (ESV) or "faultless" (NIV). It was not a "conversion from the hopeless works righteousness of Judaism into a happy justified status as a Christian."[54] Surely, then, the covenant in Torah would have operated as a positive model for understanding the covenant in Christ, not a negative one. This raises the question: what if, instead of a narrative in which as Soulen identified "God's history with Israel plays a role that is ultimately *indecisive* for shaping the canonical narrative's overarching plot,"[55] we *reversed* the expectation? What if we assumed precisely the opposite to be the case, and that in relation to soteriology God's history with Israel plays a role that is *decisive* for shaping the canonical narrative's overarching plot? This will, of course, require that we eliminate structural supersessionism and replace it, in our reconstruction, with the expectation of a positive theological contribution.

We have suggested that an obvious place to begin that reconstructive task is a fresh consideration of how we think about covenant—a concept that is self-evidently key to both Old and New Testaments and, as we have

51. Wright, *Climax*, 150.
52. Davies, *Paul and Rabbinic Judaism*, 16.
53. Stendahl, *Paul Among Jews*, 80.
54. Ibid., 15.
55. Soulen, *God of Israel*, 32.

seen, so important to the Reformed theology that underlies Evangelicalism. Karlberg's statements that "the relationship between God and humanity is, in a word, covenantal" and that "God does not deal with his creation apart from covenant"[56] are entirely appropriate, but our approach thereafter would be quite different.

Firstly, we would eliminate from the doctrinal and narrative structure all those elements that are expressly or implicitly supersessionist and/or that reflect presuppositions of theological anti-Judaism. This would, of course, result in a reconstructed covenant theology that fundamentally differs from the Reformed reading.

Secondly, we would follow this process through to its natural conclusion: rather than a *negative presumption* concerning the contrast and distinctions between "the old" covenant and "the new"—in which the *failings* of the old explain the qualities of the new—we would adopt a *positive presumption* that it is the *qualities* of the old that perform the explanatory role. As part of the rejection of supersessionism and theological anti-Judaism, we would therefore reverse the traditional approach:

- Rather than starting with a *negative* presupposition towards the covenant in Torah, instead we start with a *positive* presupposition.
- Rather than *omitting* Israel's story from the Christian account of God's consummating and redemptive purposes, we develop an overarching logic of salvation history that instead *depends* on it.
- Rather than assuming substantial *dissimilarities and contrast* between how old and new covenants operate salvifically in determining and defining relationship with God, we assume substantial *similarities and agreement*.

The logic of this methodology is underscored by Boyarin's argument that in the earliest stages of their development "Judaism and Christianity were *phenomenologically indistinguishable* as entities."[57] This lack of early distinction has profound ramifications for New Testament hermeneutics, Boyarin argues, since much traditional Christian dogma has been founded on the supposition that the two "religions" were separate and distinct from a very early date well within the first century. Since Christianity *was* a Judaism during the relevant period, it would be entirely natural for so-called "Christian" thought of the time to be profoundly informed by current Judaic thought, in which covenant would surely be central. This would have held

---

56. Karlberg, *Covenant Theology*, 11.
57. Boyarin, *Border Lines*, 89, emphasis added.

the validity of the Mosaic covenant in the highest regard, notwithstanding the variegated views amongst the various factions (Scribes, Pharisees, etc.) as to what true faithfulness to Torah should look like.

Thirdly, we would add some deeper and richer layers of meaning to our covenantal understanding by incorporating aspects of covenant identified by recent scholarship that have been insufficiently recognized in covenant theology to date—in particular, those that identify the centrality of kinship; the significance of the covenantal ratification ceremony; and the corresponding significance of the covenant meal in relation to both these aspects.

In short, we are anticipating that the effective features and qualities of Israel's history of covenantal relationship with God (as opposed to its supposed failings and weaknesses) will provide the positive explanatory lens through which we make sense of the covenantal relationship in Christ and specifically the atonement.

3.3 THE ELECTION RESULTS

Discussion of covenant cannot, of course, be detached from consideration of the party (or parties) with whom the covenant is entered into—those whom God elects, in other words. Volf has made the interesting proposal that

> If one wanted to understand in Jewish terms what drives the Christian understanding of atonement, I think it would be useful to look at one Jewish notion of election. Israel is irrevocably elect and immutably loved by God; no failure on Israel's part can change this. [. . .] At the root of the Christian understanding of atonement lies a universalized and radicalized version of Israel's election.[58]

There are several interesting aspects here. The first is that Israel's election into covenant relationship with God offers a model for understanding what is happening in atonement from the Christian perspective. This would direct our thinking about atonement towards election and away from any particular model or metaphor. Whether those remain valid (in some way) for understanding atonement thereafter is a separate and subsequent question, but in any event, election would underlie and precede them. The second is a corporate concept of election rather than a purely individual one. Israel's election was of a nation; hence, a *universalized version* of Israel's

---

58. Volf, "The Lamb of God," 316–17.

election would be one in which God elects to covenant with all nations. And the third is that Israel's status of being "irrevocably elect and immutably loved by God" within the Mosaic covenant—in which, "no failure on Israel's part can change this"—would provide the basis upon which all nations are assured of being irrevocably elect and immutably loved by God in the new covenant and that no failure on their part can change this, either. Self-evidently, for this to be true in the *new* covenant, Israel itself must have an enduring election and enduring relationship in the *old* covenant. In other words, it is the immutable nature of God's love for Israel—and the irrevocable nature of its election, notwithstanding failings on its part—that provides the theological basis for the equivalent Christian assurances. Only if these features are true of God's relationship with Israel in Torah in perpetuity do we have the basis to be sure they are true of God's relationship with the world in Christ in perpetuity.

In light of this, what if the party with whom God covenants is not "the church" (as supersessionist thinking presupposes) but "Israel and the nations"? We arrive at this conclusion by following through the logic of what we see in Israel's covenant as the model for the operation of the Christian covenant: God having now cast the covenantal boundary rope around the world just as he previously threw the covenantal boundary rope around Israel, sovereignly calling all nations into covenantal relationship with him just as he sovereignly called one nation. As with Israel, the election into covenant would be fundamentally corporate rather than individual. God elected—or "invited" or "chose"—to embrace all of the nation (singular) in the covenant in Torah and all of the nations (plural) in the covenant in Christ. This would mean that God's covenantal invitation was extended to both the faithful and the unfaithful, those who were near and those who were far off.[59] Whilst the *scope* of the covenantal offer is universal, when viewed through an Evangelical lens in which *conversionism* is considered important—i.e., the necessary exercise of a decision to "accept Christ"—it would of course also require a response. Both offer and acceptance are required in order for it to become effective. As in the covenant of marriage, an "I do" is required. Hence, the new covenant makes universal provision and yet it is not a universalism in which all will be "saved" automatically—not least because that imposes a relationship with God.[60]

---

59. Not that such terms lend themselves to ready (and still less, immutable) definition.

60. "Christ came to bring us back from the 'distant country' to our loving and waiting father (but not to force us to go with him, as universalism suggests—only to invite us to accompany him back, if we wish to)." McGrath, *Explaining Your Faith*, 102.

That the Evangelical presentation of the gospel typically focuses on individual response to a personal invitation can be unfortunate insofar as it leads to an autobiographical perspective on salvation and a corresponding unawareness of the community-transforming dimensions of God's consummative purposes (when in fact it should be "both-and"). It is important to remember as Donaldson reminds us that

> In Paul's thought, soteriology always had the community in mind. The soteriological question for him was not "How can a sinful individual find salvation?" but "How does one belong to the true community of salvation?"[61]

However, a corporate perspective on the nature of covenant does give rise to tensions, if not uncertainties, in who is within the group of the saved. This would appear to underlie Moses's exhortation to Israel in Deuteronomy 30:19: "This day I call the heavens and the earth as witnesses against you that I have set before you life and death, blessings and curses. Now choose life, so that you and your children may live." This awareness of a tension in the status of the group *versus* the individual within the covenant—and the idea of a need to choose—corresponds to that which Elliott identified in the first century.[62] He sees various factors giving rise to a greater focus on the role of the individual in the covenantal relationship. One such factor is the written Torah gaining ever-increasing importance within Judaism during the course of the Second Temple period. This resulted in an enhanced focus on attention to the requirements of the law for the individual at a personal level, and an inevitable tension between obedience to the law as an individual concern and the election of Israel as a corporate concern.[63]

We see inherent assumptions concerning the extent to which the actions of (some? many?) individuals are deemed to constitute the action of the corporate entity in Reformed assertions about Israel's covenantal failures: e.g., Horton's contention that "*the nation* had so thoroughly violated that covenant that its theocratic status was revoked."[64] Similar assumptions about *Israel's* corporate culpability have been made by Wright ("Israel had become sinful . . ." "Israel is now shown to be guilty of a kind of meta-sin . . ." Israel's "misuse of the Torah . . . ," etc.) and by Dunn (Israel's failing of "treating the realm of righteousness as exclusively Jewish territory . . ." and "a Jewish assumption of 'favoured nation' status . . ."). Clearly, if one

---

61. Donaldson, "Zealot and Convert," 679.

62. See the discussion on pages 112–17.

63. "All truly individualistic systems will eventually tend towards a downplaying of national ideas." Elliott, *Survivors of Israel*, 41.

64. Horton, *Introducing Covenant*, 47. Emphases added.

wishes to find it (and supersessionist thinking believes it has) there is *some level* of individual covenant breach by a certain number of individuals that is presumed sufficient to constitute a corporate breach by the party with which the covenant was originally made; one that negates the validity of the covenant for all individuals within it, righteous or otherwise. However, this does seem somewhat incongruous with other scriptural evidence pointing to the number of the faithful *versus* unfaithful at a particular moment *not* being a critical factor in the covenant's validity, at least so far as the faithful are concerned. For example, there is Abraham's negotiation with God over the fate of Sodom in Genesis 18; God's rejoinder to Elijah in 1 Kings 19 that there are 7,000 faithful besides himself (not a huge number, one would think, in the scheme of things, but clearly sufficient for God to find it pleasing); and faithful individuals such as Simeon in Luke 2, of whom it was said that he was "righteous and devout," "waiting for the consolation of Israel, and the Holy Spirit was on him." That "the *righteous* shall live by faith" (or "by faithfulness"[65]) suggests that there will always be a corresponding *unrighteous* within the group over whom the covenantal net is cast, who are living *other than* by faith/faithfulness.

Another area of tension that Elliott observes within Israel's understanding of the covenantal relationship is the aspect of covenant as *gift* given by God's grace *versus* that of covenant as *demand*, the requirement for obedience. All Jewish theologies, he says, embraced both aspects to some extent, but not all Jewish groups would have felt the same way about it.[66] At one extreme was the unconditional view of covenant, emphasizing its *inviolability*. At the other extreme was the view that emphasizes its *demands*, seeing covenant as *conditional* upon the performance of certain basic duties or requirements, in which failure invalidates the covenant. Hence, in the conditional understanding it would tend to be interpreted *individualistically*, with importance necessarily placed on personal behavioral choices.[67] In the words of Moses in Deuteronomy 30:15, 19-20,[68] Elliott observes that

---

65. Hab 2:4. The text can be interpreted either as "the righteous in their faith shall live" or "the righteous shall live by their faithfulness." Paul M. Cook suggests that in the immediate context the latter is more likely. Note, however, the "considerable disagreement about Paul's citation of this passage" (Rom 1:17; Gal 3:11; cf. Heb 10:38), not least because of its influence on NT understandings of "faith" and distinctions in the Hebrew and Greek (LXX) textual traditions. See P. M. Cook, "Faith," in Boda and McConville (eds.), *Dictionary of the Old Testament: Prophets*, 236-39. See also Witherington, *Paul's Letter to the Romans*, 55-56.

66. Elliot, *Survivors of Israel*, 247.

67. Ibid., 247-48.

68. "[S]ee, I set before you today life and prosperity, death and destruction." "Now choose life, so that you and your children may live and that you may love the LORD your

"what may originally have been a corporate warning to all Israel [. . .] is now interpreted as an *individual* choice between two ways."[69] In its extreme form, he says, "the corporate notion of election would be entirely subjugated to the individual's acceptance or rejection of the terms of the covenant."[70]

A further feature that Elliott identifies is how the various sects of first-century Judaism saw themselves through the lens of "the remnant"—the "true" people of God—in which God's purposes for the larger nation were being enacted by a relatively small number. This gives rise to an additional complexity beyond the binary options of the individual or the whole group. It is perhaps understandable that such streams would arise during a time of perceived national or corporate apostasy and this appears to have been the case in the divergent Judaisms (plural) of that first-century environment. It need not distract us here, but remnant thinking may be as much to do with a constructive desire to want to be part of a faithful group as it is with any destructive claim to elite or exclusive status; a sympathetic view would place the Pharisees in such a category, for example.

If Elliott is correct, we would expect to see these areas of potential tension operating below the surface of the text in the New Testament and at times breaking through. They may be particularly magnified when the subject under discussion is the covenantal status of the gentiles/pagans, with whom no divinely-initiated covenant had previously been in existence.[71]

3.4 A COVENANTAL NOMISM AS THE NEW COVENANT MODEL

Elliott's identification of covenant as gift reminds us that we may expect to see this reflected in a Christian covenantal understanding. John M. G. Barclay has recently argued that for Paul the Christ-event is both articulated and defined "as an unconditioned gift."[72] The normal ancient configuration of grace, both human and divine, was that gifts or benefactions are properly given only to the worthy and not to the unworthy. However, Paul in Galatians announces "the Christ-gift" as "that dangerous and unsettling

---

God, listen to his voice, and hold fast to him. For the LORD is your life." (NIV)

69. Elliott, *Survivors of Israel*, 278.

70. Ibid., 248.

71. Save, of course, insofar as they were proselytes within the scope of Israel's covenant or deemed a righteous gentile based upon the performance of the Noahide laws.

72. Barclay, "Grace and the Counter-Cultural Reckoning of Worth," 307. See also *Paul and the Gift*. For a review of Barclay, see Moo, "John Barclay's *Paul and the Gift* and the New Perspective on Paul."

phenomenon, the unconditioned gift."[73] Paul had experienced the divine gift, but not because he was a good Jew (even though he was)—it was "unconditioned by his ethnicity, tradition or advance in Judaism."[74] Indeed, sinful and idolatrous gentiles had been called by grace in the same way, without regard to their ethnic status or moral behavior (Gal 4:8–9). The Christ-gift "was given to Paul without regard to his Torah-excellence, and to gentiles without regard to their Torah-disobedience."[75]

In relation to the demand side of the covenant, the benefits of the gift derive from the covenanting party's obedient response to the conditions of the covenant. Morna Hooker explains it in these terms:

> Just as Palestinian Judaism understood obedience to the Law to be the proper response of Israel to the covenant on Sinai, so Paul assumes that there is an appropriate response for Christians who have experienced God's saving activity in Christ. [. . .] When Paul speaks about "the obedience of faith" in Rom. 1:5, he is clearly thinking about man's *response* to God's grace. [. . .] In many ways, the pattern which Sanders insists is the basis of Palestinian Judaism fits exactly the Pauline pattern of Christian experience: God's saving grace evokes man's answering obedience.[76]

We recall that Sanders described *covenantal nomism* in this way:

1. In Palestinian Judaism, the basis of "getting in" to the people of God (the group of the saved) is a covenant, through God's unmerited mercy in electing the nation of Israel; and

2. The appropriate individual response to that gracious election—or the means of "staying in" the covenant—is a nomism of faithful obedience to God's covenantal requirements expressed in Torah.

If we therefore follow Hooker by developing an hypothesis in which these features operate in a comparable manner to the "Pauline pattern of Christian experience," following the same precepts, it would run as follows:

1. In Paul, the basis of "getting in" to the people of God (the group of the saved) would be covenantal, through God's unmerited mercy in electing the nations; and

---

73. Barclay, "Grace," 308.
74. Ibid.
75. Ibid.
76. Hooker, "Covenantal Nomism," 48.

2. The appropriate individual response to that gracious election—or the means of "staying in" the covenant—would be a nomism of faithful obedience to God's covenantal requirements expressed in Christ.

It would be nice at this point to be able to say that Sanders has drawn the same conclusion, but he has famously and repeatedly disavowed the idea that Paul's pattern of religion is a covenantal nomism, including in his most recent work.[77] The basis of that disavowal is as follows.

Firstly, Sanders is comparing the pattern of religion he identifies in the Palestinian literature with that which he finds in Paul. Thus, considerable weight in arriving at that conclusion is borne by *what he finds in Paul*. Importantly, this centers on a universalized reading of Paul in which (i) "all are 'out' of the people of God and may enter only by faith in Christ" and (ii) "Paul does not accept the adequacy of the Jewish election for getting in; he begins the process of a theological rupture with Judaism by requiring faith in Christ."[78]

Secondly, another well-known Sanders assertion, that "Paul's thought did not run from plight to solution, but rather from solution to plight."[79] Once again, Sanders is reading Paul's perception of the plight and solution in universalized terms:

> It appears that the conclusion that all the world—both Jew and Greek—equally stands in need of a saviour *springs from* the prior conviction that God had provided such a saviour. If he did so, it follows that such a saviour *must* have been needed, and then only consequently that all other possible ways of salvation are wrong [. . .]. If his death was *necessary* for man's salvation, it follows that salvation cannot come in any other way and consequently that all were, prior to the death and resurrection, in need of a saviour. There is no reason to think that Paul felt the need of a universal saviour prior to his conviction that Jesus was such.[80]

We can therefore see that, although Sanders disavows the notion that Paul under the law saw himself as having a plight from which he needed saving, the solution that Sanders sees Paul subsequently discovering ends up corresponding to much the same problem: namely, that Paul finds something wrong with Judaism. What Sanders's Paul finds fault with—in the light

---

77. Sanders, *Comparing Judaism and Christianity*.
78. Ibid., 16–17.
79. Sanders, *Paul and Palestinian Judaism*, 443.
80. Ibid., 443.

of the solution he believes Paul has found—is "righteousness according to the law." It is "the prior fundamentals of Judaism: the election, the covenant and the law" that are wrong.[81] This for Sanders's Paul is the plight and it is universal.

The presence of these features in Sanders's reading of Paul have perceptively been noted by Mark Nanos:

> To my knowledge, what has gone unrecognized is the traditional assumption that remains necessary to Sanders' turn of phrase. It [...] requires a Paul who finds something wrong with Judaism, indeed, with the pillars of Jewish identity and religious values, such as election, covenant, Torah, and repentance—and who does so from outside Judaism rather than from on the inside, since the problem lies in the prior fundamentals of Judaism. The problem is not with some or other Judaisms, not with some Jewish people or ideas or institutions or practices, not with some or other Jewish Christians or groups, or their ways of interpreting the meaning of Jesus Christ—but with Judaism, period.[82]

Consequently, if we were to apply a post-supersessionist criterion to Sanders's covenantal nomism that assumes substantial *correspondence* in how "old" and "new" operate rather than the traditional view of substantial *dissimilarity*, that would draw us back to Hooker's reading—which we might call a "new-covenantal nomism."[83]

Once we work from an expressly non-supersessionist starting point centered in election and covenant, which affirms the divine-human relationship in Torah as a positive interpretive lens for the divine-human relationship in Christ, it can readily be seen that the features of the former can be found replicated in the latter, in terms of how that relationship is effected, maintained and where necessary restored. It suggests the divine designer intentionally used the blueprint of the covenant in Torah for the covenant in Christ and how it should be apprehended. And after all, if he loved the first design, why not?

What, then, is the *nomism* required to be in relationship with God in each of the patterns of religion? It is simply the faithful response to the

---

81. Ibid., 551–52.

82. Nanos, "Paul and Judaism," paper presented at Central States SBL, St. Louis, March 28–29, 2004, 2.

83. Interestingly, although Sanders continues to hold to his original view of Paulinism, he has more recently conceded some structural similarity: "Paul's pattern is, however, like covenantal nomism in that admission depends on the grace of God, while behavior is the responsibility of the individual." *Comparing Judaism and Christianity*, 17.

requirements of the covenant stipulated by God as the covenant-maker—whatever those are—by those to whom God has extended his covenantal offer.

With respect to the Mosaic covenant, it is faithfulness to Torah—to be and to remain "in Torah" (and, one might say, "Torah in you"). Precisely what this "faithfulness" and "remaining" looked like, of course, within then-current sociopolitical conditions, was of great concern to the conscientious first-century Jew,[84] as indeed its equivalent is to Christians today. A rehabilitated perspective on first-century Judaism also recognizes a relational and emotional center to that nomistic response, reflected in passages such as Psalm 40:8, "I desire to do your will, my God; your law is within my heart"; Psalm 119:30, "I have chosen the way of faithfulness; I have set my heart on your laws"; etc.

With respect to Christianity, if we look for the same pattern, we see that the nomism is faithfulness to Christ—to be and to remain "in Christ" (and, one might say, "Christ in you") We recognize these as familiar dual themes in Paul. It scarcely seems necessary to point to the relational and emotional center of that nomistic response in the Christian context, since Christians take this for granted. It is its equivalent in the relationship defined by Torah that they do not. However, once we restore those positive qualities, Torah—rather than Torah's antithesis—becomes the model for understanding the Christian covenant.

This reframing enables us to address Sanders's difficulty in seeing how, salvifically, one could compare being "in Christ" to being "in Israel";[85] we suggest he was failing to see that the correspondence is actually between being "in Christ" and being "in Torah."

Of course, Christianity has traditionally presumed that law and Christ have nothing in common. Thus, it may appear difficult to see how the idea of a continuity in covenantal thought between a covenant "in law" and one "in Christ" would not break down. It will therefore be helpful to explore the relationship between "law" and "Torah" a little more deeply.

---

84. E.g., in Luke 10 and 18, where Jesus is asked: "What must I do to inherit eternal life?" and in each case responds by quoting elements of the law: e.g., "You know the commandments. . . . Do this and you will live."

85. "One could not imagine a parallel formula to 'Christ is in you' (Israel is in you?)." Sanders, *Paul and Palestinian Judaism*, 547.

3.5 AN EMBODIED TORAH, PERSONIFIED IN THE MESSIAH

We have previously alluded to the inadequacy of "law," with its overtones of "legalism," as a translation of Torah.[86] George Foot Moore called it "a source of manifold misconceptions."[87] However, he noted that it is not easy to suggest an alternative, more satisfactory English word, since Torah is far more than merely "instruction" or rules for living.[88] Moore characterizes Torah as "the whole content" of divine revelation. Torah is "all that God has made known of his nature, character, and purpose, and of what he would have man be and do."[89] This broader conception of Torah as the expression of what God is like—and what humankind made in God's image should be like—leads naturally to the idea of the embodiment of Torah within the context of election and covenant:

> That God elects the Jewish people to embody his Torah or Word is already established in the election of Abraham (Gen. 17:9-12). Through the *mitsvah* of circumcision—the mark of the covenant—God commands Jewish men to embody the Torah, to inscribe the law on to their bodies. The Jews' embodiment of God's Torah has significance beyond obedience to God's will. Embodying God's Torah, the Jews become the corporeal sign of God's presence. Bearing the marks of God's Word, the people Israel become a sign or a testimony to God's reality here on earth.[90]

Embodiment of Torah is therefore the ultimate calling of Israel, intrinsic to the manifestation of God's presence in the earth and Israel's mission to be a light to the nations. In the Jewish scriptures we find the idea of Torah being so imbibed that it is spoken of in terms of being "in the heart." In Deuteronomy 30:14, for example: "The word is very near you; it is in your mouth and in your heart so you may obey it." Similarly, in Psalm 37:31, for the righteous: "The law of his God is in his heart; his steps do not slip." The

---

86. See General Introduction, n.18.

87. Moore, *Judaism*, 263.

88. Torah is a framework for knowing one is living as God intends, pleasing him and hence "right" before him. One knows one is "right with God" because one is "right with Torah" (or, "in Torah").

89. Moore, *Judaism*, 263.

90. Rashkover, "The Christian Doctrine of the Incarnation," 256.

notion of Torah as strict religious legislation entirely fails to do justice to a personal, embodied understanding.[91]

In the verses that form the basis of the *Shema*, the notion of loving God is intrinsically linked to Torah being in one's heart:

> Love the LORD your God with all your heart and with all your soul and with all your strength. These commandments that I give you today are to be on your hearts. Impress them on your children. Talk about them when you sit at home and when you walk along the road, when you lie down and when you get up. Tie them as symbols on your hands and bind them on your foreheads (Deut 6:5–8).

An important feature of Torah to which Chris Wright draws attention is that it was based on and reflected the characteristics of God himself. This is why one of the commonest expressions for obeying the law is "to walk in the ways of the LORD."[92]

> Israel was to reflect the integrity, justice, compassion and love of God in their own dealings with others. This strong motivation in OT law can also be seen in the way Leviticus 19 punctuates its demands for Israel's ethical life—on the farm, in the family, in the court, in the neighbourhood, in business, in ethnic relations—with the simple statement, "I am the LORD; I am holy, so you must be holy."[93]

Wright further observes that Torah was given for human benefit. When Jesus said "the Sabbath was made for people, not people for the Sabbath" (Mark 2:27 TNIV), he could have been speaking about the whole law. God gave it not to keep himself happy, or to take pleasure in finding fault with Israel's failures, but for its own good.[94] "They urged one another to obey it, not in order to get saved, but because God had already saved them."[95]

Rather than the cold, external formalism suggested by obedience to legislation, therefore, Torah is seen as intensely personal, relationally-centered and touching the emotions. It is the manifest embodiment of what God is like and how life should be lived, in right relationship to God and his creation. Once Torah is viewed by reference to these overarching characteristics, its personification in human life no longer seems strange; in fact, it

91. See also the passion of the Psalmist underlying Pss 19:7, 10; and 119:45, 47.
92. Wright, "Preaching from the Law," 54.
93. Ibid.
94. Ibid., 55.
95. Ibid., 56.

seems to be an entirely natural development in line with God's nature and purposes.

Against the background of the early Christians recognizing Jesus as the Jewish Messiah, it is interesting to note the role that was expected of Torah in the era of the Messiah. W. D. Davies makes a number of interesting observations in a short monograph on this subject, beginning with the idea in eschatological thought that the prophet who, in accordance with Deuteronomy 18:15, was expected to appear in the future ("The LORD your God will raise up for you a prophet like me from among you, from your fellow Israelites. You must listen to him.") is to be identified with Moses:

> The Age to Come came to be regarded as a return to two previous periods which might be regarded as "ideal," namely, the period of the sojourn in Paradise, and that when Moses lived, and the principle came to be established that the last Redeemer would correspond to the first. The marks of the Mosaic period would find their counterparts in the Age to Come.[96]

Davies was "especially concerned to discover whether Messianic speculation made the attempt to carry this correspondence to its logical conclusion and thus [. . .] to demand a *Messianic Torah* as a counterpart to the *Mosaic Torah*."[97] He explores whether, in the Old Testament and other sources, the rich complex of concepts such as the new covenant and the new exodus contained, at least implicitly, the idea of a new Torah. In Jeremiah 31, for example, although "there is a certain tension in his thought between the written Torah and the Torah to be dispensed in the 'new covenant'"—which Davies is unable to resolve into a complete distinction—it seems clear that new covenant involves also a renewal of Torah itself:

> What we are concerned to emphasize is that Torah, new in some sense and yet not divorced utterly from the old Torah, i.e., an external Torah, is part of Jeremiah's hope for "the latter days."[98]

Davies continues to imagine what this new kind of Torah required by a new covenant in Jeremiah's terms might look like. In Jeremiah's allusions to a dynamic role for the Spirit, he characterizes it as somehow "pneumatic" in that it involves "the activity of an inner, spontaneous principle":

> It is possible to argue that the covenant envisaged by Jeremiah in the future would be a new covenant demanding a new kind

---

96. Davies, *Messianic Age*, 10.
97. Ibid., 11. Emphasis added.
98. Ibid., 28.

of Torah apparently of a kind which may best perhaps be called "pneumatic" in the sense that it involved the activity of an inner, spontaneous principle. At the same time, however, we have seen reason to question that sharp antithesis to the old written Torah which this has been claimed to imply.[99]

We therefore see intrinsic to a new covenant the idea of a new Torah: one that is distinctive, yet not antithetical; dynamic and not static; new in some sense, yet not divorced utterly from the old.

A further stream of evidence, however, points to Torah ceasing in its entirety in the age to come. This was based on the notion of certain eras in Jewish history:

> At that time (i.e., the first century), the belief was widespread among the Jews that world history consisted of three epochs: first, the period of chaos—*tohubohu*; then the period of the Torah, beginning with the revelation on Mount Sinai; and finally, the hoped-for period of the Messiah [. . .]. In conformity with this, the Gospels say: "Till heaven and earth pass, one jot or one tittle shall in no wise pass from the law, till all be fulfilled" (Matt. 5:18). When all is fulfilled, and the Messiah has come, the period of the law will have come to its close.[100]

Davies therefore concludes it would be incorrect to speak of any one generally-accepted Jewish expectation as to the role of the Torah in the messianic age and/or the age to come, which, in themselves, are not always clearly distinguished in the literature. However, "we can at least affirm that there were elements inchoate in the Messianic hope of Judaism, which could make it possible for some to regard the Messianic Age as marked by a New Torah";[101] what's more, "we do know that the question of the New Torah agitated Judaism."[102] The best evidence, though, may lie in the New Testament itself, he says. We may, with some confidence assert that the Gospel of Matthew regards the words of Jesus as a New Torah; they were the Torah of the Messiah. Similarly, "Paul too found in the words of Jesus the basis of a new *halakah*: In fact, he used the phrase—*the Law of the Messiah* (Galatians

---

99. Ibid., 26.

100. Baeck, *The Pharisees, and other essays*, 72f., as cited by Davies, *Messianic Age*, 79. Davies notes that whether Paul believed that in the resurrection the final age to come had arrived, or whether the event merely inaugurated the messianic age, has an important bearing on his attitude to the law.

101. Davies, *Messianic Age*, 85.

102. Ibid., 87.

6:2)."[103] This idea goes well beyond merely Jesus's words, as Morton Smith has affirmed:

> Jesus appears in the Gospels in a number of places where the parallel passages of the Talmudic literature have God or the Law. So much is fact. A likely inference would be that Jesus occupied in the minds of the authors of the Gospels much the same place as God and the Law occupied in the minds of the authors of the Talmudic Literature.[104]

In Davies's view, then, the early church located its Torah in Jesus himself, finding not only that any possible expectations of a New Torah that Judaism may have cherished were fulfilled in him, but also that those were transcended.[105]

Portending the recent similar conclusions of Boyarin, discussed earlier, Davies suggests "it is possible that we are best to find the kind of seeds from which grew the personalization of Torah in Christ in such passages as those which speak of Wisdom (Torah) entering into men and making them friends of God (Wisdom of Solomon, 7:14; 27f)."[106]

> What makes it probable that some elements in Judaism at least may have contemplated a new Messianic Torah is the fact that early Christians, who were conscious that they were living in the Messianic Age, did in fact find room in their interpretation of the Christian Dispensation for such a concept. At this point we must insist that the New Testament must be allowed to illumine the Messianic hope of Judaism. It is surely a striking and significant fact that the New Testament presents Christianity, among other things, as a movement which not only denies the old Torah on one level, and affirms and fulfils it on another, but also introduces a New Torah.[107]

In *Paul and Rabbinic Judaism*, Davies further develops the idea that the person of Jesus is a New Torah as seen in the writings of Paul.[108] Though this is never explicitly stated in the Pauline Epistles, it is "clearly implied":

---

103. Ibid., 92.

104. Smith, *Tannaitic Parallels to the Gospels* (SBL, 1951), 159, cited by Davies, *Messianic Age*, 92n9.

105. Davies, *Messianic Age*, 93–94.

106. Ibid., 94.

107. Ibid., 90–91.

108. *Paul and Rabbinic Judaism*, 147–76, 321–24.

> It was inevitable that to regard Jesus as the Torah of God meant that Paul would be influenced in his interpretation of Jesus by those conceptions which Rabbinic Judaism cherished about the old Torah. We should expect on *a priori* grounds that attributes ascribed to the Torah revealed on Sinai would by the Apostle be transferred to Christ.[109]

For Paul, therefore, "the Torah has become 'Christified.'"[110] Furthermore, there is a strongly pneumatological element since, by the Spirit, "Christ, who was the New Torah, could dwell in the hearts of Christians"—this is because, in Paul's thought, Christ was almost identified with the Spirit.[111]

> It is in the light of this thought that we are probably to understand his references to Christ being in him and living in him, the inwardness of the New Covenant of Jeremiah's hope is achieved for Paul by the indwelling Christ, the New Torah "written in the heart." The Law within him is Christ in him; the indwelling Christ has replaced the old Torah written on tablets of stone and has become a Torah written within.[112]

By virtue of his "twofold nature" as Torah and Spirit, Christ was for Paul both the goal and the means towards that goal; hence, the Spirit is also for Paul a kind of Torah.[113] The true conditions of the messianic age, when Spirit and Torah would coincide, have been established—"We must not look for scientific precision in his use of terms, but Spirit and Torah are inextricable in his thought."[114]

Mark Edwards finds evidence for an understanding of Christ as personified Torah in Justin:

> Our conclusion, therefore, is that in the two Apologies, no less than in the Dialogue with Trypho, Christ is the Logos who personifies the Torah. In Jewish thought the Word was the source of being, the origin of Law, the written Torah and a Person next to God. Early Christianity announced the incarnation of this Person.[115]

---

109. Ibid., 148–49.
110. Ibid., 225. Also, 223.
111. Ibid., 225–26.
112. Ibid., 226.
113. Ibid.
114. Ibid.
115. Edwards, "Justin's Logos and the Word of God," 261–80. See also, Boyarin, *Border Lines*, 106: "In Justin (*Dialogue with Trypho*), the term Logos is used to confer on Christ the powers that were already attributed in Jewish literature to the spoken and

With this strongly personified element clearly established, we remind ourselves of Moore's definition of Torah: "the whole content" of divine revelation, of "all that God has made known of his nature, character, and purpose, and of what he would have man be and do"[116] This sounds extremely close to the Pauline affirmation of the person of Jesus: "The Son is the image of the invisible God" and "For in Christ all the fullness of the Deity lives in bodily form." (Col 1:15 and 2:9 NIV)

Dunn also notes in Paul's theology the personification of divine Wisdom in Jesus:

> Paul was not seeking to win men to belief in a pre-existent being. He did not have to establish the viability of speaking of pre-existent Wisdom. Such language was widely used, common ground, and was no doubt familiar to most of his readers. Nor was he arguing that Jesus is a *particular* pre-existent being; he was not arguing, for example, that of the wide variety of so-called "intermediary figures" in the ancient Near East Jesus must be identified with one and not another. What he was saying is that Wisdom, whatever precisely that term meant for his readers, is now most fully expressed in Jesus—*Jesus is the exhaustive embodiment of divine Wisdom*; *all* the divine fullness dwelt in him.[117]

In sum, Davies finds that "in wrestling to interpret the full meaning and implications" of Christ, "Paul constantly drew upon concepts derived from Rabbinic Judaism" and, specifically, the application to Christ "of those concepts which Judaism had reserved for its greatest treasure, the Torah."[118] This suggests Christ as the personification of Torah and that he features relationally within the covenant in a comparable way—namely, the relationship "in Christ" reflects the relationship "in Torah." A "new" Torah has become incarnate in Christ and through the outpoured Spirit God can be known and experienced in a way that bears direct continuity with—but is also a development from—Israel's Torah.

The radical idea that there would be an incarnation of God himself—by which he could be known personally in flesh and blood—was clearly unexpected. And yet, it may be thought far less unexpected when we bring

---

written utterances of God." According to Davies, it is probable that Trypho is another name for Rabbi Tarfon (102–40 CE), a contemporary of Justin Martyr (*Paul and Palestinian Judaism*, 280n2). Davies also notes Justin's claim in the Dialogue (chapter 11) that there shall be "an eternal and final law—namely, Christ."

116. Moore, *Judaism*, 263.
117. Dunn, *Christology in the Making*, 195, emphasis original.
118. Davies, *Paul and Rabbinic Judaism*, 323.

this background to bear. Tom Smail is surely correct to observe that "the final proof of God's covenant love to Israel is his becoming man."[119] The God of Israel had entered into the world as a human being in Jesus Christ and hence, had transformed what it meant to know him. The "wide range of speculation within early Jewish thought about God and particularly about his means of interacting and communicating with his creation and his people," noted by Dunn,[120] had been transcended and actualized through God incarnated as a person. Perhaps this is the answer to Segal's speculation as to what Paul's conversion experience meant for his understanding of Torah—namely, that "something important in the law had to be transmuted" and that transmutation involved experiencing Torah as a person.[121]

We find similar concepts identified by theologians writing from a systematic perspective. Robert Jenson speaks of Jesus in terms of "the Torah became flesh and dwelt among us" and as "the enfleshed Torah."[122]

> Undoubtedly a foundational text of Christology, of teaching about who and what the risen Jesus is, must be the first chapter of St. John's Gospel. We may summarize its teaching in this way: "The Word, that was in the beginning with God, became flesh so as to dwell among us."[123]

Jenson goes on to ask the perfectly sensible question that, if Jesus is "the Word," what does he actually *say*?

> In centuries of analysis and speculation about the nature and provenience of that "Word" it has not so often been asked what its *content* might be. God eternally speaks, and it is this speech that occurs in fleshly fashion with Jesus.[124]

In John, says Jenson, this is quickly answered: the author is plainly playing off the first chapter of Genesis.

> Though Jewish theology may not typically regard the word of Genesis 1 as Torah, in a general sense it is clear: the Word that became flesh as Jesus, according to John, is the word "from the

---

119. Smail, "Can One Man Die for the People?" 87.
120. Dunn, *Christology*, xii.
121. Segal, *Paul the Convert*, 205.
122. R. Jenson, "Toward a Christian Theology," 6, 12.
123. Ibid., 11–12.
124. Ibid., 12.

mouth of the Lord" by which God's people live, as do all his creatures; it is the Word called "Torah."[125]

We are reminded of Boyarin's claim that the Torah simply needed a better exegete: the *Logos Ensarkos* (i.e., made flesh). God first tried the text, then sent his voice, incarnated in the voice of Jesus: when the incarnate Logos speaks, he speaks Torah.[126]

Roman Catholic scholars participating in *The Commission for Religious Relations with the Jews* have similarly recognized that "God's word is one single and undivided reality which takes concrete form in each respective historical context."[127] Hence,

> In this sense, Christians affirm that Jesus Christ can be considered as "the living Torah of God." Torah and Christ are the Word of God, his revelation for us human beings as testimony of his boundless love. For Christians, the pre-existence of Christ as the Word and Son of the Father is a fundamental doctrine, and according to rabbinical tradition the Torah and the name of the Messiah exist already before creation (cf. Genesis Rabbah 1,1).[128]

Finally, Keith Ward observes that

> The New Testament could have said that Jesus is the Torah of God, as well as the Word of God and Son of God. Perhaps one reason why it did not is that there already existed a written Torah, and that may have been confusing. But it makes good (metaphorical) sense to say that Jesus is the Torah fully embodied in a person, rather than in a written text.[129]

3.6 RELATING THE WONDERFUL DIVINE GIFT OF TORAH TO THE WONDERFUL DIVINE GIFT OF CHRIST

Let us take a moment to speculate on some questions to which a fully re-pristinated view of Torah ought logically to lead. What if the "big debating point" for the early church, on which we are eavesdroppers in our reading of

---

125. Ibid.

126. Boyarin, *Border Lines*, 104.

127. "*The Gifts and the Calling of God are Irrevocable*" (*Rom. 11:29*)—*A reflection on theological questions pertaining to Catholic-Jewish relations* (10 December 2015).

128. Ibid. (no pagination).

129. Ward, *Word of God*, 79.

the New Testament, was not to do with universalized and timeless concerns over salvation by grace *versus* works but specifically first-century concerns over the correlation of God's wonderful gift of Torah with God's wonderful gift of Christ? What if the question of greatest concern was to articulate theologically the salvific connections between the elements in figure 1 (page 100)—namely, Christ, Torah, Jews, and gentiles—within one comprehensive soteriological *schema*? Might the questions under debate have arisen out of the very high rather than low regard in which Torah was held—and that even in the light of Christ, continued to be held? Questions, that are clearly interrelated, such as:

1. What are the appropriate roles of Torah and Christ, alone or in combination, in the on-going covenantal relationship of Israel with the God of Israel?

2. What is the proper interpretation of this new action in Christ on the part of the God of Israel in which he appears to have "by-passed" Torah in an eschatological outpouring of the Spirit on the gentiles (e.g., Acts 10:44–48; 11:17–18; Gal 3:2, 5)? Is this a temporary phenomenon, or the marker of a new era? And,

3. What are the implications of this new action in Christ for Torah?

Once we adopt a non-supersessionist view and eliminate theological anti-Judaism from our starting point, these questions not only engage our sympathy for the early Jesus-followers trying to grapple with them, but they become ours to grapple with too, in the present day. The supersessionism and anti-Judaic theological assumptions embedded in standard Christian thought would scarcely recognize these as conundrums—the answers would in each case be "obvious." Once we reject these supposedly obvious answers, however, it would really seem quite surprising if the questions were *not* critical ones in the early church. We would find a new respect for the theological challenge it would have been experiencing in trying to address them.

If we may go "off-piste" momentarily, into historical territory, might these questions illuminate today's debate about Paul? Perhaps Christianity has failed to identify their significance in its reading of the New Testament simply because it has taken for granted a low view of the covenant in Torah? An empathy for Jewish Jesus-followers in their genuine struggle to accept that Torah should have no relevance whatsoever for gentile believers in Christ—as it appears Paul was teaching—would, for example, lead to a new respect for the so-called "agitators" whom Paul berates in Galatians. The urgent question of how to continue living faithfully to God's wonderful gift of Torah alongside living faithfully to his wonderful new gift of Christ would be seen as a passionate and sincere debate going on within the family, rather than any timeless universal argument about salvation by grace/faith *versus* law/works.

The significance of these questions from a systematic perspective is found in their relevance to soteriology: if both Torah saves and Jesus saves, how is their salvific interaction—and their salvific distinctiveness—to be understood? This returns us to the problem of figure 5 (page 153).

We will approach this by continuing to reverse the traditional assumption that Christ and Torah relate *as rivals*, in a winner-takes-all salvific comparison. We know that traditionally the features of the covenants in Torah and in Christ have been pitched against each other in that way. Christ has been proclaimed "the winner" and Torah "the loser"—one being effective, the other not. However, a starting point that disavows theological anti-Judaism requires we reject these starting assumptions (without, in the first instance, worrying about the implications for the uniqueness and universality of the gospel of Christ, though we shall need to come back to it).

We have argued that if the history of Israel and its God is to be taken seriously in the formulation of Christian doctrine, as Soulen encourages, then so too must the efficacy and validity of Israel's covenant relationship in Torah both pre- and post-Christ. Whatever distinctions we may subsequently identify between old and new covenants, we must set aside the easy option of dismissing Torah *ab initio* on grounds of temporariness and/or ineffectuality. Since the "end" of Torah is a supersessionist presumption—in Wright's potent phrase, it's "time was up," since "all that was there in Torah that God intended to be of permanent value and intention had been transformed into the life of Messiah and Spirit"[130]—a continuing role for Torah must be our starting hypothesis. The challenge is what that role should be, and how it interacts with the role of Christ. We have seen in chapter two how some recent commentators have sought to square this particular circle by a two-track theory which "allocates" Torah to Jews and Christ to gentiles. We have argued that although this form of dualism is well-meant in affirming Torah for Jews, it is at the cost of denying the universal significance of Christ. However, the stalemate can be resolved if we begin to think about them *non-competitively* instead of either-or, winner-takes-all, comparisons.

To deal firstly with the "Torah for Jews" side of the twin-track argument, we have already seen how this is fatally flawed by the evidence of the first Christians, who were all Jewish, notably Paul. Clearly, they found in Christ something quite remarkable, that *in some way* transcended Torah as

---

130. Wright, "Whence and Whither," 265.

they knew it. We have noted that Torah already had provision for gentiles to come into the scope of Israel's covenant as proselytes; hence the coming of Christ was not necessary, in and of itself, in order for gentile inclusion in the covenant to become possible. Thus, the easy option of "Torah for Jews" and "Christ for gentiles" in which the covenantal dividing line is set according to genealogy can be excluded.

This would lead to the view that, in principle at least, both Jew and gentile can be in relationship with God through either covenant. The biblical evidence already supports this being the case: both Jews and (proselyte) gentiles came into relationship with God through the covenant in Torah; both Jews and gentiles came into relationship with God through the covenant in Christ. Thus we must conclude in the first instance that neither *salvific efficacy* nor *genealogy* are inevitable points of distinction between the covenants. We must pursue other lines of inquiry to identify the distinctives, yet still maintaining a non-supersessionist and non anti-Judaic interpretive posture.

To suggest distinctives between the covenant in Torah and the covenant in Christ is by no means synonymous with disavowing the value of Torah and still less with arguing for the necessity of its replacement. Thus we should not be precluded from proposing that there are qualitative differences in the nature of the relationship with God that each valid and continuing covenant enables. And yet, this is clearly a delicate area, with scope for supersessionism and theological anti-Judaism to raise its head. One appropriate ground for both affirming—and at the same time distinguishing—the covenants in Torah and Christ is to locate the development wholly in continuity with established Jewish eschatological expectations. Already we have seen how Christ may be understood eschatologically as a New Torah—Torah personified—in the messianic age. This would be entirely in continuity with the core features of the eschatological new covenant of which Jeremiah spoke (Jer 31:33–34.):

> "This is the covenant I will make with the people of Israel after that time," declares the Lord. "I will put my law in their minds and write it on their hearts. I will be their God, and they will be my people.
> No longer will they teach their neighbor, or say to one another, "Know the Lord," because they will all know me, from the least of them to the greatest," declares the Lord.

The thrust of the passage appears to be comparing and contrasting the nature of the eschatological new covenantal relationship with the current one—that is to say, *how* God is known. The text seems to speak of a covenant in which Torah is written in hearts and minds in a *more intimate* way.[131] The imagery suggests dynamic *versus* static. It compares and contrasts a covenant in which knowledge of God is imparted through one's neighbor in a *mediated* and hence indirect way, with a future relationship in which God is known in an *unmediated* direct way. It portends a qualitative distinction in which Torah is neither replaced nor negated but substantially enhanced in relational terms. Thus, it is speaking of a more-direct way of knowing God and yet importantly still framed in ways that remain Torah-centric.

That God should inaugurate this dramatic new way of knowing him in Christ ought not to automatically lead to the conclusion that there was any inherent necessity in nascent Jewish Christianity to give up on the practices of Torah—but it would be entirely unsurprising if it led to the conclusion that, in the light of what God had done in Christ, being in right relationship with God through the assurances offered by the *praxis* of Torah had been overshadowed.

Depending on how one saw the "balance" of a proper lifestyle that now potentially involved both Torah and Christ, it would be understandable if arguing for a more Christ-centric weighting raised concerns about inappropriate antinomianism, while arguing for a more Torah-centric weighting raised concerns over inappropriate legalism[132] (not that the true nature of either covenant inherently gives rise to those outcomes, of course). Might it perhaps be the tension in these twin concerns that we see reflected in Paul's correspondence with the churches of Corinth and Galatia, respectively?

A further logical concern for gentile believers (in particular) would be not to commingle covenantal features from Christ and Torah in some kind of pick-and-mix way. In other words, if one is to know God through Torah, one must faithfully fulfill all of its requirements, not just a selection. The point of having to perform the entire law is to do with following a consistent logic in one's response to God's covenantal initiative. To seek to relate to God through Torah requires that it be embraced *fully*, otherwise it simply does not "work" in its own terms. If one is to follow the Torah route—which one is at liberty to do, as a God-given way of relating to him (whether as a Jew or a proselyte)—then one has to do it all, not just bolt-on selected bits of Jewishness.

---

131. Perhaps there is the hint of a contrast with Deut 9:11: "The two stone tablets, the tablets of the covenant." Cf. 2 Cor 3:3: "written [...] with the Spirit of the living God, not on tablets of stone but on tablets of human hearts." (Both NIV.) Note, however, Davies's questioning of the sharp antithesis to the old written Torah that this passage has been claimed to imply (see *Paul and Rabbinic Judaism*, 228).

132. Without using law and legalism in any pejorative sense.

In sum, then, we propose to understand the operation of the new covenant in Christ in terms of a *covenantal nomism* that shares its essential features with the covenant in Torah.[133] Christ came as the personification of Torah within a new covenantal initiative that inaugurated a new way of relating to God, understood within a broader eschatological perspective. The *nomism* that is central to each lies in obedience to the terms of the covenant, as set by the covenant initiator. Hence, living "in Christ" is the direct equivalent to living "in Torah"—a Torah that has become incarnate in the person of Christ, with a knowledge of God outpoured into hearts by the Spirit, as the eschatological prophetic promises foretold. As Donaldson has observed, "there is a definite parallelism between the role of the Torah in covenantal nomism and the role of Christ in Paul's 'participationist eschatology.'"[134] What it now meant to live "in Christ"—and its counterpart, "Christ in you"—is of course one of the main preoccupations of the Pauline *corpus*.[135]

This leads us to propose that how *atonement* is provided for within the covenant in Christ should reflect how it is provided for within the covenant in Torah. Atonement in each case is "part and parcel" of a broader and wider covenantal relationship, rather than something that sits detached and theologically self-contained, as the atonement metaphors have tended to treat it.

3.7 JESUS'S DEATH CENTERED IN COVENANT

Whatever views have been taken of the atonement metaphors historically, they have always been seen as deriving from and dependent upon the work of Christ on the cross, so it is important for us now to consider in more detail how a covenantally-situated reading of the cross might pan out.

Tom Smail has suggested that situating the death of Christ in covenant should be explored for an alternative perspective to the traditional Evangelical paradigms of atonement:

> If he was not and could not be punished for our sins instead of us, if he did not and could not confess or repent of our sins vicariously on our behalf, what was it that he was doing there

---

133. Indeed, we might suggest that all God's dealings with humanity are covenantal and follow a pattern of *covenantal nomism*. God in each case sets the terms and determines the nomistic response—namely, what constitutes obedient faithfulness (leading to "righteousness")—at his discretion.

134. Donaldson, "Zealot and Convert," 667.

135. Reflected, for example, in Ephesians 1–3, with the lifestyle implications in chapters 4–6.

for us on the cross? The answer I want to suggest and explore is that he was fulfilling and renewing the covenant that we had broken.[136]

Mendenhall and Herion observe that the covenant sacrifice functions as the "ratification ceremony," the enactment of the oath of the covenant-maker—the "formal ritual by which a covenant came into force."[137]

Thomas F. Torrance identifies some important aspects of the covenant with Israel that further contribute to an understanding of how the New Testament thinks about the cross of Christ in covenantal terms.[138] One such aspect concerns the blood of the covenant as it relates to circumcision and Passover, "the two sacraments of the Old Testament," in which it functions as the divinely-given sign that "marked out the covenant and sealed it in the actual lives and homes of the people of the covenant."[139]

> In both of them, the blood of the covenant sealed the covenant, cutting it into the flesh of Israel in circumcision, and in the

---

136. Smail, "One Man Die," 87.

137. Mendenhall and Herion, "Covenant," 1182.

138. Torrance, *Atonement: The Person and Work of Christ*, is the fruit of the editorial labors of his nephew and student, Robert Walker, who compiled the book from notes of Torrance's lectures between 1952 and 1978. Though here we cite affirmatively Torrance's very helpful insights on the cross seen through the lens of covenant sacrifice, Torrance elsewhere places his perspective well within a traditional judicially-focused Reformed model, with the cross as a sin offering. At the cross, forsaken by his disciples, "the Messiah was left unutterably alone under the judgment of God upon the world's sin. [. . .] He was their representative and their very life; but in the agony of substitution he was unutterably alone, the lamb whom God had himself provided for sacrifice." In relation to Torah, meanwhile, as a result of Christ's work, "The Christian is no longer under the dominion of the law." Torrance, *Atonement*, 415–16. The little that is said about Israel focuses almost exclusively on its preparatory role and at best leaves ambiguous how the "old" relates to the "new." It is as if the question is so obvious it need not be treated. Although "the church must not forget that it has no independent existence, for through Christ it is grafted on to the trunk of Israel, nor must it imagine that God has cast off his ancient people or that the promises made to Israel as a people of divine election and institution have only a spiritualised fulfilment," quite what that means for Israel in soteriological terms is unclear. It is strongly implied that Israel's future is tied to coming under the Christian umbrella: "As God's first-born son, Israel too has part in the resurrected body of the Messiah, and grafted into it together with the Gentiles and sharing its riches, forms the one commonwealth of the people of God." According to Walker, for Torrance the church does not replace Israel; however, he quotes Torrance's paraphrase of Romans 11:15 as indicating Israel is presently "out" with the prospect of a future coming back "in": "If Israel's rejection means the reconciliation of the world, their acceptance would be an event so momentous that it means the resurrection of the dead." Torrance, *Atonement*, 348.

139. Torrance, *Atonement*, 11–15.

passover sealing the promise of redemption in the life of Israel and its seed from generation to generation.[140]

The blood of the covenant shed in the slaying of the Passover lamb was of covenantal significance in "signifying the renewal and establishment of the covenant through a mighty act of redemption."[141]

Torrance then explores more precisely what the Old Testament means by "covenant sacrifice." The Hebrew word for covenant (*berit*) is of uncertain derivation, but there are three main views.

The first is that it originates from the word "to cut." Torrance notes some eighty-six instances in the Old Testament where "cut" is used in connection with a covenant. For example, Psalm 50:5, "Gather to me my faithful ones, those that have cut (*karat*) a covenant with me by sacrifice." Both the KJV and the RSV translate the Hebrew "cut" as "made"; similarly, Psalm 105:9. It also seems evident, he says, that the same derivation is bound up with the original conception of circumcision as a seal to the covenant cut into the flesh of God's people, and so a seal of initiation into the covenant.[142]

The second view is that it derives from "to eat" or "to give to eat." This would give rise to the sense of covenant as the establishing of a bond through a fellowship meal. Torrance says that to set a meal before someone, or to partake of a meal with them, is equivalent to entering into a covenant with them. He cites Old Testament examples, especially Melchizedek and Abraham (Gen 14:18) and the covenant meal at Sinai when the covenant was established, with which the Passover meal came to be assimilated in the annual celebration of the renewal of the covenant in the homes of the people.[143]

The third view comes from the concept of "chaining" or "binding." Peterson is cited for his view that it stems from an old Semitic root meaning "oath," which speaks of the same derivation. "When the term covenant is found in the Old Testament it always or at least very frequently carries with it conceptions of the oath of the covenant, of a binding bond with its covenant promise."[144] For example, "I will bring you into the bond of the covenant" (Ezek 20:37).

Torrance believes all three views have much to say for them, since "it must be evident that the ideas involved in these various derivations are not contradictory to one another, and certainly that they all had a part to play

140. Ibid., 10.
141. Ibid.
142. Ibid., 11.
143. Ibid., 12.
144. Ibid., 13.

in the Old Testament concept of the covenant, if not through derivation at least through association."[145] Indeed it is in the coming together of the sacrifice and the covenant meal that covenant engagement and "bonding" takes place:

> Take the simplest form of covenant relation, the breaking of a piece of bread and the passing of it to the right and the left for participation. That was regarded as creating a bond of loyalty and kindness, and as involving "mercy and truth," concepts associated so many times with the covenant between God and Israel. Here the three meanings associated with the three suggested derivations are all present and are brought together into one rite. The root idea may well be to "cut" a covenant or to break into two parts, but that has just as clear a reference to a meal, to the breaking of bread as the Hebrew idiom puts it, as to the cutting of sacrifice, and both involve the conception of covenant engagement. All these elements are undoubtedly combined in the full conception of the Old Testament notion of covenant by covenant sacrifice. That is, the particular covenant rite is the breaking and dividing of a lamb or calf, the eating of it in covenant fellowship, and the cementing of a lasting bond.[146]

Torrance then turns to the application of these ideas in the new covenant in Christ. "God himself steps into the place of the sacrifice required in the making of a covenant, and offers himself in Jesus Christ as the sacrificial lamb."[147] The Last Supper is expressly spoken of as "the (new) covenant in my blood,"[148] and along with the cup Jesus distributes the bread broken in covenant enactment, as they eat in fellowship together. This is "distinctly a covenant sacrifice involving a) the breaking of the bread and the shedding of the blood, b) communion in a covenant meal, and c) commitment and solemn obligation.[149] In relation to the application of circumcision—and drawing upon its "original conception [. . .] as a seal to the covenant cut into the flesh of God's people, and so a seal of initiation into the covenant"—"the blood of the covenant is shed and the covenant is for ever cut into our human flesh" in the "total circumcision that is the crucifixion of the body of

---

145. Ibid.

146. Ibid.

147. Interestingly, Torrance notes that before it became institutionalized as a priestly role in the temple, the Passover sacrifice was originally the responsibility of the head of the household.

148. Torrance cites Matt 26:28 and Mark 14:24; the word "new" appears in some ancient versions of both Matthew and Mark. Torrance, *Atonement*, 13–14.

149. Ibid., 14.

Christ on the cross." Torrance is looking to Paul, here, in Colossians 2:11: "In him you were also circumcised with a circumcision not performed by human hands. Your whole self ruled by the flesh was *put off in the circumcision of* Christ."[150]

Hence we see again the covenantal significance of Christ's sacrifice being situated in Passover (leading up to the exodus), rather than in the Day of Atonement—which would have seemed more natural, if dealing with "sin" *per se* was the overriding divine concern. As Williamson notes:

> The hermeneutical key to the exodus event and its sequel (the Sinaitic covenant) is found in Exodus 2:23–25. From this text it is clear that God's intervention on behalf of the Israelites in Egypt was prompted by the covenant promises he had made to the patriarchs. Thus the deliverance from Egypt and God's revelation at Sinai must be interpreted in the light of the programmatic agenda set out in Genesis.[151]

We can also see how this broader covenantal context with allusions to Passover might offer fresh light on the significance of the Eucharist in the early church and New Testament thought (1 Cor 11:25). Williamson has observed how the inauguration of the Sinaitic covenant continues after the sacrificial ritual in another ceremony associated with the ratification: a covenant meal (Exod 24:9–11).[152] Stephen Finlan also sees a direct correspondence between the remembrance of the Last Supper in the Eucharist and "the covenant-creating function of a covenant sacrifice."[153] He, too, notes that the context envisaged in the Eucharist is one of covenant-making, not of sin offerings or the Day of Atonement:

> It has often been overlooked that the Eucharist could easily be intended as a new covenant ceremony, yet without any appeasing or substitutionary significance. If this is true, then he (Jesus) was intending to build on the covenant sacrifice of Exodus 24:8 but not on the sin offering. A covenant sacrifice is used to seal a treaty or agreement between groups or between a king and a subject group; it was very common in the ancient world. Abraham performs a covenant sacrifice in Genesis 15:8–18. The

---

150. The italicized language reflects the alternative reading offered by the NIV for "put off when you were circumcised by."
151. Williamson, "Covenant," 149.
152. Ibid., 151.
153. Finlan, *Options on Atonement*, 39.

"blood of the covenant" in Exodus 24:8 occurs within a ceremony of covenant between YHWH and the people of Israel.[154]

Meldenhall and Herion caution that ancient covenants are complex and do not follow a precise form: "It is not surprising that not every treaty exhibits all of the individual elements of the structure."[155] This is important for us to keep in mind as we apply a covenantal paradigm for understanding the features of the new covenant in Christ, where our primary concern is the underlying theological matrix.[156] One-to-one mapping of all of the forms and features identified in ancient covenants to the covenant in Christ is neither necessary nor appropriate. Hence we follow Shelton's more generalized proposal, of "an embracing integrative motif of covenant renewal for a biblical concept of atonement."[157]

Notwithstanding their variations of form, however, ancient covenants reflect a combination of the following features:

> (1) historical events that create relationships, usually (though not necessarily) between unequal partners; (2) customary ways of thinking characteristic of both parties, especially common religious ideas associated with deities; (3) descriptions of norms for future behavior (which are often confused with "laws"); (4) literary or oral forms in which the agreement is couched; and (5) *almost always some ritual act that is regarded as essential to the ratification of the binding promise.*[158]

---

154. Ibid., 39. In Exod 24:8, the covenantal ceremony in which the sacrifice takes place has nothing to do with a sin offering. God offers his covenant, the people bind themselves to the terms of it and the covenant is affirmed in the shed blood. "Then he [Moses] took the Book of the Covenant and read it to the people. They responded, 'We will do everything the LORD has said; we will obey.' Moses then took the blood, sprinkled it on the people and said, 'This is the blood of the covenant that the LORD has made with you in accordance with all these words.'"

155. "Covenant," 1180.

156. As Meldenhall and Herion observe, "the entire New Testament tradition points to some very important substantive connections with the type of suzerainty treaty exhibited in the Sinai covenant" but those connections "are not the external formal continuities that can be easily traced with the standard scholarly methods that compare and classify phenomena in terms of formal features and surface characteristics. For that reason, *this tradition must be explicated in terms of its underlying ideological matrix, and not in terms of any formal covenant elements* (which were already being atomized at least as early as the writings of the Deuteronomistic Historian)." "Covenant," 1199. Emphasis added.

157. Shelton, "Relational Atonement," 1.

158. Meldenhall and Herion, "Covenant," 1180, emphasis added.

Two required elements are notable for the covenant's ratification: the sacrifice and a verbal assent to the covenant: "All that the LORD has spoken we will do" (Exod 19:8; 24:3). Thus "the ratification ceremony was, in effect, the pledging of their lives as a guarantee of obedience to the divine will."[159] As Finlan notes, "Covenant blood solemnly seals an agreement; it also marks the formation of a community agreeing to that covenant."[160] "If this understanding is correct," says Finlan, "the 'blood' image is not expiatory but enacts the community-creating function of a covenant sacrifice."[161]

This would appear directly to contradict Howard Marshall's attempts to read "sacrifice for sin" into the covenant-making ceremony:

> The sacrifice which inaugurated the covenant in the wilderness was intended to atone for the sins of the people so that they might then belong to God in a covenant membership. [. . .] The sacrifice was in effect the means authorised by God for cleansing the people from their sins. By analogy, therefore, Jesus here interprets his own death as a substitutionary sacrifice for the sins of the people that they may become partakers in the covenant.[162]

Situated within a covenantal context, atonement (understood in its broad sense of bringing about an at-one relationship) can therefore be seen to originate in a "decision to covenant" in the heart of God. As James Torrance expressly affirms

> Divine covenants have their source in the divine initiative, in the loving heart of God. God conceives of the covenant, God announces it. God confirms and establishes it and carried it through to fulfilment, and the motive is love.[163]

Torrance criticizes Reformed theology (the "federal scheme") in its doctrine of atonement and penal substitution for inverting the biblical order of the relationship between forgiveness and atonement.[164]

---

159. Ibid., 1185.

160. Finlan, *Options on Atonement*, 39. This reminds us of the necessity of a nomistic response, which we see paralleled in the Evangelical expectation of a personal "yes" in acceptance of the good news of Christ. See "Why is a response to the gospel necessary?" in McGrath, *Explaining*, 102–5, e.g., 104: "You need to accept God's offer of forgiveness. You need to say 'Yes!' to God."

161. Finlan, *Options on Atonement*, 39.

162. I. H. Marshall, *Last Supper and Lord's Supper*, 92.

163. J. B. Torrance, "Covenant or Contract?" 55.

164. J. B. Torrance, "The Contribution of McLeod Campbell," 304.

> In the teaching of the Bible, there is forgiveness in God our Father who loves his world, and because there is forgiveness, he offers us a way of atonement and propitiation in Christ to cover our sins. In the federal scheme, that order is inverted. There can only be forgiveness of sins for the elect when atonement has been first made—and, because of the priority of retributive justice, there must be an equivalence of sufferings in Christ to the sufferings due as the just penalty for the sins of the elect, before forgiveness can be held out to the elect as the reward for the sufferings of Christ. In other words, the Father has to be conditioned into being gracious by the obedience and the satisfaction of the Son.[165]

This is a view, says Torrance, that both Calvin and Augustine explicitly rejected: "Atonement, Calvin argued, flows from the loving, forgiving heart of the Father" (*Institutes*, 2.xvi.4).[166]

The covenant-making ceremony can be seen to be the formal implementation of that prior decision in the heart of God, to bring it into effect. As the event that ratifies, seals or cuts a covenant, the cross of Christ assumes a positive role in establishing the relational offer from God to humanity. The cross is no longer simply about dealing with sin in a negative sense. It has a more overarching positive purpose in view—though of course, within it, that includes dealing with sin as the enemy of human life and flourishing. In both the covenants "in Torah" and "in Christ," forgiveness is announced and attested when the covenant is set in place in the covenantal sacrifice. The need for provisions to repair the relational damage done by subsequent human failings is also foreseen in the covenants' terms. Sin is certainly taken seriously, but it is not allowed to dominate the agenda.

3.8 THE KINSHIP DYNAMIC OF COVENANT

We noted in chapter one the plea of Elaine Storkey that "we need to develop an emphasis which has been there in evangelical theology from the earliest times, that at its heart atonement speaks about the deep relationality of God."[167] This understanding is developed precisely in the dynamic that covenant is an extension of the kinship relationship.[168] Scott Hahn suggests it is the "familial understanding of covenant relations and obligations" that

---

165. Ibid.
166. Ibid.
167. Storkey, "Atonement and Feminism," 233–34.
168. Hahn, *Kinship by Covenant*, 3.

"integrates and binds together the other dimensions of the covenant that scholars over the past century have identified."[169] Frank Moore Cross sees covenant as the "means by which the duties and privileges of kinship may be extended to another individual or group, including aliens."[170] The purpose of a kinship covenant "is to draw others who are potentially at enmity into a family circle where amity might prevail."[171]

> The failure to recognise the rootage of the institution of covenant and covenant obligations in the structures of kinship societies has led to confusion and even gross distortion in the scholarly discussion of the term *berit*, "covenant," and in the description of early Israelite religion.[172]

God's relationship with Israel at Sinai was a kinship-type covenant, with an emphasis on mutuality and familial relationship.[173] Within the matrix of the family, Hahn sees the "father-son relationship" as a basic category for interpreting the covenants between God and his people.[174] "The Sinai covenant represents a crucial theological adaptation of the kinship covenant, whereby a familial bond between God and Israel is established on the basis of a father-son relationship."[175] We see this imagery in Exodus 4:22, "Israel is my firstborn son," in a context where God is clearly acting for Israel against Pharaoh, as the suzerain on behalf of the vassal.

This critically important familial dimension takes us to a new level in terms of our framework for understanding the obligations that the suzerain assumes vis-à-vis the other covenant party.

> In tribal societies there were legal mechanisms or devices—we might even say legal fictions—by which outsiders, non-kin, might be incorporated into the kinship group. Those incorporated, an individual or a group, gained fictive kinship and shared the mutual obligations and privileges of real kinsmen. [. . .] In a word, *kinship-in-law became kinship-in-flesh*.[176]

These mechanisms included marriage and adoption as well as covenant *per se*.

169. Ibid., 31.
170. Cross, "Kinship and Covenant in Ancient Israel," 8.
171. Hahn, *Kinship by Covenant*, 37.
172. Cross, "Kinship and Covenant," 15.
173. Ibid., 31.
174. Ibid., 31–32.
175. Ibid., 48.
176. Ibid., 7. Emphasis added.

> The Divine Kinsman [. . .] leads in battle, redeems from slavery, loves his family, shares the land of his heritage, provides and protects. He blesses those who bless his kindred, curses those who curse his kindred.[177]

This language bears remarkable similarity to some of the customary atonement metaphors, as well as making sense of both "father-son" and "marriage" imagery applied to the divine-human relationship throughout the canonical narrative—placing it firmly within a covenantal framework that can be understood in terms of a familial kinship.

> The God of Israel adopts Israel as a "son" and is called "father," enters a marriage contract with Israel and is designated "husband," swears fealty oaths together with Israel and enters into covenant, assuming the mutual obligations of kinship, taking vengeance on Israel's enemies, going to war at the head of Israel's militia.[178]

If covenant is an extension of the family relationship, and if that is best interpreted in terms of father-and-son, then to what paradigm might we look for understanding what it means to be in covenant relationship with God as suzerain? The Parable of the Prodigal Son may be seen to offer such a paradigm.

Given that the parable is an elucidation of the nature and character of the father as much or more as it is of the younger son, it may not be inappropriate to think of it as the Parable of the Prodigal Father. After all, to many of the onlookers within that original cultural context, it would be the father who appears equally guilty of reckless, wasteful extravagance—in his case, in love, grace and mercy. Evangelicals have often struggled to interpret this parable in atonement terms, because of the absence of any judicial or penal substitutionary element in the son's restoration, but if the appropriate interpretive context is that of kinship and covenant it would be wholly unnecessary to find such features. It is simply what happens in a kinship/covenant relationship, *if the suzerain/father so chooses*. In the terms of James 2:13 it would be a case of the father's mercy sovereignly triumphing over the father's judgment, in response to the son's penitence and humble petition for restored relationship.[179] No "cosmic divine law" tells us that punish-

---

177. Ibid., 7.
178. Ibid., 13.
179. James Torrance points out the contrast with federal theology, "with its priority of justice over love" (as McLeod Campbell argued), "giving priority to the judicial over the filial [. . .] with the result that the *filial* categories, the filial purposes of the Father for mankind are, if not eclipsed, pushed into the background, in a way that is not true

ment "must" happen, if the appropriate controlling imagery is that of family and not law court. Jesus appears to be telling us that this parable reflects precisely the posture of the Father in the divine-human covenant centered in kinship. Furthermore, there seems to be no necessary reason to assume that Jesus is expounding some brand-new theological teaching that has only now become true thanks to Christ. There is every reason not to default towards a supersessionist reading that supposes Jesus's primary intention is explaining a positive feature of the new in contrast to the old. Disavowing Marcionism, we must say that the same "Father heart" underlies both the covenant in Torah and that in Christ, since God is consistent within himself.

As the parable concludes, it would be easy to revert to an anti-Judaic interpretation in which Jesus is criticizing the older brother for incorrectly conceiving the father-son relationship as centered in duty and obligation, with vengeance as the appropriate consequence of its breach (i.e., as a thinly-veiled critique of "the Jews"). Instead, we suggest that the parable is positively modelling the scale of the undeserved grace, mercy, and forgiveness that can be expected within a kinship by covenant relationship in which God is the divine Father compared to normal human expectations in that time and culture, exemplified in the older brother. If kinship by covenant is a divinely-inspired framework "to draw others who are potentially at enmity into a family circle where amity might prevail,"[180] how much more so to draw in "the son who was dead and is alive again; who was lost and is found"?

This reminds us of Horton's statement that it was always up to God what degree of disobedience God could put up with;[181] this being the case, in relation to both the covenant in Torah and in Christ we should allow God (rather than inalienable cosmic laws by which God is supposedly bound) freely to determine that. Although Klein has pointed out that "there was a freedom in God's exercise or restraint of judgment, a freedom originating in the underlying principle of sovereign grace in his rule over Israel,"[182] God has not always been granted that sovereign freedom by Reformed Evangelicalism, when it has sounded too "soft" or "liberal" to the ears of those who are more judicially-minded in their reckoning of his priorities. Yet the parable seems clearly to suggest that the father looks on the errant son with eyes of compassion, rather than eyes of punishment, and that this

---

to the New Testament. "The Contribution of McLeod Campbell," 304–5.

180. Hahn, *Kinship by Covenant*, 37.

181. Horton, *Introducing Covenant*, 32.

182. *Treaty of the Great King*, 65, as cited by Karlberg, *Covenant Theology*, 43.

is to be taken as paradigmatic of the Heavenly Father.[183] Jesus's portrayal of the nature and character of the father in the parable appears to be telling his audience something unexpected about the nature and character of the Heavenly Father. If the divine covenant is akin to bringing into a family, the parable is explaining what kind of a Father heads that family and what kind of a welcome can be expected even in a worst-case scenario.

Commensurate with this perspective, Douglas Campbell insists that "God's fundamental posture towards humanity, evident in Father, Son, and Spirit, is unconditionally benevolent."[184] This is in stark contrast to the traditional view, that he labels "Justification theory," in which the critical attribute of God is retributive justice, dictating that wrongdoing be appropriately punished.[185] Although Campbell has been criticized for setting up a "straw man" (only to then destroy it), a line of thinking which "orientates the work of Christ entirely towards God's justice and focuses significantly if not exclusively on his death" is undoubtedly prevalent within Reformed Evangelicalism. In contrast, Campbell "understands Christ's atoning work as transformational, and this work consequently encompasses his incarnation, life, death, resurrection and glorification."[186] He speaks of an alternative system characterized by grace which involves strong senses of election and assurance, is personal and intimate throughout and supplies an intimate relationship with Christ (along with a necessary and equally intimate role for the Holy Spirit).[187] Campbell is particularly prescient in identifying that these two starting points "are actually two different conceptions of God."[188]

Interestingly, Mendenhall and Herion observe that in covenant terms "there is no certain evidence for a ritual form that effectively imposed the curses [i.e., the consequences] for breach of covenant." They ask the pertinent question, "how flagrant must a violation be before the sovereign could legitimately muster his military forces and attack the recalcitrant vassal?" They note that "the treaty texts make no provision for such punitive action by the suzerain himself" since "this would negate the entire ideology of the covenant!"[189] It is therefore up to the wronged party (the father/suzerain) to

---

183. This contrasts with Reformed Evangelical thinking, in which "the justice of God is the essential attribute, and the love of God (or mercy of God) is an arbitrary attribute." J. B. Torrance, "The Contribution of McLeod Campbell," 303.

184. Campbell, *Deliverance of God*, 71, 75.

185. Ibid., 75.

186. Ibid., 76.

187. Ibid., 78.

188. Ibid., 75–76.

189. Mendenhall and Herion, "Covenant," 1182. The exclamation mark is theirs. Emphasis added.

decide what level of breach requires—as opposed to permits—any adverse consequences to be enacted upon the son/vassal, whereas as we have seen in Reformed Evangelicalism, "the demands of justice must be met before God can be merciful."[190]

This redemptive action of welcoming a stranger into the family by covenant may be seen as the expression of "the great love the Father has lavished on us, that we should be called children of God!" (1 John 3:1 NIV). Cf. Eph 2:19 (NIV): "Consequently, you are no longer foreigners and strangers, but fellow citizens with God's people and also members of his household."

3.9 A COVENANTAL FRAMEWORK SUMMARIZED

It may be helpful at this point to draw together some of these various threads concerning covenant—including how atonement features—in a summary form, beginning with its overarching framework.

An eternal divine plan (in which atonement is part-and-parcel)

We begin from Soulen's argument that the traditional "theology of redemption" reduces the soteriological account to "a story whose fundamental presupposition is the catastrophe of sin and whose goal is therefore deliverance from the negative conditions of existence."[191] Such a reductionism fails to take sufficient account of a "theology of blessing" that constitutes the canon's overarching plot. The antithesis of sin and redemption is not denied, but it is a secondary matter, operating within a more basic narrative context. That consummating work concerns "the goal and the means that God appoints for the consummation or perfection of humankind *antecedent to* all considerations of sin and the need for redemption"; God's consummating work therefore "establishes the ultimate horizon within which God's work in Christ assumes soteriological significance."[192] That there is something antecedent to the particulars of redemption is of critical interest: redemption itself is acknowledged as taking place within a grander story. God's work as consummator is the great central theme of the scriptures—its "central narrative vector"[193]—while his work as redeemer and deliverer is a subordinate theme. In other words, sin and its resolution—however necessary that

---

190. Torrance, "The Contribution of McLeod Campbell," 303.
191. Soulen, *God of Israel*, 53.
192. Ibid., 51, emphasis added.
193. Ibid., 115. On God's work as consummator, see also Kelsey, *Eccentric Existence*.

may be—are not the most fundamental feature in the story. Rather, God's overarching eternal plan is that humanity should receive life and fullness of life as his divine blessing—the rest is simply part-and-parcel of enabling it to happen. Covenant, therefore, provides the most apt biblical model for understanding both the plan and atonement's place within it.

Rejection of supersessionism and theological anti-Judaism as a base assumption

The second feature of the framework is a rejection of supersessionism and theological anti-Judaism from its starting point. Soulen speaks of the "Israel-forgetfulness" that renders God's identity as the God of Israel and the center of the Hebrew scriptures almost wholly indecisive for grasping God's antecedent purpose for human creation.[194] Following through on the full implications of this necessary correction invites us to look at the subject through the opposite end of the telescope; that is to say, with a presumption that God's identity as the God of Israel and the center of the Hebrew scriptures—an "Israel-remembrance"—is actually *decisive* for grasping his antecedent purpose.

The covenant in Torah as a positive interpretive lens

The correction of the biases of supersessionism means we now seek to understand the covenant in Christ in ways that are consonant with the covenantal relationship of God and Israel rather than placing the latter in negative contrast to it. It means affirming the covenantal history of Israel in the period prior to the birth of Jesus of Nazareth on its own terms, rather than denigrating it or making it entirely contingent on that temporally subsequent event. This is in no sense to denigrate Christ, but simply to take seriously what was said of Israel's covenant at the time, and indeed what Paul said of it in Romans 11:29. It leads to the specific proposition that the covenant in Torah provides the appropriate interpretive model for the covenant in Christ, including how atonement functions within it. Moreover, understanding Christ as the personification of Torah—best stated in George Foot Moore's terms, as "the whole content" of divine revelation, of "all that God has made known of his nature, character, and purpose, and of what he would have man be and do"[195]—further assists us in seeing a

---

194. Soulen, *God of Israel*, 49, 156.
195. Moore, *Judaism*, 263.

direct covenantal continuity with Torah, only in enhanced terms befitting its embodiment in a divine Messiah.

Atonement begins in election—a covenantal decision in the heart of God

As Volf suggests, if we seek to understand the Christian atonement in Jewish terms, we should look to a universalized and radicalized version of the Jewish notion of election.[196] Thus conceived, atonement fundamentally proceeds from a decision in the heart of God to covenant with a people and then to graciously act to bring that covenant into being, as James B. Torrance has proposed.[197] There is a synonymity between election into covenant and coming into an atoned relationship. Atonement, then, is first and foremost based in election and hence part and parcel both of God's covenant in Christ and his covenant in Torah—including the provisions within the covenants' terms for continuing relationship (relational repair) upon human failure (see below).

The cross as the ratification of the covenant

An atoned ("at-one") relationship is announced in the ratification ceremony in which the covenant sacrifice serves to "cut," "seal," or affirm the covenant. Christ on the cross is the covenant sacrifice that brings the covenantal relationship into being, that actions the atonement decision that was conceived in the heart of God to make the parties "at one." Given the covenant-making nature of this sacrifice, we note that it has *no* penal role or function. Covenant is the vehicle through which God delivers both "the now" and "the not yet" benefits of being in that covenantal relationship, which speak of what it means to be atoned. Under the covenant, God as the suzerain offers divine protection and care to his covenant people.

---

196. Volf, "The Lamb of God," 316–17.

197. "Divine covenants have their source in the divine initiative, in the loving heart of God. God conceives of the covenant, God announces it. God confirms and establishes it and carried it through to fulfilment, and the motive is love." J. B. Torrance, "Covenant or Contract?" 55.

The Mosaic covenant as the appropriate covenantal model for understanding the covenant in Christ

Already we have seen the multiple clues in the New Testament that we should relate Jesus's death to Passover rather than to sin offerings or the Day of Atonement, either of which (with their focus on sin) might sound more appropriate to Evangelical ears. As Campbell notes, however, "the atonement is [. . .] clearly an act that *rescues*, rather like the exodus."[198] This comports with Davies's depiction of Moses, noted earlier, as "the first redeemer" to whom the Messiah would correspond as "the last Redeemer," in first-century Jewish expectations.[199]

The cross, kinship, and the covenant meal

The covenant sacrifice forms the basis of the covenant meal, which is an important feature of the ratification. Eating together centers the relationship thus brought about in kinship and family. This is no commercial arrangement.

The historic explanation of the covenant meal is quite simple. It is based on the function of the meal to bring a stranger into the family circle through participating in the meal.[200]

The covenant brings us into the divine family by kinship-in-law—as if we were kinship-in-flesh. It brings us under the protection of the Divine Kinsman who leads in battle, redeems from slavery, loves, blesses, provides, and protects[201] (as, interestingly, the traditional metaphors of atonement variously picture). This kinship status bestowed by the covenant relationship is reflected in the continuing significance attaching to the Eucharist as a remembrance of the Last Supper.[202]

> [The] custom of forming a union by taking bread together is widespread; doubtless it is based on the idea that it is the family group which eats together so that admission to the meal implies admission to the family. [. . .] The implications are that sharing

---

198. Campbell, "The Current Crisis," 45.

199. Davies, *Messianic Age*, 10.

200. A. Viberg, *Symbols of Law: A Contextual Analysis of Legal Symbolic Acts in the Old Testament* (Stockholm: Almqvist & Viksell, 1992), 76, as cited by Hahn, *Kinship by Covenant*, 352n5.

201. Cross, "Kinship and Covenant," 7.

202. And we may also say, eschatologically, in the marriage supper of the Lamb in Revelation 19, since marriage also bears covenantal kinship significance.

> a meal could by itself be an effective means of constituting a covenant. [...] More, such a union must have been conceived of in terms of a family bond.[203]

Thus, a covenantal framework goes well beyond conceiving atonement just in terms of a reparative mechanism in the light of sin (though it includes that) and it does so in a context that is familial rather than legal. The covenant establishes a broader kinship relationship within which the Divine Kinsman suzerain/father acts to defend, redeem, love, bless, provide, and protect. The cross conceived as the covenant-ratifying event is creating something altogether more substantive within God's consummative purposes than simply a transaction to repair something that has gone wrong.

Given the interrelationship of covenant and kinship, it would appear that the picture of relationship between a father and son offered by Jesus's Parable of the Prodigal can legitimately serve as an interpretive paradigm for understanding God's covenantal nature, in which through kinship-in-law the alien, stranger, and even enemy is welcomed and included. The parable captures multiple aspects of a covenantal relationship in which atonement features: the bond of familial kinship which even the worst sin cannot break, under the auspices of a benign and forgiving father; the nomistic response of the returning penitent son; the response of the father in sovereignly decreeing mercy and forgiveness will triumph over judgment; the sacrifice that signifies the covenant's restoration (but which operates in a non-penal way and is not a sin-offering); and the celebratory familial banquet provided by the sacrifice.

A "new covenantal nomism" (a corporate covenant, with an individual response)

As with the Mosaic covenant in Torah, the new covenant in Christ is fundamentally corporate in scope. The former is a covenant with "the nation"; the latter, a covenant with "the nations." In each covenant, God has sovereignly decided to elect a people to be known as the people of God. However, a nomistic response is required at the individual level to actualize it and appropriate its benefits. This does not mean an individualized gospel, however; as Finlan rightly says, while "covenant blood solemnly seals an agreement [...] it also marks the formation of a community agreeing to that

---

203. McCarthy, "Three Covenants in Genesis," 185.

covenant."[204] The covenant sacrifice has "a community-creating function."[205] The covenant becomes effective upon the vassal's nomistic acceptance of the suzerain's conditions—which are, living "in Torah" or "in Christ" respectively. As Meldenhall and Herion explain:

> It would be extremely naïve to think that the mere writing of a treaty text brought into existence the treaty and the relationship it stipulated. Even today, a treaty must be signed, ratified or otherwise formally accepted before it can become binding.[206]

Faithfulness to the nomism required in relation to a covenant defines "righteousness"—namely, being in right standing with God. The righteous are those who live by faithfulness to the covenantal requirements. The divine covenant-maker sets the terms of the covenant, as he determines. In setting those terms he is not bound by immutable cosmic laws or legal *formulae* extrinsic to himself. He decides in his sovereign discretion whether they involve not eating the fruit of a certain tree, honouring the Sabbath, or practicing certain sacrifices under certain circumstances. As Jenson puts it:

> Why, after all—as David Novak once put it to me—can't Jews eat shrimp? Just to be marked off as different? [. . .] The seeming arbitrariness is much of the point. In Martin Luther's exegesis of the paradise story in Genesis, the tree of the knowledge of good and evil is so called only after the fact, in view of the consequences of disobeying God's command. In itself, the tree was just a particular tree, and the command not to eat of it gave humanity a first opportunity of obedience—the arbitrary choice of a particular tree was part of the point.[207]

Righteousness—being in right relationship with the suzerain in the covenant relationship—comes from obedience to the commands (whatever those are) rather than something intrinsic to what's commanded in isolation. This would explain why, for example, sacrifice has no *inherent* expiatory power—it gains that power by virtue of God having said that it will be so[208]—and why the apparent arbitrariness of not eating shrimp, or resting on a particular day, can be part of the definition of being "righteous."

---

204. Finlan, *Options on Atonement*, 39.
205. Ibid.
206. "Meldenhall and Herion, Covenant," 1182.
207. Jenson, "Toward a Christian Theology," 10.
208. As Stephen Holmes insightfully observes, "at times [. . .] it seems to have no meaning or context at all, except the command of God" (Holmes, *Wondrous Cross*, 22).

The need for continuing atonement is provided within the covenant's terms

Just as the covenant in Torah provided for renewed, continuing atonement in the event of human lapse, so too does the covenant in Christ. In fact, it would be better to say that in each case a renewed, continuing *atonement* comes as part-and-parcel of a renewed, continuing *covenant*. For both covenants, it is important to observe once again that how that comes about is determined by however the divine covenant-maker says it will, in the covenant's express terms—namely, by obediently embracing whatever is the required *nomistic response*.

Thus, while in the covenant "in Torah" continuing atonement upon human lapse comes through participation in its repeated sacrificial provisions,[209] in the covenant "in Christ" it comes through participation in the Eucharist as the repeated celebration of the covenantal meal that re-members Christ's once-and-for-all sacrifice to effect that covenant: *Do this in remembrance of me, as often as you shall eat and drink it.*[210] The sacramental eating of the bread and drinking of the wine in the covenant meal remember the covenantal sacrifice that brought the relationship and its benefits into being: *the proclaiming of the Lord's death until he comes*.[211] It is something that is happening within the family as a celebration of the family and it is at heart deeply relational. Again, the celebratory meal in the story of the prodigal offers a fruitful interpretive window.

The new covenant conceived in the heart of God is capacious enough to have anticipated the need for covenant restoration and renewal. Participation in the repetition of the Eucharist is the appropriate nomistic response provided for in the covenant, by which continuing, renewed atonement for sin is mediated within the bigger story.

For the avoidance of doubt, the repetition of the Eucharist is to be distinguished from any sense in which the Eucharist itself operates as a supplement to Christ's work. (We note that to speak of a sacramental efficacy in the Eucharist itself may be somewhat uncomfortable for Evangelical Protestant readers.[212]) As with the sacrificial provisions of the Mosaic covenant—and

---

209. Given the bigger context in which we are arguing that atonement takes place, the covenantal provisions for sacrifice should be understood as the required nomistic response to enable the continuation or renewal *of the covenant relationship*, rather than simply to enable atonement for sin *per se*.

210. Luke 22:19–20; 1 Cor 11:23–25.

211. 1 Cor 11:23–26.

212. Limitations of space do not permit a detailed discussion of the Reformers' perspectives on the Eucharist, save to say that their concerns appear to have been mostly

for that matter all of the provisions of all divine-human covenants—their efficacy comes about solely because God as the covenant-maker says that it can be so and will be so, rather than through any cosmic mechanism or transactional formula extrinsic to the sovereign heart of God. This is why we should resist the temptation to conceive the Eucharist in terms of a mechanism or formula, just as we resist penal substitution's attempts to do the same with what happened at the cross.

3.10 "HOW MUCH MORE GLORIOUS?" (2 COR 3:9)— THE IMPLICATIONS FOR SUPERSESSIONISM

How far have we therefore progressed in proposing a framework for thinking about the atonement that is free of supersessionism and theological anti-Judaism? This is a less than fully straightforward question to answer. If the God of Israel has become incarnate in the person of his Son in the ultimate identification with his creation, as the cornerstone of an eternal divine plan, such a momentous event cannot but lead to the God of Israel's own preceding actions in this world appearing to be of lesser import in comparison. It is hard to present his actions in Christ as anything other than "something more"—*however highly those preceding actions are regarded.* It should not be dismissive of Torah in the least to propose that Torah has become personified and enfleshed—indeed, it is surely affirming. All this being the case, though, David Novak may be right that *some form* of supersessionism is simply intrinsic to Christian belief.[213] Hopefully, however, there is a good deal that can be said about our proposal that should, at worst, significantly undermine a supersessionist or anti-Judaic tag and may, at best, be considered to escape it altogether.

The first critical step has been to fully affirm the validity and efficacy of God's preceding gift of Torah in its own terms and in its own right.[214] It draws this efficacy from the trustworthiness of the covenantal promises of God, rather than from (or contingent upon) the later coming of Christ. This contrasts with the classic Reformed proposition that the preceding covenants only foreshadow atonement in Christ and hence have only retrospective effect, which promotes the value of Christ by diminishing that of Torah.

---

to do with refuting transubstantiation and with the withholding of the elements from the people.

213. Novak, *Talking with Christians*, 41 and 164, as cited by Worthen, *Internal Foe*, 259.

214. The same would, of course, be true in relation to all of God's covenantal initiatives in scripture.

If this is the case, however, we can go further. Once we jettison supersessionist presuppositions and affirm a covenant that was never revoked, there should be no basis in principle to deny that Torah can be efficacious and valid as a way of knowing him today. If in Romans 11:29 terms the *gift of God* to Israel is Torah and the *calling of God* to Israel is to live faithfully to Torah, then surely it must indeed be irrevocable as a way of knowing him. Naturally, this raises a host of contemporaneous questions, which are beyond the scope of this present work to address. These include the implications for the salvific relationship to the God of Israel of contemporary Jewish people in Torah; the compass of Torah (Written and Oral) in the present day; and what kind of relation between Christians and Jews is consistent with this account.

Roman Catholic theologians recognize a pivotal milestone in post-Holocaust Jewish-Catholic relations in the Declaration *Nostra Aetate* issued by the Second Vatican Council ("Vatican II") on October 28, 1965.[215] Gregory Baum, who served as an expert at Vatican II and worked on *Nostro Aetate*, argued that "the Church's recognition of the spiritual status of the Jewish religion is the most dramatic example of a doctrinal turn-about in the age-old magisterium ordinarium" to occur at the Council.[216] Although there is a continuing debate over the extent to which Catholic theology post-*Nostro Aetate* is still wrestling with—and remains somewhat ambiguous on the question of—replacement theology,[217] its theologians find great significance in the statements of Pope John Paul II, when he subsequently spoke of Israel as "the people of God of the Old Covenant, which has never been revoked"[218] and similarly, in another address: "It [Israel] is the people

---

215. Commission for Religious Relations with the Jews, *Guidelines and Suggestions for Implementing the Conciliar Declaration "Nostra Aetate"* (n.4).

216. Gregory Baum, "The Social Context of American Catholic Theology," in *Proceedings of the Catholic Theological Society of America* 41 (1986), 87, as cited by Pawlikowski, "Reflections on Covenant and Mission," in Moyaert and Pollefeyt (eds.), *Never Revoked*, 58.

217. Debated, for example, in the essays in Moyaert and Pollefeyt (eds.), *Never Revoked*; e.g., "Despite the undeniable significance of *Nostra Aetate*, a critical reading demonstrates that the text still contains some elements referring to substitution theology," 163. Subsequent publications have acknowledged that "Because it was such a theological breakthrough, the Conciliar text is not infrequently over-interpreted, and things are read into it which it does not in fact contain. An important example of over-interpretation would be the following: that the covenant that God made with his people Israel perdures and is never invalidated. Although this statement is true, it cannot be explicitly read into *Nostra Aetate*." "*The Gifts and the Calling of God are Irrevocable*" (*Rom. 11:29*)—*A reflection on theological questions pertaining to Catholic-Jewish relations* (10 December 2015).

218. In a speech to Jewish leaders in Mainz, November 17, 1980. Marianne Moyaert

of the covenant, and despite human infidelities, Yahweh is faithful to his covenant."[219] A similar affirmation was made by the General Assembly of the Presbyterian Church in the USA, in 1987.[220]

Momentous though such a move is, however, it is simply a stepping-stone towards further questions that follow for Catholics and Protestants alike concerning what happens *after* supersessionism. In particular, "what is the lasting significance of the first covenant if a more complete second covenant exists"?[221] "To confirm that the *old covenant* has never been revoked is of little value as long as no theological reason is provided for the existence of Judaism after the coming of Christ."[222] Once again we see a struggle with the inherent tension in affirming the unrevoked covenant at the same time as arguing that the Christ event is the unique culmination of salvation history. Thus, "the Church confirms Israel's intrinsic value but always within the borders of particular Christian *a priori*'s [sic], such as the uniqueness of Jesus as the universal savior on God's behalf."[223] "Does [Israel's] covenanted life with God in any way involve Jesus Christ?" is an apposite question.[224] Joseph Ratzinger (Pope Benedict XVI) spoke of this tension as "an unsolvable paradox."[225] Similarly, for the Presbyterian Church:

> Christians are commissioned to witness to the whole world about the good news of Christ's atoning work for both Jew and Gentile. Difficulty arises when we acknowledge that the same Scripture which proclaims that atonement and which Christians claim as God's word clearly states that Jews are already in a covenant relationship with God who makes and keeps covenants.[226]

---

and Didier Pollefeyt, "Israel and the Church: Fulfillment beyond Supersessionism?" in Moyaert and Pollefeyt (eds.), *Never Revoked*, 165n12. See also, Christian Rutishauser, "The Old Unrevoked Covenant" and "Salvation for All Nations in Christ—Catholic Doctrines in Contradiction?" in Cunningham et al. (eds.), *Christ Jesus and the Jewish People Today*, 229.

219. Moyaert and Pollefeyt, *Never Revoked*, "Introduction," 3.

220. "A Theological Understanding of the Relationship Between Christians and Jews," the Office of the General Assembly, Presbyterian Church (USA), 1987. E.g. page 10: "When speaking with Jews about matters of faith, we must always acknowledge that Jews are already in a covenantal relationship with God."

221. Moyaert and Pollefeyt, *Never Revoked*, "Israel and the Church," 165.

222. Ibid.

223. Ibid., 166.

224. Moyaert and Pollefeyt, *Never Revoked*, "Introduction," 12.

225. Moyaert and Pollefeyt, *Never Revoked*, "Israel and the Church," 165.

226. "A Theological Understanding of the Relationship," 11.

The ecumenical statement *A Sacred Obligation*[227] accepts that "revising Christian teaching about Judaism and the Jewish people is a central and indispensable obligation of theology in our time," centering this on what it calls "a sacred obligation" to affirm that "God's covenant with the Jewish people endures forever." But this is, indeed, only a start, because as it rightly observes, "our recognition of the abiding validity of Judaism has implications for all aspects of Christian life":

> Affirming God's enduring covenant with the Jewish people has consequences for Christian understandings of salvation. If Jews, who do not share our faith in Christ, are in a saving covenant with God, then Christians need new ways of understanding the universal significance of Christ.[228]

This might be alternatively stated as the conundrum of how Torah and Christ co-exist, in divine-human relational terms, for Jew and gentile, once an enduring Jewish covenant is affirmed, i.e., the problem to which figure 1 alluded. As Ratzinger aptly observes, this will very much depend on one's stance concerning Christ:

> I have ever more come to the realization that Judaism (which strictly speaking, began with the end of the formation of the Canon, that is, in the first century after Christ) and the Christian faith described in the New Testament are two ways of appropriating Israel's Scriptures, two ways that, in the end, are both determined by the position one assumes with regard to the figure of Jesus of Nazareth. The Scripture we today call Old Testament is in itself open to both ways.[229]

Thus we are returned to the question of what it looks like to affirm God's enduring covenantal relationship in Torah at the same time as holding the new covenant in Christ in highest regard. And it is from this point on that we are at risk of some form of supersessionism, once we come to suggest that there are qualitative differences in what God has done in and through Torah compared to what God has done in and through Christ.

---

227. *A Sacred Obligation: Rethinking Christian Faith in Relation to Judaism and the Jewish People: A Statement by the Christian Scholars Group on Christian-Jewish Relation*, 1 September 2002 (Boston: Centre for Christian-Jewish Learning, Boston College). Available at http://www.bc.edu/content/dam/files/research_sites/cjl/sites/partners/csg/Sacred_Obligation.htm (accessed 9 April, 2017).

228. Ibid. (no pagination).

229. Ratzinger, *Milestones*, 53–54.

A qualitative comparison is not inherently supersessionist, of course, since no "replacement" or "taking the place of" is occurring.[230] Still less does it reflect a theological anti-Judaism. Once we understand the covenants to exist in parallel not in series and both to be valid as ways of knowing that one is in right relationship with God, albeit in different terms, then to make a direct comparison between the law and Christ—in which the salvific efficacy of each is seen as being "in competition," with Christianity finding the claims of the former wanting—would be a category error. It would mean that the law and Christ were never rivals in that sense and that the distinction between covenants is to be found in their relational character rather than their salvific efficacy. The comparison and contrast between Christ and Torah would be found in the nature of the relationship that each offers.

To say that the covenant in Christ offers something *more than* Torah would not in itself be supersessionist or anti-Judaic, whether its "more than" is understood in qualitative terms (the quality of the relationship in Christ) or quantitative terms (the breadth and depth of Christ's work). And this perhaps indicates the best way of framing this question relationally: if *both* covenant relationships are available to Jew and gentile and each is effectual in its own terms, which is the *preferred relationship* to pursue?

Might it be the case that when the early Jewish Christians were faced with such a question, they would have said to their fellow-countrymen: "Yes, both Jew and gentile can be in relationship with the God of Israel through what he did in sending Torah; but why would both Jew and gentile alike not want to be in relationship with the God of Israel through what he has now done in sending his own Son as Torah's living embodiment?" Given their own experiences as Jews of knowing God through Christ, it would surely have been inconceivable that their fellow Jews would choose knowing God through the *indirect* route of the written Torah alone when they now have the opportunity to know him *directly* through Christ. The God of Israel who had once spoken in and through the words of Torah written on stone had now spoken—and was continuing to speak—in and through the living Torah made flesh written on hearts through the Holy Spirit. "Knowing God through Torah is glorious," Paul might say, "but is it not more glorious still to know God through Christ?" This comports with Philippians 3:7–8 (NIV):

> But whatever were gains to me I now consider loss for the sake of Christ. What is more, I consider everything a loss because of the surpassing worth of knowing Christ Jesus my Lord, for

---

230. However, this may not satisfy Moyaert and Pollefeyt in their definition of supersessionism as "to be superior to." See *Never Revoked*, "Israel and the Church," 159.

whose sake I have lost all things. I consider them garbage, that I may gain Christ.

The context suggests the *previous gains* that Paul has now elected to lose are to do with the relationship with God that comes through Torah (v. 9):[231] "circumcised on the eighth day, of the people of Israel, of the tribe of Benjamin, a Hebrew of Hebrews; in regard to the law, a Pharisee; as for zeal, persecuting the church; as for righteousness based on the law, faultless." (vv. 5–6).

It is perhaps in the suggestion of a gain in the nature of the new over the old that a *hint* of supersessionism may be found, if only in the sense of a "something more," a *surpassing* of what Paul previously enjoyed.

The Philippians 3 passage has been taken to be Paul's general renunciation of his prior Judaism in favor of his new-found Christian faith. However, he appears to be using the comparison solely to highlight what he has now, not to denigrate what he had before. Hence, it falls well short of supersessionism or theological anti-Judaism. It is the greatness of what he had already that seems to provide Paul with such a valuable "more than"-based comparison to the surpassing worth of what he has now. Had the past *truly been* "garbage" then to compare his experience of Christ to it would hardly offer much of a positive endorsement![232] As Campbell observes, it therefore possesses *relative*, not *absolute*, negativity:

> The entire basis of the argument is a relative one premised upon the positive nature of the present Christian state—one of sonship, inheritance, promise, the Spirit, and so on—*in the light of which* any prior existence in the cosmos is coded negatively, with corresponding metaphors of confinement and immaturity. It follows, however, that this prior state cannot necessarily be perceived in these negative terms until the later, more positive state has been entered; *this negativity is visible only in retrospect.*[233]

---

231. The "loss" may be his sadness in setting aside Jewish lifestyle distinctives in his own life, such as food laws and Sabbath observance, and/or, the fact Paul knows he cannot teach a blending of the two ways of knowing God, in Torah and in Christ; not least because (based upon what God has already done for the gentiles outside of Torah) those lifestyle distinctives are not a feature of Paul's gospel to the gentiles and hence are "his loss" for the sake of his calling to the gentiles.

232. This proposal stands in contrast to the view that Paul had now realized that what he had thought of as "gains" were in fact not that at all, because "his attitude towards his privileges and attainments was wrong." That "when God apprehended him, Paul saw them for what they were—fleshly and therefore fallible human efforts, tainted with sin and therefore unable to receive God's approval." Thielman, *Philippians*, 170.

233. Campbell, *Deliverance of God*, 885, also 150.

Perhaps what Paul was therefore saying can be paraphrased in this way: "In terms of what I had, what I knew of God, revealed through our wonderful Torah, things could not have been better. But, when I think about it *compared to what I have now*, it's as if all that was, frankly . . . garbage!" The strength of the statement is no doubt intended to shock his audience (note the KJV's use of "dung") but this could be its impact only if both Paul and his audience held Torah in exceptionally high regard. Sanders has hinted at this same understanding: Paul is formulating "a contrast between degrees of whiteness: what was glorious and what is more glorious." "He came to relegate the Mosaic dispensation to a less glorious place *because* he found something more glorious."[234]

Choosing a metaphor to illustrate this may be invidious, but we could posit the development in television pictures. Once these were available only as relatively-blurry analogue, which in the light of ultra-high definition digital quality images have been shown to have limitations of which most viewers were previously unaware. It was only in the light of the subsequent coming of digital pictures that the difference became evident. That development did not make analogue wrong, of course, and nor did it make it unwatchable (then, or now), but given the choice most would prefer the enhanced clarity, sharpness of focus and higher definition of the new development. Might something like this be the case in relation to the eschatological development of the divine-human covenant?

Dunn notes of Paul's Damascus road encounter with the risen Christ that what we observe goes beyond the exchange of one set of cognitive beliefs for another. There is "something more" and it appears to derive from Paul's experience of knowing Christ from that time on:

> Paul's conversion must be seen as a fulcrum point or hinge on which his whole theology turned around. And certainly it was the encounter with the risen Christ (as he perceived it) which formed that fulcrum and hinge.[235]
>
> Paul's own experience played a vital role in the reconstruction of his theology as a Christian and apostle. The theology of Paul was neither born nor sustained by or as a purely cerebral exercise.[236]

Segal makes a similar point: "Paul is not converted by Jesus' teachings, but rather by an experience, a revelation of Christ, which radically reorients

---

234. Sanders, *Jewish People*, 138.
235. Dunn, *Theology of Paul*, 179.
236. Ibid.

his life."[237] Experience, rather than conversion, is the key term defining the event.

With all this in mind, how might we summarize the nature of that qualitative difference between knowing God in Torah and knowing God in Christ? We may identify two particular aspects.

Firstly, concerning Torah we may say that it is a "mediated relationship" (Gal 3:19–20; cf. Exod 19). In that sense, it is "second-hand" or "once-removed." Knowing God through Christ, on the other hand, is an "unmediated relationship." It is a "first-hand" relationship directly with the Word, rather than a "second hand" relationship indirectly with the words. The relationship is to the precepts, what God has said (past tense), rather than directly to God himself, what God is saying (present tense). In the covenant in Christ, Paul appears to see the eschatological outpouring of the Spirit as fulfilling the disintermediated way of knowing God directly of which Jeremiah spoke in Jeremiah 31. In Romans 5:5, for example, "God's love has been poured out into our hearts through the Holy Spirit, who has been given to us." (NIV).

Secondly, Torah is a relationship defined in bounded-set categories—to be relating to God "in Torah" is to be living within pre-established boundaries or boundary-markers (food laws, purity, Sabbath, circumcision, and so on). So long as you stay within them, says Torah, then by definition you know you are in right relationship with God. This inevitably carries some danger of an imbalance in focus on the boundaries *versus* the center: something of which the Psalmist and the Prophets were no doubt aware in emphasizing the relational center of the covenant and which was a frequent emphasis of Jesus in his engagements with the more boundary-focused Pharisees. In contrast, the relationship in Christ is defined in centered-set terms. One lives life defined by reference to one's closeness to the center (namely, Christ),[238] rather than by reference to being within the boundary-markers (of Torah). This carries some risk of antinomianism, of course, which is perhaps what churches such as Corinth encountered; losing sight of how to live right, when the focus shifted from boundaries to center.

We can therefore see how Paul might say "Why would you want to limit yourself to the earlier way of knowing God—effective and God-given though it is—when you have the opportunity to participate in this new way of knowing God, that he himself has clearly initiated?" This would be to commend a new and enhanced way rather than to condemn an old and

---

237. Segal, *Paul the Convert*, 3.

238. One might say that relationally, the Christian life is a journey from outer to center.

ineffectual way. Once again, the dilemma for Jews of what God has done in Christ would be not because Torah is flawed, but because Torah is wonderful. Were it otherwise—if its adherents consistently experienced it as leading to Luther's anguished conscience—there would be no dilemma! Nor would it be the case that the one offered right relationship with God while the other did not; it would rather be that the nature of each relationship was differently defined and experienced.

This would suggest that the serious challenge faced by Jews may have been how to relate the coming of Messiah Jesus—announcing a new way of knowing him in centered-set terms—to the bounded-set elements of Torah, the boundary markers and God-given lifestyle distinctives through which assurance of right-standing with God had always been found. Although in the first instance the question appears to be the same for both Jew and gentile—namely, "How to relate Jesus to Torah"—each approaches the question from a very different position. The Jew was already in a covenantal relationship in Torah, the gentile was not. Hence, if it was evident that there were now two God-given ways of effectually knowing him—indirectly "in Torah" or directly "in Christ"—why would the gentile not opt for Christ? Equally, however, there would be a both theological and practical dilemma for the faithful Jew in determining how traditional Jewish lifestyle distinctives should continue to fit with knowing God through Christ, not least because—up until now—the people of God had been wholly defined by those distinctives. (We suggest that only theological anti-Judaism would argue that such concerns of conscience should be trifling.)

That God should inaugurate this dramatic new way of knowing him should not of course lead to the automatic conclusion that there was any necessity in nascent Christianity for Jews to give up on the practices of Torah. Campbell argues that Paul was "happy for Jewish Christians to observe the law, provided that this is not, in effect, compulsory either for them or for pagan converts; it is an activity framed by freedom; see esp. 1 Cor. 9:19–22."[239] A centered-set focus does not mean that one must now live outside of the old boundaries—closeness to the center and living within the boundary markers are not inherently incompatible. Nor does it necessarily mean that Paul saw any incongruity between continuing the practices of Torah himself, for his own personal preference, as part of living respectfully to the God-given traditions ("I have done nothing against our people or against the customs of our ancestors," Acts 28:17) and disavowing the idea that they continued to function relationally, as they once did, in *uniquely* defining a person's standing before God. Yet it would surely have been clear to him in

---

239. Campbell, *Deliverance of God*, 886.

what God had done through Christ that a relationship with God that was fundamentally defined by one's place relative to boundary markers had been overshadowed.

So, in conclusion, while Jews would face an understandable dilemma in how to relate God's wonderful gift of Torah to his wonderful gift of Christ (and perhaps especially so, proselyte converts, who have already endured the literal pain of adopting circumcision), there would be no reason for gentile believers to have any such concerns absent the (well-meaning?) actions of those whom Paul called "agitators." While it seems clear that the gospel Paul had preached to the Galatians had not included any expectation that aspects of Torah-compliance be required of their faith in Christ, Paul should not be assumed to have been thereby disaffirming Torah—either for Jew or gentile—but simply following what appeared to be God's lead in what he had done among them by not requiring Torah's features to be prerequisites for a relationship in Christ.[240]

3.11 CLOSING THOUGHTS

As we began by noting, atonement theology has traditionally approached its answer to the "how?" question by reference to a range of metaphors and models that are almost entirely universalized and ahistorical in their foundations—and, we might add, that are conceived and applied in individualized, autobiographical terms. In contrast, Israel's conception of atonement was situated in a corporate election and covenantal initiation on the part of the God of Israel—with continuing atonement provided for within the covenant's terms—and an initial and continuing nomistic response by those to whom the covenant was offered. This covenantal framework was clearly conceived by Israel as a reality, not simply a "picture" to illustrate something. This being the case, one can only wonder why Christianity has expected to find the answer addressed in a manner wholly uprooted from the relational story of Israel and its God which supplies the majority of the Christian canon and within which context atonement in Christ came about. It is the argument of this book that it should not. We suggest that only a tradition that starts with a supersessionist and anti-Judaistic logic would conceive that it should be otherwise.

This, then, sums up the perspective we are proposing:

---

240. E.g., Gal 3:2–5. Hence perhaps the nature of Paul's appeal to the Galatian believers was not unnecessarily to take a specifically Jewish problem (how to relate Torah to Christ) upon themselves.

1. Atonement in Christ follows the structure and logic of atonement in Torah. In each case atonement is situated within a covenantal context.

2. Since each begins with a grace-based welcome into a covenantal relationship—"in Torah" to one nation, "in Christ" to all nations—the *naissance* of atonement derives from a prior decision in the heart of God to reach out (initially to Israel and then to the world) to offer an "at one" relationship with him.

3. The overarching purpose of God's covenantal initiatives is broader than simply dealing with the sin that has damaged creation (however necessary that may be). As Soulen observes, "redemption is for the sake of consummation, not consummation for the sake of redemption."[241] Rather than the unity of the canon being "best unlocked by insisting that everything in the Bible points towards Jesus Christ," it is more helpful to discern that unity in the recognition that both Old and New Testaments are "centrally concerned with the God of Israel and the God of Israel's coming reign of *shalom*."[242]

4. In the case of the new covenant, the divine initiative becomes a reality through its sealing or "cutting" in the death of Christ the ultimate covenantal sacrifice of the ultimate covenant.

5. God invites human acceptance of that covenantal initiative through a nomism which involves living in accordance with the terms of the covenant-maker: namely, to live "in Christ," just as in the Mosaic covenant one would live "in Torah."

6. Finally, the need for there to be continuing atonement upon inevitable human failure is divinely foreseen and hence pre-provided within the covenants' terms.

This way of positioning the atonement in covenantal context does not make the historic metaphors wrong, flawed or inapplicable to what it means to experience an atoned relationship. The metaphors are not wrong in relation to the aspects of the truth that they are conveying, and nor has the church been wrong to understand aspects of the atonement through that imagery. What *has* occurred, however, is a mismatch of "question" and "answer," because the continuity within the entire canon upon which they depend has been missed. The historic metaphors are answering a broader question than that which has been presumed—one that goes beyond a

---

241. Soulen, *God of Israel*, 175.

242. Ibid., 175. "Without doubt everything turns on Christ, but not everything concerns Christ."

dehistoricized and universalized question of how sin is dealt with at the cross. They speak of the benefits of being in an atoned relationship in a covenantal kinship setting (of which more in the next chapter).

To affirm God's relationship with Israel through Torah—including its provisions for atonement and the authenticity of the relationship with God that it offers—does not in itself do any damage to the uniqueness of Christ, to the universal offer to humanity to know God through Christ, or to what God has done for the world in Christ. Christians may continue passionately to proclaim the wonders of God's covenantal initiative in Christ and invite all people—Jews included—to respond with the nomism that gives effect to a relationship with God through Christ in individual lives. At the same time, however, we should desist from speaking contemptuously of God's covenantal initiative to Israel in Torah and should not hinder Israel—proselyte gentiles included—from engaging in its own nomistic response to an enduring covenant in Torah if it so wishes. Reconceiving the relationship of the gospel to Torah in this non-competitive way, accepting each way of relating to God—"in Torah" and "in Christ"—as valid, but different, would enable Christianity to more easily disavow supersessionism and theological anti-Judaism. At the same time, the theological anti-Judaism that cheerily denigrates Torah and the Jews of Jesus's day (and, of course, by implication, of our day) should be expelled from the Christian vocabulary, since unwittingly or otherwise, intentional or naïve, it amounts to a criticism of Torah's divine author rather than just a perceived "soft target" of Judaism.

Perhaps it is the case that the Christian tendency to default towards seeing atonement in "transactional" terms (and to pitch it against a Torah also seen in transactional terms)—"getting in," as Sanders would say—has blinded us to seeing atonement in *both* covenants in fundamentally relational terms. One of the major benefits of a covenantal framework lies in showing that it is the nature of the relationship (the basis of "knowing God") that each covenant offers which should be compared and contrasted, rather than the efficacy or permanence of one *versus* the other and still less, a reductionism that sees each covenant as largely or solely to do with addressing the problem of sin.

Lastly, how is the kind of reading we are proposing harmonious with an Evangelical lens? We may test this from the perspective of Bebbington's quadrilateral of biblicism, crucicentrism, activism and conversionism:

1. It is *biblicist* in taking seriously the God-breathed nature of the Hebrew scriptures that comprise the major portion of the Bible.[243] It is harmonious with a contemporary reading of Paul derived from

---

243. 2 Tim 3:16.

recent scholarship. It bases itself in a covenantal hermeneutic that is indisputably central to the overall scriptural narrative, in which the features of the Mosaic covenant "model" and "mirror" the features of the Christian covenant (in a thoroughly positive way). It is affirming of the full canon, in that it sees the Old Testament as a lens to illuminate the New Testament, and the New as a lens to illuminate the Old.

2. It is *crucicentric* in that it recognizes an essential role for the cross in the ratification—the ultimate sealing (or cutting)—of the ultimate covenant as an unrepeatable event. However, a covenantal framework locates Christ's work at the cross as the centerpoint of a grander story of God's overarching purposes as consummator, rather than treating its redemptive role for sin in isolation. This reading addresses sin in all its seriousness, but it does not give sin the starring role. It positions the cross at the very beginning of a relational story, the Lamb who was slain from the creation of the world.[244] Not all may agree with Rolf Rendtorff's conclusion that there is but "one, continually 'new' covenant" throughout the Old Testament,[245] but we would wish to say that there is one continual covenantal narrative throughout the canon, by which God's consummative purposes are revealed and in which individual covenants are distinguished by nuanced variation rather than fundamental difference. Dealing with sin is positioned within that overarching purpose as a means to an end rather than the end in itself.

3. It encourages *activism* in that it delivers a readily-explainable account of the good news of the new covenant without resorting to penal explanations that—if they ever did—no longer relate to contemporary western culture. Instead, it offers an account based in relationship that resonates within a society that understands both the joys of relationship and the reality and pain of relationship breakdown in a more relationally-transitory world. It also is respectful of the Jewish faith in finding supersessionist and anti-Judaic contrasts unnecessary for its explanatory power.

4. And finally, it is *conversionist* in that it requires a response—a decision to choose to accept and live in obedience to the terms of the covenant. Just as Israel's covenant was berthed in God's sovereign and unmerited decision to elect a nation, to which a nomistic response was invited, so too the covenant in Christ, only now in God's election of all nations.

---

244. Rev 13:8, for which the NIV offers as an alternative translation "written from the creation of the world in the book of life belonging to the Lamb who was slain."

245. Rendtorff, *The Covenant Formula*, 78.

In the classic terms of John 3:16, its narrative of salvation begins with God's covenantal love for the world to which a nomistic response is invited. Given that it is God's covenantal initiatives which bring the covenants into being, both "old" and "new" center not on what is involved in "getting in" as a transaction but what is involved in "staying in" as a relationship.

CHAPTER FOUR

The Continuing Place of the Traditional Ideas of Atonement

The central focus of the proclamation after Easter was that the events of Jesus' history, and particularly of the Easter period, had changed the status of believers, indeed of the whole world. The metaphors of atonement are ways of expressing the significance of what had happened and was happening. They therefore enable the Christian community to speak of God as he is found in concrete personal relationship with human beings and their world.[1]

4.1. INTRODUCTION

IT HAS BEEN OUR contention that the traditional explanatory framework on which Christian thought has relied concerning the doctrine of the atonement is rootless as regards its relationship to the history of Israel and its God. Over the course of the last half-century in particular, however, the landscape has changed, with a new scholarly awareness of Second Temple Judaism leading to a rejection of the older ideas that presupposed it to be an obsolete and even corrupt religion that primarily existed to serve as a dark background against which the light of Christ could be favorably contrasted. We have argued that once this traditional negative presumption rooted in supersessionism and theological anti-Judaism is corrected, a fresh view of Christ's atoning work becomes available.

The idea of centering atonement in a "new covenant" in Christ is scarcely novel; the difference is to understand its structure and efficacy in

---

1. Gunton, *Actuality of Atonement*, 46.

ways that are positively modelled on the structure and efficacy of the preceding covenant in Torah. This perspective on the atonement takes as its starting point a presumed *continuity* with Israel's relational history with its God, rather than the presumed *contrast* that has traditionally been supposed. It argues that that history should be a positive rather than negative lens for Christian interpretation; an approach that places God's history with Israel in high, not low, regard. It discerns a manifest coherence in the relational actions of God throughout the biblical narrative, displaying a consistency in the divine nature, character, and purposes. Israel's history is no longer seen as merely prefigurative, preparing the way for something much higher and grander.[2] Our proposal argues that the relativization of the first part of the canon causes something significant to be lost vis-à-vis the second part. A rehabilitated view of Israel—in which the supersessionist assumptions and theological anti-Judaism that have reigned for so long are eliminated—leads to a fresh validation of the entire canon. The permanence of the God of Israel's covenantal commitment to the nation of Israel in Torah becomes both the model and the assurance for the permanence of his covenantal commitment to the nations in Christ.

We began this study by questioning the assumption of Macquarrie that the best we can hope for in thinking about the atonement is "a number of analogies and metaphors, correcting and supplementing each other but together conveying something of the mystery of the cross as it has been experienced in Christian faith."[3] To recap, we have sought to mount this challenge by an argument developed on a number of levels.

Firstly, we suggested that recent new perspectives on the world of first-century Judaism provide the basis for a fundamental reconsideration of the atonement, once it is perceived in ways that are consonant with the relational history of Israel and its God centered in covenant. This requires the affirmation of Israel's covenantal relationship—in its own right, without a dependency on God's temporally subsequent actions in Christ—and the consequential elimination of supersessionism and theological anti-Judaism from our interpretive criteria.

Secondly, we proposed that atonement itself should be no mystery and nor does the New Testament speak of it in terms of a mystery. Rather, the emphasis appears to be on what once was mystery having now been revealed.[4] Matthew 13:35 specifically speaks of Jesus's teaching as *revealing* "things hidden since the creation of the world." Hence to settle for atone-

---

2. Soulen, *God of Israel*, 112.
3. Macquarrie, *Jesus Christ*, 400.
4. E.g. Rom 11:25; 16:25; 1 Cor 15:51; Eph 1:9; 3:5; and Col 1:26.

ment being inherently mysterious is both unsatisfactory and inconsistent with scripture. We suggest that a particular factor in making it mysterious has been the Israel-forgetfulness of the church's doctrinal formulations. The only mystery in atonement—albeit a profound one—is why God so loves the world that he would act as he has done.

Thirdly, that atonement conceived in covenantal terms serves as far more than an additional illustrative trope, one more metaphor alongside the many. In fact, it fails to fit the definition of metaphor at all. Israel does not appear to have understood its covenantal relation to God as purely (or primarily) an illustration of some other truth, still less an illustration to illuminate atonement for a successor that we now know to be called "the church." On the contrary, in the texts that deal with God's covenantal initiatives towards Israel there is no suggestion that the covenant functions as something being likened to something else, nor that, if applied literally, it would be obviously untrue. With respect to covenant, therefore, the Hebrew scriptures do not appear to speak metaphorically.

To doubt the effectiveness of the covenantal history of the God of Israel with Israel, on its own terms, on a plain reading, would be grounds to similarly doubt the new covenantal basis of the Christian's relationship with God through Christ, since each is equally founded upon the reliability of God's covenantal promises. God spoke the covenants into concrete existence just as he spoke creation into concrete existence. Though the Old Testament makes widespread use of metaphor in other contexts, covenant was far from merely a "picture" underlying Jewish religious thought. On the contrary, Israel's participation in the divine covenant in Torah was a daily reality—every aspect of the life of the community was being lived out in accordance with what God had said. It was not primarily a matter of belief but one of *praxis*. To do the works of the law was the faithful response to a covenant that Israel understood actually to exist. Living "in Torah" was not a *likening* to something, it was the *substance* of something—an "enacted reality":

> So long as theologians conceive their task as primarily elucidating biblical "ideas," they will continue to miss the fundamental significance of covenant in the biblical tradition. Covenant is not an "idea" to be embraced in the mind, and therefore religious community cannot be defined with respect to "orthodox" appraisals of that idea. Covenant is an "enacted reality" that is either manifested in the concrete choices individuals make, or not.[5]

5. Mendenhall and Herion, "Covenant," 1201.

God had initiated an actual covenant with tangible features—a reliable and effective covenant—to which living in accordance with what God had said, in daily life, was the obedient response called for in the covenant terms. It was not that Israel foolishly took it all literally, whereas God had intended it only metaphorically!

It is because Christian thought has failed to position atonement in a covenantal context throughout the overarching story of the canon—or more particularly, because it has relativized the first part of the canon—that atonement doctrine has ended up as a *pot pourri* of dehistoricized ideas compiled from cultural ideas and individual texts. The variegated scriptural *motifs* of atonement have been decoupled from their integrating anchor point. It is of course the case that, to varying degrees, all of the classic images of atonement can be located in scripture or logically connected to it. Hence, from a biblicist point of view, all are to be taken seriously. They have an abiding value as biblically-warranted expressions of aspects of the believer's relationship with God through Christ. The question is how the images are positioned, within an overarching covenantal understanding in which the epicenter of atonement is located as a fundamental prior decision in the heart of God to enter into a covenantal relationship affirmed in a covenantal enactment.

Before we consider how the traditional metaphors "fit" with this approach, it will be helpful to reposition the place of sin, as something that is important to the story as an enemy of human flourishing but should not be allowed to dominate its telling.

4.2. REVISITING SIN'S PLACE IN THE ATONEMENT STORY

It has seemed axiomatic in Christian theology that "the human problem" is "sin" and that atonement necessarily starts with sin and is directed towards how sin is dealt with. The definition of atonement offered by Torrance, for example, is "the divine work of covering and putting away sin."[6] In a sense this sin-focus is entirely unsurprising, since embedded within the very word "atonement" is the idea of a bringing back together—a making "at one"—of parties that have become estranged. Christian thought has traditionally identified the cause of that estrangement as the invasion and propagation of sin originating with our first parents' disobedience in the fall, in which we all become personally culpable, with Christ as the necessary and exclusive

---

6. Torrance, *Atonement*, 453.

divine remedy. In soteriological terms, of course, this amounts to moving directly from Adam to Christ: one small step for the church, with its traditional disregard for the place of Israel, but one giant leap for the church's canonical narrative. In this foreshortened telling, Christianity simply "fast forwards" through the Hebrew scriptures from creation to passion.

We recall Soulen's characterization of this giant leap as an "Israel-forgetfulness" within the foreground of the "standard model."[7] As Soulen rightly identifies, the story suffers a thematic foreshortening which is compressed into a "basic antithesis of Adam's sin and redemption in Christ."[8] The traditional metaphors to explain atonement all tend to begin with a starting point of what is bad rather than what is good. The problems of the human situation are not in doubt, of course—and nor is it in doubt that they find a corresponding solution in Christ—but this ought not to accord "the bad" a foundational standing in soteriological thought.

As Genesis 1 makes clear, each element of God's creation is good, and in its entirety it is very good. No hostile actions of any third party can change the fundamentals of that status—which is why in God's opinion it is worth "saving" in the first place. God's purposes to restore his very good creation cannot ultimately be thwarted by any enemy—whether sin, Satan, or death. One might say that the most fundamental covenantal commitment in scripture—though not articulated in these terms *per se*—is God's initiatory act of bringing into being a very good creation. The second most fundamental covenant commitment is to save and deliver it, and paramount within that creation is the divine-human relationship, which by his covenantal character he has committed himself to go—metaphorically-speaking—to the ends of the earth to sustain. The creation narrative of an "at-one" relationship between God and the human community is the *start-point* of the scriptural story. The drama surrounding its disintegration and God's sovereign plan for its restoration—with its many ups and downs as the story unfolds in God's covenantal initiatives, up to and including the ultimate "new" covenant—in the consummation that is its object and promise, is the *focal-point* of the scriptural story thereafter.

Sin is characterized by Soulen as the human family's efforts to procure blessing on its own terms, at the expense of others: turning its back on God's blessing and doing violence to the human other. As a result, an economy of blessing becomes an economy of curse—in which God's curse is, simply, "God's blessing as seen from the backside," "from the perspective

---

7. Soulen, *God of Israel*, 49.
8. Ibid., 52–3.

of the creature who has repudiated it."⁹ It remains clear that "sin, evil and oppression (and the corresponding need for redemption and liberation) are undeniable dimensions of God's history with Israel and the nations";¹⁰ nonetheless, the antithesis of sin and redemption is not the central theme and nor is it an object of concern in isolation. Rather, "liberation from powers that destroy is a matter of utmost urgency precisely because such powers threaten to cut humankind off from God's economy of consummation, where God's blessings are bestowed."¹¹

God's work as redeemer can therefore be said to be secondary in that it serves to confirm his primary objective. The theme of sin and deliverance certainly complicates the basic plot, says Soulen, but it does not supplant it; even in the narrative of the flood, "the high point of God's struggle with wickedness in the creation sagas, the narrative's prime concern remains God's blessing [. . .]. This blessing is the true cargo of the ark."¹²

It is unsurprising that this line of thought should lead Soulen to locate his theological proposal within a covenantal framework. God's purposes unfold through the covenantal promise to Abraham in Genesis 12. The promise "places the entire history that is about to unfold between the Lord, Israel, and the nations under the programmatic sign of God's covenant blessing."¹³

> Now the LORD said to Abram, "Go from your country and your kindred and your father's house to the land that I will show you. I will make of you a great nation, and I will bless you, and make your name great, so that you will be a blessing. I will bless those who bless you, and the one who curses you I will curse; and in you all the families of the earth shall be blessed."¹⁴

Thus, antecedent to the biblical narrative of redemption is a divine covenantal commitment of blessing to the human race—all the families of the earth.

> Contrary to a common Christian assumption, nothing about this passage [Genesis 12] or its immediate context suggests that God's primary motive in calling Abraham is any special concern with the problem of sin, evil, or wickedness. To the contrary,

9. Ibid., 141–42.
10. Ibid., 112.
11. Ibid.
12. Ibid., 119.
13. Ibid., 120.
14. Gen 12:1–3 (NRSV).

God's motive seems chiefly to be the sheer fecundity and capaciousness of the divine good pleasure.[15]

What we see in God's dealings with Israel in the Old Testament offers a theological framework for the interpretation of his work in Christ in the New Testament. Once again, the idea is nothing new; the newness is to propose that the proper interpretation of this framework is to see it as one in which God's new work is acknowledged to be in positive continuity with his preceding works, rather than in negative contrast to them. Hence, just as the redemptive narrative of the Old Testament takes place within an overarching prior covenantal commitment to the nation of Israel as God's chosen people, so too does the redemptive narrative of Christ in the New Testament—only now, the election and covenantal commitment is to all nations and it is ratified (made, or cut) in the ultimate covenant sacrifice on the cross. Just as the covenant "in Torah" brings about and maintains an atoned relationship, so too does the covenant "in Christ." Here once again we are conceiving atonement in a broader sense than simply a reparative action through some transaction within the Godhead.

Atonement "in Christ" defined in this manner does not start at the cross, any more than "in Torah" it starts with a sin offering. In each case, it begins with a decision in the heart of God to enter into a covenant with humanity. The covenant ratification ceremony then brings the atoned relationship into being, upon its nomistic acceptance. The covenant provides the framework and terms according to which an at-one relationship is firstly established and secondly maintained.

The terms of the covenant determine how *on-going atonement*—the maintenance of the covenant relationship after it is first brought about—is actualized for the sinner, through what the covenant-maker has provided in the covenant's terms. In the covenant in Torah, one might summarize this as faithful participation in its sacrificial provisions and Day of Atonement. In the covenant in Christ, one might summarize this as faithful participation in the Eucharist, which remembers—and sacramentally reappropriates—Christ's one-time covenantal sacrifice which is forever effective for all. Participation in that covenantal meal both renews and reminds us afresh of the familial kinship commitment, likened to a father-son relationship, which is central to our understanding of what covenant itself means and of the nature and character of the Father in that suzerain role.

However, we are still left with the question of the place and function of the traditional models and metaphors. And it is "covenant" that not only answers the question but tells us their positioning within this larger

15. Ibid., 120.

framework: *the traditional metaphors are describing the benefits of living in an atoned relationship within the covenant.*

4.3 TRADITIONAL METAPHORS RECONTEXTUALIZED WITHIN COVENANT

We have observed that the traditional atonement models and metaphors conceive the atoning work of Christ in a fragmented way, with no common *nexus* that draws them together. Each is seen in essentially isolated and self-contained terms, competing to be the "best" reading. Our proposal does not reject the traditional ideas but repositions them as *secondary* actions within a covenantal relationship entered into at the cross. Seen in this way, the models and metaphors are speaking of God's actions in *fulfilling his covenantal commitment* rather than something that sits detached and in isolation. The benefits of the atoning work of Christ that they describe come as a consequence of—as part and parcel of—the covenantal commitment. In Old Testament perspective, these actions can be described as characteristics of the Divine Kinsman who leads in battle, redeems from slavery, loves, blesses, provides, and protects. Because God has entered into a covenantal commitment to his creation he acts under the covenant to defend it against the alien powers and forces that have invaded and damaged it. Such is the nature of a suzerain's commitment to the vassal in a covenant, and all the more so the commitment of the Divine Kinsman. Hence the models and metaphors describe consequences of being in a covenantal relationship rather than simply an initial putting-right.

With this preceding covenantal relationship as their framework, God's actions in Christ acquire a basis and foundation for their interpretation—the benefits of atonement follow a decision in the heart of God that antecedes them, located in election and given effect in covenant. Thus, the atonement models and metaphors have to do with the obligations that the covenant-maker gladly and willingly assumes, to act to protect and defend the covenanted party in relation to that which attacks and threatens to do it harm. They continue to speak of Christ's work just as much or more than they ever did, but they are *repositioned* within a grander covenantal narrative.

This view also enables us to somewhat rehabilitate the notion of Christ "fulfilling" Israel's covenant, but only insofar as we conceive it as God's fulfilling of the commitment he pledged within that covenant. This should be seen not in terms of God "ending" something in relation to Israel but rather acting in Christ in on-going fulfillment of an eternal covenantal commitment—to bless, protect, and restore human life—in which the pivotal moment in the story-to-date is the first coming of Jesus the Messiah. We can see how Jesus's mission statement in his first sermon, in Luke 4, can be thought of as the outworking of precisely such a divine covenantal commitment, where God's actions in Christ are those of the divine covenant-maker vis-à-vis that which threatens his covenant people. Moreover, they are eschatologically framed by reference to Isaiah 61.

> He stood up to read, and the scroll of the prophet Isaiah was handed to him. Unrolling it, he found the place where it is written:
>
> > "The Spirit of the Lord is on me,
> > because he has anointed me
> > to proclaim good news to the poor.
> > He has sent me to proclaim freedom for the prisoners
> > and recovery of sight for the blind,
> > to set the oppressed free,
> > to proclaim the year of the Lord's favor."
>
> Then he rolled up the scroll, gave it back to the attendant and sat down. The eyes of everyone in the synagogue were fastened on him. He began by saying to them, "Today this scripture is fulfilled in your hearing."[16]

This is precisely the kind of action that the suzerain, the Divine Kinsman, would take against enemies and alien forces that have invaded the vassals' land and wreaked havoc on his covenant people's lives and experience.

Once the traditional models and metaphors are thus situated, we no longer need to see them as "competing" to establish a single winning idea that "causes" atonement to happen or best reflects what it entails. The complexities of the human situation due to sin will unsurprisingly lead to a range of concurrent divine actions. Multi-faceted problems—and the different ways that humans experience and perceive them—require more than one action in response and more than one way of apprehending that action. All such actions, however, are in fulfillment of an overarching covenantal commitment. Each metaphor illustrates, within concepts to which human understanding can relate, an aspect of what it means to be in an atoned relationship. However, there is no compelling reason why the church need necessarily promote any particular metaphor in a particular time or place, since at different times and places the enemies of human life and flourishing will be perceived in different ways. The point is that whatever those enemies are and however they are conceived and articulated—whether in terms of

---

16. Luke 4:16–21 (NIV). Cf. Isaiah 61.

sin, evil, sickness, demonic and oppressive forces, alienation, fear, or the like[17]—God acts against them on our behalf in the covenant in Christ. He acts under the covenant to do all that is needful not simply to enable us to enter into an atoned relationship at the outset of the covenant but also to maintain our at-one-ness with the Father by defeating all that would threaten and jeopardise it. Moreover, he also acts to defeat the very epitome of the consequences of human sin—death itself—leading to eternal life, since once death is vanquished there is no impediment to life being eternal for those "in Christ." The new creation of which scripture speaks describes a new world in which the covenant-maker has fulfilled every commitment he has made to his creation, pictorially reflected in, e.g., "The wolf will live with the lamb, the leopard will lie down with the goat, the calf and the lion and the yearling together" (Isa 11:6 NIV) and "'There will be no more death' or mourning or crying or pain, for the old order of things has passed away" (Rev 21:4 NIV).

A comprehensive biblical perspective on what it means to be in an atoned relationship will therefore reflect, in some measure, most of the traditional models and metaphors for understanding Christ's work. However, it is unnecessary to place them in a hierarchy. Most of the concepts through which Christ's work is articulated can be seen to speak of a particular way in which the divine covenantal commitment outworks itself:

Sacrifice: sacrificial imagery retains center stage, but is now repositioned in a way that is wholly different from penal substitution's traditional characterization of it as a sin offering. Instead, it looks to the Passover sacrifice and Jesus's re-enactment of a Passover week meal in the Last Supper to draw its meaning.

Christus Victor: God in Christ wages war against the cosmic powers and wins a triumphant victory over sin, death, and the devil,[18] rescuing human life from their power and consequences.[19] As with the actions taken by the international community to free Kuwait from Saddam Hussein's invasion in 1990, God acts in Christ as *Christus Victor* pursuant to a pre-existing covenantal commitment—in the case of Kuwait, a prior treaty mandate—to liberate humanity from the invasion of foreign, hostile forces.

---

17. This is not to promote an over-realized eschatology but simply to illustrate the range of biblical ideas that may be incorporated within God's actions in a covenantal context. In the Old Testament, too, we see a wide range of "God's attributes and actions" (including, that of being "a covenant-keeper" Deut 7:9) and illustrated in the various names of God. See e.g., Baker, "God, Names of," 359–68.

18. *Christus Victor*, 146–47.

19. Including, ultimately, death: "The last enemy to be destroyed is death" (1 Cor 15:26 NIV).

Release from slavery: The Divine Kinsman "redeems from slavery,"[20] the two principal causes of which in the ancient world were war and debt—being taken into slavery by foreign powers or sold into slavery by oppressive life circumstances.[21] Hence the Divine Kinsman/suzerain fulfills his covenantal commitment in Christ by rescuing us from enslavement to the enemies of human life and flourishing—which include the power of sin, but extend to other evil powers and spiritual agents besides sin—just as he rescued Israel from slavery in Egypt.[22] He pays our indebtedness, the price we could not pay, as our kinsman Redeemer, to release us from that enslavement.

Moral influence: in this subjective Abelardian understanding of atonement, the covenantal feature is best situated in relation to the manifestation of Christ's love by which he enters into human life to become the willing sacrifice to effect the covenantal relationship, and the overwhelming response of reciprocal love to which it gives rise in human hearts.

At the same time, in a covenantal framework in which Christ's sacrifice has no penal associations and God's actions are recognized as primarily familial rather than primarily judicial, the *penal substitutionary model* falls away. Since there is no punishment element to a covenant-creating sacrifice, it is both unnecessary and inappropriate to look for a penal substitutionary explanation within the covenantal framework.[23]

This way of conceiving the atonement answers the vast majority of the questions that we posed about it in the early part of this book:

- It addresses the multiplicity of problems identified in chapter one concerning penal substitution.
- It is wholly consonant with an "Israel-remembered" approach to doctrinal formulation.
- It recognizes a continuity within the entire canon centered in a covenantal understanding of the divine consummative plan.

---

20. Cross, "Kinship and Covenant," 7.

21. See Haas, "Slave, Slavery," in Alexander and Baker (eds.), *Dictionary of the Old Testament*, 778–83.

22. Exod 1:11–14; Exod 2:23–25 ("The Israelites groaned in their slavery and cried out, and their cry for help because of their slavery went up to God. God heard their groaning and he remembered his covenant with Abraham, with Isaac and with Jacob.") Cf. Gal 4:3; 8–9; 5:1.

23. We may, nonetheless, see a sense of *substitution* in the covenantal mechanism: God takes the initiative in establishing a covenantal relationship with us through Christ while we were dead in our transgressions and sins (Eph 2:1). He does for us what we were powerless to do for ourselves (Rom 5:6)—stepping in on our behalf—establishing a covenantal relationship with God.

- It retains a key place for the sacrifice imagery that is a dominant idea in the New Testament.
- It is fundamentally cruciform and appropriates the New Testament's texts vis-à-vis the blood of the covenant.
- The rich covenantal imagery of kinship and father-son relationship is consonant with Jesus's teaching about the nature and character of the Father and positions the Parable of the Prodigal as a key interpretive text for the nature and character of a covenant relationship with God.
- It validates the traditional metaphors—save insofar as they are penal or judicial in nature—allowing for a kaleidoscopic understanding in which the metaphors all speak of different benefits of the covenant relationship (see below).
- It finds a central place for the Eucharist as a covenantally-situated sacrament, the repetition in remembrance of which is central to our assurance of continuing atonement. It also reminds us of its foundation in the Passover.

Finally, not only is this way of conceiving the new covenant free of supersessionism and theological anti-Judaism—save insofar as it has the sense of a "something more," as described in chapter three—its explanatory power is positively rooted in and dependent upon a validation of Israel's preceding covenantal history, notably in Torah. Israel's *covenantal nomism* becomes the model for Christianity's *new covenantal nomism*. Christ is Torah personified rather than Torah's antithesis.

4.4 THE METAPHORS ADDRESS RAMIFICATIONS OF THE COVENANT

If this approach to applying an overarching covenantal framework to Christ's work were to result in a jettisoning of the traditional metaphors, then we would unquestionably lose something in the process. Their absence would leave unaddressed how, exactly, God acts within that covenant to address the damage done by sin—both to human life itself and to relationship with God. If they did not already exist, we should need to find models and metaphors to describe them! It is here that the traditional ideas help us. Atonement within the context of a divine covenantal commitment involves restorative and reparative action on the part of the suzerain to repair and restore what enemies have done or threaten to do to the vassals' land and lives. Atonement is therefore coupled to covenant as a locomotive to its carriages—covenant is the locomotive, the traditional metaphors are its train. Atonement embraces not just how an at-one relationship is brought about at the outset but also what it looks like to be atoned when one is in the covenantal relationship.

Understood in this way, the traditional metaphors answer a slightly different question from the one to which they are traditionally offered—they are positioned slightly differently in the salvific narrative. Rather than explaining how humanity is *brought into* a relationship, they are explaining what it means *to be in* a relationship, rather as Calvin spoke of "the benefits of the salvation which he [Christ] has purchased."[24] The metaphors are not speaking of divine actions to deal with the *absence* of a relationship but explanations of the divine action taken *because of* a relationship, initiated in the heart of God. They are ways of expressing the significance of God having acted within the covenantal obligations that he sovereignly authored and voluntarily assumed.

There is incalculable value in the continuing deployment of metaphors of atonement to help us to picture the benefits of Christ's work in human experience in ways we can readily relate to. It is for this reason that they must be frequently refreshed and re-imagined in response to changing cultural circumstances, so that metaphor retains its explanatory power. It explains why no single metaphor will ever be adequate in isolation, and why none can be relied upon as a universal articulation of timeless truth for all eras and contexts. The benefits may be timeless, but the communicative vehicles by which those benefits are conveyed to us must forever be subject to change. The metaphors provide gateways for understanding something beyond the gateways—through which things can be grasped that otherwise could not be grasped. They are communicating to us the efficacy of atonement in meaningful ways that we can readily enter into.

On this basis, the inability of a penal substitutionary view based in the presumed judicial appropriateness of retributive physical violence to resonate with the worldview of contemporary society is neither surprising nor need it be troublesome.[25] Once the function of metaphor within a covenantal *situs* is recognized, the discontinuation or de-emphasis of a particular metaphor is not a departure from biblical truth. At the same time, however, this reminds us of the need to do the harder work of continuously *reimagining* biblical truth in ways that remain faithful to its original expression but present the benefits of Christ's work in terms that offer accessibility

---

24. Calvin, *Institutes of the Christian Religion*, Book III, chapter 1.

25. Which is not to say that it had no resonance in past generations, or may still have in cultures further afield.

to today's audience. There is no question that to lazily repeat the metaphors and explanatory stories of past generations is easier than to deconstruct and reconstruct them in ways that speak equally powerfully—and equally "biblically"—within the current culture.

There can therefore be no objection in principle to further metaphors being developed in a continuing partnership between the biblical materials and creative human reflection on the reality of salvation in the light of changing societal perspectives on the human condition. We are not dealing with a "closed canon" of metaphors, not least because, as we noted at the outset, the church has never insisted upon a single creedal definition of Christian orthodoxy in relation to atonement.[26] No single idea has been preserved or mandated for all times and places.

4.5 CLOSING THOUGHTS

It has been our proposal that a *new covenantal nomism* serves as the framework for what, in Christ, God has done vis-à-vis the world. This is not simply a metaphorical way of speaking—just one more metaphor to add to the *smörgåsbord*. The new covenant in Christ is a concrete reality in precisely the same way that its predecessors in the story of Israel were concrete realities. It is the assurance we derive from the enduring nature of Israel's covenant that provides our assurance of the enduring nature of the new covenant. Only on the historical reliability of all God's covenant promises throughout all generations can the reliability of the new covenant be founded for Christian faith.

Atonement metaphors function as access points to help us apprehend the experiential reality of God's covenantal actions. They are describing the nature of salvation as it is experienced in a covenantal relationship, rather than explaining a cosmic mechanism or formula by which it is brought about in a divine transaction within the Godhead. God acts in accordance with his covenant, freely and unilaterally entered into, because of his love. Necessarily, therefore, we arrive at the inexorable conclusion that no single metaphor is complete in itself, none is to be privileged and none serves as primary. What *is* primary is the covenantal reality on which all metaphors that describe elements of "being atoned" depend.

---

26. Though of course this does not mean that "anything goes." On the appropriate biblical criteria to apply to any "candidate-interpretation," see McIntyre, *Shape of Soteriology*, 85–86.

Locating the atonement in something that *precedes* the work of Christ on the cross helps to explain one of the puzzles of the biblical texts to which Finlan draws attention:

> If salvation came only as a consequence of his crucifixion, Jesus certainly forgot to mention it to those people who came to him seeking salvation. They must have gone away unsaved—but then, why did he say "your faith has saved you"?[27]

The answer to Finlan's question is that faith in the reliability of the covenant promises of God—promises that underlie all his actions, whether at Sinai or Calvary—has always been the divinely-ordained basis of participating in relationship with him, whether in Torah or in Christ. Those who came to him in faith "seeking salvation" always found it assured in the present, not merely portended for the future. Human life has always been lived under the blessing of a covenant promise of God that offered relationship with him through a *covenantal nomism*. This can be said to be equally true of the covenant with Abraham—divinely initiated in God's sovereign calling and election, responded to in Abraham's nomistic obedience to the covenant-maker's requirements. This simple pattern of a divinely-authored covenant, with the required nomistic requirements for that covenant to be effectual, applies to the entire covenantal structure of the canonical story and each covenant within it.

Atonement, then, originates—and always has originated—in a covenant-making event in the heart of God. His relational, restorative work *via* an on-going covenantal relationship is the story of the scriptures, from beginning to end. The cross was the ultimate manifestation to the world of a covenantal love that began at its foundation. The cross was the consequence of a limitless divine love for God's creation seen through to its inevitable conclusion—the ultimate covenant, involving the ultimate covenant sacrifice foreseen from the foundation of the world. When we speak of the cross in isolation, however—and specifically of the function of Christ's death—it can lead towards an inappropriately transactional view, when the gospel is in reality so much more than a passion narrative with an extended introduction.[28] Though it goes beyond the scope of this present work, one might wonder whether the most astonishing idea underlying the Christian understanding of God's work in Christ ought not to be the incarnation, without

---

27. Finlan, *Options on Atonement*, 87.

28. As Martin Kähler famously described the Gospels. *The So-Called Historical Jesus and the Historic Biblical Christ* (1896), 80n11, as cited by Dunn, *Jesus, Paul and the Gospels*, 54.

which the cross would not have happened.[29] As Curtis Freeman rightly notes, "the incarnation does no theological work in evangelical theology. It only serves the functional purpose of getting Jesus to earth so he can die for our sins."[30] Mary Boys has similarly observed that in many popular understandings of salvation in our culture

> so much prominence is given to the death of Jesus that both incarnation and resurrection are largely overlooked. But the resurrection is integrally connected to the ministry, passion and death; the cross as we know it is that of the Risen One who is Emmanuel.[31]

Perhaps it is the case, then, that when Paul speaks of "the cross" he may at times be using the term *pars pro toto*.[32]

Before the events concerning Christ are climactic in world history they are climactic in the history of Israel, which provides the essential context within which God's work from beginning to end must be situated and through the lens of which it must be understood. The universal story cannot be made sense of outside the particular story—our hermeneutical lens must affirm the continuity of the salvific work of God in covenant in an unbroken process since time began. The promises of the covenantal relationship with Israel are every bit as real and effectual as the promises of the new covenant in Christ; this must be so for the latter to be reliable. The New Testament must be interpreted through the Old Testament, just as much as the other way around. Each sheds equal light on the other.

Finlan proposed that "Christianity has taken atonement as far as it can go and now stands at a crossroads where it must choose between advancing with some uncertainty without that outmoded symbol or stagnating by clinging to a symbol that can no longer be advanced."[33] We respectfully suggest that this is not the case. If we were compelled to start and end with the traditional metaphors—as our only and supposedly timeless referents to Christ's work—then Finlan's complaint could be upheld. But this book has sought to demonstrate that we are not so compelled. It is our hope that

---

29. The significance of the cross receives the bulk of Evangelical attention, but if the christology of Hebrews is taken seriously, the significance of incarnation is equally astounding, not least in the risk involved. Without that risk, which arises from Christ's humanity, his achievement would surely be a foregone conclusion rather than a victory.

30. "The Faith of Jesus Christ, An Evangelical Conundrum," 256.

31. Boys, "The *Nostra Aetate* Trajectory," 147.

32. E.g. 1 Cor 1:17–18; 2:2. Rather as Paul appears to use "circumcision" as a collective term to represent Jewish lifestyle distinctives in Torah.

33. Finlan, *Options on Atonement in Christian Thought*, 88.

symbols of atonement can be brought back to life—re-thought and re-formulated in the language of each culture, place, and time, as they must forever be on this side of eternity—to take their rightful place in a context that is re-shaped by the centering of atonement in a *new covenantal nomism*.

A final concern is a particularly Evangelical one: does the picture of covenant that we have painted contain explanatory power for today? Is it readily conveyable from the pulpit? Does it "translate" to the popular Christian world that is the concern of Evangelicalism in practice? The answer to that is somewhat uncertain. Increasingly, the communicative power of a model based in permanent commitment cannot be taken for granted in a world that seems to move ever further away from affirming that idea in human life (marriage, which itself has its origins in covenant, being perhaps the best example of that). But then again, what is true of atonement metaphors is substantially true of all scriptural ideas: we are compelled in today's world to work harder to explain them than simply citing proof texts and stock religious terminology, as if that ought to be enough. Thus, even covenant, the root of atonement in the heart of God, requires to be skillfully communicated in the language and precepts of each culture.

Our hope is that, notwithstanding the undoubted shortcomings in its articulation, this perspective on atonement centered in covenant—a "re-Judaizing" of the doctrine—can make some small contribution to the continuing rehabilitation of Israel in Christian thought and to a higher regard for the entire canon.

Bibliography

Armstrong, John H., ed. *The Coming Evangelical Crisis* Chicago: Moody, 1996.
Aulén, Gustaf. *Christus Victor: An Historical Study of the Three Main Types of the Idea of Atonement.* Translated by A. G. Herbert. London: SPCK, 1931.
Baker, David W. "God, Names of." In *Dictionary of the Old Testament: Pentateuch*, edited by T. Desmond Alexander and David W. Baker, 359–68. Downers Grove, IL: IVP Academic, 2003.
Barclay, John M. G. "Grace and the Counter-Cultural Reckoning of Worth: Community Construction in Galatians 5–6." In *Galatians and Christian Theology: Justification, the Gospel, and Ethics in Paul's Letter*, edited by Mark W. Elliott, et al., 306–17. Grand Rapids: Baker, 2014.
———. *Paul and the Gift*. Grand Rapids: Eerdmans, 2015.
Barrett, C. K. *Paul: An Introduction to his Thought*. London: Chapman, 1994.
Barrick, William. "The New Perspective and 'Works of the Law' Gal. 2:16 and Rom. 3:20." *The Master's Seminary Journal* 16 2 (2005) 277–92.
Barth, Karl. *Church Dogmatics*, III/2. Translated by Geoffrey W. Bromiley. 2nd ed. Edinburgh: T. & T. Clark, 2004.
Bartlett, Anthony. *Cross Purposes: The Violent Grammar of Christian Atonement*. Harrisburg, PA: Trinity, 2001.
Bauckham, Richard. *God Crucified: Monotheism and Christology in the New Testament*. Carlisle, UK: Paternoster, 1998.
Bebbington, David. *Evangelicalism in Modern Britain: A History from the 1730s to the 1980s*. London: Unwin Hyman, 1989.
Becker, Adam H., and Annette Yoshiko Reed, eds. *The Ways That Never Parted: Jews and Christians in Late Antiquity and the Early Middle Ages*. Minneapolis: Fortress, 2007.
Birch, Bruce, et al. *A Theological Introduction to the Old Testament*. Nashville: Abingdon, 1999.
Boccaccini, Gabriele, and Carlos A. Segovia, eds. *Paul the Jew: Rereading the Apostle as a Figure of Second Temple Judaism*. Minneapolis: Fortress, 2016.
Boda, Mark J., and J. Gordon McConville, eds. *Dictionary of the Old Testament: Prophets*. Downers Grove, IL: IVP, 2012.
Borg, Marcus, and John Dominic Crossan. *The Last Week: The Day-by-Day Account of Jesus's Final Week in Jerusalem*. San Francisco: Harper, 2006.
Boyarin, Daniel. *Border Lines: The Partition of Judaeo-Christianity*. Philadelphia: University of Pennsylvania Press, 2004.

———. *A Radical Jew: Paul and the Politics of Identity*. Berkeley: University of California Press, 1994.

Briggs, John, et al. *Crime and Punishment in England*. London: UCL, 1996.

Brown, Raymond. *The Gospel according to John, Volume 1*. London: Chapman, 1966.

Burge, Gary. *John*. The NIV Application Commentary. Grand Rapids: Zondervan, 2000.

Burns, Joshua Ezra. "God-fearers." In *The Eerdmans Dictionary of Early Judaism*, edited by John Collins and Daniel Harlow, 681–82. Grand Rapids: Eerdmans, 2010.

Byrne, Brendan. "Interpreting Romans Theologically in a 'Post-New Perspective' Perspective." *Harvard Theological Review* 94.3 (2001) 227–41.

Calvin, John. *Institutes of the Christian Religion*. Edited by John T. McNeill. Louisville: Westminster/John Knox, 1960.

Campbell, Douglas. "Beyond Justification in Paul: The Thesis of the Deliverance of God." *Scottish Journal of Theology* 65.1 (2012) 90–104.

———. "The Current Crisis: The Capture of Paul's Gospel by Methodological Arianism." In *Beyond Old and New Perspectives on Paul: Reflections on the Work of Douglas Campbell*, edited by Chris Tilling, 37–48. Eugene, OR: Cascade, 2014.

———. *The Deliverance of God: An Apocalyptic Rereading of Justification in Paul*. Grand Rapids: Eerdmans, 2009.

———. "Judaizers." In *Dictionary of Paul and his Letters*, edited by Gerald Hawthorne, et al., 512–16. Downers Grove, IL: IVP Academic, 1993.

Carlson Brown, Joanne, and Rebecca Parker. "For God So Loved the World?" In *Christianity, Patriarchy and Abuse: A Feminist Critique*, edited by Joanne Carlson Brown and Carole R. Bohm, 1–30. New York: Pilgrim, 1989.

Carson, D. A. "Summaries and Conclusions." In *Justification and Variegated Nomism: Volume 1: The Complexities of Second Temple Judaism*, edited by D. A. Carson, et al., 505–47. Grand Rapids: Baker, 2001.

Carson, D. A., et al., eds. *Justification and Variegated Nomism: Volume 1: The Complexities of Second Temple Judaism*. Grand Rapids: Baker, 2001.

———. *Justification and Variegated Nomism Volume 2: The Paradoxes of Paul*. Grand Rapids: Baker, 2004.

Chilton, Bruce, and Jacob Neusner. *Judaism in the New Testament: Practices and Beliefs*. London: Routledge, 1995.

Cohen, Shaye J. D. *From the Maccabees to the Mishnah*. Philadelphia: Westminster, 1987.

Cranfield, C. E. B. *A Critical and Exegetical Commentary on the Epistle to the Romans: Volume 1*. Edinburgh: T. & .T Clark, 1975.

———. "St. Paul and the Law." *Scottish Journal of Theology* 17 (1964) 43–68.

Crisp, Oliver. "The Logic of Penal Substitution Revisited." In *The Atonement Debate: Papers from the London Symposium on the Theology of Atonement*, edited by Derek Tidball et al., 208–27. Grand Rapids: Zondervan, 2008.

Cross, Frank Moore. "Kinship and Covenant in Ancient Israel." In *From Epic to Canon: History and Literature in Ancient Israel*. Baltimore: John Hopkins University Press, 1998.

Cunningham, Philip A., et al. *Christ Jesus and the Jewish People Today: New Explorations of Theological Interrelationships*. Grand Rapids: Eerdmans, 2011.

Dahl, N. A. *The Crucified Messiah and Other Essays*. Minneapolis: Augsburg, 1974.

Davies, W. D. *Paul and Rabbinic Judaism: Some Rabbinic Elements in Pauline Theology*. 3rd ed. London: SPCK, 1970.

---. *Torah in the Messianic Age and/or the Age to Come*. Philadelphia: SBL, 1952.
Dockery, David S., ed. *The Challenge of Postmodernism: An Evangelical Engagement*. 2nd ed. Grand Rapids: Baker Academic, 2001.
Dodd, C. H. *The Epistle of Paul to the Romans*. London: Hodder and Stoughton, 1932.
Donaldson, Terence. "Jewish Christianity, Israel's Stumbling and the *Sonderweg* Reading of Paul." *Journal for the Study of the New Testament*, 29.1 (2006) 27–54.
---. *Jews and Anti-Judaism in the New Testament: Decision Points and Divergent Interpretations*. London: SPCK, 2010.
---. *Paul and the Gentiles: Remapping the Apostle's Convictional World*. Minneapolis: Fortress, 1997.
---. "Riches for the Gentiles Rom. 11:12: Israel's Rejection and Paul's Gentile Mission." *Journal of Biblical Literature* 112 (1993) 81–98.
---. "Zealot and Convert: The Origin of Paul's Christ-Torah Antithesis." *Catholic Biblical Quarterly* 51 (1989) 655–82.
Dunn, James D. G. *Christology in the Making: A New Testament Inquiry into the Origins of the Doctrine of the Incarnation*. 2nd ed. London: SCM, 1989.
---. *The Epistle to the Galatians*. Peabody, MA: Hendrickson, 1993.
---. *Jesus, Paul and the Gospels*. Grand Rapids: Eerdmans, 2011.
---. *The New Perspective on Paul*. Grand Rapids: Eerdmans, 2008.
---. *Romans: The People's Bible Commentary*. Oxford: Bible Reading Fellowship, 2001.
---. *The Theology of Paul the Apostle*. London: T. & T. Clark, 2003.
---. "Yet Once More—'The Works of the Law': A Response." *Journal for the Study of the New Testament* 46 (1992) 99–117.
Edwards, M. J. "Justin's Logos and the Word of God." *Journal of Early Christian Studies* 3 (1995) 261–80.
Elliott, Mark Adam. *The Survivors of Israel: A Reconsideration of the Theology of Pre-Christian Judaism*. Grand Rapids: Eerdmans, 2000.
Ellison, H. L. "Judaism." In *Wycliffe Dictionary of Theology*, edited by Everett F. Harrison et al., 300–302. Peabody, MA: Hendrickson, 2000.
Fiddes, Paul S. *Past Event and Present Salvation: The Christian Idea of Atonement*. London: Darton, Longman and Todd, 1989.
---. "Salvation." In *The Oxford Handbook of Systematic Theology*, edited by John Webster et al., 176–96. Oxford: Oxford University Press, 2007.
Finlan, Stephen. *Options on Atonement in Christian Thought*. Collegeville, MN: Liturgical, 2007.
---. *Problems with Atonement: The Origins of, and Controversy about, the Atonement Doctrine*. Collegeville, IL: Liturgical, 2005.
Flusser, David. *The Sage from Galilee: Rediscovering Jesus' Genius*. Grand Rapids: Eerdmans, 2007. 4th English ed.; first published in German as *Jesus in Selbstzeugnissen und Bilddokumenten*. Hamburg: Rowalt, 1968.
Ford, David F. *Self and Salvation: Being Transformed*. Cambridge: Cambridge University Press, 1999.
Foucault, Michel. *Discipline and Punish*. New York: Vintage, 1995.
Fredriksen, Paula. *Augustine and the Jews: A Christian Defense of Jews and Judaism*. New Haven: Yale University Press, 2008.
---. "Judaism, the Circumcision of Gentiles, and Apocalyptic Hope: Another Look at Galatians 1 and 2." *Journal of Theological Studies* 42 (1991) 532–64.

———. Review of N. T. Wright, *Paul and the Faithfulness of God* in *The Catholic Biblical Quarterly* 77 (2015) 387–91.

Freeman, Curtis W. "The Faith of Jesus Christ, An Evangelical Conundrum." In *Beyond Old and New Perspectives on Paul: Reflections on the Work of Douglas Campbell*, edited by Chris Tilling, 253–59. Eugene, OR: Cascade, 2014.

Gager, John. *The Origins of Anti-Semitism—Attitudes toward Judaism in Pagan and Christian Antiquity*. Oxford: Oxford University Press, 1985.

———. *Reinventing Paul*. Oxford: Oxford University Press, 2000.

Garlington, Don. *In Defense of the New Perspective on Paul: Essays and Reviews*. Reprint. Eugene, OR: Wipf and Stock, 2005.

———. "A Review Article" (reviewing Mark Adam Elliott's *The Survivors of Israel: A Reconsideration of the Theology of Pre-Christian Judaism*). *Reformation & Revival*, 10.4 (2001) 171–83.

Gaston, Lloyd. *Paul and the Torah*. Reprint. Eugene, OR: Wipf and Stock, 2006.

Girard, René. *I See Satan Fall Like Lightning*. Maryknoll, NY: Orbis, 2001.

Glazer, Mark, "Structuralism." 1994. Available at http://www.utpa.edu/faculty/mglazer/theory/structuralism.htm, accessed February 23, 2012.

Goldingay, John. "Covenant." In *The New Interpreters Dictionary of the Bible, Volume 1*, edited by Katherine Doob Sakenfeld et al., 767–78 Nashville: Abingdon, 2006.

Green, Joel B. "Must We Imagine the Atonement in Penal Substitutionary Terms? Questions, Caveats and a Plea." In *The Atonement Debate: Papers from the London Symposium on the Theology of Atonement*, edited by Derek Tidball et al., 153–70. Grand Rapids: Zondervan, 2008.

Green, Joel B., and Mark D. Baker. *Recovering the Scandal of the Cross: Atonement in New Testament & Contemporary Contexts*. Downers Grove, IL: IVP, 2000.

Grenz, Stanley. "How Do We Know What to Believe?" In *Essentials of Christian Theology*, edited by William Placher, 11–33. Louisville: Westminster John Knox, 2003.

Grenz, Stanley, and John Franke. *Beyond Foundationalism*. Louisville: Westminster John Knox, 2001.

Grudem, Wayne. *Systematic Theology*. Leicester, UK: IVP, 1994.

Gunton, Colin. *The Actuality of Atonement*. Edinburgh: T. & T. Clark, 1988.

Haas, Guenther H. "Slave, Slavery." In *Dictionary of the Old Testament: Pentateuch*, edited by T. Desmond Alexander and David W. Baker, 778–83. Downers Grove, IL: IVP Academic, 2003.

Hafemann, Scott J. "The Covenant Relationship." In *Central Themes in Biblical Theology*, edited by Scott J. Hafemann and Paul R. House, 20–65. Grand Rapids: Baker, 2007.

Hagner, Donald. "Paul and Judaism—The Jewish Matrix of Early Christianity: Issues in the Current Debate." *Bulletin for Biblical Research* 3 (1993) 111–30.

Hahn, Scott. *Kinship by Covenant: A Canonical Approach to the Fulfillment of God's Saving Promises*. New Haven: Yale University Press, 2009.

Harink, Douglas. *Paul among the Postliberals: Pauline Theology beyond Christendom and Modernity*. Grand Rapids: Brazos, 2003.

Harrison, R. K., and F. N. Hepper. "Olive." In *The Illustrated Bible Dictionary, Part 2*, edited by Norman Hillyer et al., 1112–14 Leicester, UK: IVP, 1980.

Hartley, John. *Leviticus*. Word Biblical Commentary. Nashville: Thomas Nelson, 1992.

Haykin, Michael, and Kenneth Stewart, eds. *The Advent of Evangelicalism: Exploring Historical Continuities*. Nashville: B&H Academic, 2008.

Hays, Richard. Review of *Paul among the Postliberals*, in *Interpretation* 58 (2004) 399–402; available at http://interpretation.org/reviews/oct-04/index.htm, accessed February 24, 2012.

Heim, S. Mark. *Saved from Sacrifice: A Theology of the Cross*. Grand Rapids: Eerdmans, 2006.

Hicks, Peter. *Evangelicals & Truth: a Creative Proposal for a Postmodern Age*. Leicester, UK: Apollos, 1998.

Hiebert, Paul. *Transforming Worldviews: An Anthropological Understanding of How People Change*. Grand Rapids: Baker, 2008.

Hilborn, David, ed., *The Nature of Hell: A Report by the Evangelical Alliance Commission on Unity and Truth among Evangelicals ACUTE*. Carlisle, UK: Paternoster, 2000.

Holmes, Stephen. *The Wondrous Cross: Atonement and Penal Substitution in the Bible and History*. Milton Keynes, UK: Paternoster, 2007.

Hooker, Morna. *From Adam to Christ: Essays on Paul*. Eugene, OR: Wipf and Stock, 1990.

———. *Not Ashamed of the Gospel*. Reprint. Eugene, OR: Wipf and Stock, 1994.

———. "Paul and Covenantal Nomism." In *Paul and Paulinism: Essays in Honour of C. K. Barrett*, edited by M. D. Hooker and S. G. Wilson, 47–56. London: SPCK, 1982.

Horton, Michael. *The Christian Faith: A Systematic Theology for Pilgrims on the Way*. Grand Rapids: Zondervan, 2011.

———. "Déjà vu All Over Again." *Modern Reformation* 13.4 (2004). Available at http://www.modernreformation.org/default.php?page=articledisplay&var1=ArtRead&var2=204&var3=authorbio&var4=AutRes&var5=1, accessed February 2, 2013.

———. *Introducing Covenant Theology*. Grand Rapids: Baker, 2006.

Hugenberger, Gordon P. *Marriage as a Covenant. A Study of Biblical Law and Ethics Governing Marriage, Developed from the Perspective of Malachi*. Leiden: Brill, 1994.

Hughes, Tim. "Consuming Fire." Eastbourne, UK: Thankyou Music, 2002.

Hurtado, Larry. *Lord Jesus Christ: Devotions to Jesus in Earliest Christianity*. Grand Rapids: Eerdmans, 2003.

———. "Mediator Figures." In *The Eerdmans Dictionary of Early Judaism*, edited by John Collins and Daniel Harlow, 926–29. Grand Rapids: Eerdmans, 2010.

Jacob, Walter. *Christianity through Jewish Eyes: The Quest for Common Ground*. Cincinnati, OH: Hebrew Union College Press, 1974.

Jeffery, Steve, et al. *Pierced for our Transgressions: Rediscovering the Glory of Penal Substitution*. Wheaton, IL: Crossway, 2007.

Jenson, Philip. "The Levitical Sacrificial System." In *Sacrifice in the Bible*, edited by Roger Beckwith and Martin Selman, 25–40. Carlisle, UK: Paternoster, 1995.

Jenson, Robert W. "Toward a Christian Theology of Judaism." In *Jews and Christians: People of God*, edited by Carl E. Braaten and Robert W. Jenson, 1–13. Grand Rapids: Eerdmans, 2003.

Jenson, Robert W., and Eugene B. Korn, eds. *Covenant and Hope: Christian and Jewish Reflections*. Grand Rapids: Eerdmans, 2012.

Johnson, Gary. "Does Theology Still Matter?" In *The Coming Evangelical Crisis*, edited by John H. Armstrong, 57–73. Chicago: Moody, 1996.

Johnson, Luke Timothy. *The Acts of the Apostles*. Sacra Pagina Series. Vol. 5. Collegeville, MN: Liturgical, 1992.

———. "The New Testament's Anti-Jewish Slander and the Convention of Ancient Polemic." *Journal of Biblical Literature* 108 (1989) 419–41.

———. *Religious Experience in Earliest Christianity: A Missing Dimension in New Testament Studies*. Minneapolis: Fortress, 1998.

Käsemann, Ernst. *Commentary on Romans*. Grand Rapids: Eerdmans, 1980.

———. *Perspectives on Paul*. London: SCM, 1971.

Kelly, J. N. D. *Early Christian Doctrines*. Peabody, MA: Prince, 2003.

Kline, Meredith G. *Kingdom Prologue: Genesis Foundations for a Covenantal Worldview*. Overland Park, KS: Two Age, 2000.

Knox, John. *Theology Today* 32–33 (October 1975). Available at http://theologytoday.ptsem.edu/oct1975/v32-3-bookreview4.htm, accessed March 16, 2012.

Kramer, W. R. *Christ, Lord, Son of God*. London: SCM, 1966.

Kuhn, Thomas. *The Structure of Scientific Revolutions*. 3rd ed. Chicago: University of Chicago Press, 1996.

Leith, John H. ed. *Creeds of the Churches: A Reader in Christian Doctrine from the Bible to the Present*. Louisville, KY: John Knox, 1982.

Levine, Amy-Jill. *The Misunderstood Jew: The Church and the Scandal of the Jewish Jesus*. New York: HarperCollins, 2006.

Lieu, Judith. "Do God-Fearers Make Good Christians?" In *Crossing the Boundaries: Essays in Biblical Interpretation in Honour of Michael D. Goulder*, edited by Stanley Porter, et al., 329–45. Leiden: Brill, 1994.

———. *Neither Jew Nor Greek? Constructing Early Christianity*. London: T. & T. Clark, 2002.

———. "The Race of the God-fearers." *Journal of Theological Studies* 46 (1995) 483–501.

Lloyd-Jones, D. M. *What Is an Evangelical?* Edinburgh: Banner of Truth Trust, 1992.

Longenecker, Bruce. "On Israel's God and God's Israel: Assessing Supersessionism in Paul." *Journal of Theological Studies* 58 (2007) 26–44.

McCarthy, Dennis J. "Three Covenants in Genesis." *Catholic Biblical Quarterly* 26.2 (1964) 179–89.

McCready, Wayne, and Adele Reinhartz. "Common Judaism and Diversity within Judaism." In *Common Judaism: Explorations in Second-Temple Judaism*, edited by Wayne McCready and Adele Reinhartz, 1–10. Minneapolis: Fortress, 2008.

———. "Conclusion." In *Common Judaism: Explorations in Second-Temple Judaism*, edited by Wayne McCready and Adele Reinhartz, 215–20. Minneapolis: Fortress, 2008.

McFarlane, Graham. "Atonement, Creation and Trinity." In *The Atonement Debate: Papers from the London Symposium on the Theology of Atonement*, edited by Derek Tidball, et al., 192–207. Grand Rapids: Zondervan, 2008.

McGrath, Alister. *Evangelicalism and the Future of Christianity*. Leicester, UK: IVP, 1995.

———. *Explaining Your Faith* Leicester, UK: IVP, 1995.

———. *Historical Theology: An Introduction to the History of Christian Thought*. Oxford: Blackwell, 1998.

———. "A Particularist View." In *Four Views on Salvation in a Pluralistic World*, edited by Dennis Okholm and Timothy Phillips, 151–80. Grand Rapids: Zondervan, 1996.

McGrath, James. *The Only True God: Early Christian Monotheism in its Jewish Context.* Chicago: University of Illinois Press, 2009.

McIntyre, John. *The Shape of Soteriology: Studies in the Doctrine of the Death of Christ.* Edinburgh: T. & T. Clark, 1992.

McKnight, Scot. *A Community Called Atonement.* Nashville: Abingdon, 2007.

———. *Jesus and his Death: Historiography, the Historical Jesus and Atonement Theology.* Waco, TX: Baylor University Press, 2005.

Macleod, Donald. "The New Perspective: Paul, Luther and Judaism." In *The Scottish Bulletin of Evangelical Theology* 22 1 (2004) 4–31.

Macquarrie, John. *Jesus Christ in Modern Thought.* London: SCM, 1990.

Mann, Alan. *Atonement for a "Sinless" Society: Engaging with an Emerging Culture.* Milton Keynes, UK: Paternoster, 2005.

Marshall, I. Howard. *Acts.* Leicester, UK: IVP, 1980.

———. "The Theology of the Atonement." In *The Atonement Debate: Papers from the London Symposium on the Theology of Atonement*, edited by Derek Tidball et al., 49–68. Grand Rapids: Zondervan, 2008.

Matlock, R. Barry. "Zeal for Paul But Not According to Knowledge: Douglas Campbell's War on 'Justification Theory.'" *Journal for the Study of the New Testament* 34 (2011) 115–49.

Mendenhall, George, and Gary Herion. "Covenant." In *The Anchor Yale Bible Dictionary, Vol. 1*, edited by David Noel Freedman et al., 1179–1202. New Haven: Yale University Press, 2008.

Merrick, James. Review Article of S. Mark Heim, *Saved from Sacrifice: A Theology of the Cross.* Grand Rapids: Eerdmans, 2006. In *Journal of the Evangelical Theology Society* 50.4 (2007) 882–87.

Miller, Patrick. *The Religion of Ancient Israel.* Louisville: Westminster John Knox, 2000.

Mohler, Albert. "Evangelical: What's in a Name?" In *The Coming Evangelical Crisis*, edited by John H. Armstrong, 29–44. Chicago, Moody, 1996.

Montefiore, Claude. *Judaism and St. Paul: Two Essays.* London: Goschen, 1914.

Moo, Douglas. "Israel and the Law in Romans 5–11: Interaction with the New Perspective." In *Justification and Variegated Nomism Volume Two: The Paradoxes of Paul*, edited by D. A. Carson et al., 185–216. Grand Rapids: Baker, 2004.

———. "John Barclay's *Paul and the Gift* and the New Perspective on Paul." *Themelios* 41.2 (2016) 279–88.

———. *Romans: The NIV Application Commentary.* Grand Rapids: Zondervan, 2000.

Moore, George Foot. "Christian Writers on Judaism." *Harvard Theological Review* 14 (1921) 197–254.

———. *Judaism in the First Centuries of the Christian Era: The Age of the Tannaim.* 3 vols. 1927–30. Reprint. New York: Schocken, 1971.

Morris, Leon. "Atonement." In *New Dictionary of Theology*, edited by Sinclair Ferguson and David Wright, 54–57. Leicester, UK: IVP, 1988.

———. *The Atonement: Its Meaning and Significance.* Leicester, UK: IVP, 1983.

Motyer, Steve. "The Atonement in Hebrews." In *The Atonement Debate: Papers from the London Symposium on the Theology of Atonement*, edited by Derek Tidball et al., 136–50. Grand Rapids: Zondervan, 2008.

Moyaert, Marianne, and Didier Pollefeyt, eds. *Never Revoked: Nostra Aetate as Ongoing Challenge for Jewish-Christian Dialogue.* Grand Rapids: Eerdmans, 2010.

Nanos, Mark. "Locating Paul on a Map of First-Century Judaism." Paper delivered at the SBL Annual Meeting, Atlanta, November 22, 2010.

———. *The Mystery of Romans*. Minneapolis: Fortress, 1996.

———. "Paul and Judaism." Paper presented at Central States SBL, St. Louis, March 28–29, 2004.

———. "Rethinking the 'Paul *and* Judaism' Paradigm: Why Not 'Paul's *Judaism*'?" Paper presented at McMaster University, March 12, 2008 and elsewhere; available at www.thepaulpage.com, accessed July 13, 2012.

Nash, Ronald. *Worldviews in Conflict: Choosing Christianity in a World of Ideas*. Grand Rapids: Zondervan, 1992.

Naugle, David. *Worldview: The History of a Concept*. Grand Rapids: Eerdmans, 2002.

Neusner, Jacob. *Jews and Christians: The Myth of a Common Tradition*. Reprint. Eugene, OR: Wipf and Stock, 1991.

———. *Judaism and Christianity in the Age of Constantine: History, Messiah, Israel, and the Initial Confrontation*. Chicago: University of Chicago Press, 1987.

Newbigin, Lesslie. *Foolishness to the Greeks: The Gospel and Western Culture*. Grand Rapids: Eerdmans, 1986.

Okholm, Dennis, and Timothy Phillips eds. *Four Views on Salvation in a Pluralistic World*. Grand Rapids: Zondervan, 1996.

Pearse, Meic. *Why the Rest Hates the West: Understanding the Roots of Global Rage*. London: SPCK, 2003.

Perrin, Nicholas. "Introduction." In *Jesus, Paul and the People of God: A Theological Dialogue with N. T. Wright*, edited by Nicholas Perrin and Richard Hays, 7–17. London: SPCK, 2011.

Piper, John. *The Future of Justification: A Response to N. T. Wright*. Wheaton, IL: Crossway, 2007.

Placher, William. *The Domestication of Transcendence: How Modern Thinking about God Went Wrong*. Louisville: Westminster John Knox, 1996.

Radford Ruether, Rosemary. "The Emergence of Christian Feminist Theology." In *The Cambridge Companion to Feminist Theology*, edited by Susan Frank Parsons, 3–22. Cambridge: Cambridge University Press, 2002.

———. *Sexism and God-talk*. London: SCM, 1983.

Räisänen, Heikki. "A Controversial Jew and His Conflicting Convictions." In *Redefining First-Century Jewish and Christian Identities*, edited by Fabian Udoh, 319–35. Notre Dame, IN: University of Notre Dame Press, 2008.

———. *Paul and the Law*. Reprint. Eugene, OR: Wipf and Stock, 2010.

Rashkover, Randi. "The Christian Doctrine of the Incarnation." In *Christianity in Jewish Terms*, edited by Tikva Frymer-Kensky, 254–61. Boulder, CO: Westview, 2000.

Ratzinger, Joseph. *Milestones: Memoirs 1927–1977*. San Francisco: Ignatius, 1998.

Reasoner, Mark. "Rome and Roman Christianity." In *Dictionary of Paul and his Letters*, edited by Gerald Hawthorne et al., 850–55. Downers Grove, IL: IVP Academic, 1993.

Rendtorff, Rolf. *The Covenant Formula: An Exegetical and Theological Investigation*. Edinburgh: T. & T. Clark, 1998.

Rifkin, Ellis. "Pharisaism and the Crisis of the Individual in the Greco-Roman World." *Jewish Quarterly Review* 61 (1970) 27–53.

Robinson, J. A. T. *Redating the New Testament*. Philadelphia: Westminster, 1976.

Sanders, E. P. "Common Judaism Explored." In *Common Judaism: Explorations in Second-Temple Judaism*, edited by Wayne McCready and Adele Reinhartz, 11–25. Minneapolis: Fortress, 2008.

———. "Comparing Judaism and Christianity." In *Redefining First-Century Jewish and Christian Identities: Essays in Honor of Ed Parish Sanders*, edited by Fabian Udoh, 11–41. Notre Dame, IN: University of Notre Dame Press, 2008.

———. *Comparing Judaism and Christianity: Common Judaism, Paul, and the Inner and the Outer in Ancient Religion*. Minneapolis: Fortress, 2016.

———. "Jesus, Anti-Judaism, and Modern Christianity: The Quest Continues." In *Jesus, Judaism and Christian Anti-Judaism*, edited by Paula Fredriksen and Adele Reinhartz, 31–55. Louisville: Westminster John Knox, 2002.

———. *Judaism: Practice and Belief, 63 BCE–66 CE*. London: SCM, 1992.

———. *Paul and Palestinian Judaism: A Comparison of Patterns of Religion*. London: SCM, 1977.

———. *Paul, the Law and the Jewish People*. Philadelphia: Fortress, 1983.

Sandmel, David Fox. "Israel, Judaism and Christianity." In *Christianity in Jewish Terms*, edited by Tikva Frymer-Kensky, 159–66. Boulder, CO: Westview, 2000.

Schaff, Philip. *The Creeds of Christendom: Volume One, The History of Creeds*. Grand Rapids: Baker, 1998.

Schreiner, Thomas. *The Law and Its Fulfillment: A Pauline Theology of Law*. Grand Rapids, Eerdmans, 1993.

———. "Penal Substitution View." In *The Nature of the Atonement*, edited by J. Beilby and P. R. Eddy, 67–98. Downers Grove, IL: IVP, 2006.

Schweitzer, Albert. *Paul and His Interpreters*. Translated by W. Montgomery. London: Black, 1912.

———. *The Quest of the Historical Jesus*. Translated by W. Montgomery. London: Black, 1910.

Segal, Alan. *Paul the Convert: The Apostolate and Apostasy of Saul the Pharisee*. New Haven: Yale University Press, 1990.

———. "Paul's Jewish Presuppositions." In *The Cambridge Companion to St. Paul*, edited by James D. G. Dunn, 159–72. Cambridge: Cambridge University Press, 2003.

———. *Two Powers in Heaven: Early Rabbinic Reports about Christianity and Gnosticism*. Studies in Judaism in Late Antiquity, vol. 25. Leiden: Brill, 1977.

Shelton, R. Larry. "A Covenantal Concept of Atonement." *Wesleyan Theological Journal* 19 (1984) 91–110.

———. *Cross and Covenant: Interpreting the Atonement for 21st Century Mission*. Milton Keynes, UK: Paternoster, 2006.

———. "Relational Atonement: Covenant Renewal as a Wesleyan Integrating Motif." Paper for AAR Wesleyan Studies Group/Open and Relational Theologies Session, 2008.

Silva, Moisés. "The Law and Christianity: Dunn's New Synthesis." *Westminster Theological Journal* 53 (1991) 339–53.

Sire, James. *Naming the Elephant: Worldview as a Concept*. Downers Grove, IL: IVP, 2004.

Skarsaune, Oskar. *In the Shadow of the Temple: Jewish Influences on Early Christianity*. Downers Grove, IL: IVP Academic, 2002.

Smail, Tom. "Can One Man Die for the People?" In *Atonement Today*, edited by John Goldingay, 73–92. London: SPCK, 1995.

———. *Once and for All: A Confession of the Cross*. London: Darton, Longman and Todd, 1998.

Snyder, Graydon F. "Major Motifs in the Interpretation of Paul's Letter to the Romans." In *Celebrating Romans: Template for Pauline Theology*, edited by Sheila E. McGinn, 42–63. Grand Rapids: Eerdmans, 2004.

Sonderegger, Katherine. "Review of *The God of Israel and Christian Theology*." *Journal of Religion* 78 (1998) 454–56.

Soskice, Janet Martin. *The Kindness of God: Metaphor, Gender, and Religious Language*. Oxford: Oxford University Press, 2007.

Soulen, R. Kendall. *The God of Israel and Christian Theology*. Minneapolis: Fortress, 1996.

———. "Israel and the Church." In *Christianity in Jewish Terms*, edited by Tikva Frymer-Kensky, 167–74. Boulder, CO: Westview, 2000.

———. "Karl Barth and the Future of the God of Israel." *Pro Ecclesia* 6 4 (1997) 413–28.

Spence, Alan J. *The Promise of Peace—A Unified Theory of Atonement*. London: T. & T. Clark, 2006.

Stendahl, Krister. "The Apostle Paul and the Introspective Conscience of the West." *Harvard Theological Review* 56.3 (1963) 199–215.

———. *Paul Among Jews and Gentiles and Other Essays*. Minneapolis: Fortress, 1976.

Stott, John. *The Cross of Christ*. Leicester, UK: IVP, 1986.

———. *Evangelical Truth: A Personal Plea for Unity*. Leicester, UK: IVP, 1999.

Storkey, Elaine. "Atonement and Feminism." *Anvil* 11.3 (1994) 227–35.

Stowers, Stanley. *A Rereading of Romans: Justice, Jews and Gentiles*. New Haven: Yale University Press, 1994.

Stuhlmacher, Peter. *Revisiting Paul's Doctrine of Justification: A Challenge to the New Perspective*. Downers Grove, IL: IVP Academic, 2001.

Thielman, Frank. "Law." In *Dictionary of Paul and His Letters*, edited by Gerald Hawthorne et al., 529–42. Downers Grove, IL: IVP Academic, 1993.

———. *Philippians*. The NIV Application Commentary. Grand Rapids: Zondervan, 1995.

Thiselton, Anthony. *The Two Horizons: New Testament Hermeneutics and Philosophical Description*. Exeter, UK: Paternoster, 1980.

Thompson, Michael. *The New Perspective on Paul*. Cambridge: Grove, 2002.

Tidball, Derek, et al., eds. *The Atonement Debate: Papers from the London Symposium on the Theology of Atonement*. Grand Rapids: Zondervan, 2008.

Tilling, Chris, ed. *Beyond Old and New Perspectives on Paul: Reflections on the Work of Douglas Campbell*. Eugene, OR: Cascade, 2014.

———. "Paul and the Faithfulness of God. A Review Essay." *Anvil* 31.1 (2015) 45–56 and 57–69.

Tobin, Thomas. "Logos." In *The Eerdmans Dictionary of Early Judaism*, edited by John Collins and Daniel Harlow, 894–96. Grand Rapids: Eerdmans, 2010.

Torrance, Alan. Review Article of Douglas Campbell, *The Deliverance of God* in *Scottish Journal of Theology* 65 (2012) 82–89.

Torrance, James B. "The Contribution of McLeod Campbell to Scottish Theology." *Scottish Journal of Theology* 26 (1973) 295–311.

———. "Covenant or Contract? A Study of the Theological Background of Worship in Seventeenth-Century Scotland." *Scottish Journal of Theology* 23 (1970) 51–76

Torrance, Thomas F. *Atonement: The Person and Work of Christ*. Milton Keynes, UK: Paternoster, 2009.

Travis, Stephen. "Christ as Bearer of Divine Judgment." In *Jesus of Nazareth, Lord and Christ*, edited by Joel Green and Max Turner, 332–45. Grand Rapids: Eerdmans, 1994.

VanGemeren, Willem A. ed. *New International Dictionary of Old Testament Theology and Exegesis*. 5 vols. Grand Rapids: Zondervan, 1997.

Vanhoozer, Kevin. "Wrighting the Wrongs of the Reformation?" In *Jesus, Paul and the People of God: A Theological Dialogue with N. T. Wright*, edited by Nicholas Perrin and Richard Hays, 235–58. London: SPCK, 2011.

Vlach, Michael. *The Church as a Replacement of Israel: An Analysis of Supersessionism*. Frankfurt: Lang, 2009.

———. "Replacement Theology: Has the Church Superseded Israel as the People of God?" The William R. Rice Lecture Series, March 17, 2010. Available at http://www.dbts.edu/pdf/rls/Vlach_ReplacementTheology.pdf, accessed February 24, 2012.

Vanlaningham, Michael G. *Christ, the Savior of Israel: An Evaluation of the Dual Covenant and Sonderweg Interpretations of Paul's Letters*. Frankfurt: Lang, 2012.

Volf, Miroslav. "The Lamb of God and the Sin of the World." In *Christianity in Jewish Terms*, edited by Frymer-Kensky et al., 313–19. New York: Basic, 2002.

Walls, Andrew F. "Mystery, Mysteries." In *Wycliffe Dictionary of Theology*, edited by Everett F. Harrison et al., 366–67. Peabody, MA: Hendrickson, 1960.

Ward, Keith. *The Word of God: The Bible After Modern Scholarship*. London: SPCK, 2010.

Watson, Francis. "Not the New Perspective." Unpublished paper delivered at the British New Testament Conference, Manchester, September 2001. Available at http://www.abdn.ac.uk/divinity/staff/watsonart.shtml, accessed February 16, 2012.

———. *Paul, Judaism and the Gentiles: A Sociological Approach*. Cambridge: Cambridge University Press, 1986. (Later republished as *Paul, Judaism and the Gentiles: Beyond the New Perspective*. Grand Rapids: Eerdmans, 2007 with significantly rewritten content.)

Weaver, J. Denny. *The Nonviolent Atonement*. Grand Rapids: Eerdmans, 2001.

———. "Violence in Christian Theology." *Cross Currents* 51 (2001). Available at http://www.crosscurrents.org/weaver0701.htm#TEXT17, accessed October 4, 2011.

Webb, William J. *Slaves, Women & Homosexuals: Exploring the Hermeneutics of Cultural Analysis*. Downers Grove, IL: IVP Academic, 2001.

Weisser, Michael. *Crime and Punishment in Early Modern Europe*. Brighton, UK: Harvester, 1982.

Wenham, Gordon. "The Theology of Old Testament Sacrifice." In *Sacrifice in the Bible*, edited by Roger Beckwith and Martin Selman, 75–87. Carlisle, UK: Paternoster, 1995.

West, Nathaniel. "The Old Hebrew Theology." *The Old Testament Student* 3.1 (1883) 14–19.

Westerholm, Stephen. "The 'New Perspective' at Twenty-Five." In *Justification and Variegated Nomism: Volume 2: The Paradoxes of Paul*, edited by D. A. Carson et al., 1–38. Grand Rapids: Baker, 2004.

———. *Perspectives Old and New on Paul: The "Lutheran" Paul and His Critics*. Grand Rapids: Eerdmans, 2004.

Willard, Dallas. *The Divine Conspiracy: Rediscovering our Hidden Life in God*. San Francisco: HarperCollins, 1997.

Williams, Garry. "Penal Substitution: A Response to Recent Criticisms." In *The Atonement Debate: Papers from the London Symposium on the Theology of Atonement*, edited by Derek Tidball et al., 172–91. Grand Rapids: Zondervan, 2008.

Williams, Rowan. *On Christian Theology*. Oxford: Blackwell, 2000.

Williamson, Paul R. "Covenant." In *Dictionary of the Old Testament: Pentateuch*, edited by T. Desmond Alexander and David W. Baker, 139–55. Downers Grove, IL: IVP Academic, 2003.

Witherington III, Ben. *The Acts of the Apostles: A Socio-Rhetorical Commentary*. Grand Rapids: Eerdmans, 1998.

———. *Paul's Letter to the Romans: A Socio-Rhetorical Commentary*. Grand Rapids: Eerdmans, 2004.

Worthen, Jeremy F. *The Internal Foe: Judaism and Anti-Judaism in the Shaping of Christian Theology*. Newcastle upon Tyne, UK: Cambridge Scholars, 2009.

Wright, Chris. "Atonement in the Old Testament." In *The Atonement Debate: Papers from the London Symposium on the Theology of Atonement*, edited by Derek Tidball et al., 69–82. Grand Rapids: Zondervan, 2008.

———. *Knowing Jesus through The Old Testament*. London: Marshall Pickering, 1992.

———. "Preaching from the Law." In *Reclaiming the Old Testament for Christian Preaching*, edited by Grenville Kent et al., 47–63. Downers Grove, IL: IVP Academic, 2010.

Wright, N. T. *The Climax of the Covenant: Christ and the Law in Pauline Theology*. Minneapolis: Fortress, 1993.

———. *Jesus and the Victory of God, Christian Origins and the Question of God*. Volume Two. London: SPCK, 1996.

———. *Justification: God's Plan and Paul's Vision*. London: SPCK, 2009.

———. "Justification: The Biblical Basis & its Relevance for Contemporary Evangelicalism." In *The Great Acquittal: Justification by Faith and Current Christian Thought*, edited by Gavin Reid, 13–37. London: Collins, 1980.

———. "The Letter to the Romans: Introduction, Commentary, and Reflections." In *The New Interpreter's Bible: A Commentary in Twelve Volumes*, Vol. 10, edited by Leander Keck. Nashville: Abingdon, 2002.

———. "New Perspectives on Paul." Paper delivered at the 10th Edinburgh Dogmatics Conference, 2003. Available at http://www.ntwrightpage.com/Wright_New_Perspectives.htm, accessed February 26, 2012.

———. *The New Testament and the People of God*. Christian Origins and the Question of God, Vol. 1. London: SPCK, 1992.

———. *Paul: Fresh Perspectives*. London: SPCK, 2005.

———. "The Paul of History and the Apostle of Faith." *Tyndale Bulletin* 29 (1978) 61–88.

———. *Scripture and the Authority of God: How to Read the Bible Today*. New York: HarperCollins, 2005.

———. *Simply Christian*. London: SPCK, 2006.

———. "Two Radical Jews." *Reviews in Religion and Theology* 2.3 (1995) 15–23.

———. *What Saint Paul Really Said*. Oxford: Lion, 1997.

———. "Whence and Whither Pauline Studies in the Life of the Church." In *Jesus, Paul and the People of God: A Theological Dialogue with N. T. Wright*, edited by Nicholas Perrin and Richard Hays, 262–81. London: SPCK, 2011.

Wright, N. T., and James D. G. Dunn. "An Evening Conversation on Jesus and Paul: James Dunn and N. T. Wright." 2004. Available at http://www.ntwrightpage.com/Dunn_Wright_Conversation.pdf, accessed February 26, 2012.

Yinger, Kent. *The New Perspective on Paul: An Introduction*. Eugene, OR: Cascade, 2011.

Yoder, John Howard. *Preface to Theology: Christology and Theological Method*. Grand Rapids: Brazos, 2002.

———. *The Jewish-Christian Schism Revisited*. Edited by Michael G. Cartwright and Peter Ochs. Waterloo, Ontario: Herald, 2008.

Zetterholm, Magnus. *Approaches to Paul: A Student's Guide to Recent Scholarship*. Minneapolis: Fortress, 2009.

www.ingramcontent.com/pod-product-compliance
Lightning Source LLC
Chambersburg PA
CBHW071241230426
43668CB00011B/1532